MEDICAL ANTHROPOLOGY
AT THE INTERSECTIONS

Medical Anthropology

HISTORIES, ACTIVISMS, AND FUTURES

at the Intersections

Marcia C. Inhorn and
Emily A. Wentzell, editors

DUKE UNIVERSITY PRESS

DURHAM AND LONDON | 2012

Designed by April Leidig
Typeset in Garamond by Copperline Book Services, Inc.

Library of Congress Cataloging-in-Publication Data appear on
the last printed page of this book.

Duke University Press gratefully acknowledges the support of the
Yale University Office of the Provost, Department of Anthropology,
and Program in Reproductive Ecology, which provided funds
toward the publication of this book.

CONTENTS

ACKNOWLEDGMENTS

This book emerged from a Society for Medical Anthropology conference at Yale University (September 24–27, 2009) titled "Medical Anthropology at the Intersections: Celebrating Fifty Years of Interdisciplinarity." We want to take this opportunity to thank all of those who made that historic conference possible, including the plenary speakers who converted their presentations into the beautiful chapters of this edited volume. They are an amazing and inspirational group of medical anthropology scholars and activists.

Generous financial support for the conference and for this resulting book was provided by Yale University. Special thanks go to Ian Shapiro, Sterling Professor of Political Science, and Henry R. Luce Director of the Whitney and Betty MacMillan Center for International and Area Studies, and the MacMillan design team of Marilyn Wilkes and Lisa Brennan, who designed the conference graphics. In addition, the chair of Yale's Department of Anthropology, Richard Bribiescas, helped to support the publication of this book with a subvention through his Program in Reproductive Ecology.

Our heartfelt thanks also go to Deborah (Deb) Winslow, the director of the Cultural Anthropology Program in the Behavioral and Cognitive Sciences (BCS) Division of the National Science Foundation (NSF). Since assuming the directorship, Deb has helped to encourage and subsequently fund hundreds of faculty and doctoral research projects in medical anthropology. In so doing, she effectively doubled the number of NSF applications to the Cultural Anthropology Program. In addition, she showed great interest in this medical anthropology conference and edited volume, helping to shepherd our NSF grant proposal to a successful conclusion. We are deeply grateful to the NSF for its financial support.

A number of our colleagues helped in the preparation of the NSF grant proposal and its bibliography, including Danya Keene, Mark Padilla, Holly Peters-Golden, Elizabeth Roberts, and Amorita Valdez. We are also deeply grateful to Molly K. Moran for her exceptional editorial services.

Finally, we are glad to have found the best possible home for this book at Duke University Press. Under the visionary leadership of Duke's editorial director, Ken Wissoker, and with the editorial assistance of Leigh Barnwell and Christine Dahlin, publication has been both seamless and timely. Three anonymous readers also provided thoughtful reviews, which improved the manuscript immensely.

Medical Anthropology
at the Intersections

The First Fifty Years

In 2009 the discipline of medical anthropology celebrated approximately fifty years of existence. In 1959 one of the first references to "medical anthropology" was made in a publication by a physician-anthropologist named James Roney (1959) titled "Medical Anthropology: A Synthetic Discipline." Roney and Margaret Clark, George Foster, Charles Hughes, Charles Leslie, and Benjamin Paul were among the founders of this nascent field, which blossomed in the 1960s. Through their teaching and programmatic development, these first-generation pioneers spawned a second generation of medical anthropologists, many of whom went on to develop the field in significant new directions. When both George Foster (University of California, Berkeley) and Benjamin Paul (Stanford University) passed away in their nineties in May 2006, medical anthropologists from around the world mourned the "passing of an era" in medical anthropology. This feeling was reaffirmed in September 2009 with the death of Charles Leslie, one of the first medical anthropologists of Asia and one of the founding editors of *Social Science & Medicine*.

This "passing of an era" has caused us to reflect on how far medical anthropology has come as a discipline and on where it is headed. Our goal in this introduction is to sketch briefly the development of the field and the ways in which it has come to intersect with numerous other disciplines. These interdisciplinary intersections are the focus of the book as a whole. However, we provide this overview to orient readers to the field of medical anthropology, noting at the outset that the works cited here represent only a fraction of the huge corpus of scholarship in this burgeoning field.

Since its inception, medical anthropology has been broadly defined as the study of health, illness, and healing through time and across cultural settings (Foster and Anderson 1978; Helman 2007; Nichter 1992). Medical anthropologists study human suffering, as well as the medical systems in place to alleviate that suffering (Hahn 1995; Scheper-Hughes 1992; Strathern and Stewart 1999). Around the world, medical anthropologists analyze the relations among health, illness, social institutions, culture, and political and economic power (Baer et al. 2003; Doyal 1979), combining biomedical perspectives with those that address social and cultural problems through health advocacy and activism (Brown 1998; Singer and Baer 2007). Their work points to the differences in the ways that bodies count: who falls ill and why; who has access to health resources; and where healing is sought. Medical anthropologists have contributed to the study of the production of medical knowledge (Berg and Mol 1998; Lock and Gordon 1988) in fields ranging from reproduction (Ginsburg and Rapp 1995) to international health development (Frankenberg 1980) to the new chronic and infectious diseases (Inhorn and Brown 1990; Manderson and Smith-Morris 2010). They have examined questions of stigma, marginality, and the disabled body (Ablon 1984; Frank 2000). They have probed critical issues of biopolitics, immigration, race, citizenship, and health disparities (Fassin 2007; Good et al. 2011; Harrison 1994). They also look at the intersections of disease and environment (Leatherman 2005) and the structural violence triggered by processes of globalization, neoliberalism, and global capitalism (Farmer 2003; Janes et al. 2006). Amid these macrostructural forces, medical anthropologists have examined the social construction of illness categories, the individual illness narratives used to articulate them, and the social and political hierarchies such categories may produce or maintain (Kleinman 1988; Lindenbaum and Lock 1993; Mattingly and Garro 2000; Good and Good 2008).

On a disciplinary level in North America, medical anthropology is now very firmly entrenched within the larger field of anthropology through its Society for Medical Anthropology (SMA), which has 1,300 members, and its accompanying professional journal, *Medical Anthropology Quarterly*.[1] It is important to note that a similar disciplinary foundation has been set in Western Europe, as demonstrated by the establishment of the European Association of Social Anthropologists' Medical Anthropology Network in 2006.

The practicing side of the profession is also prospering, as seen every two years when the SMA meets with the Society for Applied Anthropology (SfAA), and medical anthropological themes are especially prominent. Given its practice orientation, medical anthropology has often been described as an applied discipline, engaging fruitfully with the allied health sciences (medicine, nursing, public health, bioethics, nutrition, occupational therapy, and social work). Medical anthropology is now well ensconced as a medical social science in universities around the world and in numerous practice settings, ranging from the World Health Organization (WHO), National Institutes of Health (NIH), and the Centers for Disease Control and Prevention (CDC) to numerous private, governmental, and nongovernmental organizations (NGOs) working around the globe.

In addition to its practice orientation, medical anthropology boasts a rich theoretical and empirical scholarly tradition. Many critically acclaimed, medical anthropological ethnographies address topics ranging from embodiment and local biologies to the health problems engendered by structural and political violence.[2] Authors of such work often engage across the social science and humanities disciplines, drawing on history, philosophy, psychology, political science, religious studies, and women's studies perspectives in their ethnographic writing (Good et al. 2010).

With its fifty-year-old foundation solidly in place, medical anthropology is currently expanding outward and interacting in many productive ways across disciplinary boundaries. In her SMA presidential address of 2006, Inhorn described ten key areas of medical anthropological interdisciplinarity (Inhorn 2007a). In 2007 the SMA Executive Board adopted the theme of interdisciplinarity and selected plenary speakers for the first international conference on medical anthropology, which was held at Yale University in September 2009, with Inhorn serving as program chair and Wentzell as co-organizer. More than one thousand scholars from forty-eight countries attended the conference, bespeaking the importance of medical anthropology as a growing global discipline. Many of the founding figures of medical anthropology, who helped to train thousands of students over the years, attended the conference. The conference clearly highlighted the importance of both mentors and students in the social reproduction of the field. In addition to the first generation, many second-, third-, and fourth-generation medical anthropologists attended the conference, as did members of the SMA's Medical Anthropology Student Association (MASA), who represent the fifth generation and the future of the field in the twenty-first century.

Interdisciplinarity

The goal of this global conference was to examine a number of key fields where some of the most exciting interdisciplinary work is emerging in medical anthropology. In this new millennium, interdisciplinarity is certainly one of the key tropes in the academy. Because medical anthropologists tend to be interdisciplinary in their outlook and training, they are often able to express multiple positionalities within their universities and practice settings. For the next generation of medical anthropologists—including students, who make up one-third of the total membership of the SMA—many of the "cutting edges" of the field of medical anthropology will be found at the intersections of many other disciplines.

Imagining the future of medical anthropology thus requires interrogation of its interdisciplinary history and future possibilities. "Interdisciplinarity" can be defined most basically as one's ability to intersect on a theoretical or methodological level with one or more academic fields. The perceived benefits of interdisciplinarity are many, including improved intellectual creativity and flexibility, the fact that some worthwhile topics of research fall in the interstices among the traditional disciplines, and the reality that many intellectual, social, and practical problems require interdisciplinary approaches (Nissani 1997). As noted by one interdisciplinary scholar, "interdisciplinarians often treat themselves to the intellectual equivalent of traveling in new lands" (Nissani 1997, 201). This practice of traveling across disciplinary boundaries to produce new knowledge resonates well with anthropology's foundational goals, including its commitment to holism and the long-standing anthropological awareness that human cultures, bodies, and experiences are generated relationally, developing at the intersections of histories, peoples, structures, and materialities (Boaz 1982; Jackson 1998; Mauss 1973; Wolf 1982). These insights have led to the development of diverse approaches within anthropology, formalized into the discipline's four subfields, and have paved the way for anthropological adoption of methods and perspectives from other disciplines.

Like any form of knowledge production, interdisciplinary research is a social act, bearing the promise and pitfalls that mark the relational development of new ways of being and thinking. Since research methods encapsulate specific worldviews, which may be differently valorized within and outside the academy, intersubdisciplinary relationships within anthropology have at times generated unease and conflict (Segal and Yanagisaki 2005). The trope of interdisciplinarity has also been critiqued as increasingly "trendy" in the academy but unhelpfully diffuse (Klein 1991) or limited by structural, cultural, and cognitive barriers in the context of academic research and institutional design (Barnes and Jentoft 2009).

Yet, the chapters presented here reveal that intersections between different forms of knowledge production have been formative in the development of medical anthropology itself. All of the authors are among the world's most prominent medical anthropologists, who have made key interdisciplinary contributions to the development of the field of medical anthropology. In each case these scholars were asked to reflect on the intersections between medical anthropology and a related discipline. In the expanded versions of their plenary addresses presented here, these researchers provide models for the practice of interdisciplinarity. Some reveal how forging relationships between disciplines shaped their own careers and anthropological commitments, while others demonstrate the ways that using tools from multiple fields can enrich anthropological analysis and stimulate medical anthropological activism in solving social problems. The contributors offer different understandings of what it means to work and think at the intersections. For example, Lynn Morgan understands these relationships through the metaphor of the "thicket," in which branches intersect both to form an environment and to obscure one's view, while Emily Martin sees them as joined through a process of "grafting."

As a whole, the contributors think through different ways that interdisciplinarity can be achieved in medical anthropology, charting paths for future interdisciplinarity by surveying the field's existing areas of disciplinary intersection. They show that the productive tensions arising when multiple approaches are combined may generate some of medical anthropology's most exciting ways forward. The book's structure provides a model for interdisciplinary engagement. Scholars working at the intersections must first martial existing knowledge produced over the history of multiple fields. Next, they must question what these intellectual histories and ways of knowing have produced as well as obscured. Finally, they must combine elements of existing approaches in order to ask new questions, generate new answers, and use their knowledge for the solution of human problems. The three parts of the book, "Histories," "Queries," and "Activisms," encapsulate these phases of interdisciplinary research.

It is important to remember that the views of interdisciplinarity presented here developed out of a specific academic and cultural context. The SMA conference attracted scholars from the Global North and the Global South, who presented a diversity of medical anthropological perspectives and approaches. However, the plenary presentations and speakers focused on concerns central to the history of medical anthropology in North America and Western Europe. This book is thus not truly global in scope, nor is it intended as an exhaustive account of all the possible interdisciplinary intersections that have shaped medical anthropology and should inform its future. Instead, it examines nine key intersections, providing a starting point for future interdisciplinary discussions in the new millennium.

Part I: Histories

This section focuses on medical anthropology's intellectual genealogy, including historical antecedents spanning two centuries. The authors demonstrate that early medical anthropology was capacious in its purview, intersecting with physical anthropology, embryology, forensics, museum studies, linguistics, Cold War development studies, and eventually second-wave feminism. As a result, the history of medical anthropology has been crucially shaped by key historical debates on issues of race, class, gender, and empire. As these debates have played out over the decades, medical anthropologists have become increasingly sophisticated in their critiques of inequality and oppression, developing a crucial subgenre known as critical medical anthropology.[3] The chapters in this section artfully blend history and critique in examining medical anthropology's early intersections with three fields: feminist technoscience studies, medical history, and international and area studies.

While the early history of a nascent medical anthropology can be traced to the first half of the twentieth century, the second half of the century saw the rise of second-wave feminism, which had major implications for medical anthropology and the discipline of anthropology as a whole. Beginning in the early 1960s, feminist writers and activists began tackling a range of issues, including women's legal rights, work for equal pay, patriarchy and the family, and sexual and reproductive rights. By the 1970s these themes began to be taken up by feminist anthropologists, including feminist medical anthropologists, who launched a major subfield in the anthropology of reproduction (Jordan 1978; Reiter 1975). Over the next decades, many feminist medical anthropologists became interested in reproductive technologies such as contraception and abortion, as well as the potential for overuse and abuse of technologies when applied to women's bodies (Davis-Floyd 1993; Ginsburg 1989; Ginsburg and Rapp 1995; Petchesky 1987; Ragoné 1994; Rapp 2000; Scheper-Hughes 1992). Feminist medical anthropologists' critical insights on patriarchy and biomedicine soon merged with the developing 1980s field of science and technology studies (STS), which also turned the critical lens on the production and reproduction of science, technology, and biomedicine. Like feminist ethnographers, many STS scholars were interested in entering the "backstage" world of laboratories, clinics, operating theaters, pharmaceutical trials, and clinical research sites to offer critical accounts of science, technology, and medicine in the making. By the early 1990s feminist technoscience studies had emerged as an interdisciplinary orientation, championed by a number of major scholars, including Donna Haraway (1985, 1988), Marilyn Strathern (1992a, 1992b), and Sarah Franklin (1995, 2007).

The emergence of this interdisciplinary field is traced by one of the group's early pioneers, Emily Martin. In her chapter, "Grafting Together Medical Anthropology, Feminism, and Technoscience," Martin uses her own biography to trace the history of the intersection between feminist medical anthropology and STS. The chapter shows how the merging of fields continuously provoked new questions and topics of inquiry; in the author's own scholarly trajectory, these topics ranged widely from reproduction to immunology to brain science. The chapter also refutes the notion that scholars work in isolation, instead showing how conversations between scholars working across fields spurred insights that profoundly influenced the field of medical anthropology. In looking back Martin also looks forward to the future of interdisciplinary work in feminist technoscience studies and medical anthropology as a whole. She argues that medical anthropologists must seek more serious engagement with problems derived from reductionism, make greater efforts to write about science and medicine for public media consumption, and ask fundamental questions about medical technology and materializing practices, guided by the history and anthropology of science. Through these avenues, Martin argues for the importance of interdisciplinary work that is both intellectually and politically significant.

MEDICAL HISTORY

Medical history may be regarded as medical anthropology's "sister discipline" in the humanities. Although medical historians' work is textually based, while medical anthropologists favor person-centered ethnography (Levy and Hollan 1998), medical historians and anthropologists have shared concerns with the history of modern epidemics (Briggs and Mantini-Briggs 2003; Farmer 1992; Ong 1987; Turshen 1989), comparative medicine in a variety of pre- and postcolonial settings (Adams 1998; Comaroff 1985; Farquhar 2002; Hunt 1999; Taussig 1987), and the emergence of new forms of medical technology (Davis-Floyd 1993; Davis-Floyd and Dumit 1998; Lock 1980, 1993). Most medical anthropologists would agree that ethnography is enriched by attention to history and historiography. Indeed, the discipline of cultural anthropology as a whole has been engaged in a "historical turn," a shift toward the humanities, from which medical anthropology has also benefited. Medical anthropologists have an important role to play at the intersection of anthropology and medical history, combining ethnographic and historiographic methods in their work on medicine, health, and the body, especially in contexts of post–Second World War humanitarian aid and development (Escobar 1995; Fassin 2007), the collapse of the Soviet Union (Kligman 1998; Petryna 2002; Rivkin-Fish 2005), and the dirty wars in Latin America, which produced untold amounts of human suffering (Bourgois 2002; Green 1999; Robben and Suarez-Orozco 2000).

In her chapter "Getting at Anthropology through Medical History: Notes on the Consumption of Chinese Embryos and Fetuses in the Western Imagination," Lynn M. Morgan uses historical sources to capture early medical anthropological interest in issues of race, ethnicity, and reproduction. Through a fascinating historical case study of early twentieth-century Chinese embryo collecting, Morgan shows how the discursive categories of "race" and "embryology" were mutually constituted through the practice of racial embryology, which held that exotic specimens might offer definitive evidence of biologically based racial variation. By creating a retrospective juxtaposition between missionaries (with their righteous abhorrence of putative Chinese "dead baby towers"), anatomists (with their blithe anatomical collecting practices), and anthropologists (who were largely oblivious to the violence engendered by their theorizing), this chapter calls for greater acknowledgment of anthropological complicity in a long-standing project to stigmatize and stereotype the Chinese.

INTERNATIONAL AND AREA STUDIES

Morgan's chapter on China also points to the ways in which medical anthropology's history has been critically influenced by the politics of Cold War engagement in international and area studies. Anthropology as a whole has always boasted of a strong area studies tradition. Since the early twentieth century, anthropologists have immersed themselves in the language, culture, history, and politics of other parts of the world. Medical anthropologists have participated in this area studies tradition through research focused heavily on non-Western medical systems, the health effects of poverty and human suffering around the globe, and the concomitant spread of Western biomedicine, technology, and humanitarian aid. Understanding health problems within their social, cultural, political, and economic matrix has required medical anthropologists to be well versed in the languages, cultures, and histories of diverse world regions. As a result, strong area studies traditions exist within the medical anthropology of sub-Saharan Africa (Boddy 2007; Comaroff 1985; Gruenbaum 2001; Janzen 1992; Smith 2004; Turner 1967), Latin America and the Caribbean (Biehl 2005; Brodwin 1996; Dressler et al. 2006; Farmer 1992; Gutmann 2007; Morgan 1993; Scheper-Hughes 1992; Whiteford and

Branch 2008), East Asia (Adams 1996, 1998; Chen 2003; Farquhar 2002; Greenhalgh 2008; Lock 1980, 1993; Kohrman 2005), and South and Southeast Asia (Cohen 1998; Das 1995, 2001; Nichter 1989; Van Hollen 2003).

However, medical anthropology's participation in area studies has not always been value neutral. Over the past fifty years, part of the field's history has been tied to larger Western political agendas, including attempts to "modernize" and "develop" the non-Western peasantry, attempts to "control" their fertility, and, most recently, efforts at "democratic nation building" through various kinds of medical humanitarian projects. In short the history of medical anthropology is tied to Cold War and post–Cold War politics, as well as the politics of war and nation building in the aftermath of September 11, 2001.

In his critical historical chapter, "Making Peasants Protestant and Other Projects: Medical Anthropology and Its Global Condition," Lawrence Cohen ties medical anthropology's emergence as an organized subdiscipline to the context of American Cold War imperatives of "containment." Against this backdrop, Cohen shows how the "culture" concept came to mark the limits of reason of the agrarian peasantry, who were at apparent risk for interpreting their social suffering as grounds to support Marxist insurrection. These imperatives intersected with the midcentury post-eugenic conception of "overpopulation" as the dominant problem facing development planning elites. This chapter argues that medical anthropology's use of culture as an analytic tool is rooted in the relation between these various political imperatives. It shows how subsequent disciplinary conversations—like the putative distinction between critical and interpretive approaches, as well as many present quandaries in the field—can be reframed in relation to the area studies' concept of "culture regions" and their disciplinary legacy.

Part II: Queries

The critical histories presented in part I underpin the questioning of key assumptions within medical anthropology posed by authors in the second part. Chapters in part II raise fundamental epistemological questions about the meanings of accepted notions within three fields: global public health, mental health, and genetics and genomics. The authors of these provocative chapters examine seemingly self-evident terms such as "global," the usefulness of medical anthropological concepts like "stigma," and the reenactment of the "nature/nurture" controversy in the move toward increasing geneticization. In each case the authors urge medical anthropologists to rethink some of the most basic assumptions within the discipline and those it engages. However, the chapters are also hopeful, charting new research trajectories for the twenty-first century.

GLOBAL PUBLIC HEALTH

Without doubt, medical anthropology has turned toward the "new" field of global public health (also called global health) with special enthusiasm and vigor.[4] Clearly, medical anthropology's passion for this kind of interdisciplinary work reflects the dire need for both compassion and humanitarian activism regarding global health inequalities and the numerous sources of disease and suffering around the globe. Such global health problems are many, including the three "global killer" infectious diseases (malaria, tuberculosis, and HIV/AIDS); maternal and neonatal mortality due to preventable conditions like malnutrition; the globalization of chronic "lifestyle" diseases such as diabetes and certain cancers; and the health problems caused by war and refugeeism. Many medical anthropologists are now undertaking work at the intersections of anthropology and global public health (Hahn and Inhorn 2009). Global health is front and center in today's public health schools, where many medical anthropologists have received dual training. Global health is also at the heart of the work being done by physician-anthropologists such as Paul Farmer and Jim Yong Kim. It is also the major focus of philanthropic initiatives by such notables as Bill and Melinda Gates, Jimmy Carter, and Bill Clinton. The new journal *Global Public Health* is edited by the medical anthropologist Richard Parker, one of the authors in this book. Numerous medical anthropologists are producing scholarship in the area of global health, particularly in response to the worldwide HIV/AIDS pandemic.[5]

In his chapter, "That Obscure Object of Global Health," Didier Fassin questions why global health has become a leitmotiv in the political and academic worlds. While global health has obvious implications in terms of the spread of infectious disease or circulation of medical knowledge, this chapter explores some of the term's less evident meanings and potentials, as well as some of the false commonsense ideas it carries. It does so through examining a series of empirical cases and posing major questions about the meaning of "global health," asking how "global" global health really is and how "health" should be understood in global health. Contrary to what is often thought, Fassin shows that the concept of global health, as well as the meanings of the terms "global" and "health," are far from clear; they must be problematized but also superseded. Fassin shows that the global meaning of health depends fundamentally on evaluations of the worth of others' lives.

MENTAL HEALTH

Over the second half of the twentieth century, some of the most important early work in medical anthropology focused on mental health and "ethno-psychiatry," or the ways in which mental health problems were expressed and healed cross-culturally (Estroff 1985; Guarnaccia 1993; Harwood 1981; Hopper 1988; Hunt 1999; Jenkins 2003; Kleinman 1980; Rhodes 1995; Rubel et al. 1991; Scheper-Hughes 1978). Medical anthropologists were interested in so-called culture-bound syndromes (Simons and Hughes 1985), as well as whether mental health conditions could be overcome through the "placebo effect" (Moerman 2002). However, in recent years, the attention to mental health within medical anthropology has shifted considerably, reflecting disciplinary concern with broader issues of social suffering (Kleinman, Lock, and Das 1997). The sources of mental illness are now often seen as rooted in conditions of poverty, homelessness, political violence, and other forms of social disruption (Bourgois 2002; Das 2001; Desjarlais 1997; Jenkins 2003; Young 1995). Led by a group of medical anthropologists, the *World Mental Health Report* (Desjarlais et al. 1995) sought to involve the World Health Organization and other global health agencies in recognizing and overcoming the burden of global mental illness wrought by war, refugeeism, genocide, sexual violence, the HIV/AIDS epidemic, and other forms of inhumanity. Given the persistence of so much human suffering in the new millennium, medical anthropology has a clear role to play in understanding and alleviating the global burden of mental health problems.

In his chapter "Medical Anthropology and Mental Health: Five Questions for the Next Fifty Years," Arthur Kleinman, one of the pioneers of this interdisciplinary field, reflects on medical anthropology and mental health's long relationship and its centrality to the development of medical anthropology as a robust discipline. Kleinman focuses on the future, drawing on the field of global mental health to present the kinds of theoretical, research, and practical policy and programmatic challenges that will be central to medical anthropology over the next fifty years. In doing so, he poses five critical questions, centering on the differences between social suffering and mental health problems; the need to redefine what is at stake in the most severe psychiatric conditions; the paradox of global pharmaceuticals and their over- or under-prescription depending upon social location; the ethics of caregiving in response to mental illness; and the need to reframe the relationship of science and society in the "golden era" of brain research in order to explore the borderland between culture and the "new" neurobiology. Kleinman argues that posing these questions prepares us to reposition medical anthropology, bringing it closer to cultural psychiatry, epidemiology, ethics, and policy in the implementation of global mental health programs. Such programs could especially benefit the poor in the most resource-constrained settings.

GENETICS AND GENOMICS

It could be argued that the "golden era" of brain research has coincided with the "golden era" of human genetics. The Human Genome Project has led to the rapid growth of genetic science and engineering (Palson 2007; Rabinow 1996b, 1999). The development of new forms of genetic technology, such as DNA and haplotype testing, is revolutionizing forensic medicine, as well as producing new knowledge about hereditary forms of risk (Finkler 2000). Assisted reproductive technologies (ARTs) are now intersecting with genetic testing, leading to the development of a field called reprogenetics (Franklin and Roberts 2006; Inhorn 2007b). Medical anthropological interest in new forms of subjectivity emerging through the rise of genetic testing is growing, particularly as anthropologists of reproduction turn their attention to genetic risk assessment within pregnancy (Browner et al. 2003; Rapp 2000; Taylor 2001, 2005).

In her chapter "From Genetics to Postgenomics and the Discovery of the New Social Body," Margaret Lock asks how the biomedical technology of genetic testing, as well as genetic and genomic research, is bringing anthropology's early interests in kinship and the so-called nature/nurture dichotomy back to the fore, demanding reinvestigation of their social ramifications. Lock's chapter opens with a discussion of the concept of "heredity" and its transformation in the scientific world in the early part of the twentieth century into the discipline of genetics. The era of Mendelian genetics has recently been radically transformed by postgenomics—described by some as a paradigm shift, in that it explicitly recognizes genetic complexity and uncertainty. Lock asks how medical anthropological research on these subjects is increasingly being used in clinical practice, highlighting the repercussions of this scholarship and its application for kinship, human affiliation and biosociality, and new forms of citizenship. The need for recognition of the inseparable entanglement of the material world with socioeconomic, political, and cultural variables is made apparent and meshes with emerging knowledge in the postgenomic era. The chapter explores the research contributions medical anthropologists can make in the understandings of this newly emerging, molecularized, "lively body."

Part III: Activisms

The final section, "Activisms," moves from the conceptual realm of disciplinary genealogies, assumptions, questions, and debates to the realm of action and advocacy. The activist impulse to "do good," "help others," "save lives," and "make a better world" has always been a running theme within medical anthropology. Variously called applied anthropology, clinically applied medical anthropology, action anthropology, and more recently, activist anthropology, medical anthropology that applies research findings to improve health and well-being has been part of the discipline since its inception more than fifty years ago. Although much of the recent advocacy and activism in medical anthropology has focused on global health interventions (Hahn and Inhorn 2009), there are many other domains in which medical anthropologists work for a better and more just world. The authors in the final section highlight medical anthropological intersections with three fields: disability studies; public policy; and gender, LGBT, and sexuality studies, where scholarly activism plays a central role.

DISABILITY STUDIES

Medical anthropology's interest in disability studies grew along with the interest in genetics and genomics described above. Early on, activist scholars, some of them disabled, formed a disability studies special interest group within SMA and began ethnographic explorations of the lifeworlds of adults whose genetic conditions had led to disability. The topics covered were wide-ranging and included classic studies of adult deafness (Becker 1983), limb reduction defects (Frank 2000), dwarfism and a variety of degenerative conditions (Ablon 1984, 2002), and autoethnography of disability experience (Murphy 2001). The seminal work *Disability in Local and Global Worlds* (Ingstad and Whyte 2007), now in its second edition, proved the importance of medical anthropological ethnography in understanding embodied difference in the lives of the disabled around the world. Still, the potential of medical anthropology to explore the world of disability studies has yet to be fully realized. This will become increasingly apparent with the global expansion of an aging and disabled population.

In their chapter "Anthropology and the Study of Disability Worlds," Rayna Rapp and Faye Ginsburg argue that anthropology has not attended well enough to disability, given that disability is one of the most universally experienced forms of difference. This neglect is apparent in spite of anthropology's foundational claim to study human diversity in all its aspects. The authors ask why anthropology seems relatively averse to focusing on disability. They then challenge medical anthropologists to incorporate disability more centrally into anthropology's canon, arguing for the value of such work on both epistemological and existential grounds. Rapp and Ginsburg also highlight their own work as "activist scholars," who are "engaged" in this field as mothers of disabled children and disability rights activists who are working for change. Their chapter highlights the problem of learning disability (LD) and describes the authors' attempts to develop innovative programs for those with LDs who are no longer children. This case study of scholarship and activism provides an inspiring example for other medical anthropologists whose personal lives can become the fodder for social change.

PUBLIC POLICY

Since the beginning of the new millennium, the official position of the SMA calls on medical anthropologists to "take a stand" against social injustices, particularly those impinging upon human health and well-being. Through its "Take a Stand" initiative begun under the presidency of Mark Nichter, the SMA has urged involvement in matters of public policy and has worked on such pressing issues as U.S. ratification of the child rights and tobacco treaties

(SMA 2006; SMA Study Group 2007) and overturning the global gag rule. Nonetheless, it can be easily argued that medical anthropology is less effective in the policy arena than it should be (Singer and Castro 2004). Perhaps if there were more medical anthropologists trained and ensconced in the policy world, the discipline would have more power to influence vital national and international health debates.

In his chapter, "Medical Anthropology and Public Policy: Using Research to Change the World from What It Is to What We Believe It Should Be," Merrill Singer argues that anthropological involvement in the policy arena has a long but conflicted history. In some areas of disciplinary concern individual anthropologists have successfully influenced public policy in productive and beneficial ways. More commonly, anthropologists have expressed frustration that their research findings, however relevant, have been ignored by policy makers. This occurs because the complex "truths" our research produces are often out of harmony with the official, usually simplistic truths formulated by those with influence in areas of anthropological interest, including health, the environment, welfare, and education. Powerful, well-funded lobbies have gained enormous control over the policy agenda, leaving little opportunity for anthropology's input. In this light, this chapter presents a strategy for expanded medical anthropological influence on health-related policy. The proposed approach involves significantly expanding relations with potential allies in the policy arena, namely community-based organizers and activists. This chapter argues that by promoting and fostering collaboration and coalition building—which are stated goals of the SMA—with the national movement of community-based organizers inspired and trained by Saul Alinsky and his descendants, we can position ourselves to participate in leveling the policy playing field and influencing the development of healthy health policy.

GENDER, LGBT, AND SEXUALITY STUDIES

Gender and health has been one of the most productive areas of medical anthropological scholarship and activism over the past four decades. Perhaps because of the aforementioned feminist movement within medical anthropology, or because of the inspiring existence (for more than two decades) of the SMA's Eileen Basker Prize for outstanding research in gender and health, medical anthropologists have produced a massive amount of scholarship in this area, including more than 150 ethnographic volumes (Inhorn 2006). By engaging in women's lives, medical anthropologists have contributed considerably to theoretical debates surrounding issues of embodiment, reproductive agency, the intersectionality of oppressions, and women's resistance to health-demoting social relations and conditions. They have also pushed for social change through involvement in feminist movements for reproductive and sexual rights. In recent years these issues and social mobilizations have also been taken up by scholars interested in masculinity (Gutmann 1996, 2003, 2007), LGBT studies (Levine 2008; Lewin and Leap 2002), and sexuality studies in the era of HIV/AIDS (Parker 1991, 1999; Parker et al. 2000). For medical anthropologists working at the crossroads of gender, LGBT, and sexuality studies, "the personal" is often "the professional"; to wit, scholarly engagements may be intertwined with life experiences involving oppression based on gender and sexual orientation. Such engagements, in turn, may produce the activist desire to agitate for greater gender, reproductive, and sexual rights.

The final chapter, "Critical Intersections and Engagements: Gender, Sexuality, Health, and Rights in Medical Anthropology" by Richard Parker, is clearly linked to the first chapter by Emily Martin, creating a kind of medical anthropological Mobius strip of interlinked histories, activisms, and futures. In his chapter, Parker surveys the wide range of intellectual and activist concerns related to gender, LGBT issues, and sexuality, as reflected in work carried out by medical anthropologists for more than four decades. Parker focuses on some of the key historical processes and events that have shaped the development of this work, including the importance of social movements in shaping the context of research and analysis; the impact of the global HIV/AIDS epidemic; the paradigm shift from population control to reproductive health and rights; and the emerging focus on sexual rights. The chapter highlights the author's own long-term activist engagements in the Brazilian HIV/AIDS movement, including his cofounding of the Brazilian Interdisciplinary AIDS Association (ABIA). The history of ABIA presented in this chapter highlights the importance of medical anthropology's activism, offering important lessons and new directions for the field in the new millennium.

The Next Fifty Years

This book traces the histories of key intersections between medical anthropology and a variety of important disciplines, pointing out the possibilities for future scholarship in these arenas and presenting hopes for the real-world consequences of such work. Each chapter offers new ways of understanding questions that have formed the ethical core of medical anthropology over the past fifty years. The book highlights nine key avenues for interdisciplinary scholarship in medical anthropology, which can advance the field as an intellectual enterprise and which can enhance the field's responsiveness to human suffering.

However, the future of medical anthropology's engagements with other fields is by no means limited to these nine interdisciplinary pathways. The intersections highlighted in this book were chosen because they have become central to the field of medical anthropology over the past half-century of existence. But the next fifty years promise a great deal more to come. Based on our thematic reading of some of the exciting new scholarship presented at the Yale SMA conference in 2009, we would like to conclude by encouraging the development of four critical pathways for future interdisciplinarity by the next generation of medical anthropology scholars and activists. Some of these areas already have rich interdisciplinary histories, while others do not. Furthermore, they do not represent the only interdisciplinary trajectories into the future. However, we believe that these four areas are especially important; thus, we would like to stress them as sites of either new or renewed interdisciplinary development for future generations of medical anthropologists.

• *Medical Anthropology and Caregiving*   Caregiving, as Arthur Kleinman (2008, 2009a) reminds us in a powerful series of recent essays, is part of what makes us human, and it is essential to twenty-first-century medicine. A medical anthropological focus on care—by kin, community, and clinicians—appears to be an ideal entry point for deepening connections between theory and practice on many levels. Medical anthropology has a role to play in the ethnographic study and analysis of caregiving (Heinemann 2011; McLean 2006; Mol 2008), as well as in facilitating the art of caregiving through clinically applied medical anthropological work in a number of allied fields. Building on existing discussions of decision making surrounding biomedical care (Kaufman 2005; Levin 1990), scholars engaging with this theme might include medical anthropologist-physicians performing primary care, as well as medical anthropologists working at the clinical crossroads of nursing, social work, bioethics, gerontology, occupational therapy, nutrition, and complementary and alternative medicine (CAM). Judging from the papers, posters, and panels at the SMA conference, there are now hundreds of medical anthropologists working at the intersections of these clinically applied fields. Together, they can move medical anthropology beyond the realm of research for research's sake to prove that medical anthropology itself is a caring profession.

• *Religious Studies and Divinity* In a world divided by ethnic and religiously based violence, it is imperative that medical anthropologists continue to be schooled in the world's religions, including their contemporary global forms and movements (Inhorn and Tremayne 2012). Religion and faith are vitally important to health and healing and are the basis for much medical humanitarianism under the aegis of so-called faith-based organizations. Religious traditions also guide the so-called local moral worlds (Kleinman 1995) of patients and healers in many forms of medical decision making, including end-of-life care. Medical anthropology has a future role to play at the intersection of religious studies, which could be undertaken not only by scholars of medicine and religion but also by medical anthropologists who are actually trained in divinity and involved in various kinds of pastoral care, hospital chaplaincies, and faith-based public health interventions.

• *Environmental Studies* The health of the environment is of particular concern in the new millennium. Medical anthropology has a major role to play in examining the health impacts of environmental degradation (Johnston 2007, 2011), including global climate change and environmental pollution. In addition, changing environments are leading to rising waters and disasters that will cause massive population disruptions and "environmental refugeeism" (Hugo 1996). Building on long-standing anthropological study of political ecology and the coconstruction of people and environments (McElroy and Townsend 2008; Turshen 1984), medical anthropology can investigate the relationships between changing environments and human health and well-being. Indeed, the intersection between medical anthropology and environmental studies may be the single most pressing direction for future scholarship and activism in the twenty-first century. Young medical anthropologists working at this intersection should consider seeking interdisciplinary training in environmental studies and/or environmental health.

• *Biocultural Medical Anthropology*   Medical anthropological questions have, and must continue to be, answered with analytic tools from both sociocultural and biological anthropology. In many ways biocultural approaches have been truly foundational in the history of medical anthropology (McElroy and Townsend 2008). Despite the potential of such research to account holistically for issues of bodily change and suffering (Armelagos et al. 1992), the proportionally small amount of biocultural work presented at the Yale SMA conference of 2009 demonstrates that this area of potential subdisciplinary intersection could be significantly enhanced. Scholars working at this intersection continue to urge further development of this approach (Goodman and Leatherman 1998; Wiley and Allen 2008), for example, reminding medical anthropologists of the importance of human ecology (McElroy and Townsend 2008); of the health risks of various forms of adversity (Panter-Brick and Fuentes 2010); of the entanglements among heredity, environment, and social context (Dressler et al. 2005; Gravlee 2009);[6] and of the importance of "local biologies" (Lock 1995) or the delicate interplay of hormones and culture (Bribiescas 2008; Panter-Brick and Worthman 2008). We, too, want to remind medical anthropologists that some of our best interdisciplinary conversations over the next fifty years may take place—indeed, *should* take place—between colleagues in biological anthropology, medical anthropology, and the related anthropological subdisciplines. Creating these intersubdisciplinary medical anthropology dialogues may be as easy as walking down the hall to a colleague's office. This, too, should be a key goal for the future of medical anthropology.

PART I

Histories

Grafting Together Medical Anthropology, Feminism, and Technoscience

Within the groves of anthropology, the many grafts between medical anthropology, feminism, and science and technology studies (STS) ✓ have borne a rich harvest. In this chapter I trace how some of these grafts came about through a historical framing of the ways my work added to and benefited from them, moving through a variety of field sites and problems, from reproduction, through HIV/AIDS, and into mental health. The topics addressed by medical anthropology were so central to the constitution of twentieth- and twenty-first-century society and culture that scholars working in feminist studies and STS were eager to address them—topics such as diverse ways of defining health, stratified access to medicine and clinics, and centralized knowledge about the health and mortality of populations, to name just a few. Medical anthropology offered scholars specialized knowledge of how to understand institutions and practices that lay at the heart of contemporary forms of power and subjectivity. In return, feminism and STS offered complementary ways to understand the topics that medical anthropologists were addressing. In particular, feminism offered a robust way of seeing how medical institutions and practices were embedded in race and gender differences rooted in the larger political economy; STS offered ways of examining the assumptions lying in the background of medical practices: such things as the experimental method, the ideal of objectivity, or the paths by which scientific knowledge is produced and changed.

The metaphor of "intersections" inspired the event behind this book because it captures some aspects of the comings and goings between medical anthropology, feminism, and technoscience. An "intersection," like a section of a road shared by two highways or a group of elements common to two sets, captures some of the developments I will sketch: it captures the sense of shared problems and shared goals among the disciplines. But I am also guided by the metaphor of a "graft" because, in the plant kingdom, a graft can lead to a new organism with higher yields and better quality. The rich contributions these three fields have made to each other have laid the groundwork for exciting "grafts" still to come. I gesture toward some of them in my conclusion.

Many of us who were trained in anthropology in the late 1960s and early 1970s were primed to engage with questions at the heart of medical anthropology, whether we knew it or not. Many of my peers' research projects dealt with questions of health and sickness, life and death, or technology and gender, inspired by the now classic writings of Edmund Leach (1964), Raymond Firth (1963), Meyer Fortes (1949), Mary Douglas (1991), Victor Turner (1967), Clifford Geertz (1973), or Claude Lévi-Strauss (1963)—even though only a minority of us would have said we were "medical anthropologists." We might not have worked in medical institutions or with trained specialists, but we often studied cosmological notions about life and death and ritual practices during birth, illness, and death wherever we did fieldwork.

For some of us, a path into a more specialized concern with the topics of medical anthropology became available during the 1970s. Despite my own lack of training, it seemed unexceptional to me that Navel Medical Research Unit No. 2 (NAMRU-2), which had moved to Taiwan years before in 1955, offered me a summer job to investigate hepatitis and other endemic diseases at the village level in Taiwan. Despite my own dismay over the war in Vietnam, NAMRU seemed like a neutral research enterprise devoted to public health measures that would reduce disease. Their explicit goal—to study infectious diseases of military significance in Asia—sounds much more ominous now. However, NAMRU support was invaluable to medical anthropology as a field, as evidenced by their support of Arthur Kleinman's early work in Taiwan.

I could not shed any light on the causes of Taiwan's hepatitis epidemic, but I did figure out why villagers would not accept measles vaccines, then available for no cost at every rural health clinic. Measles, it turned out, was regarded as a phase in the life cycle that served the beneficial purpose of letting out the polluting matter that everyone could not help having inside their bodies from passing through the "dirty" female birth canal. If you did not get rid of this pollution through the oozing pustules of measles, you would break out with it on your deathbed and be marked by dirty sores forever after in the next world. What should I do with this knowledge? If I suggested that the vaccine could have an adjuvant added to it so that it would produce a *local* pustule that people might accept as a substitute for a full course of measles, this might lead more rural people to get vaccinated. It turned out that the current version of the vaccine was just about to be withdrawn in the United States because of harmful side effects. I did not know how to negotiate this conundrum at the time because at this point, in the interactions between medical anthropology and social and cultural anthropology broadly speaking, it was acceptable to think of Western medicine (even when purveyed by the military) as a valuable resource that would benefit local populations (Ahern 1978). My understanding would crystallize later, as I describe below.

Feminism

A few years later many anthropologists were being led into the world of feminist and Marxist theory and history, and this engagement would firmly introduce issues of power, control, and class discrimination into the topics anthropologists studied, including medicine. For me this happened through the work of my colleagues at Johns Hopkins, especially Elizabeth Fee, Nancy Hartsock, David Harvey, and Donna Haraway.[1] My memory of how my fledgling acquaintance with medical anthropology connected to feminist theory centers on a lightning bolt that struck in the early 1980s when Donna Haraway, returning for a visit to Hopkins from her position at UCSC, met with some colleagues for lunch at an outdoor café. In those days, although there were no laptops, there were slides, but, of course, in the restaurant we had no projector. We were sitting in a circle outdoors and as she chatted with us about writing *Primate Visions*, she passed around the slides one by one.

It was fascinating to hear her interpret these images, while all of us were peering closely at those little slides. The one that most struck me showed Jane Goodall when she was studying the chimpanzees in the Gombe, sitting on top of a hill, eating beans out of a can. Donna's commentary on that image joins the entire history of the Second World War to Goodall eating beans. The lightning strike was: here is the scientist, in the jungle, in nature, studying nature, making science out of nature, and with her is the emblem of an incredible, mighty material force in history. The history of industrial canning, developed to serve the needs of soldiers in war, was present right in the middle of Goodall's scientific work. That was like a beacon to me. How do you see those kinds of secret forces, both cultural and political economic, hidden in plain sight?

Donna showed how this image is representational but also contains an object that was keeping Jane Goodall alive. This was literally the "material-semiotic." Donna led us from thinking, "Oh, she is eating a can of canned beans" —the prosaic—to somehow realizing what you were really looking at. I think that this lightning bolt influenced everything I did afterward. Together with scholarship like Elizabeth Fee's on the gendered dynamics of the history of science and medicine, David Harvey's on concepts and practices concerning value in capitalist societies, and Nancy Hartsock's on the gendered assumptions behind American concepts of political power, my thinking about medical practices was altered: no longer would a campaign to introduce a vaccine seem innocent, nor would cultural beliefs be positioned as obstacles to progress. The vaccine itself now could stand in for the can of beans: Whose interests were being served by its deployment? On what historical developments did it depend? What forms of power did it buttress and what forms did it weaken?

I had already been doing interviews with women, reading through obstetrics and gynecology textbooks in different editions, and going to childbirth education classes in order to get some sort of handle on what was going on with women giving birth, including myself. These years (the mid-1980s) were at the beginning of this kind of work in anthropology. Susan Harding was working in Jerry Falwell's community in Virginia, Harriet Whitehead was working with the scientologists, and Lorna Rhodes was working in a psychiatric clinic.[2] Since all of us were doing fieldwork in the Baltimore area, we met every couple of months on my row house's flat rooftop, just trying to figure out how in the world you do anthropological fieldwork in your own culture and what would make such work anthropological rather than sociological. That was the main issue we grappled with. In my head there were theorists such as Gayle Rubin (Rubin 1975) and Frederick Engels (Engels and Leacock 1972) speaking about reproduction on the one side, and the women in my fieldwork speaking about reproduction on the other. But what was I to do with this ethnographic material? It did not rush out and tell me its significance. Yet, somehow, Haraway's can of beans provided an image of the materiality of the forces of production right in the object, and I was led to think about reproduction as a form of production.

I began to hear in the language of the obstetrics textbooks that reproduction was a form of production. Reproduction was not literally the same kind of thing as production: there was not a manufactured material object like a can. But in a sense the woman's body was an analog to canned goods. It was overdetermined that the activity of birth would be seen and organized as a form of manufacturing production. Nobody—not even those of us going through it at the time—could hear that women giving birth were being held to standards of production, time management, efficiency, and all the rest. Close attention to the imagery in medical textbooks and to the language women used in describing their experiences of menstruation and menopause led me to see that there were assumptions about the necessity of producing valuable products (babies) that informed interactions between physicians and women. Menstruation was taken to be the failure of production and the casting off of the ruined debris of this failure; menopause was taken to be the breakdown of the bureaucratically organized hormonal system that governed bodily production. Like an aging and outmoded factory, the menopausal body and mind were literally described as senile.

As with any ethnographic project, this one revealed that many women actively contested the assumptions that dominated medical contexts. Women, especially working-class women, found other, less productivity-oriented ways of thinking about menstruation. Much to my surprise, when offered the hypothetical chance to eliminate menstruation with a magic wand, most women I interviewed said they would not take it. In spite of their many complaints about the mess, bother, pain, and distress of menstruating, they saw it as an important marker of being an adult woman and something they felt forged important linkages with other women. Some women found that special abilities were unleashed while they were menstruating—vivid dreaming or poetic writing, for example. This led me to speculate that a society organized along different principles might value menstruation in different ways (Martin 1987).

Other anthropologists, thinking along similar lines, were realizing that our assumptions about such apparently stigmatizing practices as seclusion in a menstrual hut might have been mistaken. Working among the Beng in

Africa, Alma Gottlieb wondered if women might relish the break from their daily routines and find pleasure in the long-simmering stews they had the leisure to cook while in menstrual seclusion (Buckley and Gottlieb 1988). And in medical anthropology proper, a number of vigorous voices that placed medical institutions and practices in the context of unevenly distributed material resources and gendered ideologies were beginning to have an impact on anthropological studies of reproduction.[3] More broadly, political economic analyses of gender, culture, and practices concerning the body were emerging at this time (Comaroff 1985; Estroff 1985; Scheper-Hughes and Lock 1987). There had begun to be, not so much neighboring "groves" of scholars working in medical anthropology and feminism, as hybrid "graft" forms. On the one hand, the early faith in the virtues of progress that could be achieved by medical technologies was turning into a more subtle awareness of the ways medical knowledge itself entailed the imposition of control over the bodies and minds of women. On the other hand, it became clear that any anthropology of contemporary society worth its salt must include sites where medical knowledge was learned, practiced, and imposed. This led more and more anthropologists to find ways of studying medical contexts ethnographically in ways that could reveal the sometimes hidden forms of power they entailed.[4]

Science and Technology Studies

Later, in the mid-1990s, the problem of how to do fieldwork in the United States was no longer an issue. So many young anthropologists had by then been doing fieldwork in the United States that there was confidence that this could be done. The problem had become how to position work on topics like HIV/AIDS that seemed to encompass more social sites than those associated with medicine or even health. A key moment was a School for American Research conference on anthropology and STS. Organized by Joe Dumit, Gary Downey, and Sharon Traweek, the conference fostered serious engagement about how feminism could be understood in the 1990s, after women's studies programs were widely established and after the language of gender and sexuality, the need for feminist classroom practices, and the imperative to combat sexist employment practices, among other things, were widely accepted and in practice. Our conclusion at this conference was that critical anthropology and critical science studies simply *were* feminist. We spoke of hybrid—but we might have said "graft"—feminist-social-cultural theories (Downey and Dumit 1997, 159). We assumed that all of our STS work would centrally engage with issues of gender and race and class and how they interrelated. Anthropological ethnographic work in the early 1990s brought together insights into how ideas about gender inflect all aspects of scientific culture, from the nature of matter to the organization of hospital birth (Davis-Floyd 1993; Traweek 1992).

Anthropologists in STS were not the only ones realizing that race, class, and gender work together, not just as separate vectors that could be separated and compared but as systematically related cultural understandings of how people are different and practices that keep them different. (Of course to these three invidious distinctions, we would now add disability, age, sexuality, and religion among others.) In 1991 Kimberle Crenshaw, acknowledging her debt to feminist writings of the 1980s, published her article in the *Stanford Law Review*, "Mapping the Margins: Intersectionality, Identity Politics, and Violence against Women of Color" (Crenshaw 1991). In the early 2000s Leith Mullings and others held a conference titled "Intersectionality and Health," in which anthropologists and public health scholars worked together (Schulz and Mullings 2006). And the UN Committee on the Elimination of Racial Discrimination published its General Recommendation No. 25 on "Gender Related Dimensions of Racial Discrimination."[5] An understanding that invidious distinctions among different kinds of people rely on each other has been growing. "Intersectionality" lies at the heart of the third wave of feminism. But parenthetically I would insist that it is a wave that rode in on much earlier understandings of how inextricable all invidious distinctions are from each other. Perhaps a kinship image would work here. Second-wave feminism always found brotherhood in the civil rights movement as it had found sisterhood in earlier moments in the feminist struggle. Feminism was never an only child.

The combination of STS and anthropology led those of us working on issues concerned with health into broader literatures in the history and sociology of science: we gobbled up Bruno Latour, Michel Callon, Lorraine Daston, and Peter Galison and realized that the scientific labs lying behind medical treatments and clinical practices were important sites for understanding medicine, that material objects like drugs had social relations embedded in them, relations that could be tracked from production and manufacturing to marketing and advertising.[6] The field of STS stirred medical anthropology's pot. In turn, STS was not well known at the time for its engagement with feminist issues on any wave, and so the anthropological engagement stirred the STS pot as well.

Feminist Reprise

All these efforts could be described as ways of pushing back the boundary of what is taken as "natural" and putting it into historical and comparative contexts. For medical anthropology it was the "natural" body; for STS the knowledge of "nature"; for feminism the "nature" of women. In the 1990s feminism had to encounter things it had inadvertently naturalized. My encounter with this moment was in Baltimore, which had long been the site of a vigorous community feminist movement, whose reading and discussion groups I frequented. I remember vividly the time, shortly after her arrival at Hopkins, that Judy Butler joined us at a meeting. I no longer remember what we were reading, but I do remember that she confronted us: weren't we being complacent to imagine that the issues of concern—reproduction, relations between men and women, and so on—mattered to all women in the same way, especially to women who desired other women? Who exactly was the "we" referred to in our texts? It was not her intent, but after her visit, this particular group did not meet again. I think it broke up, not out of rejection of her point but out of realizing that our models were too limited and had assumed far too much. New and deeper forms of analysis were being called for. We had been working with unmarked categories that served as the naturalized ground against which other kinds of bodies had to be studied (Butler 1999).

Feminism respected difference, but it had continued to make assumptions about the meanings of bodies. David Valentine asks, "If feminist anthropology has come to respect differences along lines of race, class, and culture can we also respect differences in bodies that defy what are still really the biological basis of many of our categories? It surely complicates our categories and our understandings of gender and sexuality to have gay men who call parts of their bodies clitorises; or lesbians who speak of their penises; or a person who occasionally refers to hir [spelled h-i-r] vagina as hir penis" (2007, 29). Inspired by this kind of concern, my work in HIV/AIDS was intended to broaden the canvas of the illness to include something everyone was concerned about—the immune system—and to undercut the singular association between gay men and HIV/AIDS. At this time in anthropology there was a dilemma—how to keep reiterating the importance of factors like race and gender without playing into popular conceptions that vilified groups on that basis. At one Wenner-Gren conference I remember how angry an administrator got when my paper on the assigned topic "Women and AIDS" in her view failed to address the category "women." Perhaps it was the Judy Butler moment, which forced us to confront how feminism had naturalized some of its basic categories, that led me to seek out fieldwork sites that threw the categories into question. The question was how to look at social processes obliquely, how to upend, set askew, the commonsense sociological terms like "women" that we take for granted.

I explored concepts of "the immune system," which young mothers, gay couples, and working-class community leaders could all discuss, and workplace training sites, where workers of every description were being cajoled and coerced into becoming flexible and adaptive risk takers. People drew memorable pictures of their bodies' immune systems that spoke eloquently of new concepts that were replacing the older orderly bureaucratic systems of command and control. One woman drew a picture of ocean waves to illustrate the dynamic nature of the immune system. Mothers would cavalierly allow children to eat food they had dropped on the street, saying that their child's immune system would be up to the challenge. Doctors spoke of having immune systems that could "kick ass" and of keeping them in training by drinking unpurified water while abroad. At workplace training sites, managers and workers were formed into teams and faced with the challenge of high ropes courses. They were being trained to tolerate risk, face up to their fears, and rely on the strengths of the team. This was happening on the cusp of an era in which restructuring involving downsizing became normal: the corporation was explicitly hoping to make managers and workers into new kinds of people who could "evolve" with the aid of self-study, corporate training sessions, and an insistence on self-management when they were lucky enough to be employed inside a corporation and then aggressive entrepreneurialism during the frequent periods they were now expected to spend outside. The model of the body as a complex, flexibly adapting system was being written also at the level of organizations, "bodies" on a larger scale. In both cases individuals perceived as weak and unable to swiftly adapt were considered doomed or at least impaired. Women and gay men came in for special attention as having compromised immune systems: women were seen as greatly susceptible to autoimmune diseases and gay men to HIV/AIDS (Martin 1994).

At about this time, anthropologists were developing what came to be dubbed "multi-sited ethnography," which was a term meant to capture ethnographies done in complex settings, beyond the bounds of particular locales or institutions (Marcus 1995). Anthropologists interested in medical issues were now encouraged to follow medical practices outside the clinic or laboratory into popular media, workplaces, domestic settings, and so on.[7] Since medical practices were perhaps the most obvious candidate to illuminate social processes that worked simultaneously in popular culture, formal institutions, domestic settings, and work places, among others, it could be said that the whole field of anthropology received a push in the direction of multi-sited ethnography because of methods the study of medicine made necessary.

Eventually I was able to link this ethnography on emerging concepts of immunity in U.S. society specifically to reproduction and women's bodies. I learned that cardiologists had abandoned the long-held idea that the heart beats with the regularity of a metronome in the face of new evidence that the heart responds adaptively to its environment, flexibly changing the rate of its beat in accord with the body's activity and emotional state. In fact, they now realized, the heart comes to beat with the regularity of a metronome only when it is close to death. With this in mind, the castigation of women's bodies in menopause as broken down and out of order took on new significance for me. If the medical language of obstetrics and gynecology could follow the path of cardiology, perhaps women's bodies, cycling monthly and then resetting at menopause, could be seen as paradigms of the new adaptive, ever-changing, responsive ideal. This might provide an answer to the notion that the bodies of women and gay men have inherently compromised immune systems (Martin 1999).

Future Directions

MORE ENGAGEMENT WITH HISTORY OF SCIENCE

Medical anthropology would benefit from engaging more seriously with scholarship in the history of science. Taking more leaps between medical anthropology and science studies with a historical bent would open up productive new questions. Regula Burri and Joe Dumit (2007) stress the importance of the "scientification" of medicine: medicine is increasingly intertwined with science and its technologies; medicine is increasingly implementing a science-based process of rationalization. It follows that we as medical anthropologists have to understand better what makes science tick at an epistemological level. Just as, in its early days, medical anthropology drew on neighboring sciences such as biology, medicine today is doing the same, so we need to understand better the deep assumptions that govern the scientific method. New ideas might emerge out of attention to the old material culture of medicine, the stethoscope or the thermometer, and to ancient ideas that still play a part in medical concepts of fever, pulse, muscles, and flows. At issue would be epistemological assumptions that enable historically specific understandings of number, measurement, conservation, time, space, or mass. Mauss's wonderful essay title "Conceptions Which Have Preceded the Notion of Matter" published in 1939 evokes the idea (Mauss and Schlanger 2006). Nietzsche famously said "truths are illusions of which one has forgotten they are illusions; worn out metaphors which have become powerless to affect the senses; coins with their images effaced and now no longer of account as coins but merely metal" (1979, 92). We might think of following "coins with their images effaced" into the past of medical anthropology. In *Cambridge and the Torres Straits*, edited by Anita Herle and Sandra Rouse, there are evocative photos of early measuring devices used by W. H. R. Rivers, Haddon, Seligman, and others (Herle and Rouse 1998). The color wheel is shown in a photograph with Rivers (Richards 1998, 143); Holmgren's wools (which test for color blindness) are shown in a photograph with Seligman (Richards 1998, 144). Both devices were used to test visual perception: the anthropologists' research question was whether the visual perceptions of Europeans and Torres Straits Islanders differed significantly. (Contrary to the assumptions of some, they did not.) Such habitual ways of gathering data have been called materializing devices because they are what bring things into view that we then take to be facts (Mayer 2006). They deserve our careful attention.

The photographs of early materializing devices help make the point that medical anthropology has had such practices in its history from the beginning. We could look back at Arthur Kleinman's pathbreaking early research on depression in China and Taiwan or Charles Leslie's in India (Kleinman 1980; Kleinman and Good 1985; Leslie 1998): are there equivalents to these early technologies that would help us understand the assumptions built into the field from the beginning? Like any other scientific investigators, medical anthropologists do not so much "discover" facts as "produce" them through specific technologies. We might belittle the famous "enactments" of Australian indigenous rituals staged by Spencer and Gillen, and also in the Torres Straits (Herle 1998, 93), but isn't an interview actually an enactment rather than something witnessed in real time? Could we explore the effects (enabling and limiting) of the interview itself? How is it related to the psychiatric intake interview or the physician-patient interview?

I am beginning a new project on the history of the "subject" in experimental psychology. How was (and still is) a human being held constant in time and space so that data can be extracted from him or her? My participation as a subject in psychology experiments leads me to propose a modest candidate for a scientific technology central to the psychological experiment, an example of a coin with its image effaced: the table. Obvious and overlooked, the table is nonetheless an essential accompaniment of civilized living: the first thing Robinson Crusoe did after being shipwrecked on his island was build a table. As he put it, "I could not write or eat, or do several things, with so much comfort, without a table" (Defoe 2007, 36). Early anthropological experiments depended on tables to hold their equipment steady, at eye level, and off the ground. Photographs from the Torres Straits expedition make it clear that tables played an important role in the experiments of Seligman and Rivers: Haddon draws a picture of his work table in a letter to his son.

A table is a technology that stabilizes people and things in space for a time. The table, with its chair, enforces a posture of attention to what is on it. It permits display and use of other tools and enables precise recording on paper. The photograph chosen to represent the ethnographic work of Claude Lévi-

Strauss in his obituary showed him in a Brazilian rain forest standing by a table made of sticks lashed together (Rothstein 2009). Would medical anthropologists be able to shed new light on the problems that interest them by attending to such nearly invisible (because taken for granted) technologies in medical contexts? Does medical research on microbes or with patients sometimes *depend on* the existence of such invisible apparatuses? Susan Star and Martha Lampland (2009) speak of the importance of studying infrastructures that enable and support social activities, infrastructures that are designed to become invisible as they are stabilized. What could we learn from investigating how specific technologies enable and limit medical practices, such as the hypodermic needle? The stethoscope? The thermometer?

Infrastructures like the table are not necessarily passive. Perhaps the table is even a kind of trap. Open and inviting a table might seem, but once you are sitting at it, certain forms of courtesy might serve to hold you there. Alfred Gell famously described a hunting trap as a device that embodies ideas and conveys meanings because it is a "transformed representation of its maker, the hunter, and the prey animal, its victim, and of their mutual relationship, which . . . is a complex, quintessentially social one. . . . [T]raps communicate the idea of a nexus of intentionalities between hunters and prey animals via material forms and mechanisms" (1996, 29). If the table can be thought of as a kind of trap to capture and contain a subject, it is a disarming one—it looks so placid and innocent for something that has the potential for intrusion and control. Perhaps this is one reason it has largely gone without notice. Nor need the table, or any technology, only have one use. Think about dinner tables, talk show tables, and of course medical examination tables. Nor are such tools neutral in the play of gender dynamics: think of the "head" of the table, or "high" table, both of which provide a stage for social hierarchies.

In the photo of Rivers with the color wheel, Rivers and his companion (his name is Tom) are on the same side of the table: Rivers is showing him how to use the color wheel. At this time in psychology the experimenter and subject were not separated in a stable way. We often marvel at how willing early anthropologists were to use their own bodies as research instruments. When Henry Head and Rivers experimented on nerve regeneration, Head had Rivers cut the cutaneous nerves in his own forearm (steadied by a table) in order to watch how they grew back. This is one noteworthy extreme, but there were less dramatic examples. In an item from the expedition archive, a graphical "table," we see that Rivers set his Torres Straits Islander subjects' response times alongside his fellow ethnographers' to show that there were no differences between Torres Straits Islanders and Europeans (Kuklick 1998, 177). In Rivers's time the researcher was a sampling device; participant observation was part of the accepted experimental method in science. In today's psychology both the experimenter and the subject have been firmly stabilized. But looking to the past when the lines between experimenter and subject were blurred could suggest interesting ways of exploring how scientific knowledge might be produced in new ways.

These are paths not yet—or not often—taken, potentialities not foreclosed —merely submerged. Together with the vibrant, engaged research in medical anthropology going on in every corner of the globe, exploring this terrain could yet yield new insights into the very science throbbing powerfully behind the practice of medicine. Some STS scholars are in their turn conducting studies on topics also studied by medical anthropologists. Brain imaging, heart disease, or panic disorder are some examples.[8]

TACKLING REDUCTIONISM

These kinds of explorations would allow us to tackle reductionism with greater effect. In the *New York Times Magazine* a few years ago, there was an article about the brain and mental illness. It showed a drawing of a brain, not the head but the brain, with red dots: one was labeled schizophrenia, one was labeled bipolar disorder, and one was labeled ADHD. Down below this brain there was a little old-fashioned man, apparently from the eighteenth century, looking through a telescope at this brain as though it were a sky (Raeburn 2005). It is a straightforward statement that in due course, not too far in the future, we will be able to scan the brain and find out whether someone has a bipolar brain, a schizophrenic brain, or whatever. The idea the article conveys is that the physical, material organ, the brain, is where psychiatric conditions are located. Differential diagnosis will be premised on the reading of the image of the brain, the way a nephrologist assumes the location of kidney disease is the patient's kidney. As this model of the preeminence of the material enters into psychiatry, the idea is that we will get beyond the psychiatrist asking the patient what's causing pain in his or her life—

instead, we will just scan the brain! The complete primacy of the physicality of mental illness is just assumed. It is as if Donna's "material-semiotic" were sundered and only the "material" were left. Where I can intervene as an anthropologist is to rescue the "semiotic," to take what is left over from that account, focus on what that account does not include and cannot include. To try, through descriptions and by using ethnography, to show what that account leaves out. What that account leaves out is the anthropological insight that relationships and practices imbued with meanings are a life lived, not merely a symptom of an underlying physical truth.

What would addressing those omissions do to our analysis of all the institutions that are premised on our ability to separate human from animal, rational from irrational? What would addressing those omissions do to what is perhaps the deepest trench dug between the rational and the irrational—in the form of the cultural category of "mental illness"? Perhaps the next great binary to fall, after nature/culture, male/female, and the others, is rationality/irrationality. Profound implications emerge from exploring what Ann Stoler calls the "conceit of reason," a conceit that leads us to think any institution, nation, or person could be built on a structure of the rational (1995, 165). We do not need to *add* emotions to rationality; we need to follow the consequences of realizing that rationality is a skeleton that has never actually lived on this earth: its "bones" are made up of "blood," visceral material enlivened by "irrational" emotions and sentiment.

Studies of psychiatric disorders by medical anthropologists have a particularly rich opportunity to benefit from these kinds of questions. Entering this terrain in my recent work on bipolar disorder, I found that ethnographic methods could situate the problem of mental illness in a broad cultural context and thus lead to counterintuitive insights. Participant observation in support groups for bipolar disorder enabled me to realize that the terms of the *Diagnostic and Statistical Manual of Mental Disorders* (DSM) were not always onerous labels that objectified and stigmatized people, though they have often been vilified for this. Another possibility emerged: the DSM can act as a cloak against further scrutiny of people's interior experience. Nikolas Rose writes about forms of psychological knowledge as "*techniques for the disciplining of human difference*" (1998, 105; emphasis in original). He refers to the way psychological tests of all kinds—for intelligence, personality, or cognition—as well as psychological surveys or systematic observations at work, school, or home "individualiz[e] humans through classifying them, calibrating their capacities and conducts, inscribing and recording their attributes and deficiencies, managing and utilizing their individuality and variability." Once people are given a scientific label for their pathological condition, they can use that label as protection against further scrutiny. The terms "bipolar 2" or "major depression" can bounce from one person to another without calling for examination and so allow people to keep their interior landscape closed to comparison, correction, or calibration against the norm. Instead of acting as agents of their own internalized knowledge, they may be cloaking themselves using the very terms of scientific knowledge. The terms found in the DSM can act something like an atomic table of elements for mental illness; they aim to describe the whole universe of mental illness, and every condition can therefore presumably be given a place to belong within it. Using the terms is a shorthand others can be assumed to understand, and this assumption may make further explanation of what lies within actual individual experience seem unnecessary. In this sense, the DSM would act as a shield against revealing more intimate psychic experiences.

As I pursued a detailed analysis of the history of the concepts involved in mood disorders (following the example of scholars in the history of science), I could see that a central notion in the definition of these disorders is not only mood but also motivation. Manic states are associated with unremitting energy, little need for sleep, and immense drive to throw things—money, social connections—into circulation. Depressed states, associated with lack of energy, too much sleep, and inactivity, occupy the opposite end of the scale. Together the range from high to low motivation illuminates how it is that "manic" individuals, like Ted Turner, Richard Branson, or Robin Williams, have become iconic of a certain kind of creative productive energy suited to the demands of the current economic system. The cultural desire for occupying a state imagined to be highly productive and creative joins forces with the possibility of using psychopharmaceutical means to optimize moods to that end. During my fieldwork, a psychiatrist who practices in Hollywood told me that, "Where I work, we get a lot of Hollywood comedians coming in. They are manic-depressives. There are two important things about this: first, they do not want their condition publicized, and second, their managers always get involved in the details of their treatment. The managers want the mania treated just so. They do not want it floridly out of control, but they also absolutely do not want it damped down too much."

This psychiatrist felt he was being called upon to *optimize* his patients' moods (for particular professions and for the particular kinds of creativity each requires) through proper management of their drugs. Potential new forms of subjectivity and economic pressures from the pharmaceutical industry come together to enable a new psychiatric frontier. What does it take to be the sort of person who can survive in the midst of relentless competition? How can markets for psychiatric disorders be increased lest sales and marketing departments lose jobs? On this frontier, not confined to any medical institution and often not confined to those with a psychiatric diagnosis, people are forging ways of trying to thrive in demanding neoliberal circumstances (Martin 2007, 220–21).

PUBLIC ANTHROPOLOGY

In all such potential efforts, whom are we addressing? Can we imagine reaching an audience beyond the other scholars working in similar fields or practitioners in public health or health policy? What kind of writing would work to grab and hold people's attention in public venues? What makes an op-ed work as writing that is readable and gripping? In a recent article in the *New York Times Magazine* Nicolas Kristof and Sheryl WuDunn (2009) described women's rights as the cause of our time. I am sure most of us who read it had no trouble seeing exactly how an anthropological perspective is missing from this account. But how do they write so persuasively despite such obvious illogic? What are the textual moves that allow the narrative to go along so convincingly? We need to analyze the narrative structure of publications that grab the reader as closely as we do their content. In brief my thought is that the structure often moves between individuals (Goretti Nyabenda of Burundi) and universals (promote development everywhere by providing women and girls with education, loans, and health care). How can we make it compelling to ask about intervening processes—cultural and social processes— that are anything but universal, without ending up in the weak position of saying "it's complicated"? Surely anthropologists can make the case, if only given the chance, that culturally specific family dynamics can siphon resources away from girls, or that state-level politics can divert development resources to destinations other than girls. The anthropological contribution would not be to discourage the laudable Kristof and WuDunn goals but to show that we ✓ cannot achieve them without knowledge of the intervening social structures and cultural convictions.

It goes without saying that our material practices need a material platform from which to speak. We need technologies that produce media friendly to our point of view. What can one do? Learn how to write an op-ed: take a seminar from the Op-ed Project, a social movement that offers seminars in the craft of writing and publishing an op-ed (http://www.theopedproject.org/). Support the new general interest magazine *Anthropology Now* or the UC press series in public anthropology. Blog on *Savage Minds*, *Somatosphere*, or the many other anthropological websites. Work with scholars in other countries to bring out publications friendly to the general reader or curriculum suitable for secondary education.[9]

Conclusions

I have shown how the engagement between medical anthropology and feminism led medical anthropologists to sharpen their appreciation of the ways political economic factors are present in the largest and smallest scale interactions; feminist scholars in turn were eager to apply the tools of their analysis in medical contexts because these contexts lay at the center of contemporary forms of power. Rather than simply sharing the same territory, scholars from these fields sharpened their analyses and extended their reach. In the case of STS, the exchange has also gone in both ways. We might say that medical anthropology and STS have been plucking branches from each other's groves. In the future I am hoping that some sturdy grafts will take hold.

Getting at Anthropology through Medical History

Notes on the Consumption of Chinese Embryos and Fetuses in the Western Imagination

One of anthropology's foremost goals has always been to examine meaning making in its historical and cultural contexts. Another of anthropology's goals, at least since the 1980s, has been to be reflexive and self-critical about the circumstances and truth claims of knowledge production, both inside and outside its own disciplinary confines. This chapter demonstrates the benefits and challenges of combining anthropology and history, using an empirical case study that began as an investigation of the historical emergence of embryo and fetal subjectivity in the United States. Although prompted by an anthropologist's question about the relationship between embodiment and personhood, the project took me into the archives to find evidence about a human embryo-collecting project based at Johns Hopkins in the early twentieth century. There, amid the handwritten correspondence of now-departed anatomists and anthropologists, I learned that anatomists working in China had been influenced by anthropological debates about human evolution, which in turn affected their work as archaeologists, comparative anatomists, and racial embryologists. Had I been a historian, I might have analyzed changing notions of sexuality in postimperial Chinese society, public health in the port cities, or the nationalist politics of Chinese hominid archaeology (Dikötter 1995; Rogaski 2004; Schmalzer 2008). As an anthropologist, however, I was able to range more freely, finding meaning not only in highbrow scholarly debates but in popular culture and tacking back and forth between the present and the past. The results raised questions about anthropological complicity—past and present—in casting "the Chinese" as a people who allegedly mistreat their young.

This chapter is unconventional by the standards of anthropology and history. My goal, though, was never to police, patrol, traverse, or even intentionally to transgress disciplinary boundaries; after all, as Margaret Lock points out, anthropologists have always excelled at "troubling natural categories," including those that traditionally divide the disciplines (2001, 478). This may be especially true of medical anthropologists, who seem to specialize in interrogating the boundaries between healthy and ill, sane and insane, dead and alive. Perhaps it matters in this regard that I was trained as a Latin Americanist in the materialist mold, which meant that history was never only about the past but about the literal instantiation in the present of social inequalities, material realities, and power structures. Although the disciplinary divisions between history and anthropology never held much practical importance for me, others concerned with this relationship have carried on a lively conversation. In the words of Gerald Sider and Gavin Smith, "The issue of the more or less self-conscious *construction* of histories by our subjects and by ourselves has now become the most well travelled bridge between anthropologists and historians" (1997, 5, emphasis in original; see also Axel 2002; Brieger 2004; Kalb and Tak 2005; Kertzer 2009). Instead of summarizing a long dialogue, this chapter aims rather to model a synthesis, demonstrating in the process how the methods and insights of anthropologists and historians enlivened my research and sharpened my critical and reflexive sense about the worlds within which human embryos and fetuses are "made up" (Hacking 2007). This project did not start out as a conscious effort to combine two disciplines. Rather, interdisciplinarity was forced on me as my subject matter led me into a thicket of entwined and convoluted fields: the history of physical anthropology, feminist fetal studies and the anthropology of reproduction, social studies of science and technology, changing attitudes toward racial classification, Chinese village ethnographies, and missionary reports and travelogues.

The taming of such an interdisciplinary project—even without adding a multi-sited ethnographic component—can be daunting. As Susan Erikson wisely notes, "in global ethnography we try to do too much" (2011, 25). There are many ways to approach what Erikson terms the "problems of theory and method" generated by the unshakable commitment to research problems that are both local *and* global. Several scholars have taken the approach of tracking particular scientific entities, processes, or groups through byzantine global flows and transformations, without sacrificing ethnographic specificity or our commitment to understanding local worlds of meaning making. Warwick Anderson uses this approach when he suggests putting together "a specific genealogy of metaphors, practices, and careers that links the colony with the metropole and with other colonies, that one might follow people, technologies, and ideas as they move from one site to another." The medical doctors with whom he worked, like the anatomists, anthropologists, and consumers of popular culture described in this chapter, "were itinerants, with a global view of things that historians, so preoccupied with the local and constrained by nation or region, are only now coming to appreciate" (2006, 7). Scholars of science and medicine have recently begun to embrace interdisciplinarity, reading, researching, and writing across disciplines, despite reviewers' sometimes persnickety efforts to rein them in. The ingenuity and creativity they generate has been enormously productive for our understandings of the history of dissection, fetal subjectivity, visual anatomy, and the colonial legacy of global scientific specimen collecting (see Anderson 2006, 2008; Casper 1998; Clarke 1998; Duden 1993; Landecker 2007; Sappol 2002; Starn 2004). The concept that grounded my own research was an interest in knowing how embryo and fetal specimens—those immensely interesting products of conception— "mobilized people . . . and enabled them to think differently about their bodies, social life and place in the world" (Anderson 2006, 10–11).

The Baby Towers

Around 1860 Americans and Europeans who traveled in China began to write home about the "baby towers" they encountered on the outskirts of several cities (see figure 1). These were structures of stone or brick, about twenty feet in diameter and between twelve and twenty feet high with tiled roofs. They had no doors, only a high shuttered window through which infant corpses could be placed. The only English-language ethnographic background about baby towers dates back more than a century. J. J. M. de Groot (1854–1921), a Dutch religious scholar, favored a benevolent interpretation. He described the baby towers as repositories built to keep infant bodies from being devoured by scavenging pigs or birds (1897, 1388).[1] Yet most Western writers were not so generous, and sensational reports of Chinese baby towers circulated in the Western

Figure 1. Baby tower, 1917–1919, Guan Xian (Sichuan, China), Sidney D. Gamble Photographs. Rare Book, Manuscript, and Special Collections Library, Duke University.

press well into the twentieth century. A characteristic description comes from a Western writer traveling in China in 1858, who said that he had asked for an explanation of the "more than usually pestilential stench" emanating from a nearby structure. To this his guide replied, "The Baby-tower. Look through that rent in the stonework—not too close, or the stream of effluvia may kill you. You see a mound of whisps [*sic*] of bamboo straw. It seems to move, but it is only the crawling of the worms. Sometimes a tiny leg or arm, or a little fleshless bone, protrudes from the straw. The tower is not so full now as I have seen it; they must have cleared it out recently."

The visitor inquired, "Is this a cemetery or a slaughterhouse?"

The guide replied, "The Chinese say it is only a tomb. Coffins are dear, and the peasantry are poor. When a child dies, the parents wrap it round with bamboo, throw it in at that window, and all is done. When the tower is full, the proper authorities burn the heap, and spread the ashes over the land" (Cooke 1858, 99).

Despite the qualified assurance that it was "only a tomb," most Western accounts described baby towers as places where parents could "dispose of the bodies of unwanted children," many of whom had been "starved, drowned, or poisoned" (Bennett 1918, 24). Missionaries often claimed that the baby towers were an invitation to infanticide. In 1895 the Junior Christian Endeavor Society newsletter contained this item: "May the Junior Christian Endeavor Society do something to abolish the awful disregard for infant life typified by the baby-tower. May it show to myriads of this nation the value of the soul of the little one, and inspire it with such love for little ones as He had who said, 'Suffer the little children to come unto me, and forbid them not'" (Clark 1895, 415).[2] Baby towers continued to symbolize the "awful Chinese disregard for infant life" for at least seventy years in part, perhaps, because such titillating charges loosened the purse strings of supporters back home. Missionaries were not the only ones to perpetuate word of the baby tower—W. Somerset Maugham wrote about a baby tower he found in an unnamed Chinese city in 1919 (Maugham 1922, 168; see also Mather 1910, 135).[3] Yet at that point few Chinese baby towers remained. Under intense attack from self-avowed Western civilizers, they were gradually walled up, destroyed, and forgotten.

An Appetite for Dead Babies

Although few Westerners remember the baby towers anymore,[4] the trope of Chinese "disregard for infant life" persists in the form of outrageous tales (and videos) consumed in the West about what the Chinese do (and allegedly do) to their young. Contemporary accounts focus also on the vulnerability of the unborn in China. In this climate, well-documented realities (such as the impact of China's One-Child Policy, in effect since 1979, on forced and sex-selective abortion) tend to get mixed up with fabrications, each feeding the other. Indeed, it sometimes seems that new terms and topics simply replace the old, while the moralistic messages from an earlier era remain intact: from baby towers to forced abortion, from missionary orphanages to newborns stolen for sale on the international adoption market, from female infanticide to sex-selective abortion and forty million "missing girls" (Elegant 2007; Nie 2009). As Westerners' fears of economic marginalization increasingly focus on the perceived threat posed by China, the truth of such reports tended to get exaggerated and sometimes confused with racist tabloid fantasies, to the point where it becomes very difficult to tell fact from fiction. Starting in the mid-1990s, for example, lurid rumors began to circulate on the Internet about Chinese fetal cannibalism.[5] Educated readers might be tempted to dismiss allegations about the Chinese consumption of soups and dumplings made from aborted fetuses, if elected officials in the United States had not entered the charges into the Congressional Record as fact (more on that later).[6]

The aim of this chapter is to highlight a paradoxical contradiction: while reports of baby towers and fetal dumplings circulated in the West, Westerners were (and are) engaged in their own consumption of Chinese "little ones." My primary case study centers on a little-known embryo-collecting project led by Western anatomists at the Peking Union Medical College (PUMC) in the 1910s and 1920s, during which four hundred Chinese embryos and fetuses were gathered for anatomical analysis. Nearly a century later, the Western appetite for Chinese embryos, fetuses, and infants is evident in the way that Westerners produce and consume indignant, sensationalized stories about horrors suffered by Chinese babies.[7] The discipline of anthropology, I argue, is implicated in the Western consumption of Chinese embryos and fetuses, both because anthropology provided the historical justification for the PUMC embryo-collecting project and because anthropologists are sometimes insufficiently critical of the ways in which our actions might be complicit in perpetuating pernicious stereotypes. By drawing together the discrete but contemporaneous projects of collecting embryos and condemning baby towers, I illustrate three points.

First, anthropology provided an important justification for Chinese embryo collecting in the early twentieth century, because of the discipline's concern with documenting the biological basis of racial variation. The Protestant missionary presence as well as the PUMC embryo-collecting endeavor were both born of an ideological desire to rescue Chinese children (through God and medicine, respectively) and thus to bring modernity to China. In both projects the vision of modernity was predicated on the anatomists' belief in fundamental, preexisting biological and moral differences between Euro-American and Chinese "races." Although the significance of embryology to anthropology has been largely ignored by contemporary historians of scientific racism, in fact the embryological study of human biological variation was once considered an integral part of the anthropologists' quest for human origins. The anatomists collected embryos because, as they explained it, they wanted to "get at anthropology through embryology" (Cowdry 1919a). Following Haeckel's well-known (and now discredited) postulate that "ontogeny recapitulates phylogeny," the anatomists hoped to find in human embryos empirical evidence of racial variations (and thus of disparate human origins) that might disappear later in gestation. The concern with Chinese reproduction thus has a deeper association with the discipline of anthropology than has been previously acknowledged.

Second, this chapter aims to show that the categories known as "race" and "embryo" or "fetus" were historically coproduced and mutually constituted. In other words, the discourse of race relied on that of embryology in the way it acquired its social significance and came into circulation and vice versa; the epistemological content of each category was informed by the other. The PUMC anatomists considered themselves to be specialists charged with producing knowledge about race and embryology. For this reason, they sought evidence of racial variation in human anatomy, including in the anatomical and morphological features of the embryo specimens that they were beginning to collect in large quantities (Morgan 2009). During the 1920s Western scientists were particularly interested in the "racial embryology" of the Chinese, because they thought these exotic specimens might offer definitive (that is, purer and less hybridized or contaminated) evidence of biologically based racial variation. Their desire for Chinese specimens was ideologically distinct from and yet consistent with the baby towers trope, because both projects emphasized the benefits to society of Westerners "saving" Chinese babies. Juxtaposing the practice of collecting fetal specimens with that of condemning baby towers can thus "clarify the ways in which bringing technoscientific phenomena or objects [such as "embryos" or "racial differences"] into being... require[s] the simultaneous production of scientific ideas and practices *and* other social practices... that support them" (Reardon 2005, 6). We can trace at least two antecedents of contemporary global biopolitics to the PUMC embryo-collecting and racial embryology projects: the ongoing global denigration of "unsanitary citizens" (Briggs and Mantini-Briggs 2004) that targets the Chinese for their mistreatment of "little ones" and the intellectual links between the concepts of "race" and "embryo" or "fetus" that were then emerging into sociopolitical consciousness.

Third, by creating a retrospective juxtaposition between missionaries (with their righteous abhorrence of baby towers), anatomists (with their blithe anatomical collecting practices), and anthropologists (who were largely oblivious to the violence engendered by their theorizing), this chapter calls for greater acknowledgment of the vestiges of anthropological complicity in a long-standing project to Orientalize and Other the Chinese. Yet in the spirit of reflexivity, I have to acknowledge the difficulties of the subject position I have created for myself in conducting this kind of retrospective analysis. I risk casting myself as the politically correct reader of an objectionable past, without admitting into evidence or seriously engaging claims of human rights abuses or fetal cannibalism (past or present) in China. As an ironic observer of Western excesses, I position myself outside the fray and offer instead a series of disclaimers: I am not a Sinologist, I do not speak or read Chinese, I am not denying the "violence of everyday life," including the possibility that humans might kill baby girls or consume fetal tissue (Scheper-Hughes 2002). This lets me off the hook, allowing me to say, "Let others evaluate claims about baby towers and fetus soup and listen to sobbing women describe abortions committed against their will. Let others track down the sources of journalists who write about 'Chinese citizens eating human fetuses for health reasons.'"[8] Is it ethical to leave other anthropologists to shoulder the political and professional risks of investigating the effects of China's One-Child Policy and the persecution of human rights workers and families who do (or do not) protest those policies (see Fong 2004; Greenhalgh 2008; Greenhalgh and Winckler 2005)? What legitimate claim to ethical behavior can be asserted by a writer who rehabilitates the maligned Chinese patrons of the baby towers while framing her queries safely within an anthropological "culture of critique" (Bharadwaj 2009)?[9] The story I tell below, of a long-forgotten embryo-collecting project that took place in China in the early twentieth century, raises disturbing questions about what fuels the Western appetite for Chinese fetuses, the role of anthropologists in creating and perpetuating a sanctimonious culture of critique, and just who the real "heathens" were (and are).

Bottling Babies in Peking

In the 1920s a small group of North American anatomists and anthropologists began to build a collection of Chinese embryo and fetal specimens. They were in essence constructing a far-flung outpost of a project then under way in Baltimore, where anatomists and physicians based at Johns Hopkins Medical School were collecting and sectioning thousands of human embryo and fetal specimens (Morgan 2009). The PUMC, created by the Rockefeller Foundation in 1917 to bring allopathic medicine to China, was modeled after the Johns Hopkins Medical School (Bullock 1980). One of the first faculty members to arrive in China was a Canadian-born anatomist named Edmund V. Cowdry (1888–1975),[10] who had just finished a postdoctoral residency in embryology at Johns Hopkins. His duties at the PUMC included teaching gross anatomy and dissection.

Anatomists employed in teaching hospitals were expected to have on hand a suitable collection of cadavers for dissection. In addition to the adult cadavers he would require, Cowdry also wanted to develop what he called an "embryo" collection of specimens in formaldehyde. In addition to using it for teaching purposes, he and his medical colleagues could use the collection to test their theories, advance their careers, and loosen the purse strings of donors back home. To acquire specimens, Cowdry invited Western missionary doctors to send him any remains they encountered in the clinic, and they eagerly complied with his request to participate in this scientific endeavor. The specimens they sent to Cowdry included the products of miscarriage and stillbirth, as well as fetuses obtained from operations (such as hysterectomies) and autopsies performed on pregnant women.[11] In his view dead embryos and fetuses were valuable scientific research materials that belonged within the jurisdiction of biomedical science and anthropology (Clarke 1987, 1991). He was using the same logic and techniques he had learned in Baltimore at the Carnegie Institution of Washington's Department of Embryology. That project, in turn, trained doctors around Baltimore to believe that the most enlightened way to dispose of miscarried tissue and fetal remains would be to donate them to science, where they could be used for research and teaching purposes and thus benefit the greater good.

Cowdry would have preferred to acquire *embryo* specimens from the early stages of development (technically the first eight weeks of gestational development), but in fact he willingly accepted prenatal specimens from the full gestational and even postnatal period. The majority of the four hundred specimens that Cowdry was eventually able to acquire were late-gestation fetuses, and the collection even included the remains of several *infants* that died at two, four, or eight months of age. Although the older specimens were of little use in studying embryological morphology, they could be used for dissection to demonstrate normal and pathological development to medical students and doctors. When specimens arrived at Cowdry's laboratory he stored them not in baby towers but in formaldehyde, in fancy, hand-blown jars that he ordered from Germany.

The irony should be obvious. Here was a Western anatomist who collected and "saved" (note the double-entendre, with "save" implying both "possession" and "salvation") the remains of dead Chinese "little ones" with missionary fervor in the name of science, at the same time that Western missionaries were denouncing the Chinese for collecting dead infants in baby towers. While Westerners cast the baby towers as evidence of Chinese backwardness, depravity, and godlessness, the anatomists considered specimen collecting a manifestation of medical progress and their concern for bettering human welfare through science. Contemporary accounts often continue to separate these discourses, describing Chinese population policies in moralistic terms as "humiliating," "coercive," or "extreme," while applauding "cutting edge" developments in Chinese reproductive and regenerative medicine. This chapter examines the historical role played by anthropology, both in the practice of Chinese embryo collecting and in denouncing the contemporary moral equivalents of the much-maligned Chinese baby towers.

Getting at Anthropology through Embryology

Anthropology was a capacious field of study in the early 1900s. In addition to ethnology, it encompassed the various subfields of physical anthropology: zoological anthropology, paleoanthropology, anatomical anthropology, physiological anthropology, taxonomic anthropology, racial psychology, racial pathology, and racial embryology (*American Anthropologist* 1909, 482). Racial comparisons were central to the anthropological mission, in part to address competing theories about the origin of the species and thus human identity itself (Schmalzer 2008). The polygenecists, following in the footsteps of Samuel George Morton (1799–1851) and Louis Agassiz (1807–1873), held that the modern races evolved from separate origins as distinct species. Orthogenecists posited that evolution was driven by an internal force and that modern humans were derived from a single ancestor, while other paleoanthropologists proposed that natural selection drove a single ancestral species into the diversity of modern races (Shipman 2002, 267). Evidence to resolve these questions would come from three sources: *comparative anatomy* would enable scientists to determine functional and evolutionary relationships among species, *fossil evidence* would give insight into extinct organisms and historical patterns, and *embryology* could "fill in missing data" if indeed Haeckel's biogenetic law were correct (Wolpoff and Caspari 1998, 133; see also Abu El-Haj 2007).

By the 1910s the search for human origins was shifting to China. Henry Fairfield Osborn, of the American Museum of Natural History, was convinced that humans originated in Asia (rather than Africa), and by 1916 his associate, Roy Chapman Andrews, was scouring China for evidence to support that theory. "In the second and third decades of the twentieth century," writes the historian Sigrid Schmalzer, many anthropologists were "convinced . . . of the likelihood that central Asia in particular was the birthplace of humanity" (2008, 252; see also Spencer 1997, 180).

Contemporary historians of paleoanthropology have overlooked the fact that comparative racial embryology was once considered an important component of the search for human origins. This oversight is probably attributable to the fact that embryologists have since lost "the authority to create just [or overarching] representations of human diversity" (Reardon 2005, 10). In the 1910s, however, Cowdry's embryo-collecting project occupied the same intellectual and empirical niche as the 1921–1923 excavation of Peking Man (later known as *Homo erectus*). In fact one of the paleoanthropologists who became famous for his role in the Peking Man excavations came to China as an embryologist. Davidson Black (1884–1934) was a Canadian anatomist hired by his friend Cowdry to come to China to teach neurology and embryology. Not long after Black arrived in Beijing, however, he was lured away by the news that hominid fossils had been unearthed in nearby Zhoukoudian.

Today it might seem odd that a professor of neurology and embryology would so readily abandon his post to dig for fossils. But Black was well aware that hominid fossil evidence from central Asia could shed at least as much light on human evolution as comparative embryology, and with the embryo collection well under way in Beijing, off he went. Cowdry and Black, like many other scientists of their era, hoped that embryology, paleoanthropology, and anatomy would eventually be united in a grand synthesis that would illuminate the mysteries of human evolution.

It was in the spirit of such a vast, modern, scientific synthesis to reveal the origins of the species that Cowdry tried repeatedly to elicit the cooperation of George L. Streeter, the director of Carnegie Embryology. In July 1919 he appealed to Streeter: "Now that the war is over, it occurs to me that you will be thinking of expanding the activities of your institute and I would suggest that you pay a visit to us in Peking. It is surely very desirable that you should establish personal points of contact in the Orient for the collection of embryos. Your programme of getting at anthropology through embryology appeals to me immensely" (Cowdry 1919h).

Streeter was well acquainted with both Cowdry and Black. Cowdry had just completed a three-year postdoctoral fellowship in Baltimore, and Black had visited Carnegie Embryology for two days in 1919 to study their techniques and get "ideas on the embryological side of anthropometry" in preparation for his work in China (Black 1919a). Yet Streeter declined Cowdry's invitation to come to China. Cowdry tried again, inviting Streeter to attend the joint Congress of the China Medical Missionary Association and the National Medical Society in Peking in February 1920. Again Streeter declined, suggesting instead that Cowdry send the Chinese embryos to Baltimore. But Cowdry demurred, knowing the Chinese would disapprove.[12] Cowdry suggested instead that Streeter send a delegate, who could "make adequate provision for the care of the embryos [and] for the solution of the problems which their collection makes possible." Cowdry continued, "as I understand it, one of the chief objects of your department is to *get at anthropology through embryology*" (1919i; emphasis added). This idea likewise failed to win Streeter's support.

Two years after arriving in China, Cowdry requested a leave of absence to spend the summer in the United States.[13] Back in the United States in the summer of 1920, the Cowdrys vacationed in Woods Hole, Massachusetts, which had been for many years a summer haven for anatomists and marine embryologists. There, Cowdry was inspired by conversations with his former associate from Carnegie Embryology, Warren H. Lewis (1879–1964). The two hatched a plan for the Lewises to spend the winter in Beijing (on Carnegie's dime), and Cowdry immediately wrote to request Streeter's approval (Cowdry 1920a). Predictably, Streeter torpedoed the plan. Lewis commiserated to Cowdry: "It's too bad Dr. Streeter doesn't see the Peking possibilities as you and I do. I will talk with him some more for if we could get him enthusiastic about our going I would not hesitate. I saw Dr. [Simon] Flexner in New York. He brought the matter up himself and seemed quite keen to have us go" (Lewis 1920).

In September 1920 Cowdry went to Baltimore, hoping that a personal meeting might win Streeter over. But the visit did not go well. Streeter quizzed Cowdry about his collection and concluded there was no reason to send a delegate all the way to China, at considerable expense, to examine the paltry 87 specimens—most from the fetal period—that Cowdry had by then been able to gather. To appreciate Streeter's reluctance, it is important to note that by this time the Carnegie collection had reached over 3,000 specimens (the vast majority from the United States), 760 of which had arrived in the previous year alone. The staff was hard pressed to keep up with the work of cataloging and preserving them. Under these circumstances, Cowdry's specimens—most of advanced fetal age rather than the coveted early, embryonic stages of development—held little appeal for Streeter.

Because Cowdry could not win support for the size or quality of his specimens, he changed tactics, stressing that his specimens, unlike others available to Western embryologists, were Chinese. Lewis had told him about a collaborative research project being conducted by the physical anthropologist Adolph H. Schultz (1891–1976) and Richard E. Scammon (1883–1952), a physician and fetal anatomist at the University of Minnesota. They were measuring the external morphological features of embryos and fetuses in hopes of demonstrating significant biologically based variations between "Europeans" and "Negros" (see Scammon and Calkins 1929; Schultz 1923). (They were actively trying to acquire American Indian embryo specimens as well, although without much success.) Cowdry realized that the older, whole (i.e., unsectioned),

wet tissue specimens in his collection might provide an important comparative dimension to their project and help to unravel what they called the "racial
origins of the Chinese."

The Racial Origins of the Chinese

That racial origins could be investigated through fetal measurements was obvious to anatomists and physical anthropologists of the era. Before Black left
for Beijing, he paid a visit to Aleš Hrdlička, who was an outspoken proponent
of the idea that social differences between groups could be attributed "to racial
characteristics that reflected the extent of their evolution" (Blakey 1987, 10).
Black wanted Hrdlička to show him how to conduct anthropometric measures and evaluate mixed-race anatomical specimens. He wrote to Cowdry, "I
expect to pay a visit to Hrdlička next week and to pick up pointers with regard
to his work on Negro-White crosses as I want to find out what methods they
have found to be most successful in dealing with this problem so that we may
... use their experience ... in connection with the Eurasian question" (Black
1919b), that is, with reference to the social quandaries thought to be posed by
mixed-race populations.[14]

When Cowdry made the strategic decision to reframe his collection in
terms of racial comparisons, he hired Paul Huston Stevenson (1890–1971), a
missionary doctor who had been working in China since 1917 at Luchowfu
Christian Hospital, Hofei, Anwhei (Luzhoufu, now called Hefei city, Anhui)
(Anderson n.d.). Stevenson eagerly accepted Cowdry's offer to forego clinical
work and embark on an investigation of comparative racial morphology. Cowdry wanted him to focus on the "pre-natal growth of the Chinese, particularly
in the later stages of development" (Cowdry 1920b). As he explained it, "*A
parallel study of growth of the Chinese and Americans is absolutely fundamental
to any work on the anthropology* and I feel that this is, therefore, an attractive
problem" (Cowdry 1920b; emphasis added).

The correspondence between anthropology, anatomy, and embryology
got a boost when Hrdlička visited China to preside over the first meeting
of the Anatomical and Anthropological Association there in 1920 (Hood
1964; Cowdry 1920c, 53). There, Hrdlička convinced the PUMC anatomists of
what they already knew, namely, that archaeology, pathology, and embryology

could be profitably linked. He gave several talks related to methods of anthropometry and the importance of developing anatomical and anthropological collections; he also practiced his anthropometric methods by measuring seven hundred Chinese students (Wu and Wu 1997). He said that the embryological, archaeological, and pathological investigations at the PUMC could be vital to understanding the origins and evolution of the species by shedding light on his theory that humans had evolved from "an essentially Neandertaloid population . . . [that] had slowly spread eastward into Asia and ultimately into the New World" (Spencer 1997, 504).[15]

In the wake of Hrdlička's visit, Cowdry recommended "that careful records be kept of all the dissections carried on in the principal medical schools for a period of five or six years." Cowdry adopted Hrdlička's terminology when he explained that analysis of the resulting data "will be helpful in forming an opinion as to whether the Chinese are a progressive [i.e., transforming toward the modern] or a regressive type, and will, perhaps, indicate what evolutionary tendencies they exhibit along certain lines" (Cowdry 1920c, 58–59). By immersing themselves in Hrdlička's project, the PUMC anatomists positioned themselves to address major anthropological questions, namely, the evolution and racial differentiation of the species as manifested in the structural morphology of living Chinese populations, preserved embryos, and skeletal remains.[16]

Despite his confidence and commitment to "work on the anthropology," the anatomists were vague about the specific racial differentiations they expected to find in the fetal specimens. It would be "inappropriate," Stevenson wrote, to "enter far into a discussion of the factors underlying racial differentiation and the methods of their determination. Suffice it to say . . . that the very early appearance in embryological life, as well as the subsequent disappearance, of definite morphological characteristics often reveals genetic relationships which may be entirely lost to view in later stages of development." He was certain that the specimens would "constitute a source of reliable information on the peculiar racial characteristics of the Chinese as expressed in their embryological development" (Stevenson 1921, 505). They were essentially on a fishing expedition designed to find exactly what they were looking for, namely, anatomical evidence to justify social ideologies of racialized subjects. It was for this reason that they went to such great lengths to determine the race and nationality of each specimen and to apply to each specimen labels such as "American fetus," "Australian fetus," "Chinese fetus," and "Japanese-German mixed race fetus."

These categories—and indeed the entire project of comparative racial embryology—presupposed the interchangeability of "race" with culture and nationality. Cowdry and colleagues seem not to have been aware that their categories reinscribed the racial differences they already knew to exist; they were relying uncritically on "frameworks that assumed the prior existence of [these] groups" (Reardon 2005, 161). Cowdry and colleagues also overlooked the possibility that Chinese systems of racial categorization might differ from those used by Europeans and Americans (as indeed they did; see Dikötter 1997; Eberhard 1982; Schmalzer 2008).[17] Like other students of comparative biological variation, Cowdry and Stevenson may not have been sure which "definite morphological characteristics" would constitute evidence of racial differences, but they were certain of two things: first, that racial differences would be biologically inscribed, even if they were not sure where or how (Dikötter 1997, 1); second, that they would recognize racial differences when they found them. "Upon this and other problems the collection will have its own evidence to present in the fulness [sic] of time" (Stevenson 1921, 505). In other words, they looked for ways to entwine racial presuppositions and embryological evidence as the disciplines of paleoanthropology and embryology— these "novel forms of knowing, and of governing the human"—were taking shape (Reardon 2005, 3).

Fortunately or not, the fullness of time did not bear out Stevenson's prediction, and the study of comparative racial embryology in China came to naught. One lesson we can take from this project, though, is that anthropology *as a discipline* allowed Cowdry to justify his appetite for Chinese embryos, because many anthropologists believed that comparative racial morphology held the key to understanding the evolution and origins of the species. They thought that anthropological insights would help to address urgent sociopolitical questions, including miscegenation, racial "degeneration," and the immigration policies that prohibited Chinese citizens from entering U.S. territory. By allowing theories about the biological basis of race to determine how they would narrate their specimens, Cowdry and colleagues reinforced the notion that these fetuses were special because they were Chinese.[18]

Figure 2. Fetal specimen, Peking Union Medical College, 2004. Photo taken by Juno Obedin-Maliver.

The embryo-collecting project at the PUMC ended in 1927 and faded into oblivion, along with the other projects in comparative racial embryology (Morgan 2009, 168–78). Embryo collecting is missing from most accounts of the history of physical anthropology, perhaps because by the 1920s embryology began to lose the disciplinary authority to explain population-based biological variation. This task was transferred to paleoanthropologists and later to population and molecular geneticists.[19] Selective forgetting has allowed Westerners to distance themselves from the arguably bizarre practice of pickling hundreds of dead Chinese fetuses, even though several of the specimens were still on the shelves at the PUMC when my former student, Juno Obedin-Maliver, took a picture in 2004 (see figure 2). By then, notions of racial embodiment and the racialized Chinese fetus had largely disappeared from the canons of scientific embryology. Curiously, though, vestiges of Cowdry's philosophy were still present in Western attitudes about what the Chinese do to their "little ones," as illustrated by the following example.

Art and Artifact: The Political Semiotics of Chinese Fetal Specimens

In 2005 a Chinese artist named Xiao Yu put a sculpture titled "Ruan" on exhibit at the Bern Art Museum in Switzerland. It was a cross-species anatomical pastiche submerged in formaldehyde; the human fetal head and rabbit eyes were real, as was the body of a stuffed bird (see http://www.othershore-arts

.net/xiaoyuESSAYS10.html for an image). It did not take long for the first complaint to roll in. Adrien de Riedmatten, a former candidate for the right-wing Swiss People's Party, demanded to know "where this baby comes from and if it was killed for this work. We know about the problems of late-term abortions in China," he said, "and we have the right to ask ourselves questions." At one level, Riedmatten's charge was simply an updated version of the baby tower trope. A stream of anti-Chinese news stories had been filling the newspapers: forced abortions in the countryside, Chinese prisoners executed to provide cadavers for traveling anatomy exhibits, desperate Chinese bachelors importing wives from neighboring countries, and so on (Wilson 2008). In this context Riedmatten's suspicions were aroused not only because he found the work distasteful but also because the artist was Chinese.

Riedmatten's accusation was also predicated on his apparent willingness to assume that dead fetuses must result from abortion. This assumption, I would argue, is peculiar to the contemporary era, as one outcome of nearly half a century of Western culture wars focused on abortion (Ginsburg 1989; Luker 1985; Morgan 2009, 228–42; Solinger 1998). Certainly Cowdry and his physician colleagues knew that embryos and fetuses died for all sorts of reasons, including poor maternal health and the unskilled use of forceps (Morgan 2009, 181). But Riedmatten lacked the historical referents that would have allowed him to imagine that Xiao's specimen was, say, delivered stillborn by a Western missionary doctor a hundred years ago before being recruited into anatomical service. The idea would have seemed far-fetched to Riedmatten; his suspicion that the unfortunate fetus resulted from China's coercive population policy has to be regarded as much more plausible, given the context in which he lives. Yet when Xiao was questioned about where he got the head, he told reporters he had "bought [it] in 1999 for a few dollars from a man who was cleaning out a scientific exhibition hall." The fetal head in this sculpture, in other words, was a recycled anatomical specimen. It could well have come from Cowdry's collection at the PUMC or a similar collection at another medical school. No matter. The conflict managed to both invoke and promulgate echoes of Chinese forced abortion rather than reminders of Western scientific specimen collecting. The exhibit was temporarily removed (McLean 2005), which reinforced the impression that this artist was guilty of yet another Chinese assault against a fetal soul.

The incident was ironic in several ways. First, the fetal specimen would not have existed at all, were it not for the high value placed on unborn specimens by the PUMC anatomists and their counterparts. Second, the transfer of this specimen from a "scientific exhibition hall" to a Swiss art museum would not have taken place had the scientific value attached to the specimen not plummeted throughout the latter twentieth century.[20] Third, the reaction of "righteous indignation" would have been unavailable to Riedmatten were it not for the contemporary glorification of fetal subjectivity as a form of saving babies, a concept that certainly did not exist when the specimen was acquired and that emerged, in part, because of scientific knowledge produced through the study of such collections. Fourth, the sculpture evoked a presumed association with China's draconian population policies, even though the specimen itself predated the One-Child Policy by several decades. Fifth, the entire critique allows me to maintain the position (which is both comfortable and discomfiting in its smugness) that Riedmatten's accusations are a function of his political ideology. But by refusing to entertain a discussion of forced abortion, which I have defined as outside the scope of this chapter, I am able to ignore the possibility that Riedmatten's claim might have a basis in fact (see Croll 2001). As the anthropologist Ann Anagnost explains, "The immediate problem is how to untangle the issues [of population policy and international adoption] from the representational regimes that construct China as a totalitarian state 'outside' universal values of human rights and democratic freedoms" (2004, 143). One might question whether the more ethical position is held by Riedmatten, Xiao, or myself, but it is important to go beyond the defensibility of individual positions to appreciate how Xiao's sculpture was predicated on a historically entwined and forgotten past in which Western anatomists were implicated.

As China's economic power grew in the West during the 1990s, so did anti-Chinese sentiment. The vilification took many forms, from widely disseminated stories of lead-contaminated children's toys to accounts of tainted infant formula, pet food, and toothpaste. Rumors of fetal cannibalism appeared on the websites of libertarians and antiabortion extremists, under headings like "fetus feast" and "unspeakable delicacy." Readers were encouraged to believe that people in southern China eat "fetus soup" made from aborted fetuses, pork, and ginger. The first line of a blog posting by the antiabortion activist Jill Stanek in 2007 titled, "Sweet and sour fetus: Chinese cannibalism" read,

"The following, if true, is what abortion and the dehumanization of babies has wrought. It is the most despicable outcome of abortion I have ever seen."[21]

It would be easy to dismiss such venomous accusations were it not for the fact that at least five members of the U.S. Congress repeated the charges in public. In 1995, furthermore, President Bill Clinton was presented with a Sense of Congress statement recommending "that he decline visiting China 'unless there is dramatic overall progress on human rights in China and Tibet' including an end to the use of 'human fetal remains for consumption as food'" (Dixon 2000).[22] Republican Representative Chris Smith of New Jersey used the rumor to justify withholding Most Favored Nation status for China until 1999. The fact that there was such "reciprocal interaction between popular culture and official discourse" (Dikötter 1997, 8) concerning Chinese fetal cannibalism suggests either that the rumor was a politically expedient justification for a long-standing anti-China posture or that some U.S. congressional representatives are dismayingly receptive to the inflammatory and unsubstantiated claims made by right-wing fringe groups.

We could pose the same question about Chinese fetal cannibalism that Nancy Scheper-Hughes posed in her investigation of clandestine organ sales, namely, "What truths are being served up?" (2002, 48). Scheper-Hughes found that rumors of murder and dismemberment in the Brazilian shantytowns reflected "the existential and ontological securities of poor people living on the margins of the postcolonial global economies" (2002, 36). Rumors of Chinese fetal cannibalism, in contrast, are promulgated by relatively wealthy people who live at the purported center of global power, and I confess I find it difficult to muster a Scheper-Hughesian sympathy for *their* impassioned expressions of existential and ontological insecurity. It would be much easier to cast them as xenophobic, war-mongering, fetus-worshipping fanatics willing to use whatever means at their disposal to hang onto their pathetic nationalistic pride and economic privilege in a rapidly globalizing economy.

My inclination toward moral condemnation is buttressed by the fact that the rumor mongers do not protest against the bodily transactions that involve sick Westerners traveling to China to receive embryonic stem cell and fetal cell medical treatments. Indeed, the discourse of "coercive Chinese population policies" is kept largely segregated from that of "Chinese stem cell therapy." Yet the two are linked by an uncomfortable truth: Western patients who travel to China in hopes of finding relief for degenerative diseases, developmental disorders, and neurological conditions (Gottweis, Salter, and Waldby 2009; Song 2010) constitute a growing market for Chinese embryonic and fetal tissue. Because air travel is relatively cheap, medical care is relatively expensive, and fetal tissue research has long been illegal in the United States an increasing number of patients are flying to China for treatment. Doctors' cautions do not seem to dampen the growing enthusiasm for such medical tourism, if the hundreds of patient testimonials, videos, and blogs on websites like Stemcellschina.com can be believed. Fetal tissue utilized in these therapies is acquired from induced abortion, while embryonic stem cells are generally taken from five-day old embryos fertilized in vitro. The paradox is reminiscent of what the medical historian Warwick Anderson described in his recent work on the history of kuru: "At the same time as [Carleton] Gajdusek was negotiating for the bodies of the kuru dead, then dissecting them on his dining table and ritually preparing them for scientific consumption, native cannibalism had been forbidden by the Australian authorities" (2000, 726). But in this case the "scientific consumption" of Chinese embryonic and fetal tissue has moved far beyond the activities of a small group of scientists, to a much wider constituency of very sick people who are willing to risk a great deal (and to set aside anxieties about Chinese abortion or fetal cannibalism) by pinning their hopes on miracle cures.

Conclusion

Anthropologists have tended to ignore the ways in which our disciplinary ancestors and nonacademic colleagues have built their careers on the consumption of Chinese "little ones." We have conveniently forgotten, or erased, the role of physical anthropology in justifying the practice of embryo collecting, just as we overlook the rumors of Chinese fetal cannibalism and their all too real political effects.[23] In the words of Susan Greenhalgh, one of anthropology's preeminent scholars of China, we allow "public understandings of China's population control work . . . to be dominated by a powerful narrative of coercion created by a group of conservative politicians and like-minded intellectuals located outside the academy" (2005, 354–55). In the process we overlook the conflation of anti-Chinese and antiabortion projects made possible by China's economic ascendancy and the rise of fetal fetishism. As a result, remarks such as the following, by Rod Dreher, an editorial columnist for the *Dallas Morning News*, can go unchecked. Dreher wrote in the *CrunchyCon* blog in April 2009 that the skewed sex ratio in China will lead to war: "I'm serious: for the sake of stability, the Chinese government in the future will have to find some way to channel all that masculine aggression and frustration outward. Not good for the rest of us. Just another fruit of abortion. How is it, exactly, that feminists here maintain their unqualified support for abortion rights when abortion is used to carry out a holocaust of baby girls abroad?"

On the rare occasion when an anthropologist does engage the conservative ideological position, it is to render Chinese policies more intelligible rather than to examine seriously the worldviews of right-wing ideologues, including those trained in anthropology. For example, there has not been to my knowledge a serious analysis of the consequences for anthropology of charges made by Steven W. Mosher. Since Mosher was expelled from Stanford's doctoral program in anthropology more than twenty-five years ago for revealing the identities of his informants, he has been an outspoken critic of U.S. foreign policy toward China and especially of how the Chinese use "physical force" against "fertile bodies" (Greenhalgh 2005, 354). Although Mosher arguably knows a great deal about China, his role as head of the pro-life Population Research Institute and his right-wing political affiliations have made him persona non grata among anthropologists, who have largely ostracized him by refusing to cite his writings or engage his arguments.[24] To the extent that anthropologists have constructed a moral community that ignores political and ideological challengers on the subject of how the Chinese value and treat their "little ones"—whether that challenger is Steven Mosher, Rod Dreher, or Representative Chris Smith—the discipline remains vulnerable to charges of liberal astigmatism, bigotry, or worse.

Anthropologists and others have provided well-documented and insightful critiques of the consequences of Chinese family planning policies, and social scientists have been instrumental in drawing attention to "a critique of the global processes that work to surplus these children [i.e., Chinese girls]" (Anagnost 2004, 151; see also Croll 2001; Greenhalgh 2008; Greenhalgh and Winckler 2005; Hemminki et al. 2005; Nie 2009; Rigdon 1996). Yet while social science studies on Chinese adoption emphasize the effect of the One-

Child Policy on children already born (Fong 2004; Johnson 2002), they reinscribe birth as the beginning of personhood. The focus on forced abortion, I argue, tends to reify the entities we call "embryo" and "fetus," while neglecting the technoscientific processes through which they came to be constituted as modern biopolitical subjects and signifiers of supposed ethnic and biological differences. The literature on sex-selective abortion and "missing girls" draws attention to gender disparities but devotes little attention to the social circumstances that produce pregnancy in the first place. In short, for all the ink that's been spilled about Chinese population policies and reproductive politics, the views espoused in the West sometimes carry vestiges of "baby tower" discourses that denigrate "the Chinese."

"You can tell a culture by what it can and cannot bring together," said Marilyn Strathern (qtd. in Taylor 2004, 3), and this chapter has brought together two areas of discussion that have generally been kept separate: Western denigration of how the Chinese treat their young, and the long-standing Western appetite for Chinese embryos and fetuses. Americans, in particular, seem to have a long history of relishing the horrors that the Chinese supposedly inflict upon their "little ones," while imagining themselves immune from similar behaviors. Taylor argues that "the ideological opposition between motherhood and consumption has gone unquestioned," in part because "the very suggestion seems to invoke that most frightening of all monsters, the mother who eats her own children" (2004, 10–11). Yet when American mothers occasionally do kill (and even eat) their offspring, the press labels them as pathologically disturbed "monsters" and "cannibal moms" rather than as victims of state policy (Houppert 2009; Associated Press 2009).

It is hard to escape the conclusion that Euro-Americans have sometimes seemed to enjoy "consuming" (in various senses of the word) Chinese "little ones" and that the discipline of anthropology has been implicated in the process. Yet perhaps anthropologists can also offer solutions by reframing scholarship to investigate the role of anthropology in the social lives of anatomical specimens (Anderson 2008; Landecker 2007; Starn 2004; Verdery 1999). There is room for serious anthropological studies of how Westerners satiate their appetites for embryos and fetuses, including the morbid historical fascination with baby towers and the practice of filling laboratory shelves with pickled babies. Today, the consumption of fetal tissue occurs at several levels:

literally in technoscientific and medical work (see Pfeffer and Kent 2007), metaphorically in the delectable human fetuses that are increasingly available online (in rumors about "marzipan babies" and cookie cutters in the shape of fetuses), and voyeuristically in a steady stream of news accounts about everything from forced abortion to fetal cannibalism. If the notion of "devouring fetuses" in the West sounds morbid or accusatory, then certainly anthropologists could investigate why the suggestion makes some Westerners bristle while others relish the thought.

Making Peasants Protestant and Other Projects

Medical Anthropology and Its Global Condition

Deterritorialization, or Be Careful What You Wish For

For some readers, area studies may suggest the by now ancien régime of a territorializing anthropology neatly parceled out among appropriate experts, much like the various cages in the zoo with the social scientific observer as the keeper of distinction. This postwar recasting of regional knowledge linked the imperative of security and the concept of culture to a social theory simultaneously looking forward to liberal modernization and backward to great tradition civilization. In rehabilitating the figure of civilization, area studies scaled up the taxonomic order of the culture area to encompass the supranational geopolitical theaters of the Cold War.

By the early 1990s, anthropology graduate students in several programs were being informed that the era of area studies was over, part of the apparent overturning of the Boasian culture concept (Stocking 1968), or at least its sufficiency, in the wake of important critiques of the zoo story (Abu-Lughod 1991; Asad 1973; Clifford 1988; Fabian 1983; Rabinow 1977; Said 1979; Trouillot 1991). There were sites of resistance, some notable (Sahlins 1995). But the demonstration of the *cultural* specificity of situations no longer seemed adequate to their understanding (Cohen 1998; Li 2001). Area studies as an approach was particularly challenged by postcolonial historicist critiques of anthropological knowledge formation, on the one hand, and, on the other, by political economy perspectives replacing "civilization" with "the world system" as the vehicle for scaling up.

At stake was more than the limits of the culture concept: area studies as a means of organizing conversation appeared to segregate analysis and overdetermine comparison. Arjun Appadurai (1988; and see Fardon 1990), for example, called attention to area studies' incarceration of concepts: the way varied species of typology, of problematization, and of argument become restricted to territorial expanses rendered as obvious culture areas.

During the late 1980s, a new species of critique of area studies joined these challenges, one that retained features of the culture concept but challenged its mapping onto the territory of the region or nation. Crudely, this was the challenge of what would be termed "globalization," and it attended to the intensified mobility not only of migrant populations but of capital, of media and information, and of technologies of governance and self-formation.

As the dominant logic of internationalism shifted from "development" to "globalization," the area studies model became less relevant to mainstream conversation across the social sciences, challenged by varied claims to *deterritorialize* anthropology and its allied fields (Mirsepassi et al. 2003; Mitchell 2003). In the department where I teach, job searches were less likely to be organized around an "area hire" and fewer faculty lined up to teach the "area courses" required of undergraduates. Administrators of the neoliberal university, scouting future grants and auditing teaching and research for deliverables sufficient to justify its continued existence, turned increasingly to variants of something termed global studies.

This set of turns, first toward and then away from the scaled-up figure of the "area," has particular salience for the subdiscipline of medical anthropology. It offers, not surprisingly, both promise and caution as the field apprehends its future. At this moment of writing, medical anthropologists in numerous countries find themselves asserting their relevance and utility in the face of an increasing deterritorialized field of global health. The apparent commensuration of distinctive local worlds given the mobility of capital, of context, and of organic form (pathogens, pharmaceuticals, and human organs, to name some examples of what is meant here by mobile organic form) has become as much a governing axiom as an empirical situation.

The "global," in other words, is necessarily performative: the figure does significant work in structuring a certain kind of world. It has been integral to the reorganization of medicine as humanitarianism and of medical anthropology as the critical response to structural violence. But the scale of the global can also serve as a limit to understanding and to the response to human distress and disease. In an era in which medical anthropology must accede to the embrace of global health if it hopes to stay relevant, the Cold War zoo story of area studies acquires a perverse appeal, its scaled-up areas appearing scaled-down by comparison to the global. As one of the last institutional refuges of anthropology's commitment to particular, at times incommensurable worlds, does area studies offer much more than nostalgia?

Area Studies and Temporal Incongruity

This chapter was first offered as a plenary address celebrating fifty years of institutionalized medical anthropology in the United States. In the spirit of that occasion, it looks to a past as much as it imagines a future. One of its forward-looking reviewers understandably expressed frustration with the backward orientation of it and some of its companion pieces. But area studies— its funding structures, regnant debates, and persistent congeries of interests, biographies, and commitments sustaining area centers, conferences, and journals—often appears to us as a superseded form. To be asked as I was to address area studies is to produce a Janus-faced account. This chapter works backward to plumb past materials for a possible, even hopeful future of the "area" in medical anthropology.

A model for this "backward" anthropological orientation has been offered by Hirokazu Miyazaki in a series of works (2003, 2004) drawing on Ernst Bloch's extensive writing on hope (1986 [1954–59]). Here I will limit myself to noting a central preoccupation of Miyazaki's "method of hope." Miyazaki observes how both the social actors that anthropologists study and anthropologists themselves can utilize experiences of "temporal incongruity" in orienting themselves not just to what Bloch would characterize as our ideologically determined sense of the "Now" but to the anticipatory potentiality of the "Not Yet." I have found myself turning to Miyazaki's figure of temporal incongruity in order to address the initial provocation for this chapter from the then Society for Medical Anthropology president Marcia Inhorn: that is, to attend to the future of the "area" at the very moment that future seems foreclosed by the conditions of deterritorialization and the urgent demands of the global.

Reterritorialization and the Cultural Audit

If I frame this moment of writing as finding itself in the aftermath of extensive deterritorialization, one in which area studies and the organizing value of the region are called into question, I should note that the culture concept itself has remained salient despite anthropological autocritique. If anthropologists by the early 1990s were abandoning the totalization of culture and its distribution into manageable areas of civilization like rats on an apparently sinking ship, their one-time signature concept was growing attractive to others. The attraction is particularly notable in the applied social sciences of medicine.

Long the cudgel the American anthropologist wielded against putatively universalizing discourses of medicine and psychology, culture at the moment of its disciplinary abandonment was being embraced by developmental and social psychologists and by the many clinicians, activists, and institutional auditors comprising the cultural competency industry managing both respectful and adequate care and entitlement within medicine. Laura Nader (2001) has warned that anthropology might take heed when its former reigning concepts become interdisciplinary boundary objects (Star and Griesemer 1989).

We might therefore revise any totalizing diagnosis of deterritorialization, examining the proliferation of cultural audits that accompanied the fin-de-siècle global condition. By cultural audit I mean the effort, as in cultural competency programs in medicine, to administer institutions through practices mandating and assessing the recognition and inclusion of cultural and racial distinction.

Within the social sciences of medicine and more generally in clinical research attending to "socioeconomic," "cultural," or "psychological" determinants of health, the culture concept has become closely tied to understandings (often legally mandated within the organization of governmental resource support) of ethnicity and race. Part of the power of culture has been as a site of recognition for clinically marginalized populations through proliferating pedagogies of cultural competency in patient care (Carpenter-Song et al. 2007; Jenks 2010; Kleinman and Benson 2006; Shaw 2005; Taylor 2003). As such, culture is one of several tools to disaggregate populations into distinct kinds of patient bodies, along with, for example, pharmacogenomics (Fullwiley

2007; Whitmarsh 2009), under a shared logic of clinical and social inclusion through differentiation (Epstein 2007).

Not only in the clinic, culture emerges as a key site and resource for administration and governance in the twenty-first century. Under conditions of deterritorialization, in other words, "culture" is disarticulated from territory, if to a varying extent, and can emerge as a key resource for projects of economic and biopolitical governance. It may become such a resource for the regulation of migration and citizenship. It becomes a resource for the flexible management of labor and for the assessment and creation of needs and markets. And it becomes a resource for the prognostication of crisis and management of security and war. Counterinsurgency and humanitarianism, the twin prongs of ✓ U.S. foreign policy in the early twenty-first century, are highly mobile modes of governance that yet depend upon extensive "cultural" knowledge and the utility of embedded anthropologists in managing "human terrains."

We can frame the necessity of the culture concept within deterritorialized conditions of governance—managing migration, reorganizing gender and racial inclusion in clinical research, or enabling so-called counterinsurgency —as one of several sites of "reterritorialization." As anthropology continues to trouble its relation both to counterinsurgency (Gonzalez 2009; Network of Concerned Anthropologists 2009) and humanitarianism (Butt 2002; Fassin 2011a; Redfield 2008), part of the challenge may be to imagine alternate conceptions of reterritorialization as disciplinary practice. This challenge is of salience for medical anthropology, particularly given the emergence of a parallel kind of area studies in the management of what I have termed bioavailability: individuals and populations rendered available as sources of organic form (Cohen 2004a).

Reterritorialized conceptions of culture, that is, organize not only new practices of clinical recognition and inclusion as noted above but also the *extraction* of human "biovalue" (Waldby and Mitchell 2006) across globally articulated zones of culture, vulnerability, and risk. At the same time that governmental norms under late liberalism disaggregate national populations through mingled commitments to cultural and genetic diversity, the biovalue of globally dispersed socially and economically marginal populations transforms practices of clinical drug testing of multinational pharmaceutical corporations (Petryna 2009; Prasad 2009; Sunder Rajan 2007). The creation and deployment of regionally specific knowledge becomes critical for recruiting and managing such populations by contract research organizations (CROs): Adriana Petryna argues that the "ethical variability" such area expertise can mobilize across nationally, economically, and socioculturally differentiated populations becomes a valuable resource in cutting drug development costs by outsourcing risk. Here the difference of these risk-bearing, bioavailable populations is utilized to produce universalizing norms, as opposed to minoritizing counternorms, of pharmaceutical practice.

A different government of bioavailability has emerged with the pharmaceutically created mobility of the transplant organ: tissue and organ brokers often operate outside the law and have not created the same sort of large-scale and professionalized networks of CROs (Cohen 1999, 2001; Scheper-Hughes 2000, 2004). Broker expertise in ethical variability is more idiosyncratic. But here too knowledge of regional distinctions in clinical governance is a resource for rendering tissues commensurable across social and national borders that exceed the more typical kin-based networks across which organs move.

What I am suggesting is that independent of anthropology's vexed relation to the culture concept and its bundling into geopolitically organized area studies, parallel formations of regional knowledge are being organized for the outsourcing and management of experimental risk and the extraction of biovalue. The CRO managers that Petryna studies and some of the international organs brokers with whom Scheper-Hughes works exemplify the "para-ethnographic" knowledge workers Douglas Holmes and George Marcus (2006) have described in a different context. The emergence of medical tourism leads to yet another clinical realm in which regionalized knowledge of dispersed clinical realities is being produced (Leng and Whittaker 2010; Mazzaschi and Emily McDonald 2011; Whittaker et al. 2010). The real question for the intersection of medical anthropology and area studies is less the reanimation of the Cold War corpse than both the interpretive and the critical relations to be established with this burgeoning set of para-ethnographic enterprises.

If the rigor of region-specific knowledge is to be defended within medical schools, universities, and funding agencies, such knowledge must be able to track these different deployments of cultural, political, and ethical variability in the reterritorialization of the contemporary clinic. Anthropological knowledge must be able to examine the distinctive impacts of these practices of reterritorialized knowledge upon geographically and economically dispersed populations. And anthropological knowledge must be able to examine the varied and dispersed impacts of "global health" itself: to comprehend and audit the persistent promise of deterritorialization for which we used to hope.

The Invention of Medical Anthropology, Version One

To paraphrase the old Talmudic punch line: that's the point, the rest is commentary. The commentary in this case is a set of medical anthropology origin stories, helping me produce a genealogy of territorialized knowledge in the social sciences of medicine. This backward orientation, as I suggested above, is necessary as the old territorializations have by no means simply gone away, in medical anthropology or elsewhere, and it is worth reminding ourselves of their possible entailments. The origin story for medical anthropology that I find most germane locates itself in the mid-twentieth century under the signs of decolonization and development.

Origin stories, in this genealogical sense, are partial and multiple. Many other accounts of disciplinary history are possible, each implicating our understanding, critique, and use of regionalized knowledge in different ways. For example, as many critiques of area studies are organized as responses to the colonial knowledge systems of the long nineteenth century, we could attempt the same for medical anthropology.

One could begin, in this vein, with a French physician and explorer with the nom de plume Jacobus X. Through the late nineteenth century, Dr. X published a series of books beginning with *L'Amour aux colonies* and including an English-language version with the less elegant but no less promising title *Untrodden Fields of Anthropology* (1898 [1893]; see also Proschan 2002) (see figure 1). Dr. X offered racialized anatomical descriptions, comparative genital measurements, and behavioral catalogues of the sex of French colonial subjects in North and West Africa and in Southeast Asia. For the English edition, Dr. X and his publishers justified the seriousness of this foray into sexual science by casting the book as a particular kind of archive: "documents on medical anthropology."

DOCUMENTS ON MEDICAL ANTHROPOLOGY

UNTRODDEN FIELDS

OF

ANTHROPOLOGY

OBSERVATIONS ON THE ESOTERIC

Manners and Customs of Semi-Civilized Peoples;

BEING A

RECORD OF THIRTY YEARS' EXPERIENCE IN

ASIA, AFRICA, AMERICA and OCEANIA.

By A FRENCH ARMY-SURGEON.

(IN TWO VOLUMES)

VOL. I

PRIVATELY RE-ISSUED
AMERICAN ANTHROPOLOGICAL SOCIETY
NEW YORK

Figure 1. Medical anthropology as secret knowledge.

In this account the idea of a *medical* anthropology legitimates a particular kind of invasive colonial gaze, extending beyond the already intimate conventions of a science of the human as a racialized distribution. The citation here of the physician, allowed to look and linger under norms of diagnosis and therapy that explicitly and iteratively involved touching and uncovering the body (Arnold 1987), makes possible an anthropology of the secret: all that occluded from the routine of surveillance. Yet the project cannot guarantee its morality, the possibility that its enthusiastic uncovering might not be defensible under the signs of either reason or care. It resorts to pseudonym.

This obscure gesture, in which medicine marks its relationship to anthropology through the secret, might be juxtaposed with a more familiar and later one, that of Margaret Mead's (1935) *Sex and Temperament* and more generally of the antiracist liberalism of the school of Boas in the interwar decades. Mead and her colleagues utilize the apparently differing sexual norms and gendered comportment of colonized Melanesians, Native Americans, and Pacific Islanders to promote greater respect and allowance for divergent sexual and gendered norms in the United States and for a lessening of the proscriptive and punishing norms governing youthful sexuality at home (Benedict 1934; Marcus and Fischer 1986; Mead 1928).

This juxtaposition of Dr. X and Mead enables a slender observation: if Mead's popularity was linked to her forthright account of sexual practice and gendered temperament among natives, her explication of distinction was not offered under the sign of medicine. If in this early work she implicitly called upon a cosmopolitan persona, it was not the figure of the physician but rather that of the journalist, specifically the courageous girl reporter so familiar to the American public sphere of the late nineteenth century (Fahs 2002).

The salient point is that this first moment of culture and personality was organized around an *anti-medicine*: not a catalogue or atlas of native perversions, revealed under the medical gaze, but an incorporation of the full variety of native temperament within the ever-expanding temperamental capacity of the American. Mead's work is suggestive not of a colonial empire of the secret, in which knowledge of the area requires the "medical" license to engage that which is hidden, but rather what we might call an empire of temperament. Through the Swiftian travels of Mead in New Guinea recounted in *Sex and Temperament*, each successive leg of the anthropologist's journey as she reprises United States transoceanic expansion leads to a people exhibiting a distinctive distribution of sexual and gendered norms within the far wider parameters of natural human variation.

What I am calling the anti-medicine of this first, pre–Second World War phase of culture and personality also informs the conception of the area as it intersects with the later professionalization of medical anthropology. For a strong tendency within the subdiscipline, within both its "critical" and "interpretive" camps when such labels mattered, was the critique of biomedical universalism through the invocation of culture as local knowledge (Kleinman and Good 1985; Scheper-Hughes and Lock 1987). Mead's anti-medicine and its buttressing of the empire of temperament are instructive here: for the use of the native example remained the expansion of "Western" norms of diagnosis and caregiving. Putatively a recognition of otherness, the worldliness of medical anthropology involved a persistent one-way traffic, in which culture (there) offered a powerful critique of science (here). The turn away from the culture concept in many of the subsequent generation, most notably in Paul Farmer's shift from culture to structure (particularly in his conception of structural violence) is a sharp reaction to this anti-medicine (Farmer 1999, 2003; Parker 2001). The medical anthropology that follows, to the extent that structural violence becomes an organizing concept for many entering the field, draws on a different conception of the area. To specify it, we need to turn back to a different origin story.

The Invention of Medical Anthropology, Version Two: Anthropology Gets Medical

If Mead and Ruth Benedict (1934) offered in their pedagogy of temperament what I have termed an anti-medicine, the second and postwar generation of culture and personality encountered and developed a different problematization of culture and pathology. The delineation of the pathological, in the work, for example, of Georges Devereux and G. Morris Carstairs, is less the "culturalistic" arbitrariness of the specific norm and more the impact of culture on demonstrable psychopathology.

Defending his attribution of neurosis to shamans, Devereux challenged not only his opponents but an entire style of analysis:

> They [the earlier culture and personality school] fail to differentiate between sanity and social adjustment on the diagnostic level, and between psychiatric and anthropological statements on the conceptual level; ... due to a unilaterally culturalistic ... focus of interest, they view the finding, that neurotics and/or more or less latent psychotics can perform culturally valued social functions, as a slur and as an aspersion on culture and society. As a result, they unintentionally ignore facts well known to them. (1961, 1090)

This tough-mindedness, this resolution not to ignore the facts, marks an anthropology once again organized around diagnosis and intervention. But the authority of the physician, its tough-mindedness as regards the pathology of regional types, is no longer the taxonomic gaze of Dr. X. Medicine dares to be curative: the emergent cure was modernization.

Carstairs, born in India and trained in Britain, was, given his practice as a psychiatrist, often in conversation with culture and personality anthropology. Like Devereux, he would be challenged for changing the rules of the anthropological game in his "etic" commitment to define cultural forms as pathological. In his account of widespread local tolerance in India for *hijras* or eunuchs, whom he termed homosexual prostitutes, Carstairs (1956, 1957) developed the basis for a broader pathologization of Indian Rajput masculinity. If for the previous generation of Boasian anthropology, transgendered or third-gendered roles like that of the hijra allowed for a recognition of the *natural* breadth of gendered temperament and thus a partial opening up of the norms of acceptable masculine behavior, here their deviance from the norm was linked to particularly punishing medical and psychoanalytic accounts of homosexuality. The role of the physician-anthropologist had returned.

For Devereux, like Benedict, the shaman had a role within traditional culture: the task of engaging such a culture was not to reduce it in its entirety to the disputed symptom. Carstairs, however, shared with Mead the propensity to view "pathological" temperaments as revealing of collective sickness. Though not all Rajput men became hijras, Carstairs located the emergence of the specific group in a generalized latent homosexuality he explained through Rajput and more generally Indian practices of child rearing. Most Indian men, it appeared, had a problem: only an uncompromisingly *medical* anthropology could steel itself for the diagnosis.

If the symptom of the sick human—the neurotic or homosexual—pointed toward collective pathology, a medical anthropology needed a civilizational scaling up to heal effectively. Area studies emerges as a necessity when entire culture areas become defined as pathogenic.

The Invention of Medical Anthropology, Version Two: Medicine Gets Anthropological

As formally institutionalized arrangements, both medical anthropology and area studies emerged in the milieu of the Cold War American university. The dominant paradigm offering the promise of a rapprochement of the social sciences was modernization theory, and the stakes in the new edifice were immense: modernization's promise of health and wealth was a bulwark against peasant revolt and global communism.

Post–Second World War international public health, organized around neo-Malthusian concerns for the hygiene and scale of decolonizing peasant populations (Connolly 2008), privileges anthropology as a translational apparatus: able to understand peasants and at the same time to get them to change their behavior. The anthropologists face a challenge, as they respond to the invitation to participate in the new *Pax Americana* by professionalizing medical anthropology. Their legacy is simultaneously that of an anti-medicine recognizing difference in terms of a moral and clinical relativism and of a medicine committed to tough love.

A self-consciously medical anthropology, in charter enactments like Benjamin D. Paul's (1955) collection *Culture, Health, and Community* (to which Carstairs contributes), offered expertise in culture while struggling neither to fall into the trap as Devereux had put it of becoming "culturalistic," nor to join other social scientists in condemning cultures the latter poorly understood. Culture was precisely that which seemed to many experts in the consolidating world of planned development to stand in the way of peasants and slum dwellers acting rationally and boiling their water, adopting sanitary practices of childbirth, jettisoning the medicine of superstition, and thus living longer, healthier, and (urgently) *happier* lives. The medical anthropologist had to steer a course between culture as moral alternative and culture as pathogenic.

The articles anthologized in the Paul collection are analytically sophisticated: culture and tradition are not the only frames through which the organization of norms and behavior and the distribution of life chances are understood. On the contrary, Edward Wellin's classic article on how peasants in rural Peru differently hear the message to boil water attends to many axes of difference besides that of national or peasant culture. But the narrative demands of the genre are being consolidated: *the irrationality of culture remains the key framing of the problem, and an applied psychological anthropology unafraid to name tradition as pathogenic becomes the solution.* Medical anthropology is institutionalized as a happiness machine (Grezemkovsky 2005), expected within the larger grouping of postwar disciplines to negotiate the cultural impediments to healthful behavior.

If my reduction of disciplinary origins to a kind of syllogism—(1) happy people were presumptively less prone to revolutionary sentiment, (2) illness and dead children made people unhappy, and (3) boiling water kept children alive, people happy, and societies stable—is vulgar, what I want to foreground is the necessity and urgency of vulgarity if both anthropology and America were to scale-up and make the move from documenting isolated tribes that were worlds unto themselves to the challenge of effective intercontinental governance.

Governance was at stake as peasants and other marginal subjects of decolonizing societies did not always respond positively to the rational embrace of hygienic and population control expertise. At a time when the postwar social sciences were being massively expanded and modernization theory linked them in a project promising globally distributed security, wealth, and reason, peasants and slum dwellers—the new object of this massed attention—seemed to resist their improvement.

As-if Modernity

Like medical anthropology, the interdisciplinary project of area studies reformed the project of culture in relation to rationalized imperatives of security. Faced with an imperative both medical and anti-medical, the postwar anthropologist responded by splitting culture into a more rationalized sphere of the civilization or great tradition and a more pathogenic sphere of the folk or little tradition. This split to an extent mirrored the "double discourse" by which decolonizing elites distinguished what Thomas Hansen (1999) has termed a "sublime" realm of valued tradition from a brutish condition of mass life. Culture's doublesidedness—its centrality to modernization both as resource and obstacle—could be mapped onto understanding of civilizations as containing both rationalized and irrational components. Tough love was to be lavished on the more marginal folk.

If culture was both obstacle to modern behavior and a resource for its pedagogy, it was so in a particular sense we might term "as if." To take my same vulgarized example of water boiling: textbook peasants may have particular humoral ideas of hot and cold that trouble the claims of development program "motivators" for the advantages of boiling water. But the thoughtful anthropologist can utilize these ideas (or later, with growing analytic sophistication

[Nichter 1985, 1987], these *symbols*) to achieve the aim of water boiling in the service of reduced infant mortality. Most peasants may not understand the truth of germ theory or the biophysics of microorganism death. But if the sympathetic anthropologist can manipulate their available understandings, he or she can motivate peasants to act as if they did have access to modern life and its truth. *Medical anthropology in this origin story might be defined as the practice of getting peasants and slum dwellers to act as if they were modern.*

Population Control

Just as the studies in the Paul volume offered sophisticated treatments of problems never fully reducible to the imperative of culture as obstacle to modernization, the interdisciplinary studies of "new nations" were seldom reductive analyses limited to the exigencies of modernization or the Cold War. The later political and ethical crucible of the late 1960s' social sciences, in which growing self-criticism at times came to center on an audit of anthropological involvement in "Camelot" and other Vietnam-era projects of counterinsurgency intelligence, could be met by the legitimate response of most Southeast Asian Studies scholars that their work was not implicated in military action.

Kamala Visweswaran (1999) has argued that the sophisticated tools of symbolic and hermeneutical analysis that would challenge the simplifications of modernization theory were nonetheless deeply rooted in the latter. Anthropological involvement in Cold War governance and security was never primarily a matter of military support but rather of the commitment, however nuanced, to the postcolonial obviousness of planned development and to the supplementation or even replacement of politics by the rule of experts (Ferguson 1994; Hansen 1999). Particularly in Latin America and South Asia, this refashioning came to focus on the urgent demand of population control.

The attention of governments, foundations, and anticolonial elites to the growing problem of the mass precedes the formation of area studies programs by some decades (Briggs 2003; Hodges 2008). But the historian Matthew Connelly (2008) has made a compelling case for the centrality of population control and family planning to the dominant state, multilateral, and nongovernment organization (NGO) assemblage of postwar international governance. Taking his argument further, one might situate population as the boundary object around which area studies came to cohere. Far from a unitary demand of the "periphery" by the "center," population control was an important feature of national and ethical formation for dispersed actors in decolonizing states from the 1930s through the 1980s. Anthropologists and sociologists, in encountering the renewed urgency of population in the 1960s, argued for scaled-up forms of interdisciplinary analysis to study regions in the face of global problems (Douglas 1966; Titmuss and Abel-Smith 1961).

Population control demanded a new conception of local knowledge as demographically constituted. In a manifesto in *New Society* in 1968, the anthropologist Alan Macfarlane excoriated his colleagues for failing to rise to the challenge and termed the great challenge facing the remaking of the discipline's "hunting grounds" a matter of linking the study of society and culture to a more medical and epidemiological anthropology:

> As an article in the *Biennial Review of Anthropology* for 1963 made clear, "medical anthropology" is still at a very rudimentary stage. . . . To probe further into the traditional hunting grounds of anthropologists: it is becoming clear, as V. W. Turner has pointed out, that endless discussions of witchcraft and other beliefs about the causation of illness *must* contain discussions of medical and demographic factors. How true is it, for example, that medical improvements in modern Africa will rescue the "disease-logged" societies from what many western observers consider to be "irrational" fears?

Though a later generation of medical anthropologists would return to E. E. Evans-Pritchard's *Witchcraft, Oracles, and Magic among the Azande* (1937), establishing the text and ensuing debates on illness and rationality as central to the subdiscipline's efforts to develop a body of theory, Macfarlane here argues for an account of human practices of accounting for suffering rooted not in static accounts of alternate modes of theodicy or reason but in contemporaneity, specifically the ever more crowded conditions of life among the decolonizing. If some variant of Malthusian crisis could be taken for granted, a medicalized anthropology in this call to arms had to scale-up and embrace an even more extreme version of tough love than that advocated by Devereux and Carstairs.[1]

A popularized form of Parsonian sociology (1951) with its focus on system stability was the master trope to the postwar configuration of nonsocialist planning: indeed medical anthropology, created as part of the assemblage of modernization theory, still maintains vestiges of these deep Parsonian roots. The pattern variables simplified a complex evolutionism across the social sciences (McClelland 1961; Redfield 1953, 1957; Rostow 1960; Shils 1960), a wealth of epistemologies and techniques commensurated through the systemic analysis of a cybernetic era. At the heart of this project lay a particular reading of Max Weber's *The Protestant Ethic and the Spirit of Capitalism* (2002 [1905]) in terms of Émile Durkheim's *The Division of Labor in Society* (1966 [1893]) and *Suicide* (1979 [1897]) and Sigmund Freud's *Civilization and Its Discontents* (1963 [1930]), a reading that framed Weber as the anti-Marx. Again, only vulgar restatement can convey the stakes of this reading, quickly challenged by alternative engagements with Weber (Bendix 1960), a turn to the late Durkheim (Turner 1969), and later by other readings of Freud than that of ego psychology.

We might term the stakes in this Durkheimian and ego-psychological Weber the Protestantization of peasants. These can be stated as follows: *if social stability in highly stratified societies is to be achieved, peasants need to develop better ego controls than the primitive situation of a rampant id and despotic superego allow, a kind of self-formation that in its patterning resembles the Weberian account of Calvinism in the genealogy of capitalist modernity.* Protestantism in this reading implies less a theological content than an anxious and ascetic orientation to the world that would lead one to spend less, accumulate capital, and generate the conditions for urban culture with its achievement orientation allowing capitalist takeoff.

By the mid-twentieth century, after several intensely eugenic decades and the legacy of colonial and evangelical neo-Malthusianism, wasteful expenditure implied more than rationalized household economies and the curtailment of ritual giving. Waste was bound up to the excess production of babies by the poor. Late colonial and decolonizing international governance was from the 1920s to the debt crises of the 1980s and the end of the Cold War organized in significant measure around the emergence of a network of state and foundation-based institutional forms constituting an interregional biopolitics of birth control.

As Connelly (2008, 237–326) documents, many experts across national, multilateral, and foundation-based institutions by the early 1970s were despairing of the ability of the world's masses to be motivated to have fewer children. Alternatives to family planning involving varied forms of soft or hard compulsion were increasingly mooted: the population policies of the Government of India under the 1970s' period of Emergency, linking access to state-controlled housing, jobs, and affordable commodities to proof of sterilization (Das 2004; Tarlo 2001), emerged in consequence.

If postwar medical anthropology was organized around the geopolitical urgency of subaltern child death,[2] and in its manipulation of culture offered the promise of regional stability through a commitment to achievable hygiene and more healthy children, the alarmist demography of the 1960s and 1970s came to refocus the future of the happy family and healthy economy through antinatalism, not more but less (and therefore more healthy) children. Again, development was organized around an as-if modernity: if the mass subject of the underdeveloped world subaltern could not be motivated into Protestant transformation—the cultivation of the withholding of fertility as a virtue—one could through sterilization or postnatal IUD insertion (Van Hollen 2003) cut directly into the mass body or introduce mechanical means of antinatalism, in either case producing a class of bodies refashioned to act as if they were modern. The iteration, in India, of the ideal image of the modern two-child family on roadsides and in media during the 1970s and 1980s may not have produced the "Protestant" ego controls that postwar interdisciplinarity was supposed to achieve. But if the mass subject of the new nation resisted its remaking into a "Protestant" will generative of the parsimonious family, the *body* of that mass subject at times could be claimed by the regime of expertise and rendered as if it were Protestant. Surgically or mechanically altered, the sensible body could be made into a limiting condition for the recalcitrant mass subject. It was made, at least in its all-important fertility, to act as if it were modern.

Neither medical anthropology nor area studies, as these took institutional form in the 1950s through the 1970s, were inevitably committed to the population body as the object of their expertise. But I have argued that early on both institutions encounter the recalcitrant peasant (and later the slum dweller) as a central object of knowledge. Both struggle with the simultaneous deployment of the "medicine" of urgency and the "anti-medicine" of the culture concept and U.S.-focused cultural critique. If the latter tendency will suffer from the ahistoricism and political inattentiveness of what I have termed the zoo story, the former in its necessary commitment to medical solutions will repeatedly confront local knowledge that resists a shared sense of what must be done.

The concern driving this chapter, as we work our way back to the present, is with the persistence of this internal disciplinary division between the area as the site of the mass, its need so urgent as to suspend disciplinary self-critique, and the area as the site of culture, its difference so enticing to liberal reflection so as to suspend the emergence of alternatives to the zoo story. The hope is that attention to the reterritorialized figure of the "area," in this age of scaling up to global health, might help us find other ways to imagine a medical anthropology than as a struggle between the persistence of the culture area in the interpretation of suffering and the deterritorializing clarity of tough love.

The Double Work of the Region in Second-Generation Medical Anthropology

During the 1970s, several forms of critique of the discipline's focus on the culture area as obstacle and vehicle for medical modernization emerged. In the case of population, attention to the violence and racism that population control had produced soon led to instances of sustained anthropological critique (Mamdani 1972). The period of Indian Emergency and the One-Child Policy in China—and more generally the demands placed on populations in many parts of the world to contend with antinatalist bureaucracies in the organization of care and life itself—would further the shift toward decades of critical analysis (Bledsoe, Banja, and Hill 1998; Greenhalgh 1995, 2008). This critical turn was interdisciplinary, emerging out of a decade of relative radicalization in the academy. The anthropology of fertility became a site of feminist reconceptualization and later of a focus on cultures and practices of infertility and the emergence of new technologies and forms of reproduction, relatedness, and care (Becker 2000; Ginsburg and Rapp 1995; Inhorn 1994, 2007; Kahn 2000; Sargent 1989; Strathern 1992a).

The self-criticism of medical anthropology as the proving ground of modernization theory was of course far broader: a second generation was transforming the field.[3] This second-generation critique emerged at a time of utopian commitment. It challenged the dominant modernization focus of the subdiscipline on numerous, overlapping grounds: for symbolic and phenomenological thinness, for a failure to examine "traditional" healing as radically modern and a site of colonial and postcolonial contest, for a reluctance to treat "Western" biomedicine as culture, and for an apparent inability, in framing its mission as adjunct to medicine, to attend to structural conditions in which professional medicine seemed complicit.[4] Like an earlier if arguably less sectarian split in the larger profession between symbolic and world-systems approaches, this expanded and increasingly international medical anthropology developed tensions between "interpretive" and "critical" schools. Yet among most practitioners these reflexively opposed approaches overlapped. Earlier I noted that both sets of approaches would at points maintain the "anti-medical" impetus of Ruth Benedict and Mead, troubling clinical universals. At the same time, both offered a pragmatic focus on the clinic as the site of action and were critical of the varied (political-economic and cultural) inadequacies of a "public health model."

The actual break in the discipline, in the years of its expansion in the 1970s and 1980s, was not that between critical and interpretive medical anthropologies but rather one generated by the growing dissonance between a subdiscipline ever more engaged in discovering its broader philosophical and social theoretical relevance, on the one hand, and a subdiscipline not only committed to the language of policy and pragmatic intervention but committed within the positivist framing of its funder, a biomedical social research apparatus dominated by psychology and epidemiology. The ever greater divide between so-called theoretical versus applied medical anthropologies perpetuated the challenges the subdiscipline faced in integrating both its "anti-medical" and "medical" commitments at a time, utopian only in hindsight, when anthropology promised to change the world.

The region did double labor in much of this literature. As noted above, it continued to trouble the adequacy of universalizing clinical reason much as the culture area had for the Boasians. Localized medical knowledge in its radical difference could challenge the hegemony of professional medicine as a mirror of nature or monopoly on reason (Corin and Bibeau 1975; Kleinman and Good 1985; Lock 1980; Scheper-Hughes and Lock 1987; Scheper-Hughes

1990). This reframing of "culture as obstacle to modernization" in terms of a comparative project in which *all* medical categories or bodily and healing practices are locally and historically mediated, requiring new methodologies to consider the specificities of how bodies are produced, experienced, and known, continued through the 1990s (Alter 1992; Becker 1995; Desjarlais 1992; Farquhar 1994b; Laderman 1991; Roseman 1991).

This invocation of the local might function as heir to the empire of temperament, the liberal recognition and encompassment of alternative epistemologies and clinical phenomenologies within the cosmopolitan grid of medical modernity. Less often, the local power as an alternative suggested a more radical refusal of biomedicine, at times in the spirit of anti-psychiatry or of Ivan Illich (1976). The scale of the local could vary—the neighborhood, city, tribe, or slum could in theory effect this negative labor of critique as much as the nation or global region—but particularly in the case of the scholarly medical traditions the critical use of alternatives to biomedicine seemed to demand a national scale: China, India, Mexico, Iran.

There were at least two reasons for this often unacknowledged persistence of the nation. First, the revival of "traditional" medicine and related bodily regimes was as anthropologists and historians had long argued integral to the crucible of a colonial and racialized modernity under the sign of the nation (Arnold 1987; Crozier 1968; Leslie 1976; Prakash 1999). And second, methodologically the work of studying scholarly medical practice often involved classical philological and text-historical training. The effect of such training, at points over the twentieth century, was to locate scholarly inquiry at the scale of the great tradition or civilization, as these were being mapped onto the nation. The unquestioned obviousness of national scale was furthered by a structuralist attention to langue, again and again mapped onto the nation, as opposed to the parole of the infranational little tradition. If Ayurveda could trouble the universalizing normalization of biomedical allopathy, it did so by materializing "India" as a more or less homogeneous site of alterity (and a site whose culture, as Louis Dumont [1980 (1966)] had argued, could be explained through the categories of ancient high caste Hindus).

Conversely the region did a second kind of labor for second-generation medical anthropology, not only challenging universalizing reason through national culture. In this second mode of argument, the area or region worked as the embodied site of history operating at multiple levels of scale. The focus was still totalizing. Attentiveness to the empirical conditions of illness and affliction demanded the integration of frames from world system to family system to the psychic economy of an individual's "personal symbols" (Obeyesekere 1981). "System" as the unit of analysis was retained within the medical anthropology of the 1970s and early 1980s, a survival from the earlier Parsonian moment put to work in different ways. The followers and fellow travelers of both Eric Wolf and Clifford Geertz kept the cybernetic terminology for some years.[5]

If most variants of "system" presumed some kind of totality, increasingly at stake in what I am terming the embodied site of history was less a closed universe than the figure of the afflicted body in its radical contingency, what Margaret Lock termed its "local biology" (1993). The idea of a local biology had the potential to sublate the tired opposition between (anti-medical) culture and (medical) nature, and it opened out onto the emerging field of science and technology studies as the latter was being colonized by anthropologists. The nation and traditional medicine mattered, as did the economic system and regime of technique, but not as the site of transcendent critique. The ever-increasing stress on historicism and contingency opened the discipline up to postcolonial critique (Adams 1996; Alter 2000, 2004; Cohen 1998; Farmer 1992; Farquhar 2002; Langford 2002; Pandolfo 1989). The critique of development as the dominant mode of postcolonial governance was often central to analysis. More anthropologists attended to the inadequacies of "culture-bound" analysis and of the celebration of traditional healing (Farmer 1997, 522; Pigg 1992, 1997). The "construction" of the region in historicist work could find itself in tension with both the interpretive and political demands of lived experience (Kleinman and Kleinman 1996), a tension that the project on "social suffering" attempted to address (Kleinman et al. 1997).

If medical anthropology was working to resolve those contradictions formed in response to its Cold War and area studies origins, it was engaging a world in which the organization of illness, government, and information was rapidly changing. Emergent syntheses were being just as quickly left behind.

Humanitarianism and the Death of the Clinic

One approach was to shift the temporal frame of the subdiscipline to the study of emerging forms of life. With the asymmetrically emerging deterritorializations glossed as globalization and global neoliberalism, the critical focus on development opened onto a broader effort to comprehend novel biopolitical forms. The impact of feminist, Foucauldian, and formalist analysis sharpened the analytic tools of the anthropological study of emergence within medicine and the biosciences (Fischer 2003; Ginsburg 1987; Martin 1989, 1994; Rabinow 1996a, 1999; Rapp 1988; Rose 1996; Strathern 1992a), opening up a more extensive conversation with science and technology studies.[6]

The area or region within the study of the technoscientific clinic appeared in varied ways. As with much of the sociology of science and of medicine, it could simply be ignored or assumed, one species of Occidentalism. Alternatively, studies could assume a "juxtapositional" form: technology X in (unexpected) place Y. The latter approach could reframe the "old wine in new bottles" debates of modernization theory, the life of culture inflecting the culture of life in the clinic and laboratory and vice versa (Copeman 2009; Roberts 2007). Or it could serve to decenter the assumptions of an Occidentalist field of science studies (Naraindas 2006). These approaches extended the identity of the region as nation described earlier.

Increasingly, the area became a unit of analysis reassembled at the intersection of a variably transnational biotechnology with globalizing clinical and industrial demand for bioavailable tissues and test subjects and state and humanitarian strategies for access to medication and to rights in the clinic (Biehl 2009; Cohen 2004b; Franklin 2007; Hayden 2003; Hogle 1999; Lakoff 2005; Lock 2001b; Petryna 2002, 2009; Scheper-Hughes 2004; Sunder Rajan 2006, 2007; Waldby and Mitchell 2006). These approaches extended the earlier attention to local biologies. Increasingly, however, local biology was not a concept to be fought for against a universalizing biomedicine. Rather, the *local* was itself a site of value and a commodity, a resource upon which a biological, economic, and moral assemblage of technomedicine depended. As for the culture and personality anthropologists, an expansive clinical apparatus depended on the inclusion of human difference in the development of fungible techniques (Epstein 2007).

As these varied anthropologies of the life sciences continued to expand, their shared identity as a subdiscipline was at times less clear. Medical anthropology was no longer obviously at "the borderland" between anthropology and the clinic (Kleinman 1980). The clinic itself was shifting, and the relation of a patient or care group with a healer was no longer necessarily the unit of analysis to be understood, supplemented, or critiqued. Privatization and growing costs, greater patient responsibility and activism, and the erosion of public and community health services represented part of this shift. In the wake of Cold War state planning and large-scale development programs, state-based national and international development was supplemented and in some cases encompassed by NGOs. The humanitarian gift and its governance these offered were increasingly organized less around a future promising access to basic clinical and preventive care and more around a present demanding the urgent supply of lifesaving medication or emergency supplies.

To put it in the Benjaminian terms of Susan Buck-Morss (2000), the clinic was for much of the twentieth century a key site promising a better future for the masses. Buck-Morss frames the twentieth century in terms of a linked set of "dreamworlds" of future-oriented mass utopia committed to some combination of the nation-state, socialism, and development and split by the terms of the Cold War. With the collapse of these dreamworlds—with the end not only of the Soviet system but of the mass commitment to welfare by the welfare state eroded by neoliberalism—the clinic loses its centrality in the organization of global health.

If medical anthropology in its Cold War form was nothing less than the anthropology of the dreamworld, promising the future through the critical understanding and pragmatic manipulation of culture to all those whose access to the utopia of the clinic is limited by their habitation of a culture area, what happens to the subdiscipline in the aftermath of this promise? As the structure of state and multilateral institutions of development assistance was supplanted by a diverse assemblage of banks, NGOs, state agencies, social movements, and clinical trials, as organizations like USAID increasingly outsourced their work to private corporate entities, and as the promised future tense of development gave way to the anxious present tense of humanitarian crisis (Redfield 2005), the idea of a medical anthropology demanded rethinking.

Jane Guyer (2007) has argued for a specific variant of this turning away from the future. Examining monetarist doctrine and evangelical Christianity in North America, Africa, and Europe, she suggests that a range of practices of living and modes of governance lose their grounding in the "near future" and come to depend on a split temporal register of, on the one hand, the present moment and, on the other, the infinite time of ultimate religious or economic values. Medical anthropology, as its own relation to the near future is undone, came in the early 2000s to display a formally similar splitting of its time. I have already noted the anxious turn to the emergent, to the anthropology of new biological and technical norms, that dominates many research programs across the discipline. But over the same period, an anthropology rooted in *timeless* moral demands made a cogent case for a humanitarian medical anthropology.

Amid proliferating claims for emergent diseases and novel situations, Paul Farmer, Jim Kim, and other anthropologists associated with the NGO Partners in Health troubled the idea that the world has undergone radical transformation, arguing instead for analytic "modesty" (Farmer 1999, 2003; Kim et al. 2000). Epidemic and endemic disease remained a preventable source of massive morbidity and mortality among the world's poor. Modesty as a cultivated virtue allowed the anthropologist to resist the compelling attraction of both novelty and complexity to attend to persistent inequities in the distribution of life chances. The deep and long-standing commitment of these anthropologists mobilized many scholars, clinicians, and philanthropists, creating a public for medical anthropology that far exceeded its earlier twentieth-century history.

The "time" of Partners in Health is, the cogent need for modesty notwithstanding, not simple. For Guyer the *near future* we are losing is marked by the reasoned attention to the social causes of distress that Partners in Health often exemplifies. And to the extent Partners in Health, like other humanitarian NGOs, finds itself responding to crisis after crisis, it may seem to occupy the humanitarian *present* that Peter Redfield has described. But I use this exemplary and influential NGO to stand in particular for Guyer's *infinite time*. The Partners in Health anthropologists, as I noted, have called anthropology and public health to task when they neglect persistent structural inequalities in the name of novel formations. Both Farmer's concept of structural violence and his demand for a modest condition of "moral clarity" in response draw less, I would argue, on a rationalized domain of the near future and more on a set of ultimate, often religiously framed, values. In a series of lectures in the 1990s and 2000s, Farmer challenged his fellow anthropologists to cultivate the modesty to be able to attend to a range of global situations at once persistent and urgent. Medical anthropology, in such moments, was being directed in Guyer's terms both toward the immediate moment of urgency and toward timeless values that would enable its practitioners to act.

Urgency has been a necessarily familiar theme in the discipline's brief history. If the urgency compelling earlier anthropologists toward the medicalized tough love of antinatalist governance rendering peasants into as-if moderns was based on a particular kind of near future grounded in the rational calculations of science, the urgency of humanitarian anthropology both contracts into the immediate present of masses or persons who will suffer and die without antituberculosis or antiretroviral medication and into the infinite time of the moral, increasingly linking our abilities to rise to the challenge, to our moral value as medical anthropologists worthy of the calling.

Reterritorialization in Time

A deterritorialized "global health" will produce productive reconfigurations of disciplines and problems. Anthropology need not only be the insistent voice of reterritorialization: offering regional specificity, on the one hand, and challenging the adequacy of "cultural audits," on the other. To the extent that medical anthropology's time has been split—the "now" of the emergent and urgent and the "always" of moral clarity—its responses to the professionalization of global health may be informed by this dual register.

I want in closing to note two of several ways anthropology confronts the region or area with the death of the clinic and the temporal situation of the now and always. One way is to produce a more effective form of deterritorialized knowledge.

The challenge of the now requires a scaling up of intervention to replace the lost clinic of the future. The scale of NGO-based health work continues to expand. Successful local projects are supported by ever-larger scale organizations controlling the distribution of humanitarian capital: the Gates Foundation was arguably the most prominent in the decade of the 2000s. These funders are often committed to the local: local governance, local problematization, local coalitions. But the scale of "philanthrocapitalism" requires significant deterritorialization if funding organizations are to operate efficiently and effectively on a global scale.

This scaling up draws on prior efforts to create minimalist universal forms like the humanitarian emergency "kit" that can be deployed anywhere (Redfield 2008). But many successful model projects started in the face of urgent and immediate need are intensively attuned to local worlds and cannot be easily reduced to the minimal forms of the kit. The challenge in going beyond a handful of exemplary model projects requires the implementation of an audit able to assess what configurations of techniques, personnel, and, critically, the management of these in relation to a specific local situation are effective and transportable.

Managerial rationalities have emerged as a key site for rethinking the scaling up of the local (Whitington 2008). The technical expertise that many growing NGOs and foundations turn to for this process of scaling up has been increasingly located in schools of business and administration, displacing the primacy of professional public health.[7] Regional and cultural specificity matters in business schools at a time when not only markets but production and administration are flexible and interregional, and an emergent business school para-ethnography outstrips academic anthropology in contemporary relevance.

The form of area studies and the concepts of culture that may matter the most for a contemporary anthropology of moral clarity are thus dual: on the one hand, the commitment to the ongoing engagement with local conditions through anthropological and clinical activism, and on the other, the turn away from the complexity of contemporary anthropology for the more modest— and apparently effective—analysis of culture, place, and administrative form found in professional schools of business. Not surprisingly, given the rest of the discipline's careful attention to emergent forms of medicine and of life, a number of anthropologists are currently studying this proliferation of relations linking clinical activism, philanthropic capital, and business school expertise and its possible and distributed effects.[8]

Rather than asking readers to cast their lot in with either the anthropology of moral clarity or the anthropology of emergent forms of life, I am suggesting that these both are bound up in the conditions of work when the clinic as a promissory form of modernity is called into question. Buck-Morss follows Walter Benjamin in calling attention to the *fragments* of failed dreamworlds: despite the violence that followed the varied twentieth-century dreamworlds of mass utopia—in this chapter, coercive family planning stood in for a far broader catalogue of abuses—she suggests that the commitment to reasoned efforts to make life better for many should not be abandoned to the dustbin of history.

Health activism under the sign of international development in the 1970s and 1980s centered on a variant of Buck-Morss's mass utopia, as a commitment to the provision of basic primary care—"Health for All by the Year 2000"—through the training of community health workers. The basic primary care clinic was its desideratum. The health activism of the 1990s and 2000s, by contrast, has a necessarily different goal at its core: lifesaving drugs for all. Partners in Health, for example, could not rest content with the logic of basic primary care if its goal was to take seriously the urgent situation of persons suffering and dying with MDR-TB. The struggle for health in the face of class-based, racialized, and sexualized triage mandated the provision of expensive drugs.

We might think of the pharmaceutical as a fragment, in Buck-Morss's sense, of the clinic once promised as "Health for All." The anthropology of the emergent has moved on; the anthropology of the infinite is secure in its morality. But Buck-Morss is among a number of writers who suggest the value of looking backward to recapture a lost value, in some affinity with Miyazaki's method of hope noted at the start. "Drugs for all" as the site of activism offers a mixed message: urgent in the face of the pandemics and yet arguably complicit with a neoliberal erosion of institutions and the growth of corporate power. But a commitment to the drug may reanimate some needed measure of mass utopia.

In the present, this urgent "pharmaceuticalization" (Biehl 2007) of health activism and of its clients produces new conditions of living and new kinds of politics, relations, injuries, and exclusions. The effective scaling up of drug delivery has demanded, for example, the new knowledges of business para-ethnography and "social entrepreneurship" being assembled into the field of global health. The resulting approaches to the "area" may be compelling not for their painful reminders of the culture concept at its crudest but rather for a range of managerial and audit techniques enabling the activism of pharmaceutical distribution. At the same time, despite the best practices of dedicated activists and the strengths of emergent business para-ethnography, the conjoint life of pharmaceuticals and patients may in some cases resist packaging into a scalable and nongovernmental form of clinical administration.

The caution is no reason to evade the promise of a more modest inquiry than anthropology in its radical empiricism and conceptual rigor may be able to offer. But it suggests the persistent need for regional knowledge that may exceed the purview of the new field of global health: not to reanimate the zoo story. What area-specific knowledge entails in an age of pharmaceuticalization must be determined. Recent and ongoing work is providing suggestions. Drug-based humanitarianism in relation to pharmaceutical capital and distributed ethics has entailed the reorganization of research and clinical trials, production, and marketing; of reconstituted networks of regulation, distribution, consumption, and care; and of problems of inadequate diagnosis, expense, racialized exclusion and inclusion, and property and the question of the copy (Das and Das 2005; Dumit 2005; Ecks 2005; Fullwiley 2007; Harper 2005; Hayden 2007; Lakoff 2005; Whitmarsh 2008b). The order of place and distribution of life chances these problems and networks constitute may or may not exceed the insights and achievements of the new organization of global health.

Against the securing of a timeless morality, this recasting of the area begins by recognizing the failure of our utopian projects, of a medical anthropology created to get marginal populations to act as if they were modern, and of their aftermath. Against the critical embrace of the new, this recasting of the area finds itself looking backward to dreams of health for all, everywhere, and discovering hopeful fragments in the problems and materials being assembled.

PART II

Queries

That Obscure Object of Global Health

Globalization—even if the term itself has been hotly contested—
is the modern or postmodern version of the proverbial elephant,
described by its blind observers in so many different ways. Yet
one can still posit the existence of the elephant in the absence of a
single persuasive and dominant theory; nor are blinded questions
the most unsatisfactory way to explore this kind of relational and
multileveled phenomenon. — Fredric Jameson, preface, *The
Cultures of Globalization*

Anthropology is continually confronted with the irruption into
common language of new words and notions, which emerge from the public
sphere, the political arena, or, more mundanely, the universe of social marketing, and which are claimed by their promoters to be innovative and faith-
ful descriptions of new realities. The immediate—and nevertheless highly
mediated—success of these so-called new concepts represents a challenge
for anthropologists who, like these self-designated inventors, also claim to be
legitimate commentators on the state of the world: Should they follow and
even attempt to anticipate or exaggerate the hype? Or should they resist and
denounce the empire of hollow ideologies? Few linguistic novelties have generated so much debate in academia between the enthusiasts and the skeptics as
has "globalization." Are we witnessing an unprecedented situation of mobility,
connectedness, and disappearance of borders or are we being fooled by the il-
lusion of presentism exacerbated by the cunning of capitalism? The question
has haunted many discussions in the social sciences over the past two decades.

This intellectual turmoil, however, has little affected the use of a specific
declination of globalization that has become a whole new domain: global
health. The formulation has rapidly encountered adherence from public health
specialists, international aid agencies, governments, and even medical anthro-

pologists who have heartily adopted global health as one of their fields of research and passwords for larger audiences. This is not to say that questions have not been raised about the significance, dynamics, and stakes of global health, but the "idea" of it has generally been taken for granted as the best descriptor of contemporary issues in world health, as if we all knew what it was. Yet global health has more often been defined and illustrated than problematized. Interestingly, however, when one examines the scientific literature as well as university or charity websites, we may derive the impression that the content and the contour of global health are extremely variable. Actually, aiming to grasp the object of global health can be as frustrating for the researcher as it is for the protagonist of Luis Buñuel's film *That Obscure Object of His Desire* to seize the elusive object he seeks. What I am therefore trying to do here is simply to illuminate this obscure object.

Being neither an enthusiast nor a skeptic, I will neither plead for global health nor deny its existence, but rather challenge some of the untested assumptions we may have about it: we could designate this third position as critical. First, I will show that in spite of globalization, most health issues and policies remain national, even local. Second, I will indicate two approaches, semiotics and semantics, to suggest the diversity of the significations of contemporary global health in terms of signs and meanings. Third, I will pose two symmetrical questions: In what sense is global health "global"? What does "health" mean in global health? Answering the former unveils the dialectic of spatial expansion and moral normalization. Responding to the latter brings to light the tension between the worth of lives and the value of life. Finally, I will discuss the perspectives for research in medical anthropology if one accepts the critical questioning I propose.

Prologue: *Los Olvidados*

After one year of harsh debate about health care reform, after the passing of two distinct bills in the House and the Senate, after the drafting of several versions of the White House plan, and after a final dramatic congressional vote on March 21, 2010, which was anticipated to be so close that it led to last-minute compromises, one element remained almost unchanged and unchallenged during the heated discussions about the novel social protection the

United States would allocate to its population: the existence of slightly more than twenty million people who would remain uninsured under the new legislation. Progressive constituencies legitimately rejoiced about the more than thirty million individuals who gained health coverage, but very few mentioned those who were to remain uncovered and represented a figure approximately equivalent to the population of the state of New York. Remarkably, such a huge human sacrifice and crucial social choice did not provoke major civic protests. No human rights organization or social movement expressed concern about the abandonment of this population to the goodwill of charities. For those left behind by the health reform, however, it is probable that the situation will be even worse than before, as it is to be expected that, considering the efforts made to pass the law and the debate it has raised, complaints about the condition of the uncovered will become almost inaudible and seem hardly legitimate. As it is easy to guess, most of those thus ignored or forgotten— *los olvidados*—are illegal immigrants.

One anecdotal event, too soon forgotten, may deserve attention here. During Barack Obama's much-celebrated speech to defend his health plan before Congress on September 10, 2009, Representative Joe Wilson insultingly shouted, "You lie!" Much indignation was prompted by this lack of civility or evidence of racism (depending on interpretations), but there was little comment on what provoked this gross accusation: the assertion made by the President that no illegal immigrants would ever receive benefits under the proposed plan. Whatever opinion one may have about this assertion—whether it is true or false, good or bad—the significant fact is that it seemed to take for granted that a broad political consensus existed on the exclusion of undocumented foreigners from health reform. The President thus discarded the claim made by his opponents as "bogus," just as was the claim that he was planning to set up panels of bureaucrats with the power to kill off senior citizens. In other words, saying that illegal immigrants would be included in the reform could only be a mere invention to discredit the government, as if this hypothesis were not only improbable but also unthinkable. The implicit meaning behind this reasoning is therefore that the lowest common denominator for reform was that it must draw a line within the country's population. If health was to be recognized as a common good, which was probably the most crucial issue of the bill and its major ideological innovation, then it was necessary to simultaneously define the moral community entitled to benefit from this collective solidarity. Both notions—common good and moral community—are intricately related, but they may need some theoretical clarification and even more historical perspective.

It is certainly one of the most salient features of what Karl Polanyi (2001 [1944], 141) termed the "great transformation" characteristic of modernity, and one of the most significant counterpoints to what he describes as the "liberal creed" of the market, that as a result of social struggles health may have been recognized as a public responsibility rather than a private matter. This conception derives from the fact that health has increasingly been considered a commonweal deserving a specific treatment and not just a natural given. One may remember that Jean-Jacques Rousseau (1994 [1754], 23), in the introduction to his *Discourse on Inequality*, distinguished two forms of inequality: "natural or physical inequality, because it is established by nature, and consists of differences in age, health, bodily strength, and traits of the mind," and "moral or political inequality," which "depends on a sort of convention, and is established, or at least sanctioned, by the consent of men." For him, as with most of his contemporaries, disparities inscribed in the body were excluded from the political.

Less than a century later they had become part of the progressive project of European hygienists, and it took one hundred more years to see this project formally accepted at an international level. With the birth of institutions such as the World Health Organization (WHO) in 1948, the idea of a global common good seemed to be developing just as the utopia of a worldwide moral community was inscribed in the foundational texts of the United Nations in the aftermath of the Second World War. However, six decades later, the idea and the utopia are still more present in the rhetoric of international agencies or the imaginary of nongovernmental organizations than in the empirical facts anthropologists observe in their fieldwork—what Linda Whiteford and Lenore Manderson (2000, 2) characterize as the "discordance between global ideal and local reality," and which they interpret as being much less the consequences of differences in cultures than the result of historical forces inherited from colonialism.

Without diminishing the merit of their authors, one could say that the Declaration of Alma Ata in 1978 on primary health care, essentially oriented toward the underdeveloped world, and the Ottawa Charter of 1986 for health promotion, principally dedicated to the industrialized world, have underlined more than they have transformed the global health situation, especially from the perspective of the inequalities between and within countries. Words are important indeed, but acts are even more so. From this perspective, a significant moment in the recent history of the communalization of health was the 2001 Doha Declaration on the Trade Related Aspects of Intellectual Property Rights (TRIPS), which affirmed member states' flexibility in circumventing patent rights for better access to essential medicines. As a result of intense pressures from the transnational activists that Vinh-Kim Nguyen (2005, 125–26) calls a "biological vanguard" defining "therapeutic citizenship," the wealthy states and the pharmaceutical industry had to accept what has since been referred to as the "health exception" in international trade, meaning that vital drugs should be excluded from pure market logics. However, this victory was short-lived in its effectiveness, since the United States actively engaged in a series of bilateral negotiations with Latin American, African, and Asian governments to reestablish more favorable conditions for its trade and its enterprises, in particular in the domain of medicines. The lesson should be remembered. Not only is the globalization of health as a public weal a largely unfinished business, it also appears to be an always-reversible process. Moreover, rather than being submitted to supranational political determinations and inscribed in an ethical order without borders, it continues to be principally ruled by national interests and state sovereignties primarily serving local constituencies. Instead of a uniform process, as it is often described, the globalization of health must therefore be thought of as a heterogeneous and contested historical phenomenon acknowledging common goods that can always be challenged and producing moral communities that rely on exclusion as much as inclusion.

Returning to the U.S. scene, the debate about health care reform reminds us that health remains largely seen as a national affair rather than a global question, that its recognition as a common good will come only with the conquering of individualistic conservatism, and that within each specific context the condition needed to obtain this recognition is the delimitation of a moral community that separates the entitled from the excluded, the deserving from the undeserving. The debate in Congress was illuminating. The soft—and discriminatory—position of the House bill implied that those not entitled to public social protection would still benefit from insurance if they could afford it. The hard—and ostracizing—version of the Senate counterproposition meant that excluded persons would not even be allowed to buy insurance. But with both options, it was clear that the majority of the concerned population would be left without access to prevention or treatment, merely hoping for compassionate assistance from private charities.

This point should be emphasized. That illegal immigrants are not included under the umbrella of health reform is highly significant. Far from being a marginal dimension of this important political achievement, as one might infer from the fact that the population concerned is itself marginal, it is a crucial test for policies. Just as the fate of refugees during the first half of the twentieth century was intimately related to the decline of the nation-state, as Hannah Arendt (1976 [1951], 267) asserted, we must consider the political treatment of immigrants a major challenge testing the fragility of the social state in the early twenty-first century. In fact, these two categories of population are less distinct than we might believe, since today a significant proportion of undocumented foreigners corresponds to rejected asylum-seekers. Even in a globalized world, the right to health is bound to state policies in the same way as are civil rights. The ultimate moral of the U.S. reform fable may thus be simply that global health starts at home.

But until now, the expression "global health" seems to have been considered self-evident, as if we should all know what it signifies and share what it refers to. This is also the case in many contemporary discourses, whether political or even scientific. In a sense it is true that everyone has a vague idea that global health concerns planetary issues of diseases. How to apprehend them, however, remains an unsolved question. In the field of medical anthropology, solutions range from an international collection of local health worlds, as in Faye Ginsburg and Rayna Rapp's pioneering volume (1995) on the "global politics of reproduction," to an exploration of the circulation and agglomeration of health problems, which Aihwa Ong and Stephen Collier (2005) describe as "global assemblages." I will not attempt to propose a definitive response, but rather explore what can be analyzed as the semiotic and semantic dimensions of global health.

Semiotic Perspectives

From a semiotic perspective, global health can be viewed as a sign. Its visibility has considerably increased in recent years. A Google search on April 27, 2010, yielded 99,400,000 hits. Most international agencies, national governments, pharmaceutical companies, academic institutions, and charitable organizations have created websites about activities that are not necessarily very distinct from what they had previously carried out under a different designation, such as public health, international health, health development, or health cooperation. The U.S. Agency for International Development (USAID), the Centers for Disease Control (CDC), and the World Economic Forum all have their Global Health programs, as do the Kaiser Family Foundation and the Bill and Melinda Gates Foundation, the United Methodist Church and the Seventh Day Adventist Church, Merck, and GlaxoSmithKline. Among many, the University of Washington has established a Department of Global Health, Duke has created a Global Health Institute, Johns Hopkins has developed a Center for Global Health, and Harvard has started a Global Health Initiative. Several scientific journals were recently launched, including *Global Public Health*, *Global Health Governance*, *Global Health Action*, and *International Health* in partnership with the Lancet Global Health Network. And of course Facebook and Twitter have their pages, messages, and "happy hour."

In fact, actions to eradicate malaria or filariasis, to prevent tuberculosis and AIDS, and to increase vaccination rates and drug access, all of which are undertaken under this new banner, are not so much medical novelties as semiotic innovations. Technologies have evolved little, but the message is distinctive. This is the sense of the voluntarily anachronistic title of Steven Palmer's (2010) study of the work of the Rockefeller Foundation in the early twentieth century. In other words, global health has become an effective signifier. Independent of the object to which it refers, it transmits an idea of change, of worldliness, of postmodernity. This dimension—which makes it a keyword of our time—should not be understated. In their study of the recent history of the WHO, Theodore Brown, Marcos Cueto and Elizabeth Fee (2006, 62) show how the replacement of "international health" by "global health" was part of a "strategy of survival" for this once-prestigious institution facing a profound crisis due to budget cuts, image devaluation and political marginalization. But of course, global health is not just that. There is also an idea behind the term—or beyond it. This idea is multifaceted. It refers to at least six series of phenomena: epidemiological, demographic, economic, technical, organizational, and social.

First, global health suggests the dual transformation of epidemiological profiles: on the one hand, the increasing disparities in health conditions between poor countries and the rich world, as well as within nations, which Jim Yong Kim, Joyce Millen, Alec Irwin, and John Gershman (2000) denounce in their case studies. On the other hand, Robert Desjarlais, Leon Eisenberg, Byron Good, and Arthur Kleinman (1995) established the epidemiological homogenization of disease patterns in their pioneering survey, such as the expansion of infections in the West, the increase of cardiovascular and metabolic pathology in the South, and also the progressive recognition of mental health problems that were until recently ignored in poorer countries.

Second, global health evokes the mobility of people: the millions of refugees, whether enclosed in camps in the Third World or seeking asylum in the bureaucracies of Western countries, who embody these transnational displacements submitted to the good will of humanitarian organizations, studied by Liisa Malkki (1996) in the context of post-genocide Rwanda. But migrations also concern health professionals participating in the "brain drain" from poor countries and patients from rich countries practicing "medical tourism" to obtain treatments or organs in more accessible places such as India, where Lawrence Cohen (2001) has described these new regimes of "bioavailability."

Third, global health involves the production and circulation of economic goods: medicines obviously spring to mind, since in recent years a highly disputed and conflictive market has developed, with the expansion of pharmaceutical multinationals, the dissemination of clinical trials, the competition of generic drugs, the battles over patents, and the World Trade Organization protocol of Doha, all of which are under scrutiny in the edited collection by Adriana Petryna, Andrew Lakoff, and Arthur Kleinman (2006). But these goods also include parts of the body, whether organs to be transplanted or genomes to be deciphered, processes analyzed in terms of commodification of the human body by Nancy Scheper-Hughes and Loïc Wacquant (2002).

Fourth, global health implies transnationalization of medical practices: on one side, it works as the exportation of technologies — for example, Chinese hospitals embedded in Sub-Saharan Africa or Western reproductive responses to infertility in Third World countries, as has been studied by Marcia Inhorn (2003b) in Egypt. On the other side, it also functions as an exportation of expertise, such as radiological exams performed in the United States but read in India by local physicians, or conversely, vaccines disseminated in the Third World by charities such as the Bill and Melinda Gates Foundation via the Global Alliance, which William Muraskin (2005) describes as a "virtual revolution" in the international health community.

Fifth, global health exists through an international bureaucracy: WHO, the United Nations Fund for Children (UNICEF), the Joint United Nations Program on HIV/AIDS (UNAIDS), and the Global Fund to Fight AIDS, Tuberculosis and Malaria are some of the most visible elements of so-called development programs that have had a longer history than we usually think, as Randall Packard (1996) reminds us. Beyond these global health agencies, many other organizations are implicated in the academic, philanthropic, religious, political and economic worlds—from universities to NGOs, from churches to think tanks, from banks to drug companies, all belonging to the "neoliberal world order" explored by James Ferguson (2006) in the context of contemporary Africa.

Finally, global health includes social networks that span the planet. Certainly, AIDS has been a major factor in the development of this transnational activism, as in South Africa where the Treatment Action Campaign collaborated with local actors, including the Congress of South African Trade Unions (COSATU), and international organizations, such as Médecins Sans Frontières (MSF), to facilitate access to antiretroviral drugs, as explained by Steven Robins (2009). What is more remarkable than the relationships between these agents is the common and yet heterogeneous international formation of objects of struggle, of repertoires of action, of systems of values, giving birth to what Vincanne Adams, Thomas Novotny, and Hannah Leslie (2008) call a "global health diplomacy"; that is, an activity of transforming international relations through health and vice versa.

These six dimensions of the idea of global health therefore indicate that it is not only a signifier (a slogan) but also a signified (a content) or in other words a powerful analyzer of contemporary societies.

Semantic Networks

Moving from semiotics to semantics, we can enrich and deepen our understanding of global health. The notion can be approached here not directly in
terms of what it means, but indirectly in terms of what it is associated with.
What we may learn from the uses of the expression in the public sphere is
probably less about its signification as such than about its connotation. Two
quite distinct semantic configurations can be identified. The first associates
preoccupations with security and discourses of control: talking about global
health implies responding to global threats, whether they are climate change,
viral pandemics, or even terrorist attacks, as studied by Andrew Lakoff and
Stephen Collier (2008). The second mixes sentiments of compassion and appeals to solidarity: discussing global health means underlining global inequities and their relations with violence, often embodied by victims of wars,
disasters and famines, as analyzed by Barbara Rylko-Bauer, Linda Whiteford,
and Paul Farmer (2009).

However contrasted they may at first appear, these two semantic networks
do not necessarily contradict each other. Amidst the cataclysm of the African epidemic of AIDS, during the early 2000s, I attended a seminar held in
Washington by the French Minister of Health and the U.S. Health Secretary
to harmonize the cooperative policies between the two countries. While the
theme of the discussion was how to limit the spread of the disease and treat the
increasing number of those afflicted, the central argument to justify intervention was world security, as it is in the report written by Laurie Garrett (2005)
on these issues. Significantly, high-level administrators of the Global Fund
pleading for access to antiretroviral drugs thus exchanged their views with
senior officials from the Intelligence Services, who were primarily concerned
with the risk of demographic and political destabilization on the African con-
tinent due to the epidemic. The concomitance and even convergence of the
two semantic networks—security and compassion—have become a major
element in the reconfiguration of the global order: with Mariella Pandolfi
(2010) I have analyzed the increasing confusion between humanitarian and
military interventions.

Considering the complexity but also the ambiguity of these semantic configurations should therefore render social scientists cautious in their use of the

expression "global health." One never knows what purpose this notion may serve. The mere fact of taking global health as an object worthy of academic interest and scientific publications can be seen as concordant with techno-cratic common sense or even neoliberal ideology, consequently contributing to its legitimization by science or conversely to its takeover by opinion makers.

This critique should, however, not lead to a form of nihilism. Presumably warned about the ambiguity of the expression and informed about the prob-lems of its use, we should wonder: what can we still do with it? This question implies two separate but intimately related interrogations: In what sense is global health "global"? What is meant by "health" in global health? Both sug-gest symmetrical extensions: What escapes or resists the process of globaliza-tion? And what is missed or neglected in our conception of health?

In What Sense Is Global Health Global?

Reappraising a notion that he actively contributed to introducing in anthro-pological debates, Arjun Appadurai (2001, 1) humorously observes that "glo-balization is certainly a source of anxiety in the U.S. academic world." Among the numerous reasons he proposes to explain this discomfort, however, he probably underestimates one that could be the most crucial: the confusion between two potential meanings of the word "global"—worldwide and uni-versal. The former is geographical and proposes a mere description of observed facts: global simply signifies planetary. The latter is ideological and implies a form of claimed hegemony: global here suggests superiority. We may recall the first lines of *The Protestant Ethic and the Spirit of Capitalism*, wherein Max Weber (2003 [1905], 13) poses the question of whether "Western civilization" is unique in "universal history," and he answers by asserting its "universal sig-nificance and value": here the interrogation on the spatial expansion shifts to-ward the affirmation of a moral superiority. We could see an alternative to this Eurocentrism in *The Modern World-System*, in which Immanuel Wallerstein (1974, 233) develops his apparently more neutral theory of "the core" and "the periphery," but we would thus forget his comment that the birth of the mod-ern world should be attributed to "Europe's credit," and that "for all its cruel-ties, it is better that it was born than it had not been." The Western leopard cannot change its moral spots. This simply reflects what Edward Said (1993,

65) calls "the centrality of imperialist thought in Western culture," which I believe one should consider as a fact to account for rather than a fault to expiate. What is meant by global is inextricably worldwide and universal.

Whatever uneasiness we may experience as anthropologists about this issue, it is difficult to discard the fact that globalization implies both dimensions. On the one hand, it signifies a spatial expansion, which is not mere conquest or hegemony, since it challenges us to consider what Johannes Fabian (1983, 30) calls the "coevalness" of the other and therefore makes us truly contemporaneous with the rest of the world: in this sense, globalization is both a spatial and a temporal movement, in which imperialism faces its contradictions but also its potentialities. On the other hand, it involves a moral normalization that often takes subtle and complex detours, which Homi Bhabha (1994) refers to as "mimicry" from the dominated who imitate but also transform the dominants' manners: from this perspective, globalization is a form of ambivalent alienation, in which imperialism is simultaneously confronted by adherence and difference.

Let us consider the globalization of trauma, or better said, the globalization of its clinical and political use—"the empire of trauma," as Richard Rechtman and I (2009) have phrased it. We know from Allan Young's historical study (1995) how the infamous or at least ambiguous diagnosis of trauma, particularly during the First World War when shell-shocked soldiers were suspected of simulation or hysteria, was not only reevaluated but also revalorized in the 1970s, paving the way for the recognition and rights of victims via the unlikely convergence of U.S. psychiatrists, feminists and veterans. Interestingly, however, posttraumatic stress disorder (PTSD), which started as a national success story, soon became a global enterprise. Conceived of and published by the American Psychiatric Association, the *Diagnostic and Statistical Manual of Mental Disorders* (DSM) was systematically exported into other national and international nosologies. Legitimized by this global psychiatric network, PTSD surreptitiously intervened in the theater of wars and disasters, to qualify and attest to the consequences of violence and misfortune.

This dissemination of the diagnosis is precisely at the intersection of both meanings of "global," as worldwide and universal, and thus functions simultaneously as spatial expansion and moral normalization. In the Occupied Palestinian Territories, psychologists and psychiatrists from French humanitarian organizations such as MSF or Médecins du Monde (MDM) working with adolescents and their families bring with them not only their clinical interpretation but also their political culture: limited in their therapeutic activity because of the difficulties encountered on the ground, they use the lexicon of trauma to attest to the suffering of the population and bear witness to the world about it. Therefore, as I have shown elsewhere (2008), stone-throwing *shebabs*, who consider themselves "combatants" and sometimes end up as "martyrs," become, according to the testimonies published by humanitarian workers, "traumatized" children who wet their bed at night. This representation certainly elicits more sympathy than the violent acts they may commit, but it affects the image the youth want to present of themselves and substitutes the expert's word for the victim's voice. Global health is also about competing truths and competing ethics.

Consequently, it should not be controversial to affirm that globalization is more than anything else a contemporary expression of power: the power to act on people and things as well as on ideologies and subjectivities. Power should be considered here in the sense that Michel Foucault (1994 [1973], 138) gave to it—productive as well as repressive. According to him, power relationships imply "that the 'other' [the one over whom power is exercised] is recognized and maintained to the very end as a subject who acts; and that, faced with a relationship of power, the whole field of responses, reactions, results, and possible inventions may open up." Rather than questioning this assertion it may be more interesting to analyze the failures of and resistances to the dual processes of expansion and normalization. Failures of the dominant, resistances of the dominated, one would think. However, the question of who is the dominant and who is the dominated is not always easy to determine in many situations, as ethnographic inquiry reminds us, just as it teaches that partial nonsuccess (rather than complete failure), and avoidance tactics (rather than conscious resistance), actually occur most of the time.

Thus, the exemplary Brazilian response to the AIDS epidemic, and more generally its health and social project, is mitigated by the discovery of zones of abandonment such as Vita, as studied by João Biehl (2005): the success story has its darker counterpoints. Similarly, the North American suspicion toward Haitians, initially considered responsible for the diffusion of HIV, has for its corollary rumors about the role played by the United States in the introduction of the virus to their island, as described by Paul Farmer (1992): here, power and resistance develop in the imaginary. Significantly, once more (as for the illegal immigrants previously evoked), it is through its margins, whether physical, in the case of the Brazilian charitable organizations, or symbolic, in the case of the Haitian conspiracy theories, that globalization is best grasped. And it is precisely on these margins that anthropology often makes a difference with other disciplinary knowledge, not just for empirical reasons but also for theoretical ones, since it is frequently where society is best described, as Veena Das and Deborah Poole (2004) argue.

In the end, this unique combination of expansion and normalization, of failures and resistances, of abandonments and rumors, suggests that globalization is definitely not the monolithic homogenizing process many have denounced, but rather a mélange of uniformity and distinctions, of power and innovations.

What Health Means in Global Health

If much scholarly attention has been devoted to the signification of "global," less scientific interest has been displayed toward the meaning of "health." It seems to be accepted that everyone knows what health is and that commonsense understanding suffices. From an anthropological perspective on global health, it may be, however, more problematic than often assumed. In fact, instead of the usual definitions of health as the absence of disease, the "silence of organs," according to the French physician René Leriche, or "a state of complete physical, mental and social well-being," in the WHO's definition, I suggest we shift our focus and change vocabulary. Rather than of health, I propose we speak of life. After all, life expectancy is the most utilized tool to measure health and compare it internationally—which is what global health is about.

In this reformulation, Georges Canguilhem (1989 [1943], 161) can be a useful resource. Having dedicated most of his intellectual career to the exploration of life considered in its biological forms, he did not ignore its other dimensions, proposing an original political analysis in a little-known passage of *The Normal and the Pathological*: "Everything happens as if a society had 'the mortality that suits it,' the number of the dead and their distribution into different age groups expressing the importance which the society does or does not give to the protraction of life. In short, the techniques of collective hygiene which tend to prolong human life, or the habits of negligence which result in shortening it, depending on the value attached to life in a given society, are in the end a value judgment expressed in the abstract number which is the average human life span." Adopting this view, we can assert that life expectancies and mortality rates are not only quantitative indicators giving us a demographic image of countries, they are also qualitative data offering political insights as to how societies produce and reproduce themselves, as in Colin McCord and Harold Freeman's classic study (1990) asserting that mean life duration is lower among male inhabitants of Harlem than among men in the impoverished nation of Bangladesh.

That statistics about life inform us about the treatment of lives should hardly be a surprise. As Alain Desrosières (1993) underscores, the etymological origin of the word "statistics" suggests a science of the state, which it actually was in eighteenth-century Germany: it reached its most extreme expression in Johannes Frank's six-volume *Polizeiwissenschaft*, which was no less than a treatise on the policing of all aspects of human lives. And even more explicitly, statistics' first ancestor was "political arithmetic" in seventeenth-century England, with mathematical innovations conceived by John Graunt to calculate precisely life tables for economic purposes and insurance companies. If each society therefore has the mortality that suits it, in the sense that rates correspond to decisions made in terms of social inequality and redistributive justice, in particular, then we should definitely turn to the politics of life that underlie these decisions.

Let us consider, for instance, the South African history of AIDS, of which I have made a detailed analysis (2007). The controversy surrounding Thabo Mbeki's statements concerning the social, rather than viral, cause of the disease and the danger, rather than the benefits, of antiretroviral drugs, is well known. Leaving aside the President's heterodox beliefs, wherein the tragedy of AIDS in South Africa is often reduced, a closer look at the issues at stake and at the positions defended by the numerous actors of this scene suggests a more interesting and complex political and moral landscape that is not just about truth (as opposed to error) but also about meaning and fairness. Actually two distinct, although implicit, manners of considering life can be described. Each may be apprehended on two levels, referring to causes on the one hand and values on the other.

At a first level, there is the opposition between biological etiology and social determinants. On one side, most medical discussions about the disease considered it to be a mere biological phenomenon (virus) for which mostly biochemical responses (antiretroviral drugs) had to be employed to keep patients alive; on the other, many public health professionals tried to discuss the social dimension of the disease (poverty) and of the medical response (inadequacy of the health system), therefore raising the question of the inequalities of lives afflicted by the epidemic. At a second level, there is the opposition between biological legitimacy and social justice: on the one hand, activists affirmed that each life saved counts, which implied treating patients whenever possible; on the other hand, policymakers argued that priority should be given to reducing inequity, which meant first addressing structural problems, in the health system as well as in society in general. It is clear that at both levels, the biological approach was much more popular and successful, locally and even more so internationally: the concrete efficacy of drugs and the moral evidence of saving lives swept aside the arguments about social determinants and social justice. Those who attempted to resist this powerful trend were often disqualified as dissidents even when they expressed the most orthodox beliefs about the viral etiology of the disease and the benefits of drugs.

This observation should certainly not be limited to the South African context. As I have argued elsewhere (2009), defending an individual's right to live, whether it is for a patient in need of expensive treatment or for a hostage being held by armed groups, always generates emotional consensus in a much more effective way than the revelation of massive inequalities responsible for millions of premature deaths in poor countries and among the underprivileged. We see images of the former whereas we mostly have statistics for the latter. We can give a human face to the dying patient or the suffering child, while the concreteness of disparities remains elusive. This historical trend, which lends more weight to the individual and the biological than to the collective and the social, should certainly be a concern for anthropologists (both as citizens and as scientists), since the epistemological postulate of their discipline affirms the embodiment of the social.

The distinction between the two politics of life just drawn from the South African controversy can be formulated in a more explicit and general way. It is in fact possible—and indeed crucial—to differentiate evaluations having for their object the worth of lives and judgments predicated on the value of life. The grammatical number (lives versus life) is as important here as the lexical variation (worth versus value). These distinctions deserve some explanation.

On the one hand, by evaluation of the worth of lives, I mean the practical ways in which people's lives are considered, protected and cared for, or conversely abused and sometimes eliminated. In her work on child death in Brazil, Nancy Scheper-Hughes (1992) has given a vivid description of the way children's lives may be radically devalued in the ordinary settings of everyday violence. More generally, one can think of these situations in terms of "wasted lives," as Zygmunt Bauman (2004) qualifies them. This evaluation of the worth of lives can assume statistical expressions. As I have discussed (2011a) in an analysis of epidemiological surveys and of life insurance benefits, the 2003 invasion of Iraq—an important justification of which was the improvement of the situation of the Iraqis themselves—resulted in over one hundred times more casualties among local populations, mostly civilians, than among occupying forces, almost exclusively military, and the financial compensation to families by insurance companies is one hundred and sixty times higher in the latter case than in the former. These ratios are the grim manifestation of the unequal worth of lives on a global scale.

On the other hand, by judgment of the value of life I mean the ideological and ethical grounds on which the very principle of life is affirmed or challenged, moralized, and politicized. In her analysis of the debate on abortion in Germany, Barbara Duden (1993, 2–3) evokes the recent emergence of life "as a notion" that has become an "idol" embodied in the fetus to be protected. Beyond this example, it is necessary to explore what Walter Benjamin (1978 [1921], 299) calls the "dogma of the sacredness of life." From this perspective, the symmetrical trends in immigration and asylum during the 1990s in France are remarkable, as I have shown elsewhere (2005). Legalization of immigrants based solely on the evidence of serious health problems that cannot be treated in their home countries has multiplied by seven the number of persons obtaining residence permits via this so-called humanitarian criterion. Simultaneously, the growing suspicion against asylum seekers has caused a sevenfold diminution of people granted the status of refugee. The consequence of these trends is that since the early 2000s more foreigners have obtained residence permits due to disease than have done so as refugees. Today, asylum-seekers experience increasing difficulties being acknowledged as combatants for freedom or victims of oppression, whereas immigrants tend to get documents more easily if they can display illnesses and suffering. This evolution indicates a profound change in the recognition of the value of life, which has shifted from the political to the biological.

This concept of politics of life—whether apprehended in terms of worth of lives or value of life—offers, therefore, an analytical tool quite distinct from, but complementary, to the concept of biopolitics (Foucault 2008 [2004]). Whereas biopolitics corresponds to the regulation of populations through cognitive (demography, epidemiology, economics, etc.) as well as practical (family planning, immigration control, neoliberal policies, etc.) instruments, the politics of life considers the matter and meaning of life. Rather than being about the technologies of normalization it is about the ethics of government.

Conclusion: The Discreet Charm of Critique

Global health has become a keyword of today's world (Brown and Bell 2008), an emergent discipline in academia (Macfarlane, Jacobs, and Kaaya 2008), and a new theme of research for anthropologists (Erickson 2003). Yet beyond its overwhelming presence and apparent self-evidence, it might not be irrelevant to wonder whether health was less global when we did not think of it as global health. Let us consider the already classical definition Mark Nichter (2008, 156) borrows from the Institute of Medicine of the United States National Academy of Sciences: "health problems, issues and concerns that transcend national boundaries, may be influenced by circumstances or experiences in other countries, and are best addressed by cooperative actions and solutions." Under this definition, can we be sure that "global health" refers to a new reality? While avian and swine flus have recently been threatening the world as pandemics, earlier colonization appears to have played a major role in the spread of hepatitis and tuberculosis. While preventive campaigns are currently orchestrated by the WHO and epidemiological surveys conducted by the CDC, a century ago there were hookworm eradication programs under the banner of the Rockefeller Foundation and microbiological studies by the Pasteur Institutes of the French colonies. In other words, even if we cannot deny that some problems are unprecedented and some solutions are innovative, it could be that global health is less about new problems (or solutions) than about new "problematizations," to use Michel Foucault's term (1998b); that is, new ways of describing and interpreting the world—and therefore of transforming it.

What kind of problematizations are they? And how can they be relevant for medical anthropology? Global health is not only about ideas or concerns, but about actors whom we must clearly identify and whose interests we should analyze: international institutions looking for new ways to legitimize their actions, national states demonstrating their leadership, non-governmental organizations defending their causes, pharmaceutical companies developing their markets, university professors and students opening fields and careers, academic groups or networks seeking funding in this attractive niche. But global health also signifies new hopes and old solidarities, new expectations and old condemnations: concretely, it means innovative coalitions of private and public partners involved in international health issues but also in the promotion of a research and development sector of the drug industry, genuine expression of preoccupations from Western actors regarding epidemics and tragedies in the South as well as normalization of sexual practices and imposition of development models in poor countries, and denunciation of the deleterious effects of neoliberalism simultaneously with deployment of charities based on capitalist profits. Considering this complex configuration of actors and their divergent motivations and analyzing these tensions and contradictions involved in global health may be uncomfortable, since it reveals the ambiguities of our world as well as of our own positioning in it. For that, it is all the more necessary.

Approaching global health in the way I propose is certainly challenging for the social sciences, especially when it is claimed, as in Robert Hahn and Marcia Inhorn's edited book (2009), that medical anthropology contributes to public health. In the statement prepared on behalf of the Critical Anthropology of Global Health Special Interest Group of the Society for Medical Anthropology, James Pfeiffer and Mark Nichter (2008) write that if "the flow of international aid from wealthier to poorer countries has increased over the last decade," it is "attributable in part to efforts of health activists, including medical anthropologists." This assertion is followed by a long and dense list of recommendations about what should be the role of social scientists regarding these issues. Even more explicitly, in their exhaustive review of the subject,

Craig Janes and Kitty Corbett (2009) declare that "the ultimate goal of anthropological work in and of global health is to reduce global health inequities and contribute to the development of sustainable and salutogenic sociocultural, political, and economic systems." Should medical anthropologists be activists in global health? Should their ultimate goal be to reduce global health inequities and contribute to the development of sustainable and salutogenic systems? These interrogations are crucial for medical anthropology.

In the United States, a majority in academia would possibly respond in the affirmative to both without hesitation, having in mind prominent figures in the field over the last half-century. This positioning may, however, not be shared in other subfields of the discipline. My guess is that most political anthropologists would not view themselves as activists whose ultimate goal is to establish democracy where it does not exist and to consolidate it where it is threatened. They would be concerned with the democratic progress of the country where they conduct their study but would not consider themselves missionaries of democracy. In contrast with social scientists from most other fields, medical anthropologists consider themselves both being in the position and having the obligation to change the world. The question is, therefore, why would they view themselves as global apostles of health? I suggest two levels of answers. One is specific: it has to do with the medical background and clinical practice of certain influential authors in the field, who are obviously prone to the practical issues of their theoretical thinking. The other is general: it concerns a more diffuse anxiety about the worldly engagement of the discipline against injustice, especially when disease and suffering are at stake. Both reasons are enshrined in the broader frame I have described in terms of politics of life: the contemporary contradictions between the ethical affirmation of the superior value of life and the empirical acknowledgment of the unequal worth of lives. Considered from this perspective, medical anthropologists have much in common with humanitarian workers.

The main theoretical but also political challenge for medical anthropologists may thus be to recognize the fine line between scientific detachment and moral involvement, to paraphrase Norbert Elias (1987). We can designate this line as critique. As anthropologists (as opposed to the citizens we also are and to the activists we may be), our modest but crucial contribution to society—and in the present case to global health—is the critical thinking we bring to its understanding, rather than the mere denunciation of its injustice. Making intelligible what often remains obscured, reformulating problems to allow alternative solutions, resisting individualistic and technical models to highlight the social mechanisms and political issues of global health: this is where we are able to make a difference. Indeed, we have the unique situation of being involved as social agents and detached as social scientists, on the threshold of Plato's cave where one step inside allows us to share the condition of the former and one outside gives us the distance of the latter—an uncomfortable position indeed, but the only one where we can be heard. Our sole legitimacy to speak and our sole claim to be listened to depend on our capacity to contest the untested assumptions, the most insidious being that on which we found our moral certainties.

Medical Anthropology and Mental Health

Five Questions for the Next Fifty Years

My purpose in this chapter is to ask a more general question of medical anthropology—what kind of field should it become over the next fifty years?—by raising five specific questions for one of its subfields: the medical anthropology of mental health. I am essaying the future, not the past. This is not the appropriate place to review the long and tangled history of the relationship between anthropology, psychiatry, and mental health. What can be said here is that large-scale, long-term historical forces (including colonialism, racism, the programs of modernity, wars, mass migration, and globalization) have combined with internal changes in psychiatry, psychology, global public health, and anthropology itself to reshape a chaotic, plural domain. Certain core themes that go back to the nineteenth century persist today while others have changed or disappeared; still others are newly emerging. Looking backward over the past fifty years, we can see that the central questions have concerned taxonomy (How do we classify mental health problems?); experience (What is the experience of mental illness and the mental hospital like? How do symptoms and syndromes differ for different classes, ethnic groups, and communities?); treatment systems and their interventions (How do we compare psychotherapies and folk healing practices, biomedical pharmacotherapies and traditional medicines?); culture (How do we operationalize "culture" in cross-cultural clinical settings and for cross-national comparisons?); policy (Can most mental health problems in low-resource settings be handled in primary care? Is the outcome of schizophrenia really better in poor non-Western societies?); political economy (How determinative are the structural sources of distress and disease?); and social theory (How useful is it to apply these conceptual tools—stigma, total institutions, biopower and governmentality, habitus, medicalization, etc.—to mental health?).

An earlier cultural critique of stress and its place in psychiatry has morphed into a cultural critique of PTSD and the humanitarian assistance community that has adopted it wholesale. Cultural critique itself is being supplanted by implementation and intervention studies where the anthropologist is not only a responder but, as is the case with Byron and Mary-Jo Good in Aceh, Indonesia, has developed the interventions (Good, Good, and Grayman 2009). The ethnographic study of the mental hospital has been replaced by rich ethnographies of the social course of chronic mental illness. Engagement with psychiatric and psychological science has moved beyond the problems of existing research methods to the development of new anthropologically informed research approaches. And anthropologists have interpreted entire national psychiatric training and treatment systems, as in Tanya Luhrmann's intrepid and important account of American psychiatry (2000).

It is also my personal observation that just as psychiatry has moved away from social research and the social sciences, almost turning its back on anthropology in its romance with genetics and neuroimaging, anthropology has gotten much more involved with infectious diseases, the female reproductive life cycle, transplantation surgery, biomedical research, and bioethics; and, while not turning away from global mental health, has become less excited by it. (This is visible in my own career as a teacher, where out of seventy-five former and present PhD students whom I have supervised, only a few have chosen to study psychiatry and mental health. It is also clear in my role of advocacy for mental health at global health meetings, where I am usually one of only a small number of anthropologists.)

But what should be the central questions for the anthropology of mental health over the next fifty years? And what do those questions tell us about where medical anthropology will be in that future era? The five questions I adumbrate are the ones that I believe can advance an intellectually strong, academically robust mental health subdiscipline as well as the larger field of medical anthropology. They are what excite me after four decades of thinking about this disorderly and perhaps no longer so popular, yet still highly resonant, field.

The Five Questions

QUESTION #1

What is the difference between social suffering and mental health problems (or psychiatric conditions)? And how does that difference make a difference?

The term "mental health" was developed to encompass not only dementia, psychosis and depression/anxiety disorders, but also to include a wider set of problems from substance abuse, serious school failure and family breakdown, to violence and its traumatic consequences. In extending the reach of authorized mental health categories to include both clear-cut disease and vaguer, though no less serious, problems of everyday life as well as non-medical catastrophes, "mental health" became an unwieldy, even unbelievable, odd lot—now in *DSM-IV* (and soon *DSM-V*) with hundreds of subcategories. It seems to simultaneously trivialize the most serious of medical conditions and medicalize social problems. I predict that fifty years from now this category will have been abandoned. Nonetheless, the problem it represents—what Georges Canguilhem (1989 [1943]), George Devereux (1967), and Michel Foucault (2003a) called the central theoretical problem for medicine; namely, the distinction between the normal and the pathological—will, I believe, continue to bedevil our field and the health-related social sciences, ethics and humanities, more generally.

The simple reason for this is that social suffering and illness overlap, not entirely, but substantially. Economic depression and psychological depression and societal demoralization/anomie are systematically related, as Vikram Patel and I (2003) show in our epidemiological review, and Clara Han's (2007) ethnographic research powerfully demonstrates. Political economy creates suicide just as surely as genetics does. Global social disruptions contribute to substance abuse. Political and moral processes underpin the stigma of psychosis and cognitive disability just as they provide the structural basis for psychological and family trauma. Contrary to psychiatric epidemiologists' focus on one disease at a time, in the toxic and predatory environments of urban slums and shantytowns worldwide, depression, suicide, violence, PTSD, and substance abuse cluster together—the very terrain of social exclusion, health disparities, and social suffering.

Veena Das, Margaret Lock, and I coined the term "social suffering" to emphasize how ordinary social life everywhere is experienced as pain and suffering at least as much as joy and happiness, and that such collective pain and suffering is normative and normal (Kleinman, Lock, and Das 1997). Social suffering also refers to extraordinary human experience, from the social consequences of individual catastrophes to collective disasters. The term indicates that the ethnographer of human tragedies, including serious disease and grinding poverty, almost always finds that the suffering that results is interpersonal. And it was intended to connote one other thing: that our very processes of meaning making—personal as well as cultural—grew out of, and sustained, the same societal forces that created the social and individual conditions of injury, disorder and disablement. Bureaucratic meaning making indeed rationalized social suffering as theodicy and sociodicy with all the sad implications Max Weber foresaw: an iron cage of rationality (now protocols and regulations) that replaced human emotion, spontaneity, and indigenous tradition (Diggins 1996). Institutions created to respond to suffering, say, the mental hospital or social welfare agencies or humanitarian NGOs, ended up contributing to it.

Seen this way, not all psychiatric disorder is social suffering, nor does social suffering always create or intensify psychiatric disorder. The framework of suffering also makes less useful the concept of medicalization, which has become so powerful in our time. Emphasis, I predict, will shift from psychiatric medicalization to the relationship between psychiatry and social suffering. We (medical anthropologists and global health experts, though not psychiatrists) will come to see many cases of depression and anxiety disorder as forms of social suffering as well as consequences of social suffering, as is the current case with cardiovascular disease, diabetes, and stroke. We will come to understand, too, that suicide is more often a response to social suffering than a consequence of a psychiatric disorder, though we will also be comfortable saying that it can be both.

Sociologists, anthropologists, historians, and social epidemiologists will, I predict, open the field of the embodiment of social suffering—which Joan Kleinman and I once referred to as how bodies remember—in such a large-scale way as to help psychiatry recreate a robust academic research enterprise of social and cultural psychiatry and psychosomatics (now understood as sociosomatics), as well as mental health care policy, to develop a much stronger social policy connection (Kleinman and Kleinman 1994). Indeed, anthropology's reach will be as strong in the public health side of mental health as in the clinical side.

The question for anthropology and psychiatry and public health, then, will not be on the classical order of the normal and the abnormal, but rather will involve a much deeper phenomenology of the forms of social suffering, an epidemiology of the causes and consequences of social suffering, and the implementation of policy and programs for that subset of social suffering that is represented by psychiatric disorder, as well as for psychiatric conditions that are not tied to social suffering. Either/or thinking will weaken, just as a more complex and sophisticated understanding of both societal and biological processes will advance the view that normality as well as disease embodies social suffering.

QUESTION #2

If, as I have recently argued (2009a), ground zero for patients with psychosis, globally, is moral death and social exclusion, what is the implication for medical anthropology research of going beyond stigma to redefine in cultural terms what is at stake in the most severe psychiatric conditions?

In the August 23, 2009, issue of *The Lancet*, I argued that ground zero in global health for patients with psychosis is not the 15 percent of the global burden of disease accounted for by mental health conditions, nor is it the tragic gap between that huge figure and the paltry 2 percent, and more usually 1 percent, of the funding on health that gets directed to the treatment and rehabilitation of mental health conditions in low- and middle-resource societies. Rather, ground zero in global mental health is the appalling ways in which people with psychosis are treated almost all over the world (there are a few exceptions) by professionals, family members, traditional healers, communities and the state (Patel, Saraceno, and Kleinman 2006). In China, these individuals are turned into non-persons, so that they are socially dead and morally unprotected from the most basic infringements of dignity, personal rights, even life itself. Although I have contributed to efforts to reformulate the concept of stigma to encompass this nullification of personhood and negation of moral status, I have serious doubts that this can be done (Yang and Kleinman 2008). So, I seek to question how medical anthropology will relate to the subject of stigma. And I propose that we begin to consider abandoning this concept—which has become so psychologized and conventional that it seems to me, at least, an unuseful euphemism—in favor of rethinking the catastrophic moral consequences of the dehumanization of the mentally ill (and also AIDS patients, sufferers of leprosy, those struggling with epilepsy, etc.). What happens when this failure of humanity is reinvented as social death, moral defeat, and cultural exclusion (Guo 2008)? It requires a more powerful ontological line of analysis to get at what is an entirely different way of being in the world. Biography, ethnography, and documentary film can evoke this fundamental condition of humiliation and exclusion as a non-human status. It is that ontological reality that provides a more adequate ground for research and policy responses—and also for real caregiving.

But what are the gains and losses of abandoning the concept of stigma to the psychologists and sociologists? Sadly, not much, I have come to conclude. With the exception of Bruce Link and colleagues' inclusion of power as a heretofore entirely missing social moderator of stigma, the subject is still configured in the cognitive behavioral and labeling theory approaches of the distant past (Yang et al. 2007). Neither allows the opening to experience and its ontology that medical anthropology is almost uniquely suited to advance. The impact of prioritizing the ontology of experiences of human abandonment and social death will keep medical anthropology more generally centered on experience, which I have argued and will continue to argue is its most significant object of inquiry.

QUESTION #3

How is the paradox of global pharmaceuticals for psychiatric disorders (under-diagnosis and absent treatment for the poor; over-diagnosis and abuse of treatment for the middle class and well-to-do) to be operationalized in theory and empirical studies? And where will pharmaceutical and other biomedical research end up in medical anthropology?

Like the other questions, this topic exceeds the boundaries of mental health and is important for all diseases. The paradox goes as follows: at the same moment that most people with mental illness, especially those in poor societies and in poor parts of resource-rich societies, go undiagnosed and untreated for serious yet treatable psychiatric disorders, others, especially those in high-technology and richly resourced urban centers, are being over-diagnosed and inappropriately treated with pharmaceuticals, including expensive brand name drugs, for conditions that are either minor or medicalized. The chief cultural critique of anthropologists working on either global pharmaceuticals or mental illness has focused on the latter: the misuse and abuse of psycho-pharmaceuticals (Petryna, Lakoff, and Kleinman 2006). And this is an important contribution. Relatively little ethnographic attention, in contrast, has centered on the state's (especially in middle- and low-income nations) failure of responsibility to protect the mentally ill by providing health care services such as appropriate psychopharmaceuticals, and also including resources that support families who are placed under the greatest financial, social and moral pressure. This research is urgently needed to balance the ethnographic picture. Such balance should extend to serious study of traditional pharmacology and its commercial networks, abuses, and consequences. In fact, biomedical technology and bioengineering also need to be included in this framing of the mental health paradox. And of course this is precisely where medical anthropology is enriched by the ethnography of science (see Martin 2007 and Petryna 2009).

Up until the late 1980s there was no significant stream of research in medical anthropology devoted to biomedical science (Lock and Gordon 1988). In recent years this stream has gotten stronger and stronger (see Biehl 2009; Cohen 1998; Petryna, Lakoff, and Kleinman 2006; Rabinow 1999). The study of the offshoring of pharmaceutical (especially psychopharmaceutical) research has raised basic questions about methodology (e.g., bias in sample selection, problems with randomized controlled clinical trials) and ethics (e.g., questionable use of placebo controls, conflict of interest among researchers, loss of basic medical care once studies have ended). Anthropological studies have also unpacked neuroimaging (Dumit 2003) and genetic research for neuropsychiatric conditions like dementia (Lock 2007), in so doing calling into question the ideology of evidence-based psychiatry. And yet even here, the thrust of interpretation of findings within the field as a whole has emphasized overdiagnosis and overtreatment. Medicalization still continues as the leading interpretive scheme in the ethnographic study of biotechnology in mental health (Horwitz and Wakefield 2007).

So, we can say that medical anthropologists, myself included, have seriously distorted the study of treatment for mental illness by failing to adequately examine the effects of absent or inadequate services, including as they relate to the psychiatric science industry. There is an impressive anthropological literature on the experience of psychiatric treatment in the United States and Europe, to be sure (see Bourgois and Schonberg 2009; Desjarlais 1997; Estroff 1985; Garcia 2010, Hopper 2003; Luhrmann 2000; Rhodes 2004; Scheper-Hughes 1978). But little like this literature exists for the treatment and research experiences of the mentally ill in poor and middle-income societies. If anthropology is to advance global mental health, this omission must be corrected. We need ethnographic studies, then, of the intersection of bio-technological and bio-engineering research with mental health care policies and programs.

The question, then, is: What happens when we rebalance the medical anthropological emphasis on medicalization with an equivalent emphasis on the absence of psychiatric, psychological and other professional mental health services that makes unavailable psychopharmacological, psychotherapeutic, and rehabilitation interventions? What happens when we see the state not primarily as the source of powerful control over the mentally ill and through them society at large, but rather as fragile, constrained, and almost powerless to provide the most basic care for its most impaired and vulnerable members? Some refashioning of the research agenda like this is needed if anthropology is to be serious about the study of mental illness. When it comes to the theoretical reframing of such work, it is time to supersede Foucault (1998a) and Scheff (1975), French psychoanalytic theory, labeling theory and ideas of the colony and post-colony, with a deeper, more original understanding of our unprecedented times. History continues to matter for ethnographers of the present, but so do futuristic explorations of a new age, a watershed era of transition that is creating conditions that are entirely new, including new subjectivities and new ways of living a disease. In a recent book, seven colleagues and I, all anthropologists and psychiatrists, examine the deep change in subjectivity in today's largest and most dynamic society: China (Kleinman et al. 2011). We identify a basic remaking of individuality and moral life that is associated, inter alia, with substantial rates of mental illness, substance abuse, and suicide. A parallel Chinese development is the professionalization of psychiatry and a psychotherapy boom. Tied to this is the psychopharmacology paradox, but also the development of major research programs in biotechnology, including bioscience targeting mental health problems. To understand what is happening we developed a theory of the divided self in contemporary China that ties personhood to changes in moral experience in different local worlds and that engages China's diversity and plural life worlds. This shifting moral-emotional ground is the platform on which symptoms and syndromes, ranging from neurasthenia to depression to eating disorders and psychosis, are being remade, and with them treatment and public health systems are also undergoing substantial change, change that indexes the scope and depth of China's great new cultural transformation from a primarily rural and younger to an increasingly urban and older society, from a primarily poor to an increasingly middle-class society, and from a society in which a person owes her or his life to the state to one in which the state owes each of its citizens an adequate life. To understand health and mental health in China is to come to terms with this huge transformation in ordinary life. Hence, theories of how societies change and theories of how individuals change take on a central significance for understanding changes in subjectivity, psychiatry, and the political and moral economy of health care.

QUESTION #4

How do ethics, forensics, and caregiving fit into the medical anthropology of professional psychiatric and family-based mental health care?

The 1980s and early 1990s can now be seen as the heyday for the medical anthropology of caregiving. Numerous studies focused on clinical care by physicians and nurses, and by traditional healers and laypersons (Balsham 1993; Boddy 1989; Bosk 1979; Bourgois and Schonberg 2009; Cohen 1998; Crandon-Malamud 1991; Estroff 1985; Farmer 1992; Farquhar 1994; Frankel 1986; Garcia 2010; Good 1994; Helman 1992; Ingstad 1992; Janzen 1978b; Kleinman 1980; Laderman 1991; Leslie and Young 1992; Lindenbaum and Lock 1993; MacCormack 1992; Madan 1980; Martin 1987; McGuire 1988; Rhodes 1991; Roseman 1991; Sargent 1989; Scheper-Hughes 1978, 1992; Wikan 1990). Some important work continues in areas like nursing, disability, and increasingly high-technology arenas like cancer care and transplantation (see, for example, Sharp 2006 and Kaufman 2005, among others). Yet we seem to be losing touch with this crucial subject just as we are building real strength in public health. Hence, global health seems to have almost nothing to do with caregiving. This must not happen. Medicine's failure in caregiving remains one of the great narratives in the social science and humanities' study of medicine (Kleinman 2008, 2009b). Nowhere is this failure more devastating than in the field of caregiving for psychosis, dementia, autism, and severe cognitive impairment of children (Kleinman 2009a). Where is the ethnography of today to match the works of the past? Think of William Caudill and Jules Henry's classic studies of caregiving in the mental hospital; Kim Hopper (2003), Norma Ware (Ware et al. 2007) and Sue Estroff (1985) on the chronic mentally ill; and Bob Edgerton (1993) on the cognitively impaired. Given the enormous changes in health care systems worldwide and the widespread failure of global public health workers to privilege quality caregiving, this is just the moment for such work. There are also remarkable developments that cry out for study, such as America's failure to include caregiving practices in health care financing reform and Holland's largely unsung efforts to make caregiving practices central to medical education and practice.

So my first question in this area is: Where is the ethnography of caregiving today for mental health problems (including substance abuse), and what does it tell us about the way health care—professional and family—is being transformed in our times? (For exceptions, see Bourgois and Schonberg 2009 and Garcia 2010.) Part of that professional transformation is the development of higher practice standards in psychiatry and psychiatric nursing, as well as the introduction of modern forensic and ethical approaches to mental health care. The continued misuse of psychiatry in China for political and policy purposes is not the same as the systematic abuse of psychiatry in the former Soviet Union, for example, but instead can be seen as a problem in the uneven professionalization of psychiatry, in the poor standards of professional care, in the failure to build modern forensic programs, and most notably, I believe, in the lack of serious attention to ethics—a problem found in medicine throughout East Asia. The existing evidence points to the failure of an Asian equivalent to the Nuremburg Trial and Code following the horrendous abuse of medicine through the Japanese Imperial Army's biowarfare research on Chinese civilians during the long war with Japan. The United States, Japan, and both Nationalist and Communist China are implicated in this failure of justice. But the long-term consequence seems to have retarded development of modern ethics (especially indigenously based ethics) and led to the superficial and hegemonic imposition of NIH-style bureaucratic ethics on global research (Nie et al. 2010). Much more needs to be done to unpack the question of the comparative cross-cultural ethics of caregiving. And that research will lead us not only to a new consideration of bureaucracies and institutions but also, and more radically, to a deeper appreciation of the transformation of subjectivity in our times that I have already discussed (Biehl, Good, and Kleinman 2007). Moral-political change is creating a new personhood in many societies. Here medical anthropology will return to its long-term association with psychological anthropology, a relationship that thinned out over the past decade, as medical anthropology took an increasingly "structural violence" approach and focused more on infectious disease and chronic medical conditions than on mental illness, and as psychological anthropology moved away from the study of illness toward questions of cognitive neuroscience and cognitive psychology.

QUESTION #5

Finally, how are we to reframe science and society in the golden era of brain research?

We are living through what natural scientists call the golden age of neurobiology. It is no longer reasonable for medical anthropologists to add footnotes to Marshall Sahlins's (1976) dated, not to say poorly informed, "The Use and Abuse of Biology." Cultural critique still has a place, but it must be a scientifically informed critique, otherwise we cede the field to STS program graduates, few of whom in my experience possess adequate training and real skill in ethnography to resist the imposition of a programmatic theoretical framework that represents the current-day equivalent of hegemonic political-economic frameworks of the past.

It does not take that much insight into global culture today to recognize that the new neurobiology is recasting both cultural common sense and professional scientific logic about cognition, affect and abnormality. How will anthropology's long-term interest in mental illness and psychiatry be affected by the huge wave of interest in, and great transformation of, the knowledge base of neurobiology? I myself, though medically trained and having taken a postgraduate course in neurology, albeit in 1966, feel unprepared to adequately master the new neuroscience. Just as my former students Paul Farmer and Jim Kim insist on a biosocial approach to the leading infectious diseases in global health, so too do I wish to advance a biosocial approach to global mental health. This should become—in my domain—just as core to the "Harvard School of Medical Anthropology" as are the emphases on lived experience, structural violence, and what is morally at stake for individuals and collectives.

Conclusion

These five questions are shorthand for a blueprint of what the anthropology of global mental health might become in the future. In 1995, Robert Desjarlais, Byron Good, Leon Eisenberg, Anne Becker, Mary-Jo Good, Norma Ware, Sue Levkoff, Myron Belfer, and others of my Harvard colleagues and I published *World Mental Health* as a perhaps precocious and somewhat transgressive effort at integrating anthropological and psychiatric perspectives. It may now be a more propitious time to undertake a new effort at thinking through global mental health, and medical anthropology should play a larger role in that rethinking. Because psychiatry and psychology have made such a minimal contribution to global mental health, this is a field where medical anthropology could and should play a central role in defining the subject and laying out the research questions, but also in developing the advocacy, policies, and actual interventions. Those medical anthropologists, especially, ones who are cross-trained in medicine or public health, and who focus on mental health, should feel empowered to develop the field of global mental health interventions. In this sense, the very backwardness of the field should be a spur to medical anthropologists.

To do so, of course, as in the example of the global AIDS field, is to risk being criticized for stepping out of the classroom and library and into the field, not only to do research but to link that research to interventions. Just as Paul Farmer, Jim Kim, Richard Parker, Didier Fassin, and others have created a kind of experimental anthropology based on field interventions in the area of infectious disease, this is an important direction for anthropology in global mental health.[1] Bourgois's and Schonberg's (2009) efforts to move beyond description of homeless drug-addicted people in the United States and assist them with negotiating the health care system as well as intervening on their behalf for public health practices that benefit these destitute yet difficult individuals is also a pertinent example.

The gist of my argument is that we have entered a new era in the social anthropology of mental health and in medical anthropology in general. This new era requires a rethinking of our objects of inquiry. It is an increasingly interdisciplinary era in which anthropologists must become more comfortable in collaborating across methodological and professional divides. It is an era in which anthropologists also cannot avoid contributing directly to public health (Hahn and Inhorn 2009) and clinical interventions (Farmer 2010). And it is a time when we must recreate our field through new theories, new research questions and new approaches. In my view, we are in a period of moving from the margin to the center, of our discipline and of our subject matter. Whatever uncertainty we have of taking on much greater responsibility needs to be balanced by recognition of how much interest there is in our subject and in our works by students, professionals, and laypersons who are demanding much more from us. Not the least of all, they want our contributions to make a difference out in the world. And we should, too!

From Genetics to Postgenomics and the Discovery of the New Social Body

The topics of human affiliation and the so-called nature/nurture dichotomy have provided perennial stimulus for anthropological research and debate. In the past few years this subject matter has emerged rather dramatically for renewed consideration as anthropologists examine the many social and political ramifications burgeoning knowledge in molecular genetics and genomics is currently bringing about.[1]

This chapter moves back and forth between historical and contemporary representations by scientists of genes and their assumed function and anthropological research into the social ramifications of the technology of genetic testing over the past twenty years. Anthropologists have rigorously documented how, with the expansion of scientific knowledge emerging from gene mapping and the associated application of individual genetic testing, "genetic embodiment" has been made literally knowable. Such information has the potential to produce profound effects on the lives of individuals, their families, and communities. However, the most recent transformations in molecular biology, described by many involved scientists as a paradigm shift, have brought about recognition among these scientists of a molecularized "social body" situated in time and space. This shift moves beyond genetics and genomics and explicitly demotes the reductive agency of genes. Anthropologists are now challenged to consider the social ramifications of this shift that represent the bodies of individuals and their risk for disease in terms of history, environmental exposures, individual development and life experiences, and political and economic vicissitudes, in addition to their genetic constitution. In other words, recognition of an inextricable entanglement among human activities of all kinds and molecularized human bodies incites new directions in anthropological research that takes us beyond the individualized embodiment of genetics, and the immediate social repercussions of such knowledge, to confront the complexity of emerging knowledge about "deep" embodiment of humankind in time and space.

This chapter opens with a discussion of the concept of heredity and its transformation in the scientific world in the early part of the twentieth century into the discipline of genetics. Next is a brief account of the rise of molecular genetics, culminating in the mapping of the human genome. This achievement was followed shortly thereafter by a shift on the part of a good number of scientists away from the genetic determinism associated with "classical" Mendelian genetics to a postgenomic era.[2] This shift embraces a broad array of interrelated research topics, including gene expression and function, proteomics, and epigenetics, among yet others.[3] The revitalized field of epigenetics has several branches but, in general, focuses prominently on cellular action as well as on the responses of entire organisms to their environments. Emphasis is given by certain researchers to the relationship among the expression of specific genes, the context of individual development, including environmental and political events, and intergenerational biology. Many researchers in epigenetics explicitly recognize complexity, uncertainty, and nonlinear multidirectional biological pathways.

The second section of this chapter provides an overview of the substantial body of research conducted by medical anthropologists in connection with the biomedical technology of genetic testing. This technology is increasingly being made use of in research and clinical practice and raises profound questions about concomitant transformations in kinship, human affiliation, including biosociality, and new forms of citizenship. The subsequent section is an examination of enormous social repercussions looming on the horizon as a result of rapidly accumulating research in connection with the activities of genes associated with common, complex diseases. Characterized as "susceptibility genes," they contribute to named disorders under specific developmental and environmental conditions that remain largely unknown. Many susceptibility genes are universally distributed and essential to everyday bodily functioning and are perhaps best thought of as DNA variations rather than as mutations.[4] This recent recognition of the complexity of gene function highlights an urgency to research the inseparable entanglement of the material body with environmental, socioeconomic, political, and cultural variables. Alzheimer's disease is used as an illustrative example of this point. The chapter concludes with reflections about directions for future research in medical anthropology, including comments about the potential role of medical anthropologists in researching and representing this newly embedded, lively body, continually subject to "biosocial differentiation" (Lock and Nguyen 2010, 90).

Unfortunately, space does not permit an elaboration of the extensive anthropological research being conducted in connection with the molecularization of "race" and the potential its findings have to once again essentialize the biology of human difference (see, for example, Abu El-Haj 2007; Fullwiley 2007; Montoya 2007). However, the second half of this chapter makes it clear that for anthropologists to ignore the contribution of biological difference to human health and well-being is foolhardy, especially at a time when certain basic scientists are making unreflective use of the concept of race in their research. On the other hand, to essentialize, racialize, dehistoricize, and depoliticize biological variation is entirely perverse and must be critiqued.

From Heredity to Genetics

Use of the adjective "hereditary" can be traced back to antiquity as part of popular parlance in European languages, and no doubt in many other languages as well. Obviously people everywhere have always had discussions, sometimes quite titillating, no doubt, about the similarities and differences among biological parents and their offspring. But only in the mid-nineteenth century did the noun *hérédité* first appear, when it was made use of by French physiologists and physicians and then rather rapidly adopted by several biologists of the day, including Charles Darwin and his eugenicist cousin Francis Galton (Müller-Wille and Rheinberger 2007).

It has been argued by the philosophers of biology Staffan Müller-Wille and Hans-Jörg Rheinberger that this shift, this nominalization of the adjectival term "hereditary," led to its reification as a concept and provided the opening up of a biological space in which this new, generalized notion could be made use of to "focus on elementary traits or dispositions" *independent* of the particular life forms of which they are part (2007, 13). To say that something was "hereditary" was to refer to a particular, contextualized matter relating to named families; with nominalization, the idea of heredity became thoroughly abstracted and understood as subject only to the laws of biology.

The year 1900 is widely recognized as the time when the discipline of genetics emerged, following hard on the heels of the rediscovery of Gregor Mendel's research thirty-five years after its original publication. Mendel's famous, meticulous, labor-intensive pea experiments, once their startling worth was recognized, precipitated a radical change in the "knowledge regime" of the day. This research provided the missing element needed to turn heredity into a full-blown science. The word "gene" first appears in print in 1909, replacing the vague idea of "gemmules" postulated by Darwin as the element that enables the mechanism of heredity below the level of the cell. Even before the gene concept was created, it had become apparent to nineteenth-century researchers that they would have to confront an undeniable oxymoron—an inherent contradiction between, on the one hand, the so-called hereditary dispositions clearly omnipresent within any given species believed to account for continuity and "sameness" and, on the other hand, external manifest differences, abundantly evident as a result of reproduction and already made use of extensively in classical plant and animal breeding (Franklin 2001). Once the theory of evolution was postulated, the startling idea that heredity is simultaneously timeless *and* contingent was brought to the fore, creating a new "'epistemic space' of heredity" (Müller-Wille and Rheinberger 2007, 3–25) that persists to this day and has colored both biological and anthropological debate on the subject for over a century.

The eminent Danish scientist Wilhelm Johannsen, eager to put theories about the new biology of inheritance on a sound scientific footing, argued forcibly in the early 1900s for recognition of a distinction between structure (the genotype) and its direct expression (the phenotype). Johannsen insisted that earlier ideas about inheritance were not only outmoded but also clearly wrong. In making this claim, Johannsen would become recognized as the founding father of the *science* of genetics and actively set himself apart from his predecessors, among them Gregor Mendel, Francis Galton, and August Weismann, all of whom assumed that personal qualities and behaviors were transmitted from generation to generation (Sapp 1983). By 1913 the first primitive genetic map was published, revealing what was described as the location of six specific genes on a chromosome.

Johannsen deliberately likened this new genetics to the "hard" science of chemistry, and H. E. Armstrong, a well-known chemist in the 1930s, wrote, "Some day, perhaps, biography will be written almost in terms of structural chemistry" (Gudding 1996, 526). Thus was the stage gradually set for an era that came to be dominated by genetic determinism, consolidated, as everyone knows, by the mid-twentieth-century discovery of the structure of DNA—final proof, it was assumed, of the reality of units of inheritance, the genes. The Human Genome Project, designed explicitly to expose the *structure* of the sequencing of the DNA base pairs in the human genome was, of course, the culmination of this approach. Although some outspoken scientists, James Watson among them, apparently assumed that once we had the map in hand we would in effect have a full understanding of how genes work and of what makes us human, it was evident, before the map was complete, perhaps to the majority of involved scientists, that we were in for some major surprises. An ontological shift can be detected in the mid-twentieth century in which many researchers began to be more comfortable talking and writing about DNA rather than about genes (Gudding 1996); at the same time, the very idea of the gene began to get disconcertingly fuzzy for many researchers (Stotz et al. 2006).

It is now well known that while mapping the human genome, the involved scientists set aside more than 98 percent of isolated DNA, labeling it as "junk" because it did not conform with their idea of how the blueprint for life was assumed to work. It was Richard Dawkins, author of *The Selfish Gene*, who created the term "junk DNA." In the years since the somewhat premature announcement in early 2001 that the Human Genome Project was complete, the situation has changed dramatically, and junk DNA can no longer be ignored. In 2003 an article in *Scientific American* summarized the situation, citing the work of the molecular biologist John Mattick: "New evidence . . . contradicts conventional notions that genes . . . are the sole mainspring of heredity and the complete blueprint for all life. Much as dark matter influences the fate of galaxies, dark parts of the genome exert control over the development and the distinctive traits of all organisms, from bacteria to humans" (Gibbs 2003, 48). The article continues: "some scientists now suspect that much of what makes one person, and one species, different from the next are variations in the gems hidden within our 'junk' DNA" (Gibbs 2003, 52). As yet, much of this so-called junk has no known function, although a great deal of it is remarkably "conserved" among different mammalian species, suggesting that some of it may well have functional significance, and it is now clear that some noncoding DNA acts as genetic "switches" that regulate the expression of genes. Furthermore, recent evidence suggests that, at times, noncoding DNA may also be employed by proteins to assist in their work (Mattick 2003). As Gibbs put it, we have entered an era, almost overnight, in which the "dark" parts of the genome are beginning to fluoresce (2003, 47), although much research continues to be focused entirely on genes that code for proteins.

Noncoding DNA also produces noncoding RNA, the activities of which are understood today as the most comprehensive regulatory system in complex organisms, a system that functions to create the "architecture" of organisms, without which chaos would reign. Noncoding RNA has been shown to profoundly affect the timing of processes that occur during development, including stem cell maintenance, cell proliferation, apoptosis (programmed cell death), the occurrence of cancer, and other complex ailments (Mattick 2003, 2004). The enormous task under way is to understand gene *regulation*—above all, how and under what circumstances genes are expressed and modulated. In this rapidly proliferating knowledge base, organized complexity is recognized; activities of the cell, rather than that of genes, are the primary target of investigation by an increasing number of scientists, and the effects of evolutionary, historical, environmental, and social variables on cellular activity, developmental processes, health, and disease are freely acknowledged, suggesting that it is time for anthropologists to climb on board this particular "research platform" (the trendy term for global research enterprises in the basic sciences). We are moving away rather dramatically from a belief in genetic determinism (criticized for many years by a good number of biologists, in addition to social scientists) and into the stunning world of postgenomics. The gene, Fox Keller states, can no longer be thought of as "part physicist's atom and part Plato's soul" (2000, 227).

Before pursuing further the implications for anthropologists of this shift toward the conceptualization of molecularized bodies as inextricably situated in time and space, I turn to medical anthropological findings concerned primarily with the social ramifications of genetic testing that have accumulated at an ever increasing pace over the past twenty years.

Embodied Risk

With the rapid dissemination of findings from molecular genetics a new divinatory space emerged, with the possibility of creating a highly potent zone of anxiety about what the future has in store for us all with respect to disease. This newfound ability to bring "potential futures into the present" meant from the outset that, in theory, every one of us could be, in effect, potentially constituted as part of a single population, that of the "presymptomatically ill" (Yoxen 1982). When commenting on plans by health policy makers to make genetic testing widely available in the near future, Edward Yoxen argued two decades ago that a shift in public perception would likely take place so that genes would come to be thought of as "quasi-pathogens."

Media reporting and professional publications since that time suggest that concern about genetically driven risk predictions has indeed proliferated in contemporary society, but careful observers argue that public interest and concern is not nearly so widespread as might be expected. Medical and social scientists have both been accused of genomic hype, with some justification, it seems (Franklin 1997, 178; Grace 2008; Lewontin 2000). Even so, it is clear that genetic testing of individuals and genetic screening of populations are increasingly becoming routinized as an integral part of a new "logics of vitality" (Rabinow and Rose 2006, 211) and that genetic technologies permit us to speculate with more precision than was formerly the case about who among us may be struck with misfortune. However, a characteristic feature of earlier forms of divination remains—namely, that in seeking to take control of the future, new ambiguities and uncertainties inevitably arise in association with predicted futures (Lambek 1993; Whyte 1997; Wikan 1990), and these uncertainties are abundantly evident in the rich anthropological material on genetic testing.

The idea of being "predisposed" to an illness stems from at least the eighteenth century, and some would argue much earlier. At that time there was discussion among medical professionals and lay people alike about an individual "constitution" and its contribution to disease vulnerability (Jasen 2002). But François Ewald (1991) argues that the "philosophy of risk" as we understand it today is very much a product of contemporary society—a radical epistemological transformation involving a "mutation" in attitudes toward justice, responsibility, time, causality, destiny, and even providence. This transformation is a product of a secularized approach to life where "the ills that befall us lose their old providential meaning" (Ewald 1991, 208). In a world without God, the control of events is left entirely in human hands—a logical outcome when life is transformed into a rational enterprise.

Risk, in Mary Douglas's (1990) words, becomes "a forensic resource" whereby people can be held accountable, and, as Robert Castel (1991) puts it, mobilization of the concept of risk becomes a new mode of surveillance—self-surveillance, a formidable component of the microphysics of power that Foucault (1980) noted with reference to emerging neoliberal society. Castel warns that such "hyper-rationalism" comes with a cost and that there may well be "iatrogenic aspects" to this form of prevention among which chronic anxiety is prominent.

The effect of learning about genetically "embodied risk" (Kavanagh and Broom 1998) is, in some respects, similar to monitoring high cholesterol levels or dietary habits, in which it is usually assumed that prudent behavior may well rectify the condition of risk. When the results of genetic tests are used to inform individual decisions about resorting to prophylactic measures, or when they become the driving force for making major lifestyle changes, then self-surveillance is at work. But, when decisions about reproduction are made on the basis of the results of genetic testing and screening, as is very often the case then, clearly, this entails a social, intergenerational dimension with significant repercussions that can extend as far as communities as a whole, giving the idea of "prudence" an insidious quality. There is one other important way in which "genetic risk" is special. If the involved genes are mutations with "high penetrance" (in the technical jargon of genetics) the very presence in the body of either one or two copies of the mutation (depending on the gene in question) makes the appearance of the disease highly probable and in many cases beyond doubt. Inheriting two copies of a mutated gene that causes Tay-Sachs disease, for example, determines the appearance of the disease at a young age. The only possible forms of prevention for conditions such as this are choice of a marriage partner based primarily on knowledge about genes ("genetic couple-hood," as Prainsack and Siegal [2006] term it), avoidance of pregnancy, or selective abortion once pregnant. However, in contrast to Tay-Sachs disease, for many conditions the age of onset and severity may not be highly predictable, introducing further troubling uncertainties into decision making about marriage and reproduction.

The situation becomes yet more complex when we consider common diseases to which everyone is liable—conditions in which so-called susceptibility genes are implicated. These genes have medium or low penetrance and are not necessarily implicated in disease causation; there is universal agreement that environments, lifetime exposures, experiences, and behaviors, and other genes are inevitably involved in complex disease causation, although these mechanisms are as yet rarely well understood. Such diseases can *perhaps* be averted by self-surveillance on occasion but, as we will see in the second part of this chapter, forces much greater than day-to-day lifestyles and behaviors are usually also at work.

Genetic Testing and Prudence

In the early 1990s the epidemiologist Abby Lippman coined the term "geneticization" to gloss what she perceived to be a new form of medical surveillance. Lippman characterized geneticization as a process "in which differences between individuals are reduced to their DNA codes" (1992, 1470). Above all, she was concerned about the possibilities for an indirect reinforcement of racism, social inequalities, and discrimination against those with disabilities, the result of a rekindled conflation between social realities and an essentialized biology grounded in small differences in DNA sequences.

Nikolas Rose, drawing on Foucauldian biopolitics, suggests that in advanced liberal democracies where life is "construed as a project," values such as autonomy, self-actualization, prudence, responsibility, and choice are integral to "work on the self." He argues that genetic forms of thought have become "intertwined" into this project, and the merged language of genetics and risk "increasingly supplies a grid of perception that informs decisions on how to conduct one's life, have children, get married, or pursue a career" (2007, 125). Life potentially becomes one of "optimization." But Rose is quick to add that there is little evidence to date that someone labeled as genetically at risk is reduced to a "passive body-machine that is merely to be the object of a dominating medical expertise" (2007, 129). Empirical findings strongly support this caveat.

It is estimated that only between 15 and 20 percent of adults designated at risk for a named genetic disease, or for carrying a fetus believed to be at risk for a genetic disease, have been willing thus far to undergo genetic testing, a finding that has held for over ten years (these numbers vary from country to country and differ according to the disease in question) (Beeson and Doksum 2001; Quaid and Morris 1993; Wexler 1992). It has also been shown that a good number of people, when tested, ignore or challenge the results (Hill 1994; Rapp 1999). No doubt this situation exists because uncertainty, disbelief, doubt, and kinship concerns color people's responses to test results in connection with the majority of genetic disorders. But worries about social discrimination, including stigma, insurance coverage, and possible employment difficulties, also contribute to the reluctance of many people to consider testing (Apse et al. 2004; Peterson et al. 2002). Further concerns arise because the material effects of genetic mutations are so varied and unpredictable. Responses to the possibility of undergoing genetic testing depend on the age of onset of the disease in question and whether or not reproductive decision making is implicated. Testing cannot predict the severity of many conditions or even if symptoms will manifest themselves at all, and for by far the majority of the so-called single gene disorders involving highly penetrant mutations, including, for example, Huntington's disease, neurofibromatosis, and Tay-Sachs disease, there are few if any preventive measures that can be taken and no effective treatment other than, at times, something for symptom relief. It is of note that the single gene disorders most commonly researched by anthropologists to date affect in all approximately 2 percent of the human population. This by no means diminishes the worth of the social science research, the findings of which have repercussions way beyond each disorder discussed, but nevertheless it is of note.

Of Moral Pioneers

Rayna Rapp's pathbreaking ethnography about the social impact of amniocentesis exposes many of the problems associated with genetic testing that continue to be of fundamental concern today. Amniocentesis is a technology used primarily to detect Down syndrome and also certain lethal and/or highly disabling single gene disorders. Rapp shows graphically how, despite a firm policy of nondirective counseling and a resolute belief that they are "information brokers" of "rational" knowledge, American genetic counselors convey information to women in a variety of ways that frequently depend upon the assumed ethnicity of the individual receiving the results (Rapp 1999). Counselors often encourage, apparently inadvertently, "stratified reproduction," in which "some categories of people are empowered to nurture and reproduce, while others are disempowered" (Ginsburg and Rapp 1995, 3). Rapp's ethnography also makes it clear that women and their partners must inevitably confront "the gap" created among statistical estimations of risk, their concerns about undergoing the actual test, and their doubts about the meaning of results.

Several women, including some who were well educated, misunderstood what they had been taught; however, even when the import of counseling was correctly internalized, making a "rational" decision about termination of a wanted pregnancy raised an array of difficulties. These included disbelief about the accuracy of the testing, a concern because amniocentesis can induce pregnancy loss, and a committed position on the part of some that Down syndrome is not a reason to abort a fetus. The fact that the test tells them nothing about severity of the phenotype was often noted as a reason to continue the pregnancy. Others, believing that they themselves have a healthy lifestyle, do not accept that their fetus is at risk for disease. Religious beliefs also play a part in decision making, as do family economics, the reproductive experiences of extended family members, and attitudes to disability in general. In some families the pregnant woman is made to feel responsible for the "problem" having arisen in the first place. Rapp characterizes women who have been tested as "moral pioneers" because they are expected to make rational decisions about abortion of wanted pregnancies, when in reality they are confronted with complex, heartrending decisions.

Carole Browner's work among Mexicans living in America has shown how the presence of male partners during genetic counseling sessions can have a profound effect on decision making. With few exceptions, the husband's role was understood by both partners as supportive, and facilitating of the decision that the woman herself had chosen. However, Browner found that when women appeared to be uncertain and vacillating about having a test, clinicians tended to forge alliances with the male partner whom they assumed would be more able to see reason (Browner 2007).

Several researchers, among them Rapp and Browner, have shown that when genetic information is incorporated into accounts about illness causation, such knowledge supplements rather than replaces previously held notions about kinship, heredity, and health. For example, writing about Huntington's disease, a single gene adult onset degenerative disorder for which there is no effective treatment, Cox and McKellin (1999) make it clear that lay understandings of heredity conflict with Mendelian genetics, because the scientific account does not assuage the feelings of families dealing with the lived experience of genetic risk. These authors argue on the basis of empirical findings: "theories of Mendelian inheritance frame risk in static, objective terms. They abstract risk from the messiness of human contingency and biography" (1999, 140).

People who come from families with Huntington's disease vacillate about testing, sometimes for many years, in part as a result of the uncertainties involved about age of onset and because no treatment exists (Cox and McKellin 1999). Moreover, increased knowledge about molecular genetics complicates estimations of future risk, sometimes making "educated choices" about testing problematic. For example, since the time that the Huntington's gene was mapped, it became clear that the estimations of risk that some people had previously been given based on linkage studies were incorrect, sometimes wildly so, with the result that certain individuals had to be given new estimates, on occasion entirely different from earlier information, with enormous social repercussions (Almqvist et al. 1997).

Furthermore, it is now known that there is no straightforward, unequivocal link between the presence of a Huntington's gene and the expression of the actual disease, as was formerly believed to be the case. Today, when people from Huntington's families are tested they are given one among three possible results: "No, you won't get the disease," or "yes, you will get the disease, but we cannot be sure at what age it will start to affect you," or, alternatively, to a small number of tested people, "we simply don't know. You may or you may not get Huntington's disease" (Langbehn et al. 2004). This situation applies to several other single gene disorders. The biopolitics of genetic risk is riddled with risky estimations that gloss over the uncertainties embedded in rapidly changing molecular genetic knowledge.

The anthropologist Monica Konrad (2005) in her ethnographic study describes "the making of the 'pre-symptomatic person.'" She too uses Huntington's disease as an illustrative example and is at pains to emphasize what happens in families where some people choose to be tested and others refuse. Inspired in part by anthropological research into divination, Konrad explores the "prophetic realities" unfolding in contemporary society as a result of genetic technologies. Konrad, like Rapp, is concerned with "moral decision making," and her emphasis is on how, when bodies are made into oracles, "moral systems of foreknowledge" thus produced are enacted both within and across generations. Her work, like virtually all the other social science research on genetic testing, makes it abundantly clear that the common position taken in bioethics of a "right to know" and an assumption of individual autonomy with respect to decision making in connection with genetics is extremely problematic. Konrad discusses at length the "pragmatics of uncertainty" that infuse the everyday lives of people living with genetic foreknowledge and, further, the new forms of "relational identity" that testing brings about: how and when to inform one's children of your own test results; whether to be entirely "truthful" or not or whether to say nothing at all; should the children be tested and, if so, when? Value is associated with the idea of kinship, the very ties of which are medicalized as a result of genetic testing, thus accounting for why "affectively charged kinship talk" (Konrad 2005, 145; see also Finkler 2000, 2001) consistently dominates gene talk.

When the sociologist Nina Hallowell (1999) interviewed women in the United Kingdom who come from families where cancer is very common and who were undergoing testing at a specialty clinic for the BRCA genes associated with increased risk for breast cancer, without exception she found that these women believed that it was their duty to themselves and to their children to undergo testing. Moreover, many women who had already borne children believed themselves to be responsible for having unknowingly put their children at risk. On the basis of these findings, Hallowell argued that women, more so than men, are likely to develop feelings of "genetic responsibility"—that is, experience an obligation to undergo testing and reveal the results to kin. As one woman put it, "A large proportion of my concern is a responsibility to my daughter. And I think also it's sort of a helplessness. . . . I've passed on the gene to my daughter. I must make sure now that I alert her to what might be in store for her, because I have that responsibility." Most women interviewed by Hallowell were frightened of undergoing the test, scared that it might affect their employment or health insurance, but they nevertheless went through with it. Sometimes women were pushed to do so by their spouses or sisters: "I said to my husband that I didn't want to know. I said, if I'm going to get cancer then I'm just going to get it. I don't want to go for this test. And my husband, he kept saying . . . you know, you should, because it's not just for you, but for the kids."

Kaya Finkler interviewed women who come from families designated as being "at risk" for breast cancer, some of whom had undergone genetic testing. She describes how these women become "perpetual patients" while they are healthy, undergoing extensive medicalization, and how at family events they discuss the genes they share among extended kin. Finkler concludes that families, often dispersed and no longer in contact, are reunited by medicalization: "DNA joins the compartmentalized, fragmented postmodern individual to his or her ancestors" (2001, 249), and this rejoining is accomplished most explicitly by means of medical testing, medical histories, and the storage of DNA samples. Her findings clearly document a zone of chronic anxiety that individuals and families are liable to inhabit as a result of accumulating knowledge about genes and how they function and, if they so choose, by undergoing genetic testing (Finkler et al. 2003). However, as Finkler notes, such anxiety has often been reinforced by media hype that has a tendency to misrepresent and overstate scientific findings (see also Gibbon 2007).

Mutations of BRCA genes are not involved in by far the majority of cases of breast cancer and are implicated in only approximately 5 to 10 percent of cases. It is now evident that the presence of many other genes is implicated in generating risk in addition to the BRCA genes. Even when BRCA mutations are found, this by no means determines that an individual will get breast cancer. It is estimated that, on average, such mutations, particularly common among Ashkenazi populations, place people at an increased lifetime risk as compared to the population at large, of somewhere between 50 and 80 percent. A recent important study shows that lifetime risk for breast cancer among Ashkenazi women

has apparently increased over time. Breast cancer risk by age fifty among mutation carriers born before 1940 was 24 percent, whereas among those born after
1940 the risk is 67 percent (King et al. 2003). These striking results strongly
suggest that environmental factors are implicated.

The above discussion makes clear that knowledge about genes can initiate
or inhibit action, and increase or reduce anxiety, depending on a wide range
of social factors and very often, equally, on the material effects of the genes in
question. Inevitably the future is brought into the present, and family relationships are transformed, in part by the exposure of the lines of DNA transmission. But does such knowledge result in what might be called a "genetic
subjectivity"? And is there a tight looping effect (as Ian Hacking [1995] would
put it) between genetic disclosure and a radical transformation in subjectivity?
Are people *consumed* by the idea that they *are* their genes? Or is genetic knowledge usually absorbed into preexisting beliefs about risk to self and family, as
much of the social science research suggests?

Genetic Citizenship and Future Promise

Rayna Rapp and her associates have documented how networks of families
increasingly coalesce as a result of shared knowledge about the rare single
gene disorders that afflict their children. Such groups provide mutual social
support and lobby the U.S. Congress for improved research funding (similar
activities happen in many other countries). These activists are painfully aware
that only rarely will drug companies invest in research into these kinds of
diseases because no profit is to be had in researching the so-called orphan diseases, over one thousand five hundred of which are distributed across a mere
2 percent of the world's population. Lobbying for public funding is deemed
essential, much of it directed initially at locating the relevant mutations on the
human genome. These practices often have direct links to biocapital; the state
is involved only insofar as political lobbying for recognition of the disease and
funding for it are indispensable (Rapp et al. 2001; Rapp 2003). Such alliances
constitute "genetic citizenship" in action and involve not only mobilization
of affected people but new ways of envisioning the future, when gene therapy
may *possibly* become a realistic option (Callon and Rabeharisoa 2004; Heath
et al. 2004; Rapp 2003; Taussig et al. 2003).

One of the citizen support groups investigated by Taussig and her colleagues is the Little People of America (LPA), founded in 1957. These researchers graphically demonstrate, now that biotechnology presents a possibility for normalization, the irresolvable tension that exists for people who frequently endure stigmatization in their daily lives as a result of their physical condition. Taussig and her colleagues characterize this tension as "flexible eugenics," a situation that arises when "long-standing biases against atypical bodies meet both the perils and the possibilities that spring from genetic technologies" (Taussig et al. 2003). Understanding of what is "natural" is thus subject to continuous renegotiation resulting in "flexible bodies." Members of the LPA take different subject positions with respect to the choices now available to them in connection with treatment, such as limb lengthening, and also about genetic testing. Many LPA members fear genetic testing may be used inappropriately and that pressure will be brought to bear on couples to undergo an abortion when testing is positive for dwarfing. Furthermore, when LPA couples opt to undergo genetic testing, "choice" is inevitably compounded by uncertainty, because several dwarfing conditions exist in which different genes are implicated, but there is virtually no knowledge, other than the isolated experiences of some families, about how these genes are likely to interact during reproduction (Taussig et al. 2003). Research of this kind shows how, even among politically active groups, concerns about persisting uncertainties and the outcomes of technological interventions are dominant and, further, that within activist groups people are by no means of one mind.

It is also evident from this research that the assumption of a marked distinction between lay and professional expertise is not appropriate; new forms of "entanglements" among patients, families, health care professionals, and politicians are apparent, as is the wide circulation of "expert" knowledge in many domains (Callon and Rabeharisoa 2004; Gibbon 2007; Palladino 2002; Rapp 2003). Powerful activist movements emerge around certain conditions, but there is also the danger that, in their eagerness to help in the advance of medical knowledge, people inappropriately transform themselves into experimental subjects.

Biosociality and the Affiliation of Genes

The anthropologist Paul Rabinow (1996a) created the concept of biosociality when responding to comments made in 1989 by the geneticist Neil Holtzman to the effect that early detection of genetic predisposition to diseases would shortly become routine. In delineating biosociality, Rabinow gave particular emphasis to only one of the many issues raised by Holtzman: "the likely formation of new group and individual identities and practices arising out of these new truths" (102). Rabinow is careful to note that groups formed on the basis of individual experiences with rare diseases were already in existence before genotyping became available and will clearly continue to function with respect to "pastoral" and political activities. But, he suggests, new congeries of people will emerge as a result of knowledge founded in molecular genetics. Such groups will have "medical specialists, laboratories, narrative traditions, and a heavy panoply of pastoral keepers to help them experience, share, intervene, and 'understand' their fate" (Rabinow 1996a, 102).

At the time when Rabinow first introduced the concept of biosociality the idea of groups literally coming together on the basis of a specified chromosomal abnormality as Rabinow suggested (with a touch of irony one assumes) seemed farfetched to many. In retrospect his insight has perhaps proved to be prescient. An article in the *New York Times* in December 2007 discusses the experiences of certain families with *extremely* rare genetic mutations who, as a result of a new diagnostic technology, are informed about the DNA mutation that has affected one or more of their children and, with access to email and the Internet, have made contact with similarly affected families. These families all described how contact with other affected families, even though indirect, was an extremely positive experience (Harmon 2007).

In 2007 Raspberry and Skinner carried out research with ethnically diverse families in the southeastern United States where a child had been diagnosed with a genetic disorder. Similar to the findings reported in the *New York Times*, these authors found that a genetic diagnosis frequently gives legitimacy to a disorder as being "truly" biological and allows families to escape from catchall "soft" diagnostic categories such as autism and attention deficit and hyperactivity disorder (ADHD), thus offering more hope for a "cure" in the not too distant future, perhaps by means of genetic engineering. Nevertheless, they argue that these families maintain a "hybrid notion of causality," even when it is undeniable that chromosomal deletions have brought about very real bodily changes. Inevitably, questions about the range of phenotypic expression, severity, and individual compensatory capabilities are always uppermost in mind. The "genetic body" made knowable through technology requires, then, family interpretations about the meaning of identified genes to be continually modified as a result of lived experience and ongoing uncertainties. Knowledge about genetics rarely transcends or precludes the ever present uncertainty, hope, wishful thinking, and sometimes despair that constitutes everyday life when a genetic disorder or chromosomal abnormality has been identified.

A decade on, Rabinow (2007) admits to limitations associated with the concept of biosociality, although it is a concept that has been made extensive use of by many researchers—a measured critique of which appears throughout the chapters in the edited book by Sahra Gibbon and Carlos Novas (2007). In reassessing the situation, Rabinow notes that there has been a shift in the time horizon that he formerly assumed was unfolding, brought about in large part by the demise of the gene and the emergence of the postgenomic era—to be expanded upon in the following section.

Readers will have noticed that virtually all of the research into genetic testing that I have cited has been carried out in North America and Europe. In addition, considerable work has also been done in Israel (see Rosner et al. 2009). Although genetic testing is not an inordinately expensive technology, only relatively recently has it begun to be carried out in economically deprived countries. Duana Fullwiley has carried out ethnographic research in connection with attitudes toward genetic testing in Senegal, where this technology was introduced several years ago. She notes that the physicians whom she interviewed, the majority of whom are trained in France, were frustrated with the effects of what Fullwiley describes as "discriminate biopower" (2004). Although Senegal has one of the lowest rates of HIV in Africa, at a little over 1 percent of the population, and sickle cell disease affects 10 percent or more of the population, the funding provided by NGOs, following UN and WHO directives, is almost exclusively for HIV/AIDS and not for sickle cell disease.

Fullwiley points out that Senegalese physicians with whom she talked assume that women do not want to be tested for sickle cell because abortion is not acceptable to this Muslim population and, further, Wolof "tradition" is that women should have many children. Although the majority of women interviewed by Fullwiley cited religion as a major influence on their thinking, she found that, even among those opposed to abortion, some thought that testing would be helpful in order to know what the future had in store for them. Others thought testing of male partners might give women just cause to divorce unsympathetic or disagreeable husbands. Alternatively, reluctant young women might be able to avoid entering a marriage arranged by the family in which it was proven with testing that children could well be born homozygous for sickle cell disease. Among those women who agreed that selective abortion would be acceptable, Muslim teaching was cited in which it is argued that prior to "ensoulment," embryos are simply "life." After a period of gestation (about the length of which there is some disagreement) embryos become "human life" and not simply life, and only then is abortion considered as murder.

In summary, Fullwiley found that the principal matters that concern Senegalese families when discussing genetic testing include "recent family history and present family character, spiritual conviction and religious interpretation, marital problems and familial pressure to resolve them, and the social obligation to raise healthy children" (2004, 160). These convictions, although clearly local in kind, are strikingly similar in some ways to narratives elicited by anthropologists working in the West in that the well-being of the family, and not simply the concerns of individuals, is implicated in justifying genetic testing.

I turn now to some of the significant changes that have taken place in molecular biology over the past decade and the move into a postgenomic era that has important implications for anthropological research.

Demoting the Gene

In their important book *Genomes and What to Make of Them*, the sociologist and philosopher team of Barnes and Dupré argue that DNA is not simply involved with heredity; one now has to ask what does DNA do "all the time" (2008, 50), throughout the life cycle. How, when, and under what circumstances does DNA become expressed or, alternatively, switched off? In a related vein, Richard Strohman, a Berkeley molecular biologist, asks, "If the program for life is not in our genes, then where is it?" He notes that many of his colleagues have been arguing quietly for a long time that "there *is* no program in the sense of an inherited, pre-existing script waiting to be read." Rather, he argues, "there are regulatory networks of proteins that sense or measure changes in the cellular environment and interpret those signals so that the cell makes an appropriate response." This regulatory system, a "dynamic-epigenetic network," has a life of its own, so to speak, with rules that are not specified by DNA (2001, 8).

The biologist Scott Gilbert suggests that in light of this major conceptual shift our "self" is best understood as permeable. We are each, in effect, "a complex community, indeed, a collection of ecosystems" (2002, 213). Contingency is the name of this game, and further, it is clear to perhaps the majority of researchers in molecular biology that genes do not have clearly demarcated beginnings or ends; nor are they stable, and only very rarely indeed do they *determine* either individual phenotypes or the biological makeup of future generations (Jablonka and Lamb 2005; Neumann-Held and Rehmann-Sutter 2006; Stotz et al. 2006). Quite simply, then, genes are not us, and the gene, although it continues to be a useful concept, can no longer pass as the fundamental animating force of human life, although the biological anthropologist Kenneth Weiss reports that very many researchers continue to be "in love" with the gene (personal communication). Systematic research into epigenetics is just beginning to take off, and, although genetics and genomics play an indispensable role in this research, ultimately the objective is to explain what it is about inheritance, health, and illness that genes alone cannot explain.

One well-documented example involves findings that have accumulated over the years in connection with what is known as the Dutch famine of 1944 (Lumey 1992). Thirty thousand people died from starvation as a result of a Second World War German food embargo that resulted in the complete breakdown of local food supplies, adding to the misery of an already harsh winter. Birth records collected since that time have shown that children born of women who were pregnant during the famine not only had low birth weights but also exhibited a range of developmental and adult disorders later in life, including diabetes, coronary heart disease, and breast and other cancers. Furthermore, it has been shown that this second generation, even though prosperous and well nourished, themselves produced low-birth-weight children who inherited similar health problems (Harding 2001).

Researchers argue that these findings strongly suggest that expression of crucial DNA sequences have been repressed due to radically reduced nutritional intake during pregnancy. It is now argued that such changes are the result of a molecular process known as methylation, crucial to the activation and silencing of genes; it has been shown convincingly that environmental variables can alter this complex process and, further, that the changes that result can be inherited independently of DNA. These findings are currently attracting a great deal of attention among researchers (Champagne and Meaney 2001; Szyf et al. 2008) and have opened the door to what is being described positively by some as neo-Lamarckianism. Increased knowledge about methylation and other similar key processes at the level of the cell are beginning to make clear some of the crucial mechanisms involved in dynamic epigenetics and, furthermore, are exposing both the indivisibility of culture and the material world and the means by which significant biological variation is produced over time (Jablonka and Lamb 1995; Oyama et al. 2001). However, as Strohman makes clear, scientists are currently suspended between paradigms: genetic determinism is a failed paradigm he argues (although the majority of involved scientists quite possibly disagree with him), and research into dynamic epigenetics is only just taking form—in short, we are betwixt and between, and the current generation of scientists, especially when they work in alliance with the corporate world, have, for the most part, been trained for and remain firmly embedded in a deterministic framework. Yet even Craig Venter is on record as commenting that genes cannot possibly explain what makes us what we are, and similarly, Strohman (2001) insists that while the Human Genome Project did indeed tell us a great deal about our genome, it told us nothing about who we are and how we got this way. Interpretations of this kind bring us firmly into the realms of anthropology and philosophy. The fundamental question becomes one of whether or not DNA has any "agency" or "activity" at all—concepts that Neumann-Held and Rehmann-Sutter (2006) argue are, in any case, thoroughly anthropomorphic.

The time has come to acknowledge that both environmental biology and human biology are best conceptualized as local, contingent, and ceaselessly modified by human behavior. In other words, human activities—social, cultural, political, and economic—are inextricably entangled with the ever-transforming molecularized body (Lock and Nguyen 2010). The genetics of Alzheimer's disease is set out in the following section to illustrate the complexity with which we are now confronted.

Alzheimer's Disease, Susceptibility Genes, and Risk Estimates

It was recognized as early as the 1930s by using pedigree studies that autosomal dominant genes are implicated in what is today known as early onset Alzheimer's disease (AD). This rare form of dementia, from which Alzheimer's most famous patient, Auguste D., suffered, is associated with three specific, genetic mutations, all of which have been mapped (St. George-Hyslop 2000). However, it is not strictly true to claim that the gene determines this Mendelian form of the disease, because the age of onset for identical twins can vary by as much as a decade (Tilley et al. 1998). Early onset AD usually (but not inevitably) manifests itself somewhere between the ages of thirty-five and sixty, progresses relatively quickly to death, and accounts for between 2 and 5 percent of all diagnosed cases of AD.

In 1993 the first publication appeared that explicitly made an association between a specific gene called ApoE and an increased risk for the common, late onset form of AD (Corder et al. 1993). After some initial skepticism, this finding was heralded with great excitement on the assumption that the Alzheimer's puzzle might soon be "solved." Furthermore, it forced some revisions of the received wisdom of the day—namely, that Alzheimer's disease in older people is entirely "sporadic" and does not "run in families." The ApoE gene, present in all mammals, is located in humans on chromosome 19 and is essential for lipid and cholesterol metabolism. This gene appears in three polymorphic forms in humans—ApoEε2, ApoEε3, and ApoEε4—that are universally distributed. Evidence from more than a hundred laboratories suggests that it is the ApoEε4 allele that *may* put individuals at increased risk for AD. Between 14 and 16 percent of Caucasians (the most extensively studied biological population) carry at least one ε4 allele; however, it is unanimously agreed that the presence of the allele is neither necessary nor sufficient to cause the disease, for reasons that remain poorly understood. It is estimated that *at least* 50 percent of ε4 carriers never get AD, and population studies suggest that this figure is higher (Meyers et al. 1996).

Among patients diagnosed with late onset AD, it is estimated that between 30 and 60 percent do not have the ApoEε4 allele (Myers et al. 1996), and therefore there must be at least one other, and probably several more, pathways that result in the pathology associated with AD. Moreover, researchers assume that in addition to the ApoE gene, several, perhaps many more, genes are implicated. In an effort to examine gene to gene interactions several genome wide association consortia studies (GWAS) are currently being carried out. The neurogeneticists Lars Bertram and Rudolph Tanzi argue that although the identity and total number of genes implicated in AD remain elusive "recent estimates suggest that together they have a substantial impact on disease predisposition in the general population" (Bertram and Tanzi 2009, R137). However, although GWAS have confirmed that the ApoEε4 allele is indeed a susceptibility gene for AD, no other genes have been shown thus far to have more than minimal explanatory power (Harold et al. 2009).

Molecular and population genetics have amply demonstrated that genes are shapeshifters without peer, the products of evolutionary and recent human history, dietary, and climatic patterns, toxic environments, human social behavior, and, at times, serendipitous mutations, and the ApoE gene is no exception. For example, the polymorphism ApoEε4 has been shown to work in unexpected ways in specific populations. Among Pygmies, the !Kung San and other groups of people whose subsistence economy was, until relatively recently, predominantly that of hunting and gathering, possession of an ApoEε4 genotype apparently protects against AD. This finding holds when controlled for age (Corbo and Scacchi 1999). And it is of note that the ε4 genotype is the "wild type," that is, in evolutionary terms, it was the first to come into existence and continues to be the only polymorphism found in mammals other than humans. The ε4 variation has greater prevalence among African populations than so-called Caucasian populations and is relatively low in prevalence among Chinese populations, indicating a complex human evolutionary history not well accounted for.

Low rates of AD have been reported for parts of Nigeria, and the presence of an ApoEε4 allele, although relatively high, does not appear to place individuals at increased risk (Farrer et al. 1997). On the other hand, this allele is significantly associated with dementia among African Americans, although less so than in Caucasian populations (Farrer 2000). The data are considered sufficiently robust to conclude that risk-reducing factors (in Africa) *and* risk-enhancing factors (in North America) must be implicated, among them other genes, their protein products, diet, environment, and quite possibly other variables.

Many researchers and clinicians in the Alzheimer's world argue that there has been an overemphasis on the significance of ApoEε4; they suggest that other risk factors associated with AD—toxic environments, head trauma, education levels, chronic stress, diet, prions, and so on—are obscured by ApoE hype and insist that this gene is only one factor among many. It is apparent that creating individual risk estimates for late onset AD on the basis of ApoE genotyping, age, and sex alone, as is often done, while ignoring many other possible contributing factors, makes such estimates highly questionable. Numerous researchers working on AD evidently resort to what Beck and Niewöhner have characterized as "pragmatic reductionism" (2006, 223). A further major difficulty for calculating individual risk estimates for AD on the basis of genotype is the status of the AD diagnosis itself. Not only is the genotype elusive but so, too, researchers increasingly agree, is the phenotype, making the collection of robust "cases" to form a population data base from which individual risk estimates are then calculated highly circumspect (Lock 2010).

It is also clear that an overemphasis on the genetics of Alzheimer's has ensured that family dynamics, sociopolitical and economic variables, and disadvantaged lifestyles, including extensive exposure to neurotoxins, are underreported and rarely remarked upon, even at major medical meetings, with the result that the condition is desocialized and fully located in individual molecularized, at-risk bodies, believed to be genetically predisposed to dementia.

Genetic Testing for Alzheimer's Disease

Findings from interviews with individuals who were informed about their ApoE genotype as part of a randomized controlled trial carried out in the United States over the past few years give a glimpse of possible futures filled with uncertainty, should genetic testing for susceptibility genes become routinized. For the initial phase of Risk Evaluation and Education for Alzheimer's Disease (REVEAL), subjects were recruited at Boston, Case Western, and Cornell Universities (Cupples et al. 2004). Virtually all of the subjects self-identify as "white" and are well educated, with an average of seventeen years of schooling. For the second phase of the study a fourth site, Howard University in Washington, D.C., was added. These participants are African American with, on average, fifteen years of education. Trial participants (N = 442) come from families where one or more members have been diagnosed with AD, but they themselves are healthy. They are highly motivated by what I term "corporeal citizenship," in that they are eager to assist with medical research. Many of these participants had already signed themselves up to AD research medical registries in anticipation that they could participate in a trial such as REVEAL.

Everyone was first required to attend an education session about AD in the form of a PowerPoint presentation, with emphasis on theories about AD causation, including the contribution of genes, and the uncertainties associated with the scientific knowledge to date. The participants were then asked to return to the research site at a later date for a blood draw and those in the intervention arm were informed a few weeks later about their ApoE status. People assigned to be controls were not given this information until after the trial was complete. Reactions of all the subjects were systematically monitored by means of three follow-up structured interviews conducted by genetic counselors over the course of twelve months. A subset of the sample, seventy-nine individuals, volunteered to return after the completion of the basic REVEAL study to undergo semistructured, open-ended interviews carried out between 2002 and 2003 by anthropologists.[5] This subset is 87 percent women, with an average age of fifty years.

When asked to recall their ApoE genotype, 75 percent of these participants had forgotten, mixed up, or were confused about it and about the significance of the associated risk estimates for AD that they had been given. This finding is particularly noteworthy because 91 percent of the informants stated that "wanting to know" their genotype was a major motivation for participation (although making a contribution to research was of greater importance to most people). Even though most individuals could not recall their risk estimates accurately, nearly half had retained the gist of the information—often they stated that they have a "good" or "bad" gene (Lock et al. 2007).

The majority of these research subjects had been given estimates of a lifetime risk for AD by age eighty-five of approximately 20 percent. In addition to age, these estimates were based on family history, ApoE genotype, and gender. Even among those six individuals who, because they are homozygous for the ApoEε4 allele, were given the highest risk estimates (an increased risk over a baseline population of approaching 60 percent by age eighty-five), only three were able to recall their genotype accurately, and a fourth remembered only that she has the "bad genes" and added: "I'm still totally confused, although I do know I have two of them, whatever those bad things are." Another individual who learned that she has two ε4 alleles has seven relatives affected by AD and, not surprisingly, despite learning from the education session that ε4 alleles do not *cause* the disease, she finds it difficult to come to terms with this information.

Among the majority, those who found out that their genotype is ε3/3, Adele had the following to say: "According to that test, I don't have the risk, okay? So, technically I should feel better. But I don't believe it, given that there are four people in my family with the disease." Of course, it could be that her affected family members are also ε3/3, because at least half of all patients diagnosed with AD do not have ε4 alleles. Furthermore, Adele has been taught as part of the education session she underwent that she does indeed have increased risk, whatever her genotype, because her relatives have the disease. Knowledge of her genotype and of what she has been taught as part of REVEAL is, it seems, confusing and/or counterintuitive.

Other informants clearly express their confusion about the test results: "From one meeting to the next I would come in and I couldn't remember what my risk was. And to this day, I'm not 100 percent sure. But I know that it's elevated." A second stated: "I don't remember much . . . to be truthful, not much. I'm sure I have it (my risk estimate) somewhere, but I don't remember where." Some people were explicit about their frustration with the project: "Well, I know where I am at, where I stand. I can let my kids know where we stand. You know, I mean, maybe get it, maybe not."

Low levels of accurate genotype recall cannot be accounted for as due to limited formal education or, for that matter, as a result of early signs of AD (as some individuals commenting on these findings have jokingly suggested is the case). Rather, they illustrate the way in which people often nest genotype information into their experience of AD in the family (Lock 2007); as we have seen this is also the case when people learn about single gene disorders. Furthermore, because these individuals are predominantly in their forties and fifties and, for most of them, the increased risk estimate appears negligible prior to old age, and even then not very disturbing, in part because it is associated with so much uncertainty about which one can do nothing, there is no logical reason why they should treat this information as singularly important or predictive of their futures.

The concept of "blended inheritance," adapted by Martin Richards (1996, 222) from thinking derived from the early years of the discipline of genetics, refers to a common understanding he documented among the British public in which people believe that they inherit a mix or blend of genetically produced characteristics from each parent. Such ideas stem from a long tradition of such reasoning evident as early as classical times (Turney 1995, 12), reasoning that is evident in a good number of the individuals who underwent ApoE testing. For example, Katherine said: "I showed you the picture of me and my dad. We look like clones, practically, physically. And nobody's really said—I don't know whether or not that makes a difference, a person's physical appearance. But I have a suspicion that it does." And Robert commented: "Do I think I have a higher than normal chance? Yes. Heredity. And also I'm so much like my mother, who had Alzheimer's. There's a very high likelihood that one or more of her children will have a predisposition toward it. And I would say I'm frontrunner because of so many other characteristics that are very much like my mother's." Clearly, the risk estimates these individuals had been given have not displaced their informal thinking, already well established, about whom in their family is likely to be afflicted with AD. It is perhaps not surprising that when these interviewees talked about theories of causation, multicausal explanations were common, and genetics did not dominate the exchanges. It was evident that people already held complex models about AD causation before participating in the trial, and this understanding was reinforced because, as part of the required education session, they had been taught that the ApoE gene does not *cause* AD. When asked what brought about her father's illness Caroline responded: "I can't pinpoint any one thing." And Martha replied: "I think [genetics] plays a part, but I don't think that's all. I'm sure that a lot of the diet, and the health, and the exercise that we do today will prolong life and mental acuity."

Professional knowledge about late onset AD is riddled with uncertainties that are becoming ever more marked in light of recent technological advances and postgenomic insights (Lock 2011). Many of these research subjects are exquisitely aware of this complexity, having imbibed this message from their personal physicians, AD societies, some media sources, and from the RCT education session (Lock et al. 2007). Almost without exception, their responses make it clear that they are pragmatic in the face of this uncertainty and retain an intuitive awareness that their family histories are almost certainly of more relevance in predicting the future than are their genotypes, a position taken by many clinicians working with AD families (Clarke 2009). For the majority, "gene talk" is simply incorporated into their already existing thoughts and concerns about what is in store for them; in effect, genes are "familiarized" (Chilibeck et al. 2011) and absorbed into the encompassing vital entity of the "social body."

The genetic counselors who are part of the REVEAL study emphasize the possible fallibility of the calculations about genetic risk estimates when talking to participants, and it appears that most REVEAL participants have listened to these cautionary warnings. The level of uncertainty involved in susceptibility gene testing coupled with the limitations of the predictive power of the ApoE test no doubt dissuade people from giving up alternative theories about AD causation based on other sources of information or family history. Probabilistic estimates are not sufficiently authoritative to displace preexisting ideas and beliefs about who in the family is at risk. As fifty-one-year-old Rosie, who has two affected relatives, says of her results: "I thought it was interesting. But you know, I've looked at this knowledge not as *the* answer to anything. And I just take what I want and leave the rest. . . . I don't take anything anybody tells me as God's truth! . . . It's good to know, but I'm not going to do anything with it."

And fifty-seven-year-old Elizabeth says: "I don't like being kept in the dark—you get a tendency to go off the deep end when you're in the dark, you know? . . . Nothing is black and white—everything is like grey. But it's just good to know. I knew about my Dad's AD [although not about his genotype], I knew about my grandfather, I also know that they had a lot of siblings and that it wasn't showing up all that great, you know, but you never really know, okay?"

A good number of people in effect took control over their interviews, talking expansively about the emotional trauma of watching a close relative succumb to Alzheimer's, their struggles with caregiving, and other enormous stressors in daily life. Vicki, interviewed at Howard University, poured out a heartrending story about her life over the past decades. Her concern for her own risk for AD is eclipsed by her experience of caring for her ailing father with no support from her siblings who declared they were too busy to get involved. At the same time she struggled with her mother who was "in denial," resentful of her husband's forgetfulness and erratic behavior. It was Vicki who took him to doctor's appointments, dealt with his wandering, and found him a nursing home when she could no longer care for him. For nearly seven years until his death she went through the ordeal of "caring for this man that was no longer my Dad." Her mother was diagnosed with Lou Gehrig's disease just a year and a half after her father's death, and so she started "retraining again, to learn about Lou Gehrig's." While her parents were alive, Vicki was also caring for a demented aunt and uncle, struggling to make important financial and legal decisions for them with no input from their own children who lived far away. Her uncle died three years after Vicki took on the prime responsibility for his care, but care of her aunt continued at the time of the interview, and Vicki said she was feeling guilty for not spending more time with her. Vicki herself has diabetes and is concerned about her blood sugar levels and cholesterol.

Amidst this illness and death, daily life goes on. Vicki and her husband have raised three children and she has worked with only occasional leave from her full-time government job. She recently took an early retirement package: "Retirement suits me," she says. She is fully occupied with her family, church activities, and a local advocacy group for homelessness. She is excited about the future and says: "If I do [get AD], then I do. . . . I told my husband about my results [Vicki learned that she is homozygous for ε3] and he's been through as much as I have and he was like, 'well, whatever, we'll deal with it.'"

These interviews afford just a glimpse into people's lives, a delimited static picture, frustrating because there is no possibility for future encounters, but they suggest that for those who are living in a "zone of chronic anxiety" it is not due to knowledge about their genetic embodiment but, rather, to the social and economic deprivations associated with everyday life. Whether, as the REVEAL participants approach their late sixties and seventies, knowledge about their genotypes will become more significant is open to question. Meantime, before participating in REVEAL, everyone gave permission for their donated blood to be stored and used in basic science research in connection with AD.

Future Directions and Challenges

The significant questions currently being posed by many researchers in connection with the expression and action of susceptibility genes involve social and environmental contexts, toxic onslaughts, and other happenings that have occurred and accumulated over past generations and throughout individual life cycles. It is increasingly evident to many that embodied risk calculations made on the basis of susceptibility genotyping alone is an exceptionally crude and highly misleading exercise. The presence of specific genes informs only about potentiality and nothing more. In the case of AD, aging, above all else, is the most significant factor for increased risk, implicating every one of us, and it is well established that aging itself is profoundly influenced by lifelong events of numerous kinds (Butler 2008), a finding rapidly being consolidated with emerging epigenetic findings (see, for example, Abraham 2011).

Most susceptibility genes have less predictive power than does the ApoE gene, suggesting that for the majority of complex diseases, even though genetic testing may well help research to move ahead, decontextualized segments of DNA are unlikely to become powerful instruments for predicting future disease in individuals. This implies that activities associated with genetic citizenship, biosociality, and even the ripple effects among kin of individual genetic testing are unlikely to be the focus for anthropological research into the genetics of complex conditions. Of course, the *experience* of dealing with single gene disorders in affected families and communities continues to demand the attention of anthropologists, not only in clinical settings but even more so in daily life. And, as genetic testing and screening for conditions such as sickle cell anemia attain a global reach, ethnographic research embedded in local medical, political and economic contexts will be invaluable in assessing its social repercussions.

One major task ahead for anthropologists will be to track the content of the various forms of dissemination of postgenomic thinking into the public domain, and what effects this has on the uptake of technologies, including genetic testing and screening and preimplantation genetic diagnosis (see, for example, Franklin and Roberts 2006). More challenging will be to demonstrate the inextricable entanglement of human activities—environmental, historical, social, cultural, political, and economic—with the molecularized body (Lock 2009). Such research will expose the very process of biosocial differentiation in which genes participate but by no means determine the body in health and illness. An approach such as this, integrated with one that relentlessly reveals the enduring bodily effects of social inequality and developmental disadvantages in daily life, has the possibility of moving the anthropology of genetics and genomics into some exciting new directions that will build on work already accomplished. Epigenetics is receiving a great deal of coverage in scientific journals at present and is being incorporated in the research design of numerous projects, including the investigation of AD. But a good number of scientists caution that the findings so far are largely limited to animal modeling, and those that apply to human populations are frequently overly simplistic and/or do not result in substantial findings (Miller 2010). At present, much of what is being researched is grounded in a neoreductionism that has shifted attention away from genes alone but failed to engage more than perfunctorily with social, political, and economic dynamics that profoundly affect both individual bodies and the family milieu.

For example, the effects of early childhood experiences, notably abuse, on adult well-being, and an apparent increased risk for suicidal behavior recently reported by epigenetic researchers, has received much publicity. Specific molecular markers that the researchers argue had affected the emotional and behavioral states of these individuals have been isolated in the brains of abused individuals whose bodies were autopsied following death (McGowan et al. 2009). However, the findings are accrued from a very small sample and focus exclusively on molecular biology, setting completely to one side the socioeconomic and political milieus in which their research subjects had lived their lives. This project and others like it will continue to attract a great deal of attention but ultimately will founder badly, as does current research that draws unquestioningly on racialized categories of difference, because crucial ontological, epistemological, and sociopolitical matters have been overlooked.

Much more promising is the work of the medical anthropologist Daniel

Benyshek whose research findings call into question the long-standing theory of the "thrifty gene" associated with high rates of diabetes and obesity in contemporary populations. This research complements a body of emerging research in which an "epigenetic memory" is believed to be at work—one that links maternal deprivation to fetal vulnerability in a similar manner as does the Dutch famine research. The broader sociopolitical and environmental implications of the origins of the so-called epidemics of diabetes and obesity that confront us today are made immediately apparent by this research that, by extension, is also relevant for a contextualized understanding of dementia causation.

The promise of the postgenomic era is enormous and presents an urgent challenge to medical anthropologists to openly confront and critique the obvious limits of narrowly defined deterministic genetics and epigenetics. On the other hand, the possibility of engaging actively with postgenomic researchers by drawing on ethnographic methods and a sociopolitical approach to generate rich, embedded accounts of lived bodies is seemingly boundless. Such an engagement directly exposes social and political inequalities that result in the persistent and unequal distribution of health across populations. Also laid bare are unexamined biases and hardened false assumptions about the origins and best management of ill health, assumptions that often contribute to its very persistence among individuals and populations. A move away from the overused concept of individualized risk and from a confined understanding of embodied genetics is overdue. The time has come for the new entangled, social bodies to take center stage.

PART III

Activisms

Anthropology and the Study of Disability Worlds

In June 2007 we joined the many New Yorkers waiting to get into the East Coast premiere of the documentary *Autism: The Musical* (Reagan 2007). The queue stretched around the block—far outnumbering the other festival lines at one of the many venues for the trendy Tribeca Film Festival. People who could not catch the sold-out screening of this moving and humorous film were able to see it at home when HBO had the premiere broadcast the following year. The documentary, which follows five Los Angeles children on the autism spectrum and their families over the course of six months as they work together to produce a musical, went on to garner two Emmys.

The next spring, we had a déjà vu, once again joining a New York City ticket line that snaked far beyond the space around the Cinema Village theater for the theatrical opening of *Praying with Lior* (Trachtman 2008), another award-winning documentary feature that focuses on Lior, a young Jewish man with Down syndrome, and the world that nurtures him—and that he in turn inspires—as he moves toward his Bar Mitzvah.

Despite our awareness of a growing movement, especially among media activists, for more public and multidimensional representations of life with disabilities, we were nonetheless astonished at the drawing power of these admittedly outstanding films, a genre that has been evolving over the last two decades from a few singular works to a recognizable category in mainstream film festivals. This is the kind of change that the disability scholar Rosemarie Garland-Thomson identifies as "visual activism" that is reshaping the politics of recognition for those with disabilities and their supporters (Garland-Thomson 2009, 193).[1]

Ever the field-ready anthropologists, we chatted with people around us to see what brought them there: unsurprisingly, the answer was almost always kinship. "When have I seen a film with another kid like my darling [pick one: son, grandson, niece, cousin], where people get to see what life is like instead of feeling like you have to hide?" was a typical response.

Such encounters are increasingly exemplary of how we—and many others in the United States—experience "disability worlds" in the early part of the twenty-first century. In the 1950s and 1960s, when we were coming of age, we rarely encountered children with disabilities in our classrooms, neighborhoods, or places of worship, let alone at the movie theater. Looking back we now understand that many if not most disabled children were institutionalized, medicalized, and often hidden from public view. Their stunning absence from public space left us particularly unprepared for the unanticipated roles—and a remarkably changed universe—that we stepped into as adults when we both became parents of children with disabilities. Lacking models in our own intergenerational experience for managing the intimacy of family life "with a difference," we found ourselves reinventing the cultural assumptions and temporalities of the taken for granted world of kinship. As we moved from these insights into research, we quickly discovered that this was a widespread response among many parents managing the complexities of raising an atypical child; we have come to understand this process as the creation of what we call a "new kinship imaginary" (Rapp and Ginsburg 2001).

In the interests of full disclosure, our research began as a result of our many years of experience as mothers of children with learning disabilities.[2] Ginsburg's daughter has a rare genetic disorder, familial dysautonomia, which affects her autonomic nervous system and has consequences for learning that are not well understood along with her more global medical problems.[3] Rapp's son has classic dyslexia, and he requires accommodations for reading and writing. We became interested in this topic because of our own difficulties navigating the educational system on behalf of our children. As a result, we have been carrying out multi-sited ethnographic participant observation research on cultural innovation and learning disabilities since 2007. Our current fieldwork carries us in many directions as we track sites where the landscape of learning disabilities is transforming most rapidly. Despite our best efforts to contain it, we have found the categories that we are studying to be promiscuous violators of the walls erected by medical manuals and school bureaucracies. For example, the "visual activism" of the films and filmmakers discussed in our opening paragraphs are part of a disability media world (Ginsburg et al. 2002) ranging from books to documentary work to disability film festivals and screening series to YouTube uploads. These new kinds of visual and narrative mediations of the experience of disability are rapidly transforming contemporary American public culture; impairments that were once hidden are now increasingly rendered visible and sometimes celebrated.

Our research also includes fieldwork in neuroscience and epidemiological psychiatric research labs, where scientists use technologies such as genome analysis and functional magnetic resonance imaging (fMRI) to understand brain differences among children. Additionally, we have been carrying out interviews with heads of schools and programs—both public and private—that are particularly accommodating to children who struggle with conventional educational skills and demands. Much of our work is directed toward understanding the experiences of families whose children are labeled and remediated through their Individual Education Plans (IEPs, the school district-issued educational passport to special ed services). As engaged researchers, we are also participating in two post–secondary school projects. The first is the creation of a "transition program" for students who have grown up with the institutionalized benefits and burdens of federally mandated special education labels, only to find themselves without continued support or a clear pathway toward a fulfilling adult life as they leave high school. The second is supportive work with the NYU branch of Project Eye-to-Eye, the first national organization created by and for college students with learning disabilities (LDs), as they develop mentoring relationships with LD students at local middle schools. We discuss both in greater detail below.

In the world beyond the family, disability is no longer defined simply by diagnoses and medical models. We found that this category has burst all prior conceptual boundaries, appearing across many cultural fields. As anthropologists, we found this irresistible as a new territory to explore and inaugurated a research project titled Cultural Innovation and Learning Disabilities. We quickly discovered a rich tradition of work by anthropologists studying a variety of disabilities cross-culturally and at home. Ironically, while most of these works were conceived as broad cultural projects, often with a critique of medicalization, this work was nonetheless often identified as medical anthropology, the subfield that had embraced such research at a time when disability studies was just finding its own location in academia. We want to acknowledge the significance of that history; medical anthropology was one of the few locations in the field that offered an intellectual home to scholars working on disability and a full-fledged recognition of what inclusion entails, from publishing research to providing ramps and other accommodations at conferences. Now, as the intersection of anthropology and disability studies becomes ever more robust, medical anthropologists themselves have appropriately called for ethnographic research on disability to move beyond the confines of this single subdiscipline.

In this chapter, we first index the key processes that led to the increased presence and awareness of disability that characterizes contemporary American life from enhanced medical technologies to civil rights legislation. We then address the emergence of the study of disability both in the growing field of disability studies and by anthropologists whose intellectual and advocacy projects increasingly intersected the same terrain. Why, we ask, has anthropology confined much of the study of disability to medical anthropology— a hospitable home but one that now needs expansion? Finally, we use our own research on the transformation of the place of LDs in the United States since the 1960s to show the impossibility of containing such a widespread form of experience within medical categories alone. We thus argue for a framework that puts such research in conversation with disability studies, expanding a key concern for anthropology: what it means to be human.

Emergence of Disability

What has happened in the last several decades that helped to create this change, rendering disability increasingly visible—albeit slowly—as part of American cultural life? While we cannot fully recount the rich history of the growth of the movement for disability rights and its unexpected allies in sufficient detail here (see Charlton 1998; Linton 1998; Shapiro 1993), below we sketch the following deeply interdependent structural changes that helped bring this about.

First, starting in the 1970s, the movement for deinstitutionalization returned several generations of children with disabilities both young and older to communities and especially families from which they had once been removed. Additionally, the widespread dissemination of neonatal intensive care units (NICUs) beginning in the 1960s, led to the increased survival rate of preterm and low-birth-weight newborns, a population that has grown with the routinization of in vitro fertilization (IVF) and other assisted reproductive technologies (ARTs).

Many of these children—now surviving and living at home, often with mild to moderate impairments—required not only medical supports at home but also school placements, raising questions about the segregation (and need for integration) of differently abled children in the public school system of the United States. By the 1970s, groundbreaking legislation required educational rights for those with disabilities. Notably, the passage in 1975 of the Individuals with Disabilities Education Act (IDEA), and its periodic renewals, mandated a free and appropriate education for all of America's children. A parallel series of landmark Supreme Court cases spelled out the obligation of states and municipalities to provide public education for children with disabilities in "the least restrictive environment"[4] or fund its delivery in the private sector. The pioneering enactment in 1990 of the Americans with Disabilities Act (ADA) set the stage for a range of other challenges to discrimination in the public arena.

Second, the emergence of a late twentieth-century version of "special education" to accommodate this growing population was accompanied by the increased categorization of different "problematic" learning styles and medicalized behaviors. These ranged from LDs to attention deficit hyperactivity disorder (ADHD) to the increasing numbers of children assigned to the autism spectrum. The escalating presence of "all kinds of minds" in American classrooms helped catalyze a range of curricular innovations to meet the needs of diverse learners (Levine 1992).

More recently, public awareness of LDs has reverberated into a number of cultural domains beyond classrooms. For example, the growing fields of neuroscience and genetics offer new scientific explanations of atypical learning patterns, while simultaneously reinforcing diagnostic categories. In the world of popular culture, the increasingly widespread and positive presence of disability-related topics and characters—in mainstream books, cinema and television, independent film and educational documentaries, and digital interactive forms such as websites and blogs—has played a foundational role in changing broader cultural narratives.

Of course, the movement for disability rights both contributed to and benefited from the emergence of these large-scale social transformations. In its wake, the growth of an exciting, impassioned, and engaged disability studies scholarship grew more visible and widespread. The heady atmosphere of activism served as a crucible in which the demand for a new, inclusive, and critical scholarship emerged. In disability studies scholarship, recognition and analysis of systemic "disabling social conditions" has enriched the many fields from which the first wave of work emerged. This in turn contributed to an expanded understanding of civil rights, from the classroom to the courtroom. Much like prior innovative work in women's studies and gender studies and critical race studies, those working in disability studies made claims for cultural citizenship that extended the reach of the social movement from which it emerged.

Close Relatives: The Emergence of Disability Studies and Anthropological Work on Disability

In its Anglo-American form, disability scholarship has been highly interdisciplinary, emerging first in the humanities and later in the social sciences. In describing the field's epistemological approach, the foundational disability scholar and activist Simi Linton describes the work of disability studies as "creating theories that conceptualize disabled and nondisabled people as integral, complementary parts of a whole universe [showing] the historical and cross-cultural research on practices that divide communities along disability lines, as well as those that unite people and promote equity . . . [creating] a cohesive knowledge base that positions disability as the central vector of analysis" (1998, 129). Linton's fellow scholars in this ambitious and visionary enterprise have contributed to the paradigm shift that takes disability from margin to center, using the expertise of their respective fields, beginning with literary studies and history, that reread everything from popular culture to academic language while also narrating the little-known story of an emerging movement (e.g., Charlton 1998; Corker and Shakespeare 2002; Davis 2010; Garland-Thomson 2009; Longmore 2003; Mitchell 1997; Schweik 2009; Siebers 2006; Snyder 2006; Umansky 2001).

This proliferation of interdisciplinary scholarship addressed the need for the demedicalization of disability, insisting on a recognition of how the category of disability is socially constructed. The pages of journals such as *Disability Studies Quarterly* were home to debates on the value and limits of identity politics, interrogating the politics of language, such as "disabling conditions" versus "impairments." Writers weighed in on the benefits and burdens of using disability in the singular or plural, arguing that a united front was a key political move in fighting the stratification of human difference in which certain "kinds" of human beings are privileged over others. Despite the political merits of a "united front," the questions raised by different kinds of disabilities demand different responses. For example, the field is now actively wrestling with how to encompass mind and body splits: emotional and cognitive disabilities are frequently treated and experienced quite differently from the embodied, sensory differences that dominated the first wave of scholarship, perhaps because of the demands for intellectual achievement as a ground rule for academic recognition.

Anthropologists were among the early contributors in the social sciences to disability research and writing, focusing on how persons are constructed locally, inevitably bringing a cross-cultural perspective to the field. Indeed, anthropologists—long accustomed to questioning cultural categories—were quick to point out that what "counts" as a disability varies across social contexts as do the practices by which children and adults with disabilities are integrated, sequestered, shunned, or denied an integrated life. These vary enormously with other sociocultural rationalities (and cruelties). Intersecting relations obviously include gender, racial, ethnic, and class or caste differences, rural and urban locations, and concrete state policies. The immense and growing importance of international movements for claiming rights for the disabled is illustrated in the rapid passage of the UN Convention for Persons with Disabilities with a record number of signatories.[5] However, as many activists have recognized, such "global" statements have very little efficacy in daily life at the local level, a point that underscores the significance of ethnographic research.

Anthropological scholarship on disabilities spans at least four decades and is characterized by close attention to local cultural conditions, placed in their widest national and transnational contexts. According to the anthropologists and disability studies scholars Devva Kasnitz and Russell Shuttleworth, the

Disability Research Interest Group of the Society for Medical Anthropology began in the 1980s under the leadership of Dr. Louise Duval, with Carol Goldin and Devva Kasnitz. As the group grew over the next two decades, it regularly sponsored sessions at the American Anthropological Association (AAA) meetings and participated in policy formulation, including the President's Commission on Disability chaired by Gerry Gold (Kasnitz 2001; Kasnitz and Shuttleworth 2001, 4).

For many, the foundational ethnographies focused on disability began with the publication of Robert Edgerton's groundbreaking monograph *The Cloak of Competence* (1993 [1967]), his term for the strategies deployed by those who learned behaviors that enabled them to manage when they were repatriated to "their" communities after long-term institutionalization. Sixteen years later, Gay Becker's (1983) book on deafness and aging, *Growing Old in Silence*, inaugurated a new wave of U.S.-based research in which the impact of living with embodied difference in a less-than-accommodating world is the primary focus. Pioneering scholar Joan Ablon authored her first of several studies on the social consequences of genetic differences, with the publication of *Little People in America: The Social Dimension of Dwarfism* (1984), followed by *Living with Difference: Families with Dwarf Children* (1988), and most recently *Brittle Bones, Stout Hearts and Minds: Adults with Osteogenesis Imperfecta* (2009).

This literature was quickly claimed and supported by scholars within medical anthropology, who recognized its creative opening of larger arenas involved in the study of human diversity as well as the activist implications of many of the insights these works generated (see Singer and Parker, this edited volume). It is important to point out that much of the work by anthropologists on disability never fit directly into the medical anthropological paradigm; indeed, a number of key works rely heavily on the impact of communicative differences on the formation of stigma and/or the segregation of particular communities. For example, Nora Groce and John Gwaltney were particularly attentive to different communicative practices entailed in impaired hearing (Groce 1985) and sight (Gwaltney 1980). Gwaltney's own blindness gave him a particularly rich understanding of the lives of the blind people he studied. Stratification by testing—a supposedly objective measure of intelligence—is central to the cultural and linguistic analyses of learning disabilities in the educational ethnography *Successful Failures* (Varenne and McDermott 1998).

Karen Nakamura's *Deaf in Japan* (2007) raises important issues concerning normative personhood, language, and the roles available to those with disabilities in specific cultural settings, without focusing on the medical domain.

In turning their attention to specific international cultural contexts, Benedicte Ingstad and Susan Whyte's first coedited volume, *Disability and Culture* (1995), highlighted the social circumstances in which people with impairments survive and are integrated or dis-integrated from their natal groups; by their second volume, *Disability in Local and Global Worlds* (2007), social movements, eugenics, and human rights were all present in the case studies they collected. These concerns are also central to Matthew Kohrman's *Bodies of Difference: Experience of Disability and Institutional Advocacy in the Making of Modern China* (2005).

The field has also been enriched by another time-honored ethnographic strategy. Some anthropologists, when confronted with their own chronic disabling conditions, use an auto-ethnographic lens to offer powerful insights; the classic case is Robert Murphy's *The Body Silent* (1987) and his discussion of his experience of the cultural norms that disable the social status of those using wheelchairs. Later, investigations into living with chronic pain grew out of the authors' firsthand experiences: Jean Jackson's *Camp Pain* (1999), and Susan Greenhalgh's *Under the Medical Gaze: Facts and Fictions of Chronic Pain* (2001). Both situate their own medical journeys in the larger context of an American discourse in which individuals are responsible for overcoming adversity. More broadly, many ethnographic studies not only drew attention to the cultural construction of a range of conditions; they also offered a sociological analysis and critique of the consequences of medical models for their subjects in at least two ways. First, they had to address health care and medicalization as an important aspect of their specific experience. Second, they tended to be self-reflexive, placing themselves as Americans participating in the stereotypes, services, and social movements that framed the lives of their subjects, embedding them into the ethnographic picture. For example, Gelya Frank's *Venus on Wheels* (2000) addresses the life of Diane deVries, a woman born without arms and legs, and also reflexively explores the long-term psychodynamics of their relationship. Gail Landsman used her own experience as a mother of a child with a disability to conduct the research that informs *Reconstructing Motherhood and Disability in the Age of "Perfect"*

Children (2009). In trying to reach a broad literate public that includes people intimately affected by the disabilities of which they write, auto-ethnography has also been central to the work of Roy Richard Grinker's *Unstrange Minds* (2007) and Emily Martin's *Bi-Polar Expeditions* (2008).

As disability has become a more prominent topic in and beyond anthropology, medical anthropologists increasingly are recognizing a disability component in their research while bringing a critical analysis to the social framing of disease and disorders. Margaret Lock's (1993, 2001b, 2006) comparative work in North America and Japan on aging, brain death, and most recently on Alzheimer's disease, offers a cultural critique of assumptions about life, death, and living with disability. Similarly, Lawrence Cohen's book *No Aging in India* (1998) situates and contrasts South Asian and American assumptions about cultural understandings of senility, as does the edited collection *Thinking about Dementia* (Leibing and Cohen 2006). Julie Livingston's book *Debility and the Moral Imagination in Botswana* (2009) explores the lives of newly "debilitated persons" who are suffering from the influx of chronic disease and the changing medical and social networks of caregiving. The disabling consequences of poverty are addressed in Nancy Scheper-Hughes's *Death without Weeping* (1992) and in her activist work on the impact of the "organ market" on those who sell their body parts to survive (2000). All such studies complicate any simple notion of personhood and disability, while situating the specificity of impairment and its impact on embodiment in its capacious social and comparative setting.[6]

In this too-brief glance at the literature, we underscore how ethnographic accounts of disability often take shape within an expanding field of medical anthropology, even when the studies are built on a foundational critique of medical categories, making this a particularly ironic home for this work. To reiterate, the field of disability studies was founded on the explicit demedicalization of the categories and description of disability in favor of a social analysis of how impairments and diversity are linked or decoupled by the institutional and cultural frameworks within which they are embedded. While the replacement of the medical model with a social model is now widely accepted, those anthropological studies that address the social construction of disability in local contexts have nonetheless flourished inside the shelter historically provided by medical anthropology.

Anthropology's Reluctant Embrace of Disability

Despite these exemplary studies cited above, the field of anthropology as a whole has exhibited relatively little curiosity about disability as a social and lived category fundamental to the human experience.[7] This is surprising—and problematic—given anthropology's rapid embrace of gender as well as its foundational obsession with race. As Devva Kasnitz and Russell Shuttleworth (2001) so tellingly analyzed the situation almost a decade ago, "Anthropology's genuine fascination with otherness and the thickness of the ethnographic stance should be a boon to international disability studies. However, this promise is late in coming. . . . [And] compared to the plethora of work on illness and healing, medical anthropological research on disability has been minimal" (2001, 3, 5).

Given the centrality of diversity to our epistemology, why has the subject of disability not been a central topic for our discipline? Anthropology is well known for its capacious and ever-expanding framework for understanding "human nature." Why then has anthropology as a discipline been relatively reluctant to embrace the study of disability as another aspect of its romance with and professional curiosity about human difference and humanity in its widest, most philosophical sense? Surely, this form of difference, so often stigmatized by social hierarchies, is a universal aspect of human life. As we have learned from studies of early and latter-day eugenics and histories of institutionalization, the label of disability has been used to dehumanize populations across the globe. Such knowledge invites anthropological research on disability, daily life, and governance, work that should be used to reshape academic and public debates (Rapp and Ginsburg 2010).

At the same time, disability is a different form of difference: unlike the deeply embodied categories of race and gender, from which one can only enter or exit very rarely and with enormous and conscious effort ("passing," "transgendering," cutting yourself off from your own social and cultural legacy), disability can happen in a heartbeat, turning one's vantage point around and implicating others: the birth of a child with unanticipated health problems; the slip of a wheel on an icy road; the consequences of being an unwilling recruit to an epidemic or a war; the frailties of old age, for those lucky enough to get there. It may be a truism but it is worth repeating: because disability is not easily bounded as someone else's life experience, those without disabilities live in unconscious fear and denial of their "temporarily able-bodied person" status, as is too often made clear to those claiming citizenship in the disability community. In the words of the disability scholar Rosemarie Garland-Thomson: "Each one of us ineluctably acquires one or more disabilities—naming them variably as illness, disease, injury, old age, failure, dysfunction, or dependence. This inconvenient truth nudges most of us who think of ourselves as able-bodied towards imagining disability as an uncommon visitation that mostly happens to someone else, as a fate somehow elective rather than inevitable" (2009, 19). We return to this dilemma as a problem for anthropology at the end of this chapter.

Thus, it is the unavoidable premise of our work that anthropologists—like many others of similar class and cultural background—have a substantial fear of the random loss and stigma that disability brings. Additionally, the presence of disability as a topic too often signals a lack of cultural capital and social reproduction in a field where intelligence and "heroism" (as Susan Sontag [1963] noted of Lévi-Strauss) are so highly valorized. Employment statistics on those with disabilities are dismal. It is hard to get in and around the academy if one uses a wheelchair or other form of assistive technology, and the problem for field-working anthropologists is highlighted in its stereotypes: "Indiana Jones in a wheelchair?" to cite Devva Kasnitz and Russell Shuttleworth once again (2001)—unlikely! Moreover, our children with disabilities may never live in the lifestyle that we ourselves inhabit; many of them may be downwardly mobile. Some of them may not ever give the gift of grandchildren: these are conundrums for social reproduction. The litany of potential losses, conditions that might marginalize, is substantial. Despite our hesitation to adopt potentially reductive Freudian approaches, it is hard not to assume that perspective on this form of denial.

Some of disability's differences lie close to home, with enormous personal and systematic consequences. Speaking analytically about their own painful experiences as anthropologists with learning disabilities, for example, Dana Raphael, Mike Salovesh, and Martha Laclave write:

> Brain different people need to become their own most intense listeners, powerfully sensitive to what is happening inside their body, their brain. . . .
> If and when its presence is diagnosed, LD still is an invisible condition. Its

carriers do not move in wheelchairs or use other aids that can be seen. Their bodies present no recognizable signs of any impairment or disability. Having an invisible impairment carries annoying disadvantages.... People with LD manage to make some sort of adjustment to the world around them. It may not be the most effective or the most efficient solution to their particular problem(s), but most find a way to function on par with those around them. Accommodation is frequently accompanied by concealment. After all, we hear accusations of stubborn, obstinate and worse so often that passing as normal or even "faking" can come to be more important than getting help. (159)

It is on that vertiginous and shifting terrain of visible and invisible difference and disability so aptly described by these anthropologists that we travel daily as parents of "atypicals," and on which we are building our current research (Rapp and Ginsburg 2011).

We initially began our investigation of LD as an emergent, largely invisible category of disabling difference but quickly discovered that neither the children so labeled nor the label itself are easily domesticated nor reified. We therefore have accepted into our study any child, family, school or other institution for which an IEP is relevant. There is, of course, a social and historical context for our emergent work. Most obviously and importantly, the shadow of powerful structural changes in economy, policy, and medicine looms over our research. As mentioned earlier, deinstitutionalization brought children old and young back to their families and into their communities. The effects of civil rights legislation and struggles on the intersecting grounds of race and disability, and a shift toward a high-literacy service economy, all played a part in transforming the experience of people with disabilities and their families. Specific transformations in schooling fueled a shift in the diagnostic categories of special education, causing them to mutate over short periods of time.

The Invention of Learning Disabilities

The concept of the LD was invented by Samuel Kirk (1962, 1963) in 1963, who later went on to serve in the U.S. government as an educational adviser. Now, 15 percent of school-age children in the United States are marked for special education, and LD has become the fastest growing category within IDEA's fourteen diagnostic categories, doubling in each decade and accounting for almost half of all special education diagnoses. These diagnostic-bureaucratic categories require unpacking for their slippery-slope Foucauldian effects. Indeed, Paul Shattock, a British autism pharmacology researcher, notes the uneven process of diagnoses, in which some of his subjects moved from being labeled as having mental retardation (MR) to having LD to having autism spectrum disorder (ASD) over the course of their lifetimes.[8]

This transformation of special education is bolstered and sometimes contradicted by the work of scientists focused on brain variation in children; our fieldwork takes place among two laboratory teams, one in pediatric neuroscience and the other in psychiatric epidemiology. Both are attuned to neuroplasticity and variation among children and adolescents. Among those we have been tracking, the very thoughtful words of Dr. Dolores Malaspina, Steckler Professor of Psychiatry at NYU-Langone Medical Center and a world-renowned researcher in psychiatric problems of childhood, demonstrate an evolutionary perspective on the mass production of the temporalities of maturation and the burden this places on families whose children are atypical learners. Excerpts from her interview with us in 2007 reveal this antistandardizing perspective toward human growth:

> we need to have an appreciation that adolescence and young adulthood go through their mid 20s and that some people will take that long to amass the information that they need to be successful in society. . . . Now, people feel that unless they have kept up at a certain rate [in school], they have dropped out completely. . . . Whereas if we had an appreciation that learning occurs at different rates for different people then we wouldn't need to push them into a diagnosis and into a special ed track. We would have tracks that went forward at a different rate. . . . But the reality is that contemporary families have to adjust to the world of school bureaucracies and the transition to the unstructured life beyond schooling.

Dr. Malaspina's thoughtful view of how differential brain development affects education and social life for atypical learners synthesizes scientific and cultural meanings. Its wisdom surely draws from her own familial experiences: as the sister of someone diagnosed as a teenager with schizophrenia, and the stepmother of a now-grown young woman with LDs, she has considerable appreciation of the work of kinship in remaking the life cycle of those whose diagnoses reframe their educational, work, and community lives. As a scientist with a recognition of the cognitive diversity of the human species, she articulates a keen appreciation of the "unruliness" of developmental temporality that cannot always be squeezed into the lockstep grid of educational regulation. Like many others who have been touched by the difference of disability as it reverberates from life experience to public work, Dr. Malaspina uses the idiom she knows best—biomedical research—as a basis for constructing a counternarrative that will contribute to a more capacious social order.

The New Kinship Imaginary

Our work has beckoned us to develop descriptions of some new forms of domestic citizenship (Das 2001), part of what we call a "new kinship imaginary" (Rapp and Ginsburg 2001). We are particularly committed to documenting how families mediate and rewrite kinship to accommodate their own intimate "unnatural histories" that incorporate the experience of living with disability. We also note the narrative urgency that catalyzes these culturally unanticipated stories—told in books, movies, websites, IEPs, and scientific publications whose creation and impact we are documenting.

Kinship and the temporality of the life cycle are not the only issues to which anthropological attention needs to be paid. Not surprisingly, generational location matters. The gravitas of Malaspina's discussion matches the approach of our own generation. As disability increasingly becomes "the elephant in the playroom" (the title of a recent book by Denise Brodey [2007]), other strategies typical of Gen Xers are emerging, to our delight. For example, the parodic—but heartfelt—resistance of the Shut Up Moms and their hilarious DIY videos along with their book and website are both entitled *Shut Up About Your Perfect Kid* (Gallagher and Konjoian 2010).[9] A quote from their YouTube video renders their rhetorical position (and humorous style) clear: "There is a powerful movement sweeping across America. Imperfect parents . . . are coming out of their messy closets and boasting about the accomplishments of their imperfect children." This follows a scene around a kitchen table where a group of suburban mothers brag about their brilliant children and their accomplishments while the two mothers of the children with disabilities (the authors) fortify themselves with shots of vodka under the table to endure this ritual of middle-class female domination. Finally, they tear open their blouses to reveal T-shirts with the slogan that they also shout: "Shut Up About Your Perfect Kid." Their "imperfect" and wacky video, making good use of satire and irreverence, underscores an entertaining but powerful point confirmed in our research. Their work gets at fundamental truths about the complexities of raising children with disabilities in a world that valorizes a narrow range of achievements. As the authors Gina Gallagher and Patricia Konjoian made clear to us in an interview, the book is also a serious resource by and for parents learning to navigate the complex new world they have entered with their atypical child: "We are not in any way saying that parents shouldn't be proud of their children. Most days (like those rare ones when they actually help with the housework), we're quite proud of ours. But as sisters and parents of two daughters with disabilities—bipolar disorder and Asperger's syndrome—we're proud of our kids for a completely different set of reasons. Reasons that sadly don't measure up to most people's high standards of imperfection."

They went on to explain the experiences that motivated them to write their originally self-published book: "There is no book out there on special needs like this. Most of them are so depressing. They portray the worst case scenario. It's not a death sentence—some of them make you feel that way—we talk about that—it's a mourning period that you have to get over that loss—not only are they not going to do that—they are going to have struggles. You talk and you see people of all economic, ethnic, religious backgrounds . . . we are all the same." The authors' spirited resistance to the stigmatized categories imposed on their children is clearly more than idiosyncratic. It is concrete evidence of what we call "the social distribution of moxie" among the many parents of disabled kids who become "accidental activists" on behalf of their children (Ginsburg and Rapp 2010). The fact that the book was picked up by an imprint of Random House suggests that this stance has broad appeal that brings a new parental discourse into public visibility.

These cases are evidence of a widespread new kinship imaginary that we have been encountering in our work, an imaginary that positively embraces family members with disabilities. We argue that this alternative model of kinship ("the movement of imperfection," to use the words of Gallagher and

Konjoian) is emerging—if unevenly—across America and through a variety of idioms. If social mores once dictated that family members with disabilities be hidden from view and stories about them silenced, our research strongly suggests that this cultural script is being revised on a daily basis, creating a seismic sea change felt across multiple locations, from the intimacy of kinship to the public world of educational policy, research, and popular media.

Reshaping the Social Landscape of Learning Disabilities

Two final examples drawn from our fieldwork focus on longitudinal and developmental change in the embodied differences experienced by diagnosed children who have now graduated from their IEP labels to confront what one mother identified as "the unlatched window" of life beyond the mandated services of high school. Project Eye-to-Eye is a national organization of students with learning disabilities who have made it to college where they "come out" and bond via a mentoring program they run with middle school kids who are also labeled with LD. The chapter at NYU that we are tracking runs the Beyond Normal Art Club to preserve and enhance children's self-esteem by demonstrating the skills, creativity, and humor that the young adult Project Eye-to-Eye mentors have learned to deploy along their own slower route to success. This is the first national organization created for, about, and, most importantly, by young adults with LDs, building, as one of their T-shirts says, "a revolution in special education one classroom at a time." Thinking ahead, Jon Mooney, founder of Project Eye-to-Eye, now works as a liaison in Los Angeles between public utility companies and technical colleges, designing certificate programs that are committed to bringing young adults with LDs into the skilled workforce.

Our second example flows from our work as engaged and activist scholars. We helped to inaugurate and now document a pilot transition program—the Skills Program—that brings together two local independent high schools working with LD pupils with the support of interested faculty at NYU. Through this program, a small group (fifteen) of graduating LD seniors have had an opportunity to experience life on a college campus while continuing focused studies, internships in the community, and person-centered planning for the social support and services they require to live a fulfilling life. Overall, the goal is to help them launch what some call "enviable lives" structured around their interests and capacities, rather than their limits, and that puts their goals at the center rather than dropping young adults into existing social service agency structures. Internships, for example, range from work at local branches of disability friendly companies such as CVS or Trader Joe's, while others are working in self-advocacy organizations where they are trained in public speaking or in professional offices of photographers, lawyers, and occupational therapists. Like the Project Eye-to-Eye philosophy, these internships constitute their own revolution "one workplace at a time." For example, a disability friendly colleague at the American Museum of Natural History took on one young man with Asperger's syndrome and an encyclopedic knowledge of film to archive films from the Margaret Mead Film Festival. Her initial concerns disappeared after his first hour as an intern when he stood up and proclaimed loudly to no one in particular, "I love this job." Everyone in the collective office space immediately became supporters of his presence.

Such projects are all too rare; far too many LD high school graduates and dropouts are stuck in dead-end jobs or institutional settings, results that renege on the promissory note imagined by progressive legislation mandating inclusive education.

The Future of Anthropology and the Study of Disability Worlds

How might the study of disability inform the future work of anthropology as well as the reworking of classic anthropological concepts? The conceptual framework sketched above touches on many key themes familiar to cultural anthropologists: the social construction of childhood and personhood; nature and culture boundary formation in the explication, representation, and experience of atypical minds; diversity in embodiment; kinship relations and their claims on intimate differences; and emergent biosociality and its sometimes resistant demedicalization.

Research on disability allows us to build fresh perspectives on how human diversity is accommodated, resisted, humanized, satirized, problematized, and made more inclusive. Exemplary of this, we note that in 2008 Devva Kasnitz presented a paper at the AAA meetings in which she placed the communicative practices of people diagnosed with autism spectrum and cognitive impairments into systematic conversation with those labeled speech disabled, thus shaking up the boundaries across categories: the "R" word (mental retardation) —long anathema in the disability rights community—was thereby subsumed into a larger, more interesting problematic of I and thou communication, with or without a technological assist. In other words, Kasnitz offered a direct intervention into assumptions about the social nature of communicative practices, focusing on the diversity of available language styles beyond a conventional perspective on individual mind and body limitations. This engagement with the taken-for-granted categories of anthropology and sociolinguistics through insights built on disability studies is exemplary of how this work can push the field into a future in which the recognition of difference is continuously renewed.[10]

Unsurprisingly, this lesson is not lost on the emergent generation coming into anthropology, perhaps in part because they grew up in worlds where their own differences were recognized or their differently abled siblings and other relatives who survived fragile experiences of infancy were not hidden away in institutions. After reading Gail Landsman's *Reconstructing Motherhood and Disability in the Age of "Perfect" Babies* and watching the documentary *My Flesh and Blood* (Karsh 2003), our graduate students queried in a spring of 2009 seminar, why isn't this book—or disability—being taught in every introductory anthropology class? It's a good question.

Our post-ADA students, who grew up with disability present in their families and communities, have taught us that the next generation has already accepted the demedicalization of disability. This in no way diminishes the significance of medical anthropology's historical role in launching research in this area. Instead, they readily recognize disability as a widespread aspect of human diversity that should be part of the foundational anthropological repertoire. People with disabilities do not fit neatly into medical anthropological tropes of "the search for healing and cures," nor is "suffering" the primary dynamic that organizes their subjectivity. In contrast, our colleague, the disability activist and arts advocate Lawrence Carter-Long, describes an alternative approach to representing disability: "No handkerchief necessary, no heroism required. This is *disability through a whole new lens.*" His "disTHIS" attitude represents a sea change in contemporary cosmopolitan consciousness of the experience of disability as a fundamental fact of life.[11] Taking the difference that disability makes seriously depends upon our collective insistence that it be recognized as a foundational concern and theorized and embraced by the field of anthropology as an essential form of human diversity.

Medical Anthropology and Public Policy

Using Research to Change the World from What It Is to What We Believe It Should Be

A nation that continues year after year to spend more money on military defense than on programs of social uplift is approaching spiritual doom.— Martin Luther King Jr., "Beyond Vietnam— A Time to Break Silence"

If the subtitle of this chapter sounds familiar, you heard it in 2008 during the Democratic National Convention. It appeared in the speech by Michelle Obama (2008), when she told the assemblage and millions of TV viewers that after graduating:

> Instead of heading to Wall Street, Barack had gone to work in neighborhoods devastated when steel plants shut down, and jobs dried up. And he'd been invited back to speak to people from those neighborhoods about how to rebuild their community. . . . Barack stood up that day, and spoke words that have stayed with me ever since. He talked about "The world as it is" and "The world as it should be." And he said that all too often, we accept the distance between the two, and settle for the world as it is—even when it doesn't reflect our values and aspirations.

Actually, Obama was not the original author of those words. He learned them by reading Saul Alinsky's important activist volume *Rules for Radicals*. Alinsky (1971, 3) introduced his subject with the explanation: "What follows is for those who want to change the world from what it is to what they believe it should be." A consideration of the role of medical anthropology in what has been called the "policy arena"—perhaps in part because arenas historically are sites of both spectacle and contestation—is unavoidably an engagement with the issue of change, change from what we believe is wrong to something we believe will be better. The Irish literary critic and playwright George Bernard Shaw said, "If there was nothing wrong in the world there wouldn't be anything for us to do" (2006, 55). If this is true, in this world, at least we need never fear there is nothing worth doing.

In this light the purpose of this chapter is to analyze the anthropology of engagement in the policy arena. Anthropological involvement in this domain has a long but conflicted history. In some areas of disciplinary concern individual anthropologists have been successful in influencing public policy in productive and beneficial ways. Anthropologists, for example, through their research, framing of issues from an anthropological perspective, and presentation of evidence, played a role in the passage and subsequent improvement of the American Indian Religious Freedom Act, a federal law designed to "protect and preserve for American Indians their inherent right of freedom to believe, express and exercise the traditional religions of the American Indian, Eskimo, Aleut, and Native Hawaiians" (United States Code, Public Law 95–341 1978). Covered by this statute was the right of members of the Native American Church to consume peyote as a religious sacrament. More commonly, anthropologists have expressed frustration that their research findings, however relevant, have not reached the eyes and ears of decision makers or have been ignored in the policy-making process. With reference to the issue of access to local health care and public health systems by immigrants, Willen and Castañeda (2008) observe that in a number of receiving countries medical anthropologists among others (e.g., human rights and migrant advocacy organizations) have called for increased attention to the health consequences of lack of access, but their arguments have largely failed to persuade policy makers. Moreover, anthropology has not generally gained recognition as a policy-oriented discipline, despite a growing recognition and discussion that the field is positioned by its work to provide needed evidence-based information and conceptual insight that is pertinent to effective and beneficial policy development in health and other domains. Exemplary of this point is the effort by medical anthropologists engaged in the U.S. health care debate who have pointed out the middle-class bias that informs basing policy decisions on the dominant economist model of the autonomous consumer rationally seeking health care (Sarah and Lamphere 2006).

Specifically, within the context of current rethinking about the relationship of anthropology to the policy process, this chapter seeks to suggest a strategy for moving medical anthropology toward more meaningfully influencing health-related policy development. The proposed approach involves significantly expanding relations with a potential ally in the policy arena. By promoting and fostering collaboration and coalition building, which are stated goals of the Society for Medical Anthropology (SMA), with the national and international movement of community-based organizers inspired and trained by Saul Alinsky and his descendants, we position ourselves to participate in leveling the policy playing field and influencing the development of healthy health policy.

Obama in the Garden

Choosing to start with Saul Alinsky and Barack Obama in a discussion of medical anthropology and policy, at a time described by the president during his victory speech as a defining moment of change in American history, is, of course, not accidental. Obama, the son of an anthropologist, was trained at Gerald Kellman's Developing Communities Project in Chicago in the Alinsky methodology of grassroots community-based organizing for social change. Kellman assigned Obama to work in Altgeld Gardens, a 1,998-unit public housing project populated by blue-collar African American families reeling from a steel mill closing, a nearby health-threatening landfill, a putrid sewage treatment plant, and homes filled with asbestos. As Michael Kranish (2008) describes it, Altgeld lies twenty miles "from the glittering center of Chicago, at the farthest edge of the South Side" and consists of "dozens of two-story brick buildings [that] stretch for block after weary block." It was built to provide public housing for African American veterans of the Second World War, but because of government neglect it had deteriorated over the years and become an unhealthy place for most residents by the time Obama arrived.

Like many first time ethnographers beginning their research careers, Obama came to "the Gardens" as an outsider. He really did not speak the language of the street or understand the local way of life and the values that guided community members, nor did he know much about the lay of the local social landscape. As Walsh (2007) reports, "To accomplish his mission, Obama spent hours with Altgeld residents one on one, learning their problems and their dreams." This he did by conducting interviews in people's homes, sitting at their kitchen tables listening to their concerns, eating the food they offered in hopes of fattening up their energetic and talkative but very skinny visitor, and recording their answers to his many questions; all of these, of course, are behaviors that are very well known to medical anthropologists doing field research.

Eventually, by utilizing the community organizing tools he had been taught, Obama was able to help unite several hundred residents to demand improvements in the housing project. Included among his accomplishments, which even he admits were modest in light of the level of need, were obtaining grant funding for a jobs program, sparking a community push for asbestos removal, and the development of a group of activist mothers who continued to press for improvements long after Obama's time at Altgeld was over. One of the local residents Obama worked with during those years, Linda Randle, has commented, "What he brought to the effort was he helped [residents] to step into themselves to do things they weren't going to do and that the establishment here was not going to get done" (qtd. in Kranish 2008). Of these events, Obama has written, "It was the sort of change that's important not because it alters your concrete circumstances in some ways (wealth, security, fame) but because it hints at what might be possible and therefore spurs you on, beyond the immediate exhilaration, beyond any subsequent disappointments." Specifically, it was important, argues Obama, because organized community efforts broke down internal walls "into a reservoir of hope, allowing people of Altgeld to reclaim a power they had had all along" (2004: 242).

Interestingly, it has been said that Obama's approach to issues since moving into the Oval Office has continued to be that of a community organizer. Thus Reverend Alvin Love, whom Obama recruited into community organizing during the 1980s, has said of Obama as president, "I think at his heart Barack is a community organizer. I think what he's doing now is that. It's just a larger community to be organized" (qtd. in Moberg 2007).

Admittedly, it is not always clear what community Obama is now trying to organize. If it was the majority of poor, working-class, and middle-class people, I suspect Obama's strategy for addressing the health crisis facing this country would be different than what we have seen. Instead of trying to find common ground with the representatives of the medical-industrial complex, he might, as Vicente Navarro (2009) asserts, have initiated a popular, community-based "mobilization against the medical-industrial complex [that was designed] to ensure that everyone has the same benefits that their representatives in Congress have, broadening and improving Medicare for all. . . . And to achieve this goal—which the majority of the population supports—he should have stressed the need for government to ensure that this extension of benefits to everyone will occur."

Of course, such an approach, appealing as it sounds, would have produced howls of opposition from expectable quarters. As we all well remember, the president's opponents in the election campaign of 2008 tried to use his earlier involvement in community organizing against him. They did this by making the cynical and high-handed claim that up-from-the-bottom change is somehow bad, menacing, corrupt, or out of control. There is in this a lesson for a medical anthropology intent on improving health-related policy in light of the findings of our research.

Saul Alinsky and His Anthropological Descendants

Community organizing, of course, is no less complex and no less varied in its focus than medical anthropology. It is notable that during his life, Saul Alinsky (the topic of Hillary Clinton's senior thesis at Wellesley College) organized neighborhood groups in Chicago to fight against government indifference over the decline of their communities; the African American community of Rochester to pressure the Eastman Kodak company to end discrimination in hiring; steelworkers in Pittsburgh; First Americans in Canada; and Chicanos in the Southwest, including providing training to Cesar Chavez, who went on to found the first successful labor organization, the UFW, among California farmworkers, the organization that provided my own training and first involvement in community organizing.

As aptly described by Reverend John E. Gibbons (1995) in a sermon at First Parish Unitarian Church in Bedford, Massachusetts, on February 26, 1995, Saul Alinsky "was an American original, a radical, an irascible free-thinking visionary. He devoted his life to sharing the struggle of the 'have-nots' who would claim—in housing, in jobs, in fair-treatment—their share of the American dream. And, until he died in 1972, Saul Alinsky merrily went on the hunt for the 'haves' who would exploit, pollute, discriminate, and otherwise diminish that dream." During his sermon, Reverend Gibbons also noted that Alinsky graduated cum laude from the University of Chicago in 1930, having studied archaeology and sociology. Alinsky, he reported, enjoyed archaeology but worried about job opportunities for an archeologist during a depression, a sentiment no doubt shared by more than a few young archeologists and other anthropologists in the middle of the current recession. As for sociology, and reflective of his up-from-the-bottom perspective, Alinsky liked to quote Jimmy Farrell's observation that the sociology department at the University of Chicago "spent $100,000 on research to find out the location of houses of prostitution which any taxi driver could tell them for nothing" (qtd. in Gibbon 1995).

Upon graduating, Alinsky was rescued from unemployment when he received a graduate Social Science Fellowship in criminology, which paid his tuition, room, and board. He was surprised to learn he had been awarded the fellowship because, as he later explained in an interview: "I still don't know why they gave it to me—maybe because I hadn't taken a criminology course in my life and didn't know one goddamn thing about the subject—But this was the Depression and I felt like someone had tossed me a life preserver—Hell, if it had been in shirt cleaning, I would have taken it" (Norton 1972). Alinsky soon developed an interest in street crime, but finding that the usual methods employed in criminology at the time were too far removed from the places the kind of crimes that interested him actually occur, he decided to use ethnographic methods in his doctoral study of Al Capone and organized crime in Chicago: "I went over to the old Lexington Hotel, which was the gang's headquarters, and I hung around the lobby and the restaurant. I'd spot one of the mobsters whose picture I'd seen in the papers and go up to him and say, 'I'm Saul Alinsky, I'm studying criminology, do you mind if I hang around with you?' And he'd look me over and say, 'Get lost, punk.' This happened again and again, and I began to feel I'd never get anywhere" (Norton 1972).

In a pattern well known to ethnographers, Alinsky's persistence paid off and he eventually found a key informant who shared his criminal experiences and introduced him to other members of Capone's gang in his social network. Although Alinsky did not finish his dissertation and dropped out of graduate school, he later reported, "I learned a hell of a lot about the uses and abuses of power from the mob, lessons that stood me in good stead later on, when I was organizing" (Norton 1972).

In each of the settings where Alinsky later worked as a community organizer, somewhat different approaches to community action were needed (Rothman 1974). Of particular concern here is "social action," which is defined as an approach "that seeks to alter institutional policies and to make changes in the distribution of power" (Brager, Specht, and Torczyne 1987, 54). This is precisely one of the key strategies needed in the skill set of policy-oriented medical anthropologists. In fact it is not an unfamiliar tactic within anthropology, although it remains a somewhat forgotten fact that the first professional positions for members of our discipline in the United States were not in universities and colleges but in government policy research settings (Rylko-Bauer et al. 2006; Singer 2008).

Thus, anthropological work at the Bureau of American Ethnology (BAE), an institution established in 1879 by an act of Congress, began a decade before the opening of the first university department of anthropology. While not its primary focus, health behaviors of Indian peoples were at times a topic of research by the BAE (e.g., the mythical origins of curing practices [BAE 1880–81], examination of medicinal plants and practices [BAE 1908–9]). Similarly, the emergence of the American Anthropological Association (AAA), the parent organization of the SMA, was linked to the already existing Anthropological Society of Washington (ASW), established in 1879, the institutional founder of the AAA's flagship journal *American Anthropologist*. Notably, the ASW had an early involvement in carrying out applied research on social inequality and health among the poor of Washington, D.C. These efforts were spurred by the election of George Martin Kober, a physician and anthropologist, to the presidency of the ASW in 1906 and again in 1918 and 1919. Kober was very active in issues of public hygiene and investigated the emergence of typhoid during a local epidemic at the request of the District of Columbia Health Officer.

Another issue of his concern was the condition of housing for impoverished African American families in the back alleys of Washington, D.C. Toward the end of the nineteenth century, there were over twenty thousand people, primarily former slaves who had migrated from the South after the Civil War, living in very crowded and unsanitary secreted arteries of the city

(Gillette 2006). This population, Kober (1908, 122) observed, was forced "to find shelter in houses unfit for human habitation," which accounted for why "the mortality of children under one year of age is 115.50 per 1,000 among the white, and 334.86 among the colored." A report issued by the Associated Charities in 1896 led to media coverage that lamented that, "No human being could be other than stunted physically and morally amid such surroundings" (qtd. in Gillette 2006, 112). The Washington Civic Center, a coalition of civic and charitable organizations, for which Kober, as chair of the organization's committee on housing, was active, stressed the weight of environmental factors as determinants of health and well-being. The Civic Center launched a study of social conditions in the back allies of the capital that was intended to impact public opinion and to promote legislation to improve living conditions for the poor in the city (Gillette 2006; Schensul and Schensul 1978). Specific policy recommendations to the president and Congress included the enactment of more stringent laws regulating milk production to protect the public from milk-borne diseases, the removal of slum areas, the control of exploitation and usury, public announcement of harmful ingredients found in foods and patent medicines, and the enlargement in the number of city sanitation inspectors (Kober 1908). Importantly, Kober and his colleagues did not stop at research; they also issued reports and developed policy recommendations. Their activist strategy, in fact, incorporated some of the features of community organizing for change that were systematized, expanded, and scaled-up nationally by Alinsky fifty years later.

Following in this tradition is the much more recent work by the anthropologist Anna Lou Dehavenon, author of *There's No Place Like Home* (1999). She founded the Action Research Project on Hunger, Homelessness, and Family Health in New York, an organization that continues what is now a century long anthropological tradition of linking local research to advocacy for change in public policy on the health and well-being of the poor and homeless. In an interview in 2000, Dehavenon noted (qtd. in Fisher 2000), "I never started out to do good.... My primary responsibility was to good research, not advocacy." But, as Dehavenon soon realized, good research on the challenging health and social problems facing communities can gather dust on library shelves or it can be mobilized to make a difference in the world. In her work, she chose the latter option. For example, on twenty-five nights between January 7 and August

26, 1991, Dehavenon observed and documented the experiences of families waiting for shelter placements at city facilities and monitored the degree of city compliance with relevant court rulings concerning the administration of the welfare and emergency shelter system. Among the policy recommendations she made (Dehavenon 1999, 63) based on this research was that "public health and housing authorities at all levels of government should evaluate the significance for family health and child development of the overcrowding and lack of privacy experienced by homeless families" who are forced by city practices to live "doubled-up," that is, locating two or more families in a single-family dwelling. Findings were also used in Dehavenon's testimony as an expert witness in several cases brought on behalf of the homeless by the Legal Aid Society. In one of these cases, the New York Supreme Court's favorable ruling enabled thirty thousand families to remain in apartments from which they would have been evicted because of inability to pay.

Beyond work on homelessness, anthropologists over the years have worked on many health policy issues, including the South to North global trade in organs, body tissues, and body fluids; sterile syringe access, harm reduction, and HIV/AIDS prevention; diet, food insecurity, and nutrition; environmental health and environmental justice; cancer; reproductive health; and health and human rights, among other issues. Still, some anthropologists define policy as beyond their scope of expertise. Of equal importance in our policy shyness, I believe, is the sense that many anthropologists feel that we cannot make a difference. We have either experienced directly, or heard the stories of our colleagues, having research findings and policy recommendations ignored because they did not support the prevailing opinions of policy makers. There is also recognition that findings can be misused by policy makers. It was Laura Nader who reminded us, for example, that research on the poor is often used against them, and hence her urge that we study up, including research on policy makers.

Struggles in Community Organizing

In this regard it must be admitted that those who embrace a hostile view of Alinsky's methods and goals are correct: the empowerment of the many through on-the-ground community organizing is a very real threat to control by the few and to the continued hegemony of what Linda Whiteford and Lenore Manderson (2000) in their book, *Global Health Policy, Local Realities*, fittingly call the fallacy of the level playing field. As noted by Oxfam (2009), the cause of problems like poverty "isn't just about lack of resources. In a wealthy world it's about bad decisions made by powerful people."

The seriousness of the threat posed by community organizing to the maintenance of an unlevel playing field in health and beyond is seen in recent conservative attacks on the Association of Community Organizations for Reform Now (ACORN), an activist policy-oriented organization that Obama represented in a lawsuit and taught community organizing techniques for during the 1990s. The most recent round of attacks on ACORN began during the presidential election campaign of 2008 when authorities in Nevada, claiming that employees of the group had filed false voting registration forms, raided the group's state headquarters. This led quickly to Senator John McCain's public claim that ACORN was both out to disrupt the U.S. political system and, because it allegedly had "bullied" banks into making bad home loans to the poor, was an important contributor to the mounting economic recession. In the view of Congressman Jesse Jackson Jr., however, the real issue, aside from scattered voter registration problems—which ACORN readily admitted and assisted in investigating—was that the rich are "scared of too many poor people preparing to vote this year" (qtd. in Burns 2008).

Founded in Arkansas in 1970 by Wade Rathke, ACORN, which describes itself as a coalition of local groups advocating for election, economic, and social equity, has deep philosophical roots in the perspective of Saul Alinsky. With over five hundred thousand dues-paying members across the United States, by the end of 2009 ACORN employed community organizing strategies to secure a series of landmark victories in areas like community reinvestment policies, fair lending practices, living wages standards, education reform, free school lunches, Vietnam veterans' rights, and environmental justice. Consequently, there is a long history of conservative efforts to defund and demonize ACORN (usually around the time of elections) (Maddow 2009), a pattern that is reminiscent of efforts prior to the passage of the Voting Rights Act of 1965 to prevent the voting registration of African Americans in the South.

After the election in September 2009, Fox News featured several hidden-camera videotapes produced by James O'Keefe, a conservative activist (known for having attempted a similar but failed "expose" of Planned Parenthood in previous years), in which he and a female colleague, Hannah Giles, posing as a pimp and a prostitute, seek assistance in tax preparation or in receiving a mortgage loan from ACORN employees. In the videos, shot in several cities, O'Keefe and Giles state that they need ACORN's help to support their illegal prostitution business, leading to various suggestions and advice from some ACORN employees, although no actual applications were completed. Not shown were videos shot in those cities where no advice was provided or, as was the case in Philadelphia, where ACORN staff called the police. Although all of the employees involved in providing advice were fired, and the behavior was roundly condemned by ACORN directors as a violation of organizational policy, on September 17, 2009, Congress voted (via H.R.3571—the Defund ACORN Act and a parallel Senate bill) to eliminate federal funding for ACORN. In response, the Center for Constitutional Rights (2009) brought a lawsuit against the U.S. government on behalf of ACORN, charging Congress with having violated the U.S. Constitution. The lawsuit was based on an explicit constitutional prohibition against "Bills of Attainder," which are laws that single out an individual or group for punishment without an investigation and trial. Despite this effort to defend itself, and the subsequent arrest of James O'Keefe and conviction for attempting to tamper with the phones in Senator Mary Landrieu's (D-La.) office, loss of donor and government funding forced ACORN to disband as a national organization in 2010 (although local and state organizations continue to function under various names). Subsequently, the district attorney in Brooklyn concluded that staff in the Brooklyn ACORN office had not been involved in the violation of any laws, the attorney general of California found that videos made by O'Keefe in several ACORN offices in the state were significantly edited prior to public release, and the U.S. Government Accountability Office reported that there was no evidence that ACORN misused federal dollars.

As this example suggests, community organizing is seen to be such a sufficient threat to the status quo of inequality that it motivates resorting to even the most extreme measures. Put otherwise, community organizing is seen by those who oppose it as a very effective method for leveling the playing field, and hence it is a method worthy of consideration by medical anthropologists interested in playing a role in influencing health policy.

Community Organizing and Anthropology:
Implications for Policy Work

What is the relationship of the anthropological approach as it has evolved over time to community organizing? If the practice of community organizing is to reach out to and continually bring in new people, broadening the networks of communication and change-oriented activism, the dominant practice in anthropology, the one that has tended to gain the most recognition and disciplinary reward, is in the opposite direction. Generally, as Okongwu and Mencher (2000, 109) observe, "Anthropologists have tended to write mainly for other anthropologists, not for those who have the power to change the world." As a result, Stull and Moos (1981, 18) remarked a number of years ago that "in comparison with other social and behavior sciences, anthropology . . . has been conspicuously absent in the policy process." In this, medical and other anthropologists have been like most other people in society who have for many years felt "alienated from an increasingly remote and commercialized policy-making process" (Shore and Wright 1997, 3).

Notably, however, public reaction to the Obama presidential victory in 2008, as was well expressed by the scale of popular involvement in his inauguration, has been interpreted as an expressed hope for empowerment, as a desire to end alienation of the masses. Whether this optimism will be realized remains to be seen, although there is uncertainty aplenty among progressives based on events since the swearing in of the forty-fourth president of the United States. The way over the top, and in equal parts vicious and wacky, backlash against Obama that we have witnessed since he took office, however, shows how even the hint of more equitable policies afflicts the comfortable. This merits our attention as we are likely to see challenges from the same quarters concerning the right of a field like medical anthropology to have a policy role.

Of course, the ability and desirability of anthropology being active in policy has been an issue of contestation. Despite a sense of rarely having a dependable seat at the policy table, some anthropologists certainly have been drawn to policy making as an activity that appears to have the potential to make a difference in the world. As Hamann et al. (2007, ii) observe, in the twenty-first century, "'policy' has become an immensely powerful almost magical word."

In seeking entry to the policy arena, however, we encounter immediately a fundamental dilemma. As Peter Marris (qtd. in Singer and Castro 2004, xvi) has said, "Policy is governed by entrenched myth." Consequently, the relationship of anthropologists and their colleagues in allied disciplines with policy makers historically has been conflicted, a thing of starts and stops, and at times a merry-go-round. As noted above, many anthropologists, including those with a health focus, who have ventured into this domain, soon realized that their findings, gained through endless hours of work under, at times, the most difficult of on-the-ground conditions, may be ignored and that their research-informed recommendations go unheeded. One reason for this is that the complex "truths" our research produces often are out of harmony with the official and usually simplistic truths formulated by the few who have tended to control the health, environmental, educational, and social policy arenas (Lee and Goodman 2002; Nichter 2008), overtly or implicitly in the interests of the capitalist class (Janes and Corbett 2009; Singer and Castro 2004).

Perhaps the closest I personally have come to witnessing this process in action occurred in 1994, when, through a curious quirk of circumstance I was invited with many others to a meeting with Hillary Clinton at the White House. At the time, Clinton, who was heading a presidential task force, was struggling to overcome the staunch opposition led by the Project for the Republican Future, the Heritage Foundation, and the Health Insurance Association of America to the implementation of a comprehensive national policy on universal health care. At the meeting, Clinton stressed that the assembled, representatives of health-focused NGOs from the Northeast had been called together because she and her husband were encountering immense difficulty in getting their message about the benefits of universal health care out to the American people. Indeed, during this period, media powerhouses like *Time*, CBS News, CNN, the *Wall Street Journal,* and the *Christian Science Monitor,* among others, were all running stories questioning whether there really was a health care crisis in America. Clinton's words were sobering. If the president of the United States and the head of a presidential task force could not make their voices heard on a key national policy issue that was contested by powerful economic interests, how can medical anthropologists, relatively few in number and having a celebrated tendency to resist being herded, have any organized effect at all on health policy?

This example underlines what has become a painful reality in the formation of American policy, especially with reference to health-related issues: powerful, well-funded lobbies have gained enormous control over the policy agenda, especially at the federal level (Singer 2010). As Robert Kaiser (2009), a *Washington Post* associate editor, has written, "Forty years ago, lobbying was the work of a small group of lawyers and fixers; today, it is a multibillion-dollar industry involving thousands of people, including nearly two hundred ex-senators and former House members from both parties. . . . When asked to explain why lobbying had grown so dramatically during the four decades in which he has thrived in the business, Robert Strauss, the former chairman of the Democratic National Committee, had a simple explanation: 'There's just so damn much money in it.'" By way of example, Kaiser pointed to the bill of 2003 that created a drug benefit for Medicare recipients, a piece of legislation that was directly written by lobbyists for the pharmaceutical industry according to Representative Walter Jones of North Carolina. The bill blocked the federal government from negotiating with drug companies over the prices that would be paid for drugs purchased through Medicare, a process that had previously been a routine way of lowering prices to the consumer. To shore up its support for this unhealthy health policy, the pharmaceutical industry donated tens of millions of dollars to the campaign efforts of members of Congress, two thirds of it to Republicans between 2000 and 2006.

More recently, in the great national health insurance debates of 2009–10, sparked by Obama's drive to dramatically reform health care coverage for the American population, the health insurance industry mobilized its army of lobbyists to oppose the inclusion of a government backed "public option" as a competitive alternative to insurance company control of people's access to health care. Despite a track record, since the failed Clinton effort to reform health care coverage, of dramatic rises in costs of privatized health care at a pace that outstrips increases in personal income and overall economic growth, the industry publically announced and publically argued (through a well-managed and heavily funded public relations effort) that it is the public option that will cause health costs to rise. This is typical, according to Wendell Potter, the former head of corporate communications at Cigna, who asserts that the industry routinely engages in duplicitous public relations and lobbying campaigns (see Hilzenrath 2009).

Exemplary of this practice is the industry's publicity campaign, led by America's Health Insurance Plans (AHIP)—a lobbying group that represents over one thousand two hundred member companies—in opposition to the public option. Repeatedly AHIP, which spent over six million dollars on lobbying efforts in the first half of 2009 (OpenSecrets.org 2009), claimed that research showed that over 75 percent of Americans were happy with their health insurance coverage. The poll cited to support this assertion, a *New York* ✓ *Times* and CBS News survey of June 2009, actually found that 72 percent of participants favored a public option. In this survey participants also said that they believed the government would do a better job than private insurers of holding health care costs down and providing fuller coverage (Hilzenrath 2009). Nonetheless, the airwaves were filled with industry advertisements that distorted the findings of the survey.

As Linda Whiteford and Cecilia Vindrola Padros (2011, 210) have observed, "by analyzing who makes policies and how they make them," one thing anthropologists can do is to "show that policies are not neutral, but rather reflect and represent the concepts and ideas of the groups that have the power to make them." As things stand now in the United States, as Vicente Navarro (2009) stresses, "the enormous power of the insurance and pharmaceutical industries corrupts the nature of our democracy and shapes the frontiers of what is possible in the U.S." Thus, while the national health reform legislation that passed in 2010 includes important healthy provisions, like banning insurance companies from denying coverage to people with preexisting conditions, the continued reliance on private for-profit companies to provide insurance coverage for both the existing and thirty-two million additional insurance customers ensures that there will be ongoing efforts to find loopholes that allow increased charges and reduced benefits to the public. Contrary to conservative criticism of the new law, as the political commentator and comedian Bill Maher (2009) aptly observes, "The problem with President Obama's health care plan isn't socialism, it's capitalism."

This discussion returns us to the central problems of this chapter: How can we, as medical anthropologists, have impact in the perverse, unjust, and iniquitous world of health policy? How can we participate in meaningfully reshaping the frontiers of what is possible? And why would we want to? The issue of anthropological motivation for policy involvement is laid out clearly by Cris Shore and Susan Wright in their book *Anthropology of Policy: Critical Perspectives on Governance and Power* (1997). As they stress (Shore and Wright 1997, 4), "Policy has become an increasingly central concept and instrument in the organization of contemporary societies. Like the modern state . . . policy now impinges on all areas of life so that it is virtually impossible to ignore or escape its influence. More than this, policy increasingly shapes the way individuals construct themselves as subjects. Through policy, the individual is categorized and given such statuses and roles as 'subject,' 'citizen,' 'professional,' 'national,' 'criminal' and 'deviant.' From the cradle to the grave, people are classified, shaped, and ordered according to policies, but they may have little consciousness of or control over the processes at work." As a consequence, policy immediately impacts issues long central to anthropology, while the study of policy "leads straight into issues at the heart of anthropology: norms and institutions; ideology and consciousness; knowledge and power; rhetoric and discourse; meaning and interpretations; the global and the local—to mention but a few" (Shore and Wright 1997, 4).

Until now, however, most of our responses to this realization have been confined to analyses of the policy process and critiques of its often problematic effects. Far less common is the effort to systematically and effectively translate research into policy development (Van Willigen 2002). If the latter is part of our defined professional mission then we must begin to explore ways to overcome past obstacles. In this venture Davis and Matthews (1999) offer cogent advice. In the past, they note, anthropologists seeking to influence policy have played the role of data generators who provide information for the decisions made by those in a position to formulate or revise social policies. As an alternative, they propose assessment of policy-related issues in light of the role that policy plays in the operation of structures of power. By aligning themselves with those most negatively impacted by prevailing practices and policies, anthropologists can ensure that the results of their work are directed to the hands of citizens and community groups struggling for access, rights, and resources to address their needs.

One starting point for successfully carrying out the program proposed by Davis and Matthews (1999) lies in the very important and very needed work of creating expanded training of students, getting them to think regularly about the nature, formation, and effects of health policy, the policy implications of their research, and new approaches for the mobilization of research into meaningful policy change. As Sawchuck (1993, 286) stresses, while "our anthropological training leaves us with little understanding of the inside workings of the government or of the constraints or needs of policy makers," it equips us with the skills to learn this information using the holistic and grounded approach to knowledge characteristic of the discipline. While policy issues are taught currently in some anthropology courses, particularly those within the field of applied anthropology, an enhanced focus on health policy as a fundamental topic within medical anthropology courses is critical to our ability to move from occasional to regular influence in health policy decisions and to break free of the traditional narrow characterizations of anthropology as the study of the exotic and the obscure. One option for medical anthropology students to receive policy training is through programs like the Public Policy Project, which offers an eight-week, hands-on learning program designed to examine the policy process, aid strategic planning, facilitate policy issues identification, build community organizing and civic engagement, and provide skills for advocacy campaign management. Similarly, some colleges and universities offer summer training in policy issues that might be assessed for relevance by medical anthropology programs.

Beyond encouraging policy training for medical anthropology students, in light of the discussion that has been presented, this chapter is primarily concerned with proposing an approach for enhancing the role of anthropologists in policy. This approach involves linking with citizen and community efforts and the development of working allies in the policy arena. Here, I am concerned especially with developing strong relations with a specific ally, the very one brought into action by Alinsky's initiatives, the same one that gave Obama his on-the-job training in working for change, and the one embodied in the civil rights movement: namely, community-based organizers and activists. On the campaign trail, as his opponents tried to turn community organizing into a dirty word and a grave and looming threat to the democratic election process, Obama responded by saying that many people do not know what community organizing is and that he himself had an incomplete understanding of it when he became a community organizer. In time he came to understand that community organizing is "people working at the grassroots level to bring about change" (Obama 2008). Through community organizing, he explained at a presidential campaign news conference, "you can . . . match the power of corporations and lobbyists to actually influence what is going on in a place like Washington" (Obama 2008).

These remarks are reminiscent of a paper on community organizing that Obama wrote almost twenty years earlier in which he argued that many of our persistent problems "do not result from a lack of effective solutions, but from a lack of power to implement these solutions" (Obama 1990, 36). If this is true, then finding a way to make mutually beneficial common cause with community organizers makes a lot of sense as medical anthropologists seek to make their voices heard on key health-related policy issues. To reiterate a point made at the outset of this chapter, by promoting and fostering collaboration and coalition building, which are stated goals of the SMA, with the national movement of community-based organizers inspired and trained by Saul Alinsky and his descendants, we position ourselves to participate in leveling the playing field.

There is a natural basis for such unity born of the relative strengths and weaknesses of community organizing and medical anthropology. The strength of community organizing, of course, is its ability to mobilize on behalf of an issue of heartfelt and just concern. Its Achilles' heel, as Alinsky well knew, is the ever-present danger that the ideology that motivates movements for social change will deteriorate into dogma. In his disdain for dogma, Alinsky turned to the words of the atomic physicist Niels Bohr, who stressed that "every sentence I utter must be understood not as an affirmation, but as a question" (qtd. in Alinsky 1971, 4). This is, of course, a basic principle and strength of science and of research, namely that while certainty is pursued, it is never achieved. At the same time, a limitation in the arsenal of most researchers is our ability to translate insight into concrete action for a common good. As noted in the NIH Roadmap for Medical Research, "To improve human health, scientific discoveries must be translated into practical applications." Yet, argues Carmen Head (2008), a granddaughter of a survivor of the infamous Tuskegee syphilis study, one of the difficult questions we face is how to successfully "engage and influence the world's policymakers, religious, and opinion leaders in an effort to create new laws and regulations, provide resources where lacking, and promote political and moral will." In their respective arrays of strengths and fragilities medical anthropology and community organizing appear as compatible allies for achieving this objective. Experience suggests that collaboration is facilitated when associates share common goals, but supplement rather than duplicate each other's capacities. Such an alliance in the pursuit of public health policy change exemplifies the kind of exciting intersectorial work in the new millennium that the SMA aimed to promote through its conference "Medical Anthropology at the Intersections: Celebrating 50 Years of Interdisciplinarity," upon which this volume is based.

Community-Based Collaboration

It is in part to overcome this danger, as well as to expand the policy impact of medical anthropology, that I see value in collaboration with community organizers. My views on this are influenced by many years of experience working in a direct service, policy- and advocacy-oriented, and research-driven community-based health organization, the Hispanic Health Council in Hartford, Connecticut. One of the lessons of that experience is captured in a comparison made by Labonte (1996), who said that the process of policy change can be likened to a nutcracker, with one arm comprised of data-rich research and policy reports and the other consisting of organized community pressure. Cracking entrenched, outdated, and unhealthy health policy requires both arms working together. For example, there is the issue of preventing the spread of HIV/AIDS among injection drug users through the development of sterile syringe access policies. Efforts to initiate syringe exchange in Hartford, an undertaking with which anthropologists have been consistently involved, date to the latter years of the 1980s (Singer, Irizarry, and Schensul 1991; Singer 1991). This work began as part of a statewide community-based initiative aimed at changing Connecticut state laws banning syringe purchase or possession without a prescription. As part of this grassroots effort, an ad hoc community coalition of concerned individuals and groups interested in syringe exchange was formed in Hartford in the early 1990s. This coalition had its roots in a citywide community meeting organized by a group of social work students and their professor, but it attracted a broad range of representatives from community-based organizations as well as AIDS advocates. Shortly thereafter, several CBOs, including the Hispanic Health Council, publicly endorsed syringe exchange and urged that its operation be community directed.

Subsequently, a community organizing effort was launched to enhance public awareness of syringe exchange, address various concerns people had about providing syringes to drug injectors, and build a broad base of support for policy changes needed to allow the implementation of syringe exchange. Anthropologists already working in AIDS research were able to help this grassroots effort by providing research findings showing that: (1) over 50 percent of injection drug users tested in an AIDS outreach project in the city were seropositive for HIV infection, suggesting the critical importance of prevention efforts for this population; (2) the vast majority of drug users interviewed in this project both supported and said they would make use of syringe exchange if it were available; and (3) there was considerable popular support for syringe exchange in all neighborhoods of the city based on door-to-door community surveys. These data, collected, analyzed, and assembled by community-based anthropologists, were shared with partner organizations and presented at public hearings called by state legislative committees and subsequently the Hartford City Council concerning existing syringe access policies. Furthermore, anthropologists publicly testified at state and city hearings in support of syringe exchange and arranged for HIV-infected drug users to testify at a City Council meeting called to review the implementation of syringe exchange. During the legislative session of 1992, the state's fourteen-year-old drug paraphernalia law (that criminalized possession of a syringe without a prescription) was rescinded, a syringe exchange authorization bill was passed, and funds were made available through both the Connecticut Department of Health Services and the Hartford Health Department to implement a syringe exchange program in Hartford. Nineteen years later this program is still in operation and rates of new HIV/AIDS infection among injection drug users are significantly lower than before the program was put into operation (Heimer et al. 2002).

To cite another example of the successful marriage of medical anthropology and community organizing, there is Merrill Eisenberg's work for over ten years on disability policy issues. This work began when she was hired as an advocacy coordinator at a newly developed Independent Living Center (ILC) in Hartford. Funded through Title VII of the federal Rehabilitation Act, ILCs were designed to assist people with disabilities with housing, transportation, and personal care so that they could live independently in communities. Further, ILCs were organized to help empower program participants to advocate for themselves. In Connecticut this was interpreted to mean building political advocacy on behalf of people with disabilities as well, which was the assignment given to Eisenberg.

To begin her work, after gaining a better understanding of the lay of the land in the Connecticut disabilities community, Eisenberg conducted a series of semistructured interviews and engaged in participant observation with people who had experience in disability policy, including the lobbyists and executive directors of disability service agencies. To gain a better understanding of the views and experiences of the population being served, she also conducted semistructured interviews and helped to organize a day-long community meeting to discuss program and policy concerns with people who had a wide range of disabilities. During the meeting, participants told their personal stories, discussed their perspectives, and offered policy recommendations. These she assembled into a brochure, which was nationally distributed by the Easter Seals Society.

At a subsequent meeting with a state legislator, the issue was raised about the need, in light of the conservative swing at the federal level that was likely to usher in cuts in disabilities funding, to change state policy by inserting the words "physical or mental disability" into the equal protection clause of the Connecticut state constitution, a passage intended to bar discrimination against identified vulnerable groups.

Eisenberg's next task was to investigate all of the political, legal, and judicial implications of amending the state constitution to win the support of a key legislator, the chairman of the Judiciary Committee. While this entailed engaging in types of research that were new to her, ultimately the concerns of the committee chairman were satisfied and a bill was developed that proposed changing the state constitution. To support passage of the bill, Eisenberg helped to organize a statewide education campaign and a set of "democracy skills" training workshops for people with disabilities so that they were prepared to advocate for the bill with their state senators and representatives. A grassroots advocacy network was also established to facilitate people with disabilities and their supporters contacting elected officials, and speakers were recruited for public hearings on the amendment. As a result of this activist campaign, the bill passed the House and was referred to the Senate, where a lower key approach was successfully implemented. This enabled the bill to be placed on the ballot for state voters to decide, which they did, in support of amending the state constitution. Notes Eisenberg (2010, 8), the "infrastructure that was created in order to pass the constitutional amendment and the success of that effort contributed to increased feelings of political empowerment and participation in policy issues by people with disabilities across the state," which fueled a series of subsequent initiatives to address the rights and needs of people with disabilities in the state of Connecticut.

Conclusion

There has been considerable discussion in recent years about the need to close the gap between public health practice and research evidence, as well as substantial uncertainty about how this goal is best accomplished. A parallel gap exists between health policy and research, and similar hesitation prevails about how to narrow this divide. Medical anthropologists are keenly aware of the later issue, and they believe our discipline has something to offer the effort to create beneficial and research-informed health policy at local, regional, national, and global levels (e.g., with reference to responding to the multiple and unequally distributed health challenges of global warming and other anthropogenic ecocrises). While discussions about the need for identifying strategic allies to achieve imperative social goals often is phrased as a search for friends in high places, an alternative approach is the development of friends in more marginal places but with high aspirations. While medical anthropology and community organizing have their similarities and differences, their specific strengths and their unfortunate weaknesses, and, no doubt, more than a few points of tension and potential areas of disagreement, a strategic alliance, seen as a respectful meeting of equals with complementary resources, offers one road to the achievement of shared health policy objectives. As Pol De Vos and coworkers (2009, 32) have recently noted, "If marginalized groups and classes organize, they can influence power relations and pressure the state into action. Such popular pressure through organized communities and people's organizations can play an essential role in ensuring the implementation of adequate government policies to address health inequities." This is what is required to assert the "right to health," and this approach, which they label "health through people's empowerment," provides common ground for the collaboration of policy-oriented anthropological researchers and change-oriented community organizers. While different contexts offer varied opportunities and challenges for such collaboration (e.g., the ability for the medical anthropologist to engage policy issues differs in domestic versus foreign settings), globalization and flows of people, commodities, production, and pathogens create transnational fields (e.g., border areas) where the policies of one country impact the health of another.

Earlier, George Bernard Shaw was quoted with regard to the shortcomings of our world and our need to be active in it. An even more famous quote of his, one picked up and effectively used by a president of the United States is this: "You see things and you wonder, 'Why?' I dream of things that never were and wonder, 'Why not?'" (Shaw 1949, 7). This seems an appropriate foundation for anthropological work in policy.

Critical Intersections and Engagements

Gender, Sexuality, Health, and Rights in Medical Anthropology

A key theme throughout this book is the extent to which the field of medical anthropology has been shaped by its fundamental interdisciplinarity —by its connections and intersections with a range of related fields and disciplines. If this is undeniably true of medical anthropology as a whole, perhaps nowhere is it more clearly evident than in medical anthropology's engagement with issues related to gender and sexuality. Indeed, in the medical anthropological work that has been carried out on these issues over the course of the past fifty years, what I view as one of the truly defining characteristics of the field emerges with particular clarity: its intersection not only with related academic disciplines but also with emerging activist movements that have shaped the topics that it has examined, the issues that it has prioritized, and even the "ways of knowing" that it has developed. Throughout this chapter, while focusing broadly on gender and sexuality and their relation to both health and rights, I want to emphasize the embeddedness of medical anthropology in activism: feminist activism, AIDS activism, population and reproductive rights activism, and, most recently, sexual rights activism. I want to highlight the ways in which our engagement in activism and in political critique has given the field not only much of its intellectual energy but also a significant part of its practical impact.

In order to make this case, it is especially important to trace the historical developments and trends over time leading up to the contemporary moment in gender and sexuality research in medical anthropology. In particular I want to emphasize the importance of four major movements that have shaped work in this area. First, I will highlight the importance of feminism, and of related social movements, in shaping the context of research and analysis from the early 1970s up to the present. Second, I will examine the role of HIV and AIDS, and of engagement with AIDS activism beginning in the 1980s and continuing up to the present day, in providing an ongoing focus for medical anthropological attention. Third, I will look at the ways in which medical anthropology has been part of an important shift in paradigms from a focus on population control, which dominated much of the mid-twentieth century, to a new emphasis on reproductive health and rights, which began to emerge in the late 1980s and early 1990s and has continued to influence the field up to the present. Finally, I will turn to an emerging focus, since the mid- to late 1990s and more clearly during the first decade of the twenty-first century, on what has increasingly been described as the area of sexual rights, building on, yet distinct from, the earlier focus on reproductive rights.

Throughout the following discussion, my goal will be to highlight not only much of the most important scholarship that emerged in relation to these various topics but also the contested character of the construction of knowledge in these areas. I will also offer at least some sense of the ways in which theory is inevitably linked to practice, often in deeply personal ways, for those of us working in this field—and will suggest that this linkage is of no small importance for understanding the ways in which our work has developed. Finally, I will present a number of the key challenges facing the field and discuss the ways in which these challenges might shape an agenda for medical anthropology as it moves into the future.

Feminism, Gender and Sexuality Studies, and Medical Anthropology

The connections between activism and the production of knowledge in medical anthropology are clearly demonstrated by the influence that the new wave of feminism that emerged in the 1960s had on anthropological work on gender beginning in the 1970s and early 1980s, as well as by the impact of the slightly later lesbian, gay, bisexual, and transgender (LGBT) movements on the field over the course of the 1980s and beyond. As I will suggest below, over time other newer social movements have also become increasingly important, but the work inspired by feminism in the 1970s and 1980s is a clear point of departure for thinking about this field of work within medical anthropology.

The key contributions that medical anthropology has made to work on women's health, and the interface between feminism and medical anthropology, is surely subject enough for any number of different analyses—and is highlighted in this book's first chapter by Emily Martin.

My task has also been made much easier because of the important review published just a few years ago by Marcia Inhorn in *Medical Anthropology Quarterly* that highlighted the key contributions of medical anthropology to the field of women's health based on a review of more than 150 ethnographic studies (Inhorn 2006). In this review, Inhorn emphasized the importance of anthropological work in listening to women's voices to determine their own health priorities, in understanding that women's health cannot be separated from the social, cultural, political, and economic context in which it is shaped, and in critiquing the inequalities that exist in health care services and service delivery. If not for the impact of feminism and a new generation of scholars in the 1970s and 1980s, and continuing on up to the present, it is impossible to imagine that such work would have been carried out.

While this body of work is by now quite extensive, it is worth calling attention to some of the groundbreaking ethnographic studies that paved the way for the development of a feminist medical anthropology and that have continued to sustain it over the course of recent decades. Key studies such as Emily Martin's *The Woman in the Body: A Cultural Analysis of Reproduction* (1987) and Faye Ginsburg's *Contested Lives: The Abortion Debate in an American Community* (1989), for example, engaged with the broader feminist project of critical analysis of women's health and reproduction in contemporary North American society. Studies such as Nancy Scheper-Hughes's *Death without Weeping: The Structural Violence of Everyday Life in Brazil* (1992) explored similar issues in the Global South, linking the examination of women's experiences to a deep concern with structures of inequality and social exclusion. Robbie Davis-Floyd's *Birth as an American Rite of Passage* (1992) and Margaret Lock's *Encounters with Aging: Mythologies of Menopause in Japan and North America* (1995) explored social and cultural constructions of women's health at widely different points in the life course, while Marcia Inhorn's *Quest for Conception: Gender, Infertility, and Egyptian Medical Traditions* (1994) and Rayna Rapp's *Testing Women, Testing the Fetus: The Social Impact of Amniocentesis in America* (1999) examined the complex construction of women's bodies in relation to cultural understandings of reproduction, as well as of science and technology.

In seeking to map the complex intellectual landscape of these works, and many others like them, Inhorn's review details a wide range of messages and themes that emerged from medical anthropological work on women's health in recent decades. While the limitations of space make it impossible to cover all of them here (see Inhorn 2006 for the full review), I want to emphasize at least a few of the most influential: the social and cultural construction of women's bodies (see, for example, Martin 1987; Rapp 1999); the reproductive essentialization of women's bodies (see Browner 2000; Inhorn 1994; Rapp 1999; Scheper-Hughes 1992); the biomedicalization of women's lives (Davis-Floyd 1992; Hunt 1999; Inhorn 1996; Sargent 1989); the negative health effects of patriarchy (Croll 2000; Inhorn 1996); the politics of women's health (Anagnost 1995; Ginsburg 1989; Ginsburg and Rapp 1991, 1995; Gruenbaum 2001; Maternowska 2006); and the importance of women's local moral worlds (Hirsch 2003; Inhorn 2003a; Kahn 2000; Rapp 1999). Inhorn's review also calls special attention to work in medical anthropology that has drawn on and contributed to intersectionality theory in feminist scholarship (Crenshaw 1991). Intersectionality theory, which highlights the intersection of gender with race, class, and other axes of inequality (Maternowska 2006; Mullings 1997; Schulz and Mullings 2006; Sobo 1995; Sterk 1999; Viveros Vigoya 2002; White 1999), is a particularly important line of inquiry that has significantly influenced both medical anthropology and other fields of inquiry for a number of decades. I emphasize these themes, among others, precisely because they give a good sense of what I think is the most important abiding legacy of the feminist roots of this whole area of work: their critical stance in relation to social inequality generally and in relation to the reproduction of inequalities in the fields of biomedicine, the health sciences, and the social sciences as they address issues of health and illness (see Inhorn 2006). It is this ongoing emphasis over the course of the past four decades that has most clearly driven our research agendas and analyses, and it is among the most important contributions of work in this area (and at this intersection) to medical anthropology more generally.

It is also this legacy, inspired by feminist critique, that I think drives much of the most important work that has been done as we shift from women's health to the health of a wide range of sexual *others*. Many of the same themes are reproduced here, with slightly different but nonetheless important inflections: the medicalization of nonnormative sexualities (Blackwood 1986; Fry 1982; Perlongher 1987); the negative health effects of patriarchy as it interfaces with compulsory heterosexuality (Carrier 1995; Gutmann 1996); the stigmatization of sexual difference (Lancaster 1988, 1992, 1995; Parker and Aggleton 2003; Plummer 1975; Tan 1995, 1996); the often tragic impact of sexual discrimination and violence (Epprecht 2004; Nanda 1990; Prieur 1998); and the intersectionality of sexuality with gender, race, class, and other axes of inequality (Blackwood and Wieringa 1999; Hawkeswood 1996; Manderson and Jolly 1997; Parker 1999; Tan 2001). Much of the most important work that has been carried out on nonnormative genders and sexualities across cultures and in diverse communities, and on the ways in which medicine and medical sciences have impacted on sexual diversity, has operated in the same spaces originally opened up by feminist concerns; until very recently, however, it has been if anything even more marginalized than early feminist work. Indeed, it is worth remembering that while many of the earliest feminist scholars in anthropology had to confront male-dominated departments and barriers at every turn, many of the earliest lesbian and gay scholars, working openly on lesbian and gay issues, were not even able to work within the academy and for the most part had to carry out their work as independent scholars, at least in the 1980s and early 1990s (Carrier 2001; Murray 1992; Taylor 1985).

Much has, of course, changed over the course of the past decade, or decade and a half, but the ongoing influence of social movements and social mobilization more broadly on this field of research and analysis is certainly one of the ongoing continuities. The breadth and diversity of movements has changed over time—to the early influence of second-wave feminism and an emerging LGBT movement, we might add AIDS activist and later treatment access movements starting in the mid-1980s and continuing to exert influence up to the present (Robins 2006), transnational women's health movements that gained force in the late 1980s and early 1990s (Turshen 2007), the health and human rights movement that began to take shape in the 1990s (Farmer 1999), and, as I will discuss below, the emerging sexual rights movement that has grown significantly during the past decade (Corrêa, Petchesky, and Parker 2008; Parker 1997; Petchesky 2000). The key point that I want to make is that the interface with social movements and political critique has given this area of work its most special quality. For better or worse, it has perhaps made us vulnerable to the criticism of those who favor a less engaged academic pursuit or who believe that scientific objectivity is somehow compromised by political engagement. But it has also been a source of inspiration for those of us who believe that values matter and that the role of the university is to engage with society and raise critical questions that matter beyond the exigencies of the present.

The Impact of HIV and AIDS

Having briefly laid out a number of issues related to the first major influence that I see in relation to work on gender, sexuality, LGBT issues, and related questions within medical anthropology, let me turn to the second: the impact of HIV and AIDS since the early 1980s. While many of the leading medical anthropologists in the past two decades have made major contributions to AIDS research (see, for example, Biehl 2007; Farmer 1992; Fassin 2007; Singer 1998; Susser 2009), the importance of HIV and AIDS research in medical anthropology appears to have been in decline in recent years, and work focusing primarily on the epidemic was not chosen as one of the main topics of intersection in structuring the present book. Yet HIV and AIDS continue to be major areas of concern for work in medical anthropology (Hirsch et al. 2010; Schoepf 2001; Singer et al. 2006; Thornton 2008) and important areas of engagement for anthropologists both inside and outside the academy. And the impact of HIV and AIDS has undeniably been especially important in the areas of gender, LGBT studies, and sexuality studies more generally (Brummelhuis and Herdt 1995; Herdt 1997; Parker 2001; Parker and Gagnon 1995).

It is important to emphasize that anthropology as a discipline was relatively slow to respond during the earliest years of the HIV epidemic. It may be that the discipline's traditional emphasis on cross-cultural research proved to be a disadvantage in the context of a crisis that was initially perceived to be concentrated primarily in the gay communities of the United States. Whatever the cause, psychologists and psychologically inclined behavioral scientists in applied public health research settings tended to enter into HIV and AIDS research before anthropologists did and quickly began to shape epidemiological as well as social and behavioral research (see Turner, Miller, and Moses 1989, including the section authored by Shirley Lindenbaum on relevant anthropological research). While the geographic focus may have been an early impediment to anthropological research on HIV, there is no doubt that stigma, discrimination and homophobia within the discipline (and within the academy more generally) also played an important role. It should not be forgotten that the first significant anthropological collection of cross-cultural research on homosexuality was published only in the mid-1980s, five years after the earliest cases of AIDS had been reported (see Blackwood 1986).

Early resistance to conducting anthropological research on HIV was overcome only with a great deal of struggle and with concerted effort, particularly on the part of those from affected communities (Herdt 1987). Over time, the HIV epidemic has stimulated the expansion of research in medical anthropology on sexuality and, although slightly later, on gender as well (Herdt 1997; Parker 2001, 2009; Parker and Gagnon 1995). The evolving field of medical anthropology has come to be characterized by sharp critiques of epidemiological and biomedical categories and epistemologies, as well as by comparable critiques of behavioral science research and research methods (Bastos 1999; Brummelhuis and Herdt 1995; Clatts 1995; de Zalduondo 1991; Kane and Mason 1992; Parker 2001). More than any other discipline, medical anthropology has offered a key alternative to these approaches through its emphasis on the ethnographic study of local sexual and drug-using cultures and on the social and cultural construction of sexual and drug use experience (Feldman 2008; Herdt and Lindenbaum 1992; Singer 1998; Singer et al. 1992).

Starting in the late 1980s, a concern with HIV and AIDS unleashed a new wave of important empirical investigation in medical anthropology in the United States and around the world. Studies of same-sex relations between men, injecting drug users and their relationships with sexual partners of diverse types, the social organization of prostitution and sex work, female as well as male and transgender, and the sexual experience and sexual cultures of young people all became important contributions of medical anthropology and areas of work that were furthered in major ways by the application of anthropologically inspired ethnographic methods (see, for example, Aggleton 1996, 1999; Amuchástegui 2001; de Zalduondo 1991; Heilborn et al. 2006; Hunter 2002, 2005; Katsulis 2009; Kuklick 1998; Lorway 2006, 2008a, 2009; Lorway, Sushena, and Pasha 2008b; Marshall, Singer, and Clatts 1999; Parker

1987). While such approaches have never been in what might be described as the mainstream of AIDS research (psychologists and behavioral scientists in public health have continued to play a more central role in epidemiological, social, and behavioral research, as well as to dominate review committees and available research funding), ethnographically grounded studies of local experience, and of the social, cultural, economic, and political forces and contexts that shape practice in meaningful ways, have nonetheless provided an important alternative to mainstream social and behavioral research on the epidemic and its consequences (Bolton and Singer 1992; Herdt and Lindenbaum 1992; Setel 1999).

While much of the earliest ethnographic and medical anthropological work on HIV was focused on understanding sexual diversity and differing patterns of socially constituted risk—and then deconstructing the often ethnocentric use of categories such as "homosexuality" or "prostitution"—an early focus on the relation between culture and power quickly translated into a perception of the importance of gender power inequalities in shaping women's vulnerability to HIV infection. Indeed, anthropology was out in front of virtually every other academic discipline in terms of calling attention to women and AIDS early in the epidemic, and both ethnographic accounts and anthropologically informed comparative analyses were extremely important in calling broader attention to the risks faced by women in the epidemic (Farmer, Connors, and Simmons 1996; Schoepf 1992; Sobo 1995). And this was as true outside of the United States as it was in medical anthropology in this country, as anthropologists from Latin America, Africa, and Asia played key roles in documenting women's vulnerability in those regions (Amuchástegui 2001; Parker and Galvão 1996; Preston-Whyte 1995; Singhanetra-Renard 1997).

Such work had a major impact on the field more broadly in at least two especially important ways. First, it opened up a new understanding of the relationship between gender inequality and a range of other structural forces such as race, ethnicity, and class, captured in the notion of structural violence (in its own way reflecting a theoretical focus on intersectionality) (Farmer 2004; Farmer, Connors, and Simmons 1996; Hirsch et al. 2010; Lyttleton 2000). By examining multiple axes of inequality, and the synergies produced by their interaction, such work helped to call attention to the structural drivers of HIV infection, as well as to the interaction of multiple epidemics (related to HIV and other infectious diseases but also to drug use, violence, and a host of others health issues) in what Merrill Singer and colleagues have described as "syndemics" (Singer and Clair 2003; Singer et al. 2006). Also (and in part precisely as a result of such concerns), it helped to initiate and push forward a broader shift from the conception of "behavioral risk" to the conception of "social vulnerability"—a strategic framing in relation to the epidemic that would also prove crucial in terms of mobilizing resources not just for research but for scaling up the policy and programmatic responses to the epidemic globally (Ayres et al. 2006). But medical anthropological work was not limited to looking at social epidemiology or the factors structuring social risk in people's lives. It was also crucial and has continued to play an important, ongoing role in documenting, witnessing, and analyzing the experience of people living with HIV and AIDS and in providing important analytic resources in dialogue with AIDS activism (Daniel and Parker 1993; Galvão 2000; Robins 2004, 2006; Robins and von Lieres 2005; Susser 2009; Terto Jr. 1999, 2000; Terto Jr. and García 2008).

The concept of "social death," mentioned by Arthur Kleinman in this book as especially important in work on mental health, was elaborated early in the epidemic by AIDS activists such as my Brazilian colleague Herbert Daniel and was further elaborated in a number of our coauthored essays in the early 1990s (see Daniel and Parker 1993; see also Terto Jr. and García 2008). More recent explorations of the many struggles around treatment access, and the transformation of living with HIV, at least for some who are fortunate enough to have guaranteed treatment access, into a chronic condition have led to the development of key concepts. One key example is Vinh-Kim Nguyen's notion of "therapeutic citizenship"—his focus on the ways in which access to treatment, involvement in research, and engagement with activist organizations can empower people living with HIV by involving them in research in meaningful ways, offering them new understandings of the political, as well as the experiential reality of living in the epidemic (Nguyen 2005; Nguyen et al. 2007). Another is João Biehl's important exploration of the lived experience of what he describes as "pharmaceuticalization"—the emergence of a pharmaceutically centered model of public health as a byproduct of HIV treatment scale-up—and its impact over an extended period on those excluded in multiple ways from the full experience of citizenship in their societies (Biehl 2004, 2006, 2007).

Work on the experience of living with HIV has also gone hand in hand with work on the broader politics of the epidemic—research on policy debates and policy battles, on the political mobilization of affected communities and populations, on AIDS activism and how it has affected the epidemic—and the study of the politics of HIV and AIDS has typically been linked to a broader critique of dominant patterns of governance in global health (Parker 2000a). In the crowded and complicated field of research on policy and politics in relation to the epidemic, medical anthropological work on the politics of AIDS has perhaps been less visible than some of our work on the structural factors shaping the movement of the virus through populations and communities. Medical anthropologists' conceptual creativity and ability to capture the multidimensional complexity of social processes and the fundamental importance of values in driving politics is striking when compared to the more narrow approaches of some of our social science colleagues from other disciplines (Biehl 2005; Fassin 2007; Galvão 2000).

That said, it is also true that medical anthropological work on HIV and AIDS has tended to operate at the margins and even outside the mainstreams of power—both academic and political—in relation to the epidemic. In recent years, as some anthropologists have ridden the tide of conservative U.S. aid programs such as the President's Emergency Plan for AIDS Relief (PEPFAR), launched under the Bush administration and extended by the Obama administration,[1] becoming apologists for abstinence-only strategies and prevention programs, the denial of rights to sex workers, and other similar policy tragedies (see, for example, Green 2003), there have been times when I have wondered when the real values that drive our field will reassert themselves. But the lasting impact of the epidemic on medical anthropology, and of medical anthropological work on HIV and AIDS, I believe, will be our continuing focus on the politics of the epidemic. It will be our ability to contribute to a fuller understanding of what Paula Treichler described more than twenty years ago as an "epidemic of signification" (see Treichler 1987, and more generally, 1999)—and what my colleague Herbert Daniel described as the "ideological virus" that is every bit as dangerous and insidious as the biological virus

(Daniel and Parker 1993)—and our consistently critical engagement with dominant biomedical and epidemiological categories and understandings, as well as with mainstream behavioral research.[2] Working at the margins, we may not have had the impact on policy making that we ideally would like to, probably for a number of different reasons (see, for example, the analysis in Singer's chapter in this book). But it is worth remembering that we have made occasional forays into policy making positions of some importance in agencies such as the World Health Organization (WHO) and in the trenches at UNAIDS, as well as in some national AIDS programs, to highlight the fact that medical anthropologists have played an important policy role even in some highly official settings. We have been most at home, though, in building activist and civil society projects aimed at challenging the status quo—ranging from Paul Farmer and Jim Kim at Partners In Health (PIH) to Merrill Singer and other anthropologists at the Hartford Hispanic Health Council (HHHC) to my Brazilian colleagues and I at the Brazilian Interdisciplinary AIDS Association (ABIA) to community-based organizations and activists groups in Burkina Faso, Côte d'Ivoire, South Africa, India, Thailand, and so many other places.

From Population Control to Reproductive Health and Rights

The third major set of events that I think has had an especially important impact in relation to work on gender, sexuality, and related issues in medical anthropology emerged slightly later than the HIV epidemic, though its roots could surely be traced further back in the long-term criticism of the population control strategies that had emerged as part of the development industry after the Second World War (Corrêa, Petchesky, and Parker 2008; Greenhalgh 1996; Maternowska 2006). This critique began to come to a head, however, in the late 1980s and then especially in the early 1990s through a series of events leading up to the International Conference on Population and Development, held in Cairo in 1994 (Corrêa 1994; Lane 1994). Once again, social movement involvement was critical; feminism gained strength within the field of international development, and the emerging transnational women's health movement began to mobilize in anticipation of the Cairo conference and the International Conference on Women to be held in Beijing in 1995 (Corrêa 1994).

At the heart of this mobilization was bringing women and women's empowerment to the center of the population debate and challenging the way in which the control of women's bodies—and women's subjectivities—had been exercised at the height of the population control movement (Lane 1994; Obermeyer 1999). As part of this broader mobilization, new emphasis was given to the development of applied social science research, including medical anthropology, in countries around the world. Important nongovernmental donors such as the Ford Foundation, the Rockefeller Foundation, and the MacArthur Foundation pledged support for such research, as well as for research training, a key priority, and research and training centers based at universities in every region of the Global South were established and began to train a new generation of researchers in medical anthropology and related disciplines (see Ford Foundation 1991). The WHO program of population and reproductive health began to fund researchers working on these issues based in the Global South, and even bilateral aid programs such as USAID provided support for work that fed into these major trends (see Corrêa, Petchesky, and Parker 2008; Petchesky 2003; Petchesky and Judd 1998).

The direct involvement of anthropologists and other social scientists in the preparation for the Cairo and Beijing conferences was an important part of the intellectual movement taking place in the early 1990s, and while this was not always noticed by academics based in the Global North, the intellectual center of gravity defining the key problems and political perspectives driving work in this area was gradually beginning to shift (Corrêa 1994; Parker et al. 2000; Petchesky 2003). While these changes are still very much in process even today, medical anthropology was going global, and was doing so with consequences that I think we are still seeing even today, almost two decades later. Perhaps somewhat ironically—though also strangely logically—one of the important consequences of rethinking the field of population and seeking to transform it through a new understanding of reproductive health was in fact a new emphasis on the study of masculinity (Cornwall and Lindisfarne 1994; Gutmann 1997; Inhorn 2012; Inhorn et al. 2009). Men's studies had begun to take shape in Global North–centered social sciences during much the same time, but literally exploded in the Global South as a result of the shift to a focus on reproductive health (Jones 2006). "Male involvement" in reproduction and reproductive health research was identified as a high priority, and funding for a new wave of research carried out by anthropologists and other social scientists in Latin America, Asia, and sub-Saharan Africa underwent a kind of boom in the mid-1990s (Gutmann 2003; Louie 2002; Morrell 2001; Ouzgane and Morrell 2005; Osella and Osella 2006; Valdés and Olavarria 1998; Viveros 2001). This development linked up closely to a new wave of theorization, particularly in sociology and anthropology, around hegemonic and nonhegemonic masculinities, normative and nonnormative masculinities (Connell 1995). As part of this broader trend, or set of trends, the social construction of masculinity and men's socialization in relation to both gender and sexuality increasingly came to be understood as key risk factors for men's health, and a body of work in many ways similar to the work that had been carried out for some time in medical anthropology on women's health began to take shape in relation to men's health (Gutmann 2007).

Finally, with the growing influence of reproductive health as a new conceptual framework, there has also been new emphasis on the issue of reproductive rights as a field not only for advocacy but also for research (Rapp and Ginsburg 1995). Ethnographic research on reproductive rights movements—as well as on opposition movements aimed at rolling back reproductive rights (Ginsburg 1989)—had been an important area of medical anthropology work on women's health for some time, but it expanded significantly over the course of the 1990s, particularly with the boom in reproductive health and rights movements that took place in the Global South (Corrêa 1994). A whole new wave of reproductive health and rights research with strong influences from medical anthropological approaches has emerged, particularly across Latin America and many parts of Asia but also in many sub-Saharan African countries (see Petchesky and Judd 1998). This work has of course been deeply intertwined with the feminist and women's health movements, and it has been far more characteristic for researchers in the Global South to have one foot in the academy and another in advocacy settings (Petchesky 2003). Precisely because so much of this work has taken place as part of transnational organizing around reproductive health and rights, one of the key roles for research in medical anthropology has been to document and analyze what might be described as grassroots understandings of reproductive rights—the understandings of women and men in local communities as opposed to those more deeply embedded in or linked to transnational networks.

The Emerging Terrain of Sexual Rights

Finally, the fourth and last of the events or processes that I think has had a key role in shaping the development of work in medical anthropology on gender, sexuality, and LGBT issues has been the development of sexual rights, linked to but nonetheless distinct from reproductive rights, as a newly emerging battleground in the late 1990s and continuing in the past decade. It is important to emphasize that the whole terrain of sexual rights is a conceptual and discursive field that is still in formation, one that is taking shape simultaneously at local, national, regional, and global levels, and because it is a field in the process of construction, it may ultimately move in directions that are still difficult to fully predict. Yet its potential is especially interesting precisely because it suggests a set of convergences between different social and political movements and fields of work that may offer the possibility for developing important new alliances and coalitions (see Corrêa, Petchesky, and Parker 2008; Terto Jr., Victora, and Knauth 2004).

Most directly, we can see a convergence between an important feminist stream (or streams) emerging out of the struggles around the Cairo and Beijing conferences—where the very terminology of sexual rights first ventured onto the battlefield (Petchesky 2000)—with another stream from the multiple LGBT movements (Adam et al. 1999). Indeed, this focus on sexual rights has opened up new possibilities for redressing the long-standing marginalization of lesbian sexualities that existed in work on both HIV and reproductive health (see, for example, Blackwood and Wieringa 1999). It has also been important in drawing new attention to those sexual orientations and gender identities—such as transsexual, two-spirited, queer, and intersexed—that are sometimes wiped away by acronyms such as LGBTTTQI and so forth. While the combination of these diverse categories under an expanding acronym can in some instances represent a powerful statement of explicit political solidarity, its own internal diversity also highlights complex tensions in relation to both meaning and power that medical anthropology has long sought to comprehend as part of its own unique contribution to struggles for greater social inclusion (Corrêa, Petchesky, and Parker 2008).

As these points highlight, the possibilities for broadening this discursive field are hardly limited to mainstream feminist or lesbian and gay activism. In recent years, transgender communities and movements (Currah, Juang, and Price Minter 2006; Valentine 2007), sex worker movements (Agustín 2007; Kempadoo and Doazema 1999), the mobilization of HIV-positive persons and networks (Terto Jr. 1999; Whittaker 1992), and most recently, intersex persons and communities (Cabral and Benzur 2006; Machado 2009)—to name but a few of the newcomers asking for a seat at the table or a voice at the rally—have all grown in importance both in international organizing and international research around sexual rights. As Gayle Rubin noted twenty-five years ago in her classic article, "Thinking Sex," "sexualities keep marching out of the pages of the *Diagnostic and Statistical Manual* and onto the pages of social history" (1984, 287). And just as a growing array of diverse populations and communities has truly given content to the term "sexual diversity," work around sexual rights has provided a forum for building consensus and moving toward coalition. The importance, and the immense difficulties, of such consensus—and coalition—building are perhaps already illustrated by the rapidly expanding acronym of LGBTTTQI, which continues to grow as new letters are added. While the use of this strategy can easily be called into question for obscuring, or even wiping away, important differences between the diverse groups that it encompasses and sometimes appears to conflate (see Corrêa, Petchesky, and Parker 2008), it is also important to acknowledge that rather than simply conflating difference, this acronym and this new LGBTTTQI identity is also another way of creating solidarity in a queer movement. As a strategy for forging solidarity within the otherwise fragmented world of identity politics, it may thus exemplify an important development that is itself aimed at building broader coalitions and alliances rather than at minimizing differences. Efforts to construct the field of sexual rights even more broadly, and through this construct to link LGBTTTQI rights to women's rights, the rights of people living with (or vulnerable in the face of) HIV and AIDS, the rights of people with disabilities, and so on, face immense challenges within the current hegemonic world in which identity politics makes intermovement consensus exceptionally difficult (while intramovement consensus, on the other hand, tends to be driven by neoliberalism and heteronormative [for example, gay marriage] arguments and frameworks).

Constructing a meaningful definition of sexual rights, building an effective movement for advocacy around sexual rights (out of the immense diversity spread out upon this complicated playing field), and developing a research agenda both to understand the social forces and historical processes at play, and to contribute to them in meaningful ways, are by no means easy challenges. Just some of the issues that must be addressed can be found laid out in the results of a WHO consultation in the early part of this decade in which medical anthropologists and their colleagues from a number of related disciplines came together with activists and advocates from around the world to try to hash out some of these problems. They concluded that sexual rights include the right of all persons, free of coercion, discrimination, and violence, to attain the highest possible standard of health in relation to sexuality, including access to sexual and reproductive health services (WHO 2002). Sexual rights also include the right to seek, receive, and pass on information in relation to sexuality, and the right to sexuality education. They are based, above all else, on respect and choice: respect for bodily integrity, the right to decide whether or not to be sexually active, to choose one's sexual partners, to enter into consensual sexual relations and relationships, and the right to decide whether or not and when to have children.

Just how hard it is to move such an agenda forward is confirmed by the fact that even as it places these definitions on its website, the WHO explicitly declines responsibility or ownership for them, clearly emphasizing that they are the result of work being carried out outside of the organization by activists and academics. The challenges that currently confront this area of work are by no means insignificant; fundamental issues, such as whether to emphasize what have been described as "negative" rights (such as protection from violence and discrimination) or "positive" rights (such as the right to pleasure and erotic satisfaction), have at best only been thrown up into the air for debate, and the results are still impossible to foresee or predict (Corrêa, Petchesky, and Parker 2008). The one thing that I can say with relative confidence, however, is that medical anthropology and medical anthropologists are part of the discussion—that the work we do will have an impact on how such questions are answered both today and in the future.

Theory and Practice

Throughout the discussion above, I have emphasized that the historical development of thinking in these areas—the historical processes that have led to the current moment in gender, LGBT, and sexuality research in medical anthropology—has been far more than simply a history of ideas that have taken shape in the rarefied world of academic institutions. On the contrary, it has been shaped by the active engagement of medical anthropologists in social movements, in program design and implementation, and on the front lines of political struggles taking place in diverse settings around the world. Nearly all areas of medical anthropology are characterized by a unique connection between theory and practice—between what is understood to be happening "in theory," and hence assumed to offer a more removed, objective, or scientific perspective, and what is happening on the ground in lived reality. This engagement is perhaps especially evident, however, in work on gender, sexuality, health, and rights. Our ability to move forward intellectually in this field is shaped to a remarkable degree by the lives that we lead and by our personal, social, and political commitments and experiences.

Examples of engaged medical anthropology are numerous; many of them are well known both nationally and internationally, and at least a few of them have already been cited above in this chapter or are present in other chapters in this book (see, for example, the chapters by Rayna Rapp and Faye Ginsburg and Merrill Singer). In my own experience, the linkages between theory and practice have been forged most clearly in my long history of work in Brazil and in the ways in which my personal experiences have intersected with my research and political activities.

I first traveled to Brazil in 1982 as a doctoral student in social and cultural anthropology at the University of California, Berkeley, to begin research for my doctoral dissertation on the politics of popular culture (Parker 1991, 1999). At the time, the idea of focusing my research on sexuality or homosexuality seemed highly unlikely. In the face of a shrinking job market and the marginalization of such issues within the homophobic environment of most academic institutions, for any graduate student concerned about developing a professional career, the notion of specializing in such topics seemed almost suicidal. But thanks to a series of what can best be described as historical accidents, my plans changed rapidly in ways that reconfigured not only my personal life but also my career over the course of the next three decades.

On the one hand, and probably most importantly, fairly early in my fieldwork, I met Vagner de Almeida, a Brazilian playwright and filmmaker, my partner in work as well as in life (for more than twenty-eight years now). The challenges of building a relationship, of bridging cultural differences, of trying to mediate them without either ignoring or disrespecting them, and of finding ways to construct a life across the boundaries of two different societies —each with its own complex forms of discrimination in relation to nonnormative expressions of gender and sexuality—became part of my personal as well as my professional life in ways that I never would have expected. Other kinds of concerns (like worries about my professional future) somehow seemed inconsequential in relation to the more immediate challenges of finding a way to build a life together in the face of substantial odds (see Parker 1999).

As any readers attentive to history will have already realized, at virtually the same moment the HIV epidemic also fell into our lives, disrupting nearly every aspect of our existence. The very first cases of what would come to be called AIDS had been reported in the San Francisco Bay Area just shortly before my departure for the field, and the first cases in both São Paulo and Rio de Janeiro were reported early on in the initial period of my field research. By the time that I was ready to return to the United States in 1984, at the end of my first period of extended field research in Brazil, for both personal and professional reasons, my work had become focused on what I described as "Brazilian sexual culture" (Parker 1991, 2009), as well as on the impact of HIV and AIDS on Brazilian society as a whole and on vulnerable populations and communities in particular (Daniel and Parker 1993).

Much of our time over the next few years was spent moving back and forth between the United States and Brazil. At the same time that I was trying to finish my doctoral dissertation in anthropology at Berkeley, I was convinced that what I was trying to understand about the relative fluidity of cultural boundaries regulating sexual interaction between same-sex as well as opposite-sex partners in Brazil would have important implications for understanding the HIV epidemic—and, possibly, for responding to it in meaningful ways (Parker 1987). As I worked closely with Vagner on his play *Adeus Irmão, Durma Sossegado* (Goodbye My Brother, Sleep Peacefully), the first theater production on AIDS to be staged in Brazil, we began to become deeply engaged in building that response, particularly through cultural activism (Almeida and Parker 1989).

By the time we returned to Rio in 1988, both to produce *Adeus Irmão,*

Durma Sossegado and for me to begin work on a new study of the politics of HIV and AIDS in Brazil (funded by the Social Science Research Council and the Wenner-Gren Foundation for Anthropological Research), I had become close friends with a number of key AIDS activists in Brazil—especially the writer and early gay activist Herbert Daniel and the sociologist and long-time progressive leader Herbert de Souza (better known popularly as Betinho; see figure 1) (see Galvão 2008; Howes 2001). Both had been deeply involved in the resistance to the military dictatorship and spent long periods in political exile, returning to Brazil only at the beginning of the 1980s when the dictatorship began to give up its hold on the government and approved amnesty for political exiles. Betinho and his two brothers all had hemophilia and were among the earliest public figures to identify themselves as HIV positive (*New York Times* 1987, 1997). Beginning in 1986, Betinho had begun to bring together a diverse group of concerned citizens, health professionals, intellectuals, and researchers to discuss how to mobilize politically in response to the epidemic in Brazil. In 1987 they formally created ABIA as a nationwide AIDS advocacy organization.[3] Its aim was not to develop a structure parallel to the government to provide services that the state itself should have been providing, but rather it was to apply political pressure on the state so that it would assume responsibility for the development and provision of those policies and services needed in order to respond to the epidemic (de Souza 1994).[4]

In 1988, shortly after our return to Rio, I began working as a consultant to the Ford Foundation's field office in Brazil, where Peter Fry, a British anthropologist who had been based in Brazil for many years and who had been active both in the Brazilian gay rights movement and in the early discussions that led to the creation of ABIA, was then the foundation's representative and began to develop a number of grants to support work on HIV and AIDS (Brier 2009). As part of my work with Ford, I began interacting with a group of social scientists (including the medical anthropologists Sérgio Carrara, who had also been involved in the creation of ABIA, and Maria Andrea Loyola, among others) in the Institute of Social Medicine at the State University of Rio de Janeiro, which wanted to start a new research program on the social dimensions of the epidemic. I was recruited to a faculty position at the institute in 1989 and was given a lead role in coordinating their new research program, as well as in maintaining external relations with the growing number of civil society

Figure 1. Herbert de Souza (Betinho)
in 1994. Brazilian Interdisciplinary
AIDS Association.

organizations working on HIV and AIDS and the local and national governmental programs focusing on the epidemic. It was this work that led me to
serve as chief of the Prevention Unit of the Brazilian National AIDS Program
in 1992, when the State University of Rio de Janeiro lent me to the Ministry of
Health to help restructure the national response to the epidemic and to begin
preparing an application to the World Bank for the first in a series of loans
that would play a key role in supporting Brazil's response to the epidemic up
to the present (see Berkman et al. 2005; Parker 2003).

It was also in this role at the Institute of Social Medicine that I first joined
an advisory committee at ABIA and began to work closely with Herbert Daniel
(known to everyone as Daniel, his pen name), who had joined ABIA's full-time
staff as the organization's lead writer and who, over time, became their second
most important public spokesperson, together with Betinho. In 1989 Daniel
was diagnosed with HIV and TB and asked me to work with him on a number
of writing projects that he had taken on but was too weak to carry out on his
own. The next three years were especially intense. Daniel brought together a

Figure 2. AIDS and Solidarity Corcovado Protest in 1989. Brazilian Interdisciplinary AIDS Association.

range of friends and colleagues to form the Grupo Pela VIDDA (loosely translated as the Group for LIFE), the first organization of people living with HIV in Brazil, and he, Betinho, and others (including myself) waged an increasingly aggressive campaign against what they saw as the federal government's neglect of its responsibility to provide services needed to prevent transmission of HIV and to care for those already infected (see figure 2).

This period was also the most remarkable education that I ever received on the power of activism to reinvent the social imaginary. At a time when biomedical technologies and public health techniques still offered almost nothing in the way of a meaningful response to the epidemic, cultural, institutional, and ideological constructions were among the most powerful weapons that were available to us. Much like groups such as ACT-UP in the United States (and at roughly the same period in time), ABIA, Pela VIDDA, and other emerging AIDS organizations in Brazil began to articulate what I can only describe as

Figure 3. AIDS and Solidarity Corcovado Protest in 1989. Brazilian Interdisciplinary AIDS Association.

a set of ethical-political principles to serve as the basis for a meaningful social response to the epidemic. By far the most powerful of these was the conception of *solidariedade* or "solidarity"—our ability to comprehend the pain and suffering of others as if it were our own, and, precisely because we understand it as our own, our obligation to take collective responsibility for the struggle to change it (see figure 3) (Daniel 1989; Daniel and Parker 1993; de Souza 1994; Parker 1994, 1996). Understood along these lines, solidarity took on both ethical *and* political dimensions. Articulating a vision of responding to AIDS through solidarity was fundamentally a reaffirmation of the rights of citizenship—in particular, the right of all citizens to health—and about the struggle to combat the stigma, discrimination, and marginalization related to the HIV epidemic that denied those rights to those infected and affected by HIV (Daniel and Parker 1993).[5]

Over the next few years, after his diagnosis in 1989, Daniel became the most visible and important leader of the movement of people living with HIV and AIDS in Brazil, but his health also declined rapidly at a time when almost no medical therapies other than AZT were available for HIV treatment. In 1991, hospitalized and unable to work (and with ABIA embroiled in a series of internal financial and political crises), he asked me to join ABIA's staff full-time as its executive director, a position that I finally took on publicly after his death in early 1992 (Parker and Terto Jr. 2001).[6] Over the course of the 1990s, we developed a number of major lines of work that were shaped by, and that also helped to shape, thinking about the intersections between gender, sexuality, and HIV. Indeed, the very notion of intersectionality, discussed above, was central to our broader institutional project. Beginning in the early 1990s, and extending over the course of the next two decades, creating opportunities for dialogue across sectors—and building alliances around progressive policies emerging from such intersectoral dialogues—became our primary way of advancing political debates around the response to HIV and AIDS as well as its relationship to issues of gender, sexuality, health, and rights. Through seminars and workshops that brought together researchers, policy makers, practitioners, and activists, we sought to open up spaces for public debate and to use those spaces to shift the dominant paradigms employed in thinking about the epidemic (for example, from "risk" to "vulnerability"; see Ayres, França Júnior, and Calazans 1997) as well as the dominant practices employed in responding to it (for example, from interventions at the level of "behavior" to interventions at the level of "structure"; see Parker 2000b).

This work was consistently driven by the initial thinking (articulated most clearly by Betinho) behind the founding of ABIA—that it should not serve as a substitute for the state but should instead pressure the state to fulfill its responsibility in confronting the epidemic. In the early 1990s this work was carried out largely from the outside, funded by private donors. Government officials were asked to sit at a table that had been set by activists and researchers. Over time, however, as intersectoral dialogue deepened and government programs began to adopt a rights-based approach, the nature of the partnership began to shift, and by the late 1990s, the National AIDS Program (NAP) asked us to organize a series of "itinerant seminars" held in cities around the country with the goal of "refining the debate" about the policy response to the epidemic—a line of work that we continue to develop in partnership with the NAP today (Parker, Terto Jr., and Pimenta 2002; Pimenta, Raxach, and Terto Jr. 2010).

This same basic model was also employed in work that ABIA carried out

ABIA Associação Brasileira Interdisciplinar de AIDS

Figure 4. "Enjoy" poster, originally developed for Eco 92 NGO parallel conference and reissued multiple times since.

both at the interface of the HIV epidemic and reproductive health and rights and in mobilizing emerging LGBT communities in response to the epidemic. Beginning in 1992 and growing out of a consultancy that I had coordinated for the Ford Foundation in 1991 to explore the interface between HIV/AIDS and population and reproductive health and largely as a result of discussions with the feminist thinker Sonia Corrêa, ABIA embarked on a series of projects aimed at building bridges between the world of HIV and AIDS and the world of women's reproductive health and rights (see Brier 2009). Initially, the steps that we took were cautious and relatively modest. Projects, such as a translation into Portuguese of the Panos Institute's dossier on women and AIDS, *Triple Jeopardy* (Panos 1990; ABIA and SOS Corpo 1993), developed as a collaboration between ABIA and the leading feminist organization in northeastern Brazil, SOS Corpo, and a project aimed at raising awareness within women's organizations of women's vulnerability to HIV infection and at proposing sexual liberty and empowerment as alternatives to oppression and repression, developed together with ECOS, one of the leading feminist NGOs in São Paulo.

As this line of work evolved, largely thanks to ongoing support from Ford, it became increasingly complex and multifaceted. We recruited the anthropologist Jane Galvão to lead a series of projects that stretched over the rest of the decade with the goal of bringing together researchers, women's health and AIDS activists, health practitioners, and policy makers to develop a knowledge base on gender power relations, women's vulnerability to HIV infection, and possible approaches to prevention and to living with HIV among women already infected (*New York Times* 1993). Over roughly the next six years, we organized a series of seminars and training workshops around the country. We published *Quebrando o Silêncio: Mulheres e AIDS no Brasil* (Breaking the Silence: Women and AIDS in Brazil) (Parker and Galvão 1996), the first book on women and AIDS based on empirical research carried out in Brazil. Perhaps most importantly, this publication built a case for the inclusion—and centrality—of reproductive rights within the broader framework of health and human rights that was being elaborated by Brazilian AIDS activists and increasingly adopted by the Brazilian National AIDS Program and the Brazilian government more broadly (ABIA and IMS/UERJ 1997).

Beginning in 1993, in partnership with the Grupo Pela VIDDA in both Rio de Janeiro and São Paulo, we designed and implemented the first large-scale prevention program for gay, bisexual, and other men who have sex with men in Brazil (see figure 5) (see Parker and Terto Jr. 1997). Designed as a multilevel intervention working at individual, community, and broader social levels, it used extensive ethnographic mapping as a way of understanding the world of same-sex interactions in both cities. The program also developed outreach work in public sites and commercial venues, as well as a range of ongoing activities such as safer sex and expressionist theater workshops, psychosocial counseling services for the HIV positive and those at risk, and the development of visual materials, theatrical productions, books, and videos aimed at pushing the limits of HIV prevention practice (see, for example, Almeida 1997; Parker and Terto 1997; Rios et al. 2004).

At least three major dimensions of this work distinguished it from more traditional public health approaches and underscored its deeply anthropological roots. First, it maintained an ongoing commitment to building partnerships across the boundaries of seemingly separate identity-based communities and social universes—between men who have sex with men and self-identified gay and bisexual men; between gay men, male sex workers, and transgender women; between gay and other men who have sex with men and

Figure 5. "It Doesn't Matter with Whom" poster, developed for the Homosexualities Project for prevention among men who have sex with men in 1994.

lesbian women; and between HIV negative and HIV positive men—as well as between community activists and the owners and managers of commercial venues (such as discos or saunas) catering to a gay or queer clientele; between community-based organizations and public health services (such as STD treatment clinics, HIV testing centers, and HIV treatment providers); and between community representatives and local governmental AIDS programs. Second, it emphasized what we described as "cultural activism": the strategic use of cultural forms and frameworks as interventions aimed not simply at changing behaviors but at changing mindsets and political structures (see figure 6) (Almeida et al. 1998; Rios et al. 2004).

Finally, it stressed the importance of ongoing ethnographic research and cultural analysis and highlighted the role of activist organizations in the production of knowledge about the worlds in which they work (Parker and Terto Jr. 1998). It also provided the broader context within which my own book *Beneath the Equator: Cultures of Desire, Male Homosexuality, and Emerging*

Figure 6. Cabaret Prevenção theater production, 1995.

Gay Communities in Brazil (Parker 1999) was researched and written over the course of the 1990s, suggesting some of the ways in which an emerging dialogue in anthropology and related social sciences about the changing shape of same-sex relations under conditions of globalization must necessarily exist in dialogue with deeply rooted experiences of local communities and local cultures if it is to be truly meaningful.

Over the course of the late 1990s and the 2000s, we have continued to prioritize many of the same projects and areas that were the primary focus of ABIA's work in the 1990s. Our work with men who have sex with men, for example, has continued throughout this period, though the sources of funding have changed over time, and we have incorporated new projects seeking to reach specific subpopulations such as young gay men, transgender youth, and male sex workers (see figure 7). We have also continued to develop a series of ongoing prevention projects for young people using techniques such as popular street theater—again, with an evolving focus over time and, in

Figure 7. "Accept Diversity" poster, 2002.

particular, with increased emphasis on Afro-Brazilian populations. But we also have developed new initiatives in response to the changing shape of the HIV epidemic as well as changing circumstances in global policy debates and transnational activist movements that have been closely linked to the changes in medical anthropology. One key area of work that has evolved as part of ABIA's broader engagement with HIV treatment activism has been intellectual property rights and advocacy aimed at pushing the Brazilian government (and other relevant actors) to utilize international trade agreements to guarantee access to the most effective treatment options for all people living with HIV who need them, available at the lowest possible cost to the Brazilian state (Reis, Terto Jr., and Pimenta 2009).[7]

Especially deeply rooted in medical anthropology, and as a critical analytical response to the (all too often uncritical) promotion of faith-based organizations' involvement in HIV prevention and control activities by the United States and other governments, we carried out an extended five-year, multi-sited ethnographic study in Brasília, Porto Alegre, Recife, Rio de Janeiro, and São Paulo and developed a comparative analysis of the responses to HIV and

AIDS in Brazil on the part of Catholic, Evangelical, and Afro-Brazilian religious institutions and traditions, focusing on the ways in which social actors from each of these traditions have engaged politically with other civil society organizations and with the state at municipal, state, and federal levels (see, for example, García et al. 2009).[8] Also, for nearly a decade now, we have worked on Sexuality Policy Watch (SPW), a coalition of researchers, activists, and policy makers focusing on sexual rights and the interface between sexuality and politics globally. With two secretariats, one based at ABIA in Rio de Janeiro and the other at Columbia University in New York City, SPW's work seeks to communicate research findings on sexuality and sexual politics to advocacy communities in ways that will more effectively contribute to struggles for erotic justice—in Brazil, as well as around the world (see www.sxpolitics.org).[9]

As I look back over the development of my work and thinking on medical anthropology in relation to gender, sexuality, health, and rights over the course of nearly three decades, it is impossible for me to imagine it outside of or disconnected from my own experiences of engagement, largely through ABIA, in struggles at the intersections of medical anthropology, feminism, and women's health, HIV and AIDS, reproductive health and rights, and sexual rights more broadly. While it may seem obvious to speak of a dialectical movement between theory and practice, in which each shapes the other over time, in few other areas of anthropological work is this so clearly realized. It is this combination of *critical social analysis* and *social movement activism* that has opened up the greatest potential for medical anthropological work on gender, sexuality, LGBT issues, and related topics and that has made this work such an important part of life for so many of us working in this field. It is this combination as well that propels us to confront what I see as some of the key challenges facing the field of medical anthropology.

Key Challenges for the Future

While this chapter has covered a fair amount of terrain and a number of different areas of work, before closing, I would like to call attention not only to some of our key contributions to the field but also to a number of challenges that should concern us as we move forward.

In medical anthropology more generally, and in work on gender, sexuality, health, and rights in particular, I am convinced that we have made key contributions to both theory and practice by deconstructing the impact of medicalization and biomedicine, prioritizing local knowledge and grounded social and cultural constructions, documenting grassroots understandings of the key issues being explored in international debates and by transnational networks operating far from the grassroots, and investigating key struggles taking place on the ground in ways that may help to keep transnational debates and processes honest and responsive to the people in greatest need. It is our particular view, from a very localized position, together with our values and our commitment to a set of moral, ethical, and political principles, that provides our most important contribution across these areas of work.

While many of our key contributions are clear, however, so too are some of our most important challenges—in particular, the challenge to make medical anthropology as global as the transnational fields of gender, sexuality, health, and rights are in the early twenty-first century. The greatest developments in these fields recently have been in the Global South, where a boom in medical anthropology has taken place. Yet in the Global North it sometimes appears that we have still not been able to fully engage with our colleagues around the world. There is still much to be done to make our Society for Medical Anthropology truly representative of the diversity in our field. Work on gender, sexuality, health, and rights is an area in which the growing leadership of researchers and advocates from the Global South offers especially rich potential for moving medical anthropology in the direction of global diversity.[10]

The second key challenge, I think, is to develop a new set of horizontal collaborations between researchers across communities, cultures, and countries in ways that surpass current limitations. The traditional anthropological approach of traveling to the field, working individually with our informants and in their communities, and returning to our academic institutions to write up our findings, publish them for our academic audiences, and further our academic careers is clearly a model that cannot be sustained—at least in this area of work—in the world in which we live today. Increasingly, work carried out on these issues in other disciplines, and in countries and cultures around the work, has become more interdisciplinary and more collaborative—often involving activists, as well as academics, and drawing on models from community-based and participatory research approaches. While there are many challenges involved in developing such approaches, there can be no doubt about their importance. We urgently need to develop new models, new forms of collaboration on equal footing, if we are to address issues that are global and that can only be addressed through struggles for equity.

The final challenge that I would like to emphasize is the need to build on the kinds of critical engagements that I have described here in relation to gender, sexuality, health, and rights to further projects aimed not just at the construction of knowledge but also at building meaningful social and political change. Anyone who works on these issues should be acutely aware of their moral responsibility in a world that has for too long been characterized by inequality, violence, and oppression. While our ability to confront such issues directly is necessarily conditioned by our positions as researchers and academics, one of the key legacies of the first fifty years of medical anthropology is unquestionably our deep embeddedness in activism, which is quite explicitly aimed at transforming the world around us—at confronting all forms of oppression and the suffering that they cause. Building upon our activist past—and extending its legacy by continuing to contribute to ongoing struggles for social and political change—remains perhaps our highest moral calling and our greatest challenge for the future.

Throughout this chapter, I have highlighted the many ways in which connections with work on gender, sexuality, health, and rights have contributed to the field of medical anthropology. I have also emphasized the ways in which our engagement with social movements, political critiques, and activism— feminist activism, AIDS activism, reproductive health and rights activism, LGBT activism, and sexual rights activism—has given work on these issues both intellectual power and political importance. I have described the historical development of work on these various topics, highlighting what I view as some of the most important scholarship that has emerged in medical anthropology, as well as the contested nature of what constitutes knowledge and how knowledge is attained on such relatively controversial issues. Drawing on some of my own experience working in Brazil—experience that is surely paralleled by other medical anthropologists working in their own field sites—I have also tried to offer a sense of how deeply our theoretical perspectives and our thinking *about* the world are linked to our own experiences and to our practice *in* the world. While I am convinced that this is true throughout the broader field of medical anthropology, I also think that it is particularly relevant to work on gender, sexuality, health, and rights. The unique ways in which our personal experiences intersect with our academic work, our engagement as activists, our work as policy makers or practitioners—and, often, a number of these roles all at the same time—have, to a remarkable degree, shaped the development of work on these issues in medical anthropology. In my view, this intersection of critical social analysis and social movement activism is among the most important legacies that those of us laboring in these areas can offer to those who will take up this work in the future. As we celebrate the fiftieth anniversary of medical anthropology, it is important to recognize that the advancement of medical anthropology in the areas of gender, sexuality, health, and rights is no small accomplishment, and one that has been achieved often in the face of significant odds. But it is also equally important to remember that history will judge us on the ways in which we collectively carry this legacy forward into the next fifty years—by the ways in which we use it to continue to construct this field in the future.

Introduction: Medical Anthropology at the Intersections

1. Many other journals are largely devoted to medical anthropology, including *Medical Anthropology*; *Culture, Medicine and Psychiatry*; *Anthropology and Medicine*; *Body and Society*; *Global Public Health*; and *Social Science & Medicine*.

2. Among the prizes won by medical anthropologists are the J. R. Staley Prize of the School of Advanced Research; the SMA's Eileen Basker Prize and New Millennium Book Award; SfAA's Margaret Mead Award; the Diana Forsythe Prize; and the Robert J. Textor Family Prize for Anticipatory Anthropology. Many of these award-winning books are now in their second editions. Some key examples of award-winning ethnographies include those by Adams (1995, 1998), Becker (2000), Biehl (2005, 2007), Boddy (1989), Bourgois (2003), Briggs and Mantini-Briggs (2004), Cohen (2000), Davis-Floyd ([1992] 2003), Dumit (2003), Farmer ([1992] 2006), Fassin (2007), Frank (2000), Ginsburg (1998), Inhorn (1994, 2003), Janzen (1978), Kaufman (2005), Kleinman (1980), Lock (1995, 2001), Martin (1995, [1987] 2001), Mol (2002), Morgan (2009), Parker ([1991] 2009), Petryna (2002), Rapp (1999), Scheper-Hughes (1992), Sharp (2006), and Young (1995).

3. The SMA's Rudolph Virchow Prize celebrates the best essay in this genre.

4. Global health is the new trope that is now replacing what was once known as international health or tropical medicine. This name change reflects growing concern with processes of globalization, including those that cause disease and suffering.

5. A few key examples include works by Biehl (2005, 2007), Castro (2004), Coreil (1990), Fassin (2007), Green (1994), Hunter (2003), Janes (1999), Kendall (1998), Nguyen (2005), Nichter (1992), Padilla (2007), Parker (2001), Petryna (2002, 2006), Schensul and Schensul (1990), Schensul (2008), Schoepf (2001), Trostle (2004), and Whiteford (2008).

6. We thank one of the anonymous reviewers for suggesting this provocative notion of "entanglements."

One. Grafting Together Medical Anthropology, Feminism, and Technoscience

1. Representative works include Fee (1973); Haraway (1989); Hartsock (2004); and Harvey (1985).

2. These projects were eventually published as Harding (2000); Martin (1987); Rhodes (1991); and Whitehead (1987).

3. See work by Merrill Singer, Carolyn Sargent, or Carol Browner, for example.

Some of their publications are Browner and Sargent (1990); Sargent (1989); and Singer and Baer (1995).

4. Some noteworthy examples of anthropologists who moved into the study of biomedical topics after doing research in other areas are Veena Das, Rayna Rapp, Faye Ginsburg, Lesley Sharp, and Paul Rabinow. Some of their works are Das (2007); Ginsburg and Rapp (1995); Rabinow (1992); and Sharp (2006).

5. Officer of the High Commissioner for Human Rights, "General Recommendation No. 25: Gender Related Dimensions of Racial Discrimination: 03/20/2000. Gen. Rec. No. 25. (General Comments)," March 20, 2000, http://www.unhchr.ch/tbs/doc.nsf/(Symbol)/76a293e49a88bd23802568bd00538d83?Opendocument.

6. See, for example, Callon (1986); Daston (2004); Daston and Gailson (2007); and Latour and Biezunski (1994).

7. For example, see Taussig (2009); Oaks (2001); Whitmarsh (2008a); Oldani (2004); or Pinto (2008).

8. Consider Joyce (2008); Mol (2002); and Orr (2006). The topic is too complex for the space available here, but it would be interesting to ask whether the concept of ethnography or of culture in works like these differs from an anthropological one.

9. *Anthropology Today* has announced that anthropology will soon be included in A-level exams in the United Kingdom.

Two. Getting at Anthropology through Medical History

Thanks to Marcia Inhorn and Emily Wentzell for the opportunity to present this material and to the China scholars, archivists, anthropologists, and historians who so generously shared their knowledge, including Paul G. Anderson, Bridie Andrews, Ina Asim, Robert Bickers, Joseph Bosco, Peter Carini, Julie Cormack, E. Grey Dimond, Frank Dikötter, Jackie Eng, Vanessa Fong, Sara Friedman, Charlotte Furth, Alan Goodman, Gerry Groot, D. E. Mungello, Beth Notar, Ruth Rogaski, M. Roy Schwarz, and Sigrid Schmalzer. I am grateful to Debbora Battaglia, Monica Casper, Jonathan Lipman, Meredith Michaels, Beth Notar, Alan Swedlund, James Trostle, and especially to Jackie Eng, Adi Bharadwaj, and the reviewers for their insightful comments and suggestions on an earlier version of this chapter.

1. In de Groot's words: "They are of stone blocks or of brick, and measure some five metres in diameter; their shape is either round, polygonal or square, and they form a single compartment with a tiled roof. [Infant] corpses are to be dropped in through a window-like aperture, from which the winds, birds and bats are warded off by a square wooden shutter, turning in hinges fixed in the lintel.... Baby-towers have no doors, never being entered by living man" (de Groot 1897, 3:1388; see also Mungello 2008, 66; Watson 1988, 182; Eitel 1885, 423–24).

2. Westerners were arguably overeager to find evidence of infanticide among the Chinese, sometimes basing their conclusions on iconography rather than direct observation or firsthand reports (see Mungello 2008, 14).

3. I thank Dr. Ina Asim for bringing the de Groot and Maugham references to my attention.

4. For an exception, see Mungello (2008, 10).

5. Results of a Google image search using the English-language phrase "Chinese fetus" on September 15, 2009, showed that nine of the first ten entries made specific reference to *eating* Chinese fetuses. In an article titled "[How] America Is Exacerbating China's Abortion Problems," Damjan DeNoble writes, "I began to explore the links between the American abortion debate and China's abortion problems after coming across a wide swath of misconceptions about Chinese attitudes towards prenatal life; from unrepentant Chinese and Taiwanese baby fetus eaters, to super secret Chinese government conspiracies which encourage the aborting of female babies in order to amass testosterone for a future global war" (*Asia Healthcare Blog*, http://www.asiahealthcareblog.com/2009/10/07/america-is-not-helping-china%E2%80%99s-abortion-problems/).

6. Although outside the scope of this chapter, the potential for misinterpreting others affected the Chinese as well. After an epidemic killed thirty-four Chinese children living in a Catholic orphanage in the 1870s, "many Chinese [reportedly] believed that the missionaries wanted to dismember the children and mix their hearts, eyes, and brains with opium to make a medicine that could be sold for a financial profit" (Mungello 2008, 58).

7. Due to space considerations, this chapter omits from consideration the complicated politics of international adoption of Chinese babies (see Dorow 2006; Volkman 2005; Anagnost 2004).

8. "In China they are eating babies, in Loma Linda, they are harvesting organs," (http://www.sdadefend.com/Abortion/Harvest-organs.pdf). The same article appears on several pro-life and evangelical Christian websites.

9. I am indebted to Adi Bharadwaj for his critique of an earlier version of this chapter and for encouraging me to consider the ramifications of the subject position I created for myself. His caution ("don't do a Rosaldo on Evans-Pritchard!") prompted me to be more reflexive, although of course I realize that any rhetorical reflexivity I may have achieved on the page remains ethically "easy" and ultimately cowardly.

10. Biographical information pertaining to Edmund Vincent Cowdry can be found at the Washington University School of Medicine and the Bernard Becker Medical Library's website, http://beckerexhibits.wustl.edu/mig/bios/cowdry.html, although it makes no mention of his embryological work. The finding aid to E. V. Cowdry's papers at the Bernard Becker Medical Library of the School of Medicine at Washington

University in St. Louis can be found at http://becker.wustl.edu/libdept/arb/findaid/FC008.html.

11. For the acquisition of embryo specimens from hysterectomies performed on pregnant women, see Morgan (2009, 126–30).

12. Cowdry and Black were both sensitive to Chinese concerns about "Western scientists who were shipping large numbers of artifacts and fossils out of the country" (Schmalzer 2008, 44).

13. Cowdry's wife, Alice Hanford Smith Cowdry (1892–1974), was ill, having lost thirty pounds during her two years in China; she was also pregnant with their first child (Anderson 1983, 19).

14. The "Eurasian question" was purely academic in Black's view. His concern with the evolutionary implications of "Negro-White crosses" did not affect his social relationships with people of other races; in fact Schmalzer reports that he was "dearest to the hearts of the Chinese colleagues" and a man known for "his respect for China and for Chinese scientists" (Schmalzer 2008, 42).

15. Hrdlička's vision of physical anthropology centered on the origins and migration of various races in Asia and elsewhere and in human variation as manifested through anthropometry. Adolph Schultz wrote of Hrdlička after his death: "In his capacity as editor of the *American Journal of Physical Anthropology*, Hrdlička persisted in discouraging studies of a statistical nature and under his management morphological papers left very little space for contributions from other fields" (1945, 313).

16. Today it is difficult to appreciate the seriousness with which scientists pondered the racial questions that the "Chinese material" would be called upon to answer. For example, a historian of the era, testing an entirely different theory about racial qualities, set out to document each recorded instance of multiple births in China. His goal was to test an "anthropological theory to the effect that the phenomenon of multiple births in man represents a survival of or reversal to his former animal state and that with the advance of civilization the number of such births is liable to decline" (Laufer 1920, 122). Embryologists were certain that their specimens would offer "scientific information of a fundamental character regarding the Chinese as a race" (Cowdry 1925, 375).

17. It was not until much later in the twentieth century that Western scholars began to contemplate Chinese notions of racial differentiation. In 1982 Eberhard wrote, "In China, in contrast to the West, the question of minorities is not a question of race.... As the term is usually used today, race refers to physical traits observed by others. In China, however, what are commonly called races do not necessarily have any visible biological uniqueness; their identity is defined by social perceptions" (1982, 3). Later, the historian Frank Dikötter argued that the "notion of a 'yellow race'" was not imposed on China by Europeans (1997, 12). He writes, "Chinese reformers in the

1890s were active agents who participated in the invention of their identities. They were not the passive recipients of a 'derivative discourse,' but creative individuals who selectively appropriated elements of foreign thought systems in a process of cultural interaction. More important, the reform movement which contributed so much to the invention of racial identities in China was largely the product of complex interactions and fusions of different indigenous schools of thought, such as New Text Confucianism, statecraft scholarship (*jingshi*), classical non-canonical philosophies (*zhuzixue*) and Mahayana Buddhism, all of which had virtually nothing to do with Western learning" (1997, 14–15).

18. Cowdry and Black were not racists. Both were known for their sensitive, respectful treatment of Chinese associates, and as Reardon says of a later generation of geneticists interested in biological variation, "it would be historically inaccurate, and morally insensitive," to accuse them of "wielding the power of science to objectify and exploit marginalized groups" (2005, 2–3). The point here is not to portray them or their project as exemplars of a discredited form of racist Orientalism but to show the extent to which social ideologies and scientific projects are intertwined (2005, 9).

19. There was a resurgence of embryological interest in biologically based differences with the development of ultrasonography as a new measuring device in the 1980s, which resulted in references to population-based differences among "ethnic groups" rather than "races" (see Walton 1981). In 2008 the accurate dating of pregnancy was given as a justification for measuring "ethnic Chinese" fetuses and comparing them to "populations" from the United Kingdom and France (see Leung et al. 2008).

20. A similar exhibit is on display in Mexico's Museo Nacional de Antropología. It is labeled as an offering to the dead, consisting of a mask made from an infant skull (*cráneo infantil*). The Aztec-era dry bone mask, with its bulging eyes, looks like Xiao's sculpture, except that his is a wet tissue specimen from China.

21. Jill Stanek, "Sweet and sour fetus: Chinese cannibalism," April 9, 2007, http:// www.jillstanek.com/archives/2007/04/sweet_and_sour.html.

22. Allegations of Chinese fetal cannibalism were also reported from other regions of the world. In the Hong Kong filmmaker Fruit Chan's 2004 movie *Dumplings,* an aging Hong Kong movie star purchases dumplings—made from human fetal remains—from a beautiful, mysteriously ageless immigrant from the Chinese mainland. Sigrid Schmalzer reported hearing a similar rumor in Fiji (ironically once known to Westerners as the "Cannibal Isles"), where it was said that "Chinese scientists have been acquiring Polynesian fetuses for use in genetic experiments to create a race of superhumans" (2008, 264). The theme of Chinese cannibalism extended also to a reanalysis of Peking Man evidence. The physical anthropologists Noel Boaz and Russell Ciochon resuscitated old suspicions (dating from the 1930s, according

to Schmalzer) that *Homo erectus* may have practiced cannibalism. In reexamining a "first generation cast" of a *Homo erectus* skull from Longgushan, they concluded that "stone flake tools" were used "not to study anatomy or to deflesh the body for burial. . . , but to eat it." Chinese hominid ancestors, they continued, "very likely engaged in cannibalism" (2004, 135).

23. Scholars have given greater attention to the role of anthropologists in collecting other kinds of anatomical specimens, including brains, skulls, and the skeletal remains of Native Americans (see Fabian 2010; Starn 2004).

24. Thanks to Vanessa Fong for sharing references by Horowitz (1983), Sun (1983), and Whyte (1984) regarding the Mosher controversy.

Three. Making Peasants Protestant and Other Projects

1. Much of the social anthropology of population acceded, under the sign of urgency, to a plethora of such tough-minded solutions. See for example, B. Benedict (1961), a review of Titmuss and Abel-Smith cited above, in which he suggests that given how population control measures, necessary to prevent an "Orwellian" future, run against the interests of Mauritians, the only option to save Mauritians from their Orwellian future will be "a very authoritarian government." The irony seems lost on Professor Benedict. Medical anthropology, as the anthropological subdiscipline most committed to terrains of urgency, might be cautious when the need to act creates this kind of uncritical commitment to the clarity of one's own position. I return to contemporary terrains of urgency in closing.

2. Even the critiques of neo-Malthusian assumptions retained the imperative of "the urgent task of population planning" (Polgar 1972, 211) and with it the figure of the mass, simultaneously pathogen and patient.

3. The danger of producing Whig history is great in internal disciplinary narratives such as my own here. As the student or long-time colleague of many of these scholars, my "feel" for the history of disciplinary production is biased toward personalistic and progressive historical accounts. Moving beyond such accounts, one would need to argue for yet a third origin story, one that locates this moment of critical expansion not simply as an ideological response to the discipline's Cold War origins or neo-Malthusian dalliances but in relation to the later expansion of social science research in the clinical sciences in the 1970s and 1980s. I am indebted to Tobias Rees for conversation in regards to what I am here calling the third moment of disciplinary creation, not late nineteenth-century colonial governance nor the Cold War scaling up. Most non-Whig histories of this period, however, continue to focus on Cold War legacies. My sense is that a different account, one more attentive to multiple conditions for the resurgence of utopia in the 1970s, is needed. But the latter lies beyond the proverbial scope of this chapter.

4. From 1976 to 1986, some of the many contributors to what were by then international debates included Baer (1985), Bibeau (1982), Boddy (1982), Comaroff (1985), Devisch (1983), Favret-Saada (1977), Frankenberg (1976), Gaines (1982), B. Good (1977), B. Good and M. Good (1981), Helman (1982), Janzen (1978a), Kapferer (1983), Kaufman (1986), A. Kleinman (1980, 1985), Last (1976), Leslie (1976), Littlewood (1986), Lock (1980), Morsy (1979), Obeyesekere (1981), Pandolfi (1986), Scheper-Hughes (1978, 1985), Singer (1986), M. Taussig (1980), and Young (1981, 1982).

5. The language of traditional, modern, or modernizing medical systems (Bibeau 1982; Leslie 1976) progressively gave way, first as noted above to a nonevolutionary comparativism (A. Kleinman 1980) and then in the wake of a broad epistemological turn (Bates 1995; Farquhar 1994b; B. Good 1994; Kuriyama 1994; Leslie and Young 1992; Young 1981), to an engagement with questions of embodiment, affect, and sensation (Csordas 1990, 1993; Desjarlais 1992; A. Kleinman and J. Kleinman 1996; Kuriyama 1999; Farquhar 1994a; French 1994).

6. By "formalist" I group together a variety of responses to the work of Marilyn Strathern (1985). Among the efflorescence of work between 2000 and 2010, one could inadequately mention that of Biehl (2005), Brodwin (2000), Cooper (2008), Dumit (2004), Fortun (2001), Hyde (2007), Jain (2006), Kohrman (2005), Lakoff and Collier (2008), Landecker (2007), Nguyen (2005), Povinelli (2006), Schull (2010), Sharp (2006), and K. Taussig (2009).

7. One prominent example of the restructuring of necessary expertise is the Global Health Delivery Project, chaired by Kim and Michael Porter of the Institute for Strategy and Competitiveness, linking Harvard's schools of business and medicine and adopting the para-ethnographic form developed at the former of field-based case studies.

8. Of the many scholars engaging related questions, I am particularly indebted to conversations with Andrew Hao, Pierre Minn, Tobias Rees, China Scherz, and Bhavat Venkat.

Four. That Obscure Object of Global Health

My gratitude goes to Linda Garat for her revision of an earlier version of this chapter as well as to the anonymous reviewers who have contributed to its improvement.

Five. Medical Anthropology and Mental Health

1. I am thinking here of work with Partners in Health, Médecins Sans Frontières, the World Health Organization, NGOs in Brazil, and other intervention programs.

Six. From Genetics to Postgenomics and the Discovery of the New Social Body

Parts of this chapter also appear in Chapter 12, *An Anthology of Biomedicine*, by M. Lock and V. Nguyen. Oxford: Wiley-Blackwell, 2010.

1. The investigation of the roles and functions of single genes is a primary focus of molecular biology. In contrast, genomics is the study of the genomes of cells and of whole organisms. There are several current definitions of the term "genome" presently in use. Following Barry Barnes and John Dupré, *Genomes and What to Make of Them* (2008, 9) a genome is best understood as a "real" material object constituted out of DNA. Research about single genes does not fall into the field of genomics unless the aim is to elucidate the effect of a specific gene on and its response to the activity of the genome as a whole.

2. I use the term "postgenomics" to signify the present era in which many scientists involved with molecular biology presently focus their attention, in addition to genes and genomes, on numerous variables that are understood as contributing to life itself, human development, and to health and disease.

3. Proteomics is the study of the structure and function of proteins. Epigenetics has several definitions, some of which are limited to technical usage. In general terms epigenetics is the study of those variables both external and internal to the body that contribute, in addition to DNA, to human development, inheritance, and to health and disease.

4. Personal communication, William Foulkes, specialist in cancer genetics.

5. The author and three research assistants, Janalyn Prest, Stephanie Lloyd, and Gillian Chilibeck, were responsible for developing, carrying out, and transcribing these interviews. Heather Lindstrom assisted with interviewing at Case Western University. The software NVivo was used to systematize emergent themes.

Seven. Anthropology and the Study of Disability Worlds

We would like to thank the editors, Marcia Inhorn and Emily Wentzell, as well as two anonymous readers for Duke University Press, for their encouragement for and insights into this chapter. Portions of this research were carried out with the support of the Spencer Foundation and New York University's Institute for the Study of Human Development and Social Change. We thank them both; interpretations, of course, remain our own.

1. In the 1980s, there were only a few notable positive public representations of disability circulating in American popular culture. In 1979 Ira Wohl's direct cinema documentary *Best Boy*—focusing on the fate of his developmentally disabled cousin "Philly" Wohl who spent his first fifty years at home with his aging working-class Jewish parents in Queens—won the Academy Award for Best Documentary. Soon after, Jason Kingsley, a child with Down syndrome, appeared on Sesame Street, due to the tireless efforts of his mother, Emily Perl Kingsley, a long-standing scriptwriter for the show and activist for inclusion of people with disabilities in the arts.

2. Of course, we are not alone in turning unexpected family circumstances into research topics. See, for example, Linda Layne's (1990) writings on her "miscarriage years" and Gail Landsman's (2009) expansion of her own experience parenting a child with cerebral palsy into a study of how mothers reorganize their identities in the face of diagnoses of their infants as disabled.

3. For more information, see the Dysautonomia Foundation's website at http://www.familialdysautonomia.org.

4. This legislative and judicial history is available at http://www.wrightslaw.com/, the website of Peter W. D. Wright and Pamela Darr Wright, where its implications are explained for the benefit of families.

5. A history and current signatories to the UN Convention on Persons with Disabilities can be accessed at http://www.un.org/disabilities/convention/conventionfull .shtml.

6. As we have argued elsewhere (Rapp and Ginsburg 2006), another strand of medical anthropology—the "politics of reproduction" literature—also highlights the profoundly social nature of disability. Recent research on infertility, for example, stresses how socially disabling involuntary childlessness and reproductive loss may be, especially although not exclusively for women (e.g., Becker 2000; Birenbaum-Carmeli 2009; Franklin 1997, 2006; Inhorn 1996, 2003, 2012; Inhorn et al. 2009; Layne 1990; Sandelowski 1993).

7. We thank one of the anonymous reviewers of this book for his or her insights into this issue. As she or he wrote: "I could not help but think that when these authors asked why anthropology has neglected disability studies, the answer that sprang to mind was 'because it involves children,' and children are of little interest within anthropology. And . . . disability appears to be 'mothers' work,' where already savvy women within medical anthropology meld their activist work for their children with academic concerns."

8. Interview with the authors, 2 April 2010.

9. "Shut Up About Your Perfect Kid!" YouTube video, 3:35, posted by shutupabtperfectkid, 3 December 2007, http://www.youtube.com/watch?v=N_I3PMB30boSMA.

10. Of course, there is a substantial academic literature on autism spectrum disorders, including notable work by anthropologists, e.g., the work of linguistic anthropologist Elinor Ochs and her team at UCLA whose many publications are listed at this website, http://www.sscnet.ucla.edu/anthro/faculty/ochs/publish.htm; see also Ochs et al. (2004) and Grinker (2007).

11. Disabilities Network of New York City, "disTHIS! Film Series," http://www.disthis.org/index.htm.

Nine. Critical Intersections and Engagements: Gender, Sexuality,
Health, and Rights in Medical Anthropology

Thanks to Marcia Inhorn and Emily Wentzell for all that they have done in organizing the SMA Conference and in preparing this book—and, in particular, for their
very helpful editorial suggestions on this chapter. Thanks as well to Jonathan García,
Jennifer Hirsch, Laura Murray, and Elanah Uretsky, who were kind enough to offer
comments on earlier drafts of this chapter, and to Natalie Wittlin for her excellent
editorial assistance.

1. For a fuller discussion of PEPFAR and some of its impacts, see www.pepfarwatch
.org.

2. Treichler's notion of an epidemic of signification has been especially influential
in drawing attention to the cultural dimensions of the HIV epidemic—and to the
need for cultural analysis as part of a broader political critique of the ways in which
societies and political systems have confronted it.

3. The most complete description of the early history of ABIA can be found in Portuguese in Parker and Terto Jr. (2001). Useful English sources include Parker (2003)
and Brier (2009).

4. The model of action developed by ABIA, which has continued to guide its work
up to the present, is thus in many ways very different from that used by many other
AIDS service organizations (ASOs) in Brazil and elsewhere; it is far more focused on
advocacy, together with occasional demonstration projects, than on service provision.
In addition, ABIA's national focus distinguishes it from the many international NGOs
that have sprung up in response to the global HIV epidemic. In contrast to organizations like Partners In Health (PIH), which have made key contributions by using
international resources to guarantee service provision in places where services are
absent or inadequate, ABIA has offered an alternative model of locally based expertise
and advocacy. It has also consistently taken a critical stance on the importation of
public health models from the Global North and has been exceptionally concerned
about developing equitable horizontal collaborations with organizations in other
parts of Latin America and Lusophone Africa.

5. For further English-language discussions of HIV and AIDS in Brazil, and on
the Brazilian response to the epidemic, see, for example, Biehl (2004, 2007); Brier
(2009); Inciardi, Surratt, and Telles (2000); Lieberman (2009); Nunn (2009); and
Parker (2003). Specific references to ABIA's work can be found in the indexes of all
of these works.

6. At the end of 1995, after working with ABIA in this capacity for three years, I
resigned from this paid position to become general secretary of ABIA's board of directors. After Betinho's death in 1997, at the end of his elected term, I was then elected

ABIA's president—a position that I still hold today, after having been reelected five times. Having moved to take a faculty position at Columbia University at roughly the same time, since 1999, I have divided my time between New York City and Rio de Janeiro more or less equally, traveling back and forth on average six to seven times a year, and spending longer or shorter periods in each place depending on the flow of the academic calendar and the exigencies of trying to integrate research and political practice. For nearly two decades now, ABIA has thus provided the institutional platform for virtually all of my research in Brazil, as well as for the political work that has been most meaningful to me. It is also worth highlighting that ABIA has been able to play a key role in training medical anthropologists in Brazil (and on Brazil). While working with ABIA, I continued to hold an academic appointment at the Institute of Social Medicine at the State University of Rio de Janeiro until 2005, and nearly all of my doctoral students in medical anthropology worked at ABIA as staff members or consultants during and often after completing their doctoral studies. Veriano Terto Jr., Regina Maria Barbosa, Jane Galvão, Luis Felipe Rios, and Maria Cristina Pimenta, among others, went on to make major contributions to HIV-related work, women's health and reproductive health and rights, and sexual rights advocacy. ABIA has also served as the institutional base for nearly all of my graduate research assistants in medical anthropology who have worked on Brazil since I joined the faculty at Columbia University.

7. For more information in Portuguese, see ABIA's website, http://www.abiaids .org.br/projetos/projetoView.aspx?lang=pt&seq=11025&mid=5&fg=Projetos.

8. For more information in Portuguese on this work, see ABIA's website, http://www .abiaids.org.br/projetos/projetoView.aspx?lang=pt&seq=11848&mid=5&fg=Projetos.

9. In much the same way as my work with ABIA on evolving same-sex relations and gay communities provided the foundation for my academic work in publications such as *Beneath the Equator* (Parker 1999), these projects, which mix research with political action, have been the point of departure for nearly everything that I have written over the course of the past decade, including more empirical collections such as *SexPolitics: Reports from the Front Lines* (Parker, Petchesky, and Sember 2007) and more theoretical works such as *Sexuality, Health, and Human Rights* (Corrêa, Petchesky, and Parker 2008).

10. Especially in an information age dominated by the Internet, it is important to emphasize just how much the dominance of English as the global language of scientific and scholarly exchange limits our ability to realize this goal of fully engaging with colleagues from the Global South. It is impossible for me to adequately do justice, for example, to just how much my own work and thinking has been enriched by the work of Brazilian anthropologists, almost entirely written in Portuguese and inaccessible to most people working in medical anthropology outside of the Lusophone

world. It should also be noted, however, that it is possible to imagine mechanisms that may be used to change this situation—for example, the launch by the Brazilian Anthropological Association of the English-language, open-access electronic journal *Vibrant (Virtual Brazilian Anthropology)*, see http://www.vibrant.org.br/index_ english.html.

ABIA and IMS/UERJ. 1997. *Saúde reprodutiva em tempos de AIDS*. Rio de Janeiro: ABIA e IMS/UERJ.

Ablon, J. 1984. *Little People in America: The Social Dimension of Dwarfism*. New York: Praeger.

———. 1988. *Living with Difference: Families with Dwarf Children*. New York: Praeger.

———. 2002. "The Nature of Stigma and Medical Conditions." *Epilepsy and Behavior*, 3, S2-S9.

———. 2009. *Brittle Bones, Stout Hearts and Minds: Adults with Osteogenesis Imperfecta*. Sudbury: Jones and Bartlett.

Abraham, C. 2011. "Goodbye, Thrift Gene, and Hello to a New Prime Suspect behind the Global Upsurge in Obesity and Diabetics: The Womb." *Globe and Mail*, March 5, F6–7.

Abu El-Haj, N. 2007. "The Genetic Reinscription of Race." *Annual Review of Anthropology* 36: 283–300.

Abu-Lughod, L. 1991. "Writing against Culture." In *Recapturing Anthropology*, edited by R. G. Fox, 137–62. Santa Fe: School of American Research Press.

Adam, B., J. W. Duyvendak, and A. Krouwel. 1999. *The Global Emergence of Gay and Lesbian Politics: National Imprints of a Worldwide Movement*. Philadelphia: Temple University Press.

Adams, V. 1996. *Tigers of the Snow and Other Virtual Sherpas: An Ethnography of Himalayan Encounters*. Princeton: Princeton University Press.

———. 1998. *Doctors for Democracy: Health Professionals in the Nepal Revolution*. Cambridge: Cambridge University Press.

Adams, V., T. E. Novotny, and H. Leslie. 2008. "Global Health Diplomacy." *Medical Anthropology* 27: 315–23.

Aggleton, P. 1996. *Bisexualities and AIDS: International Perspectives*. London: Taylor and Francis.

———. 1999. *Men Who Sell Sex: International Perspectives on Male Prostitution and HIV/AIDS*. London: UCL Press.

Agustín, L. 2007. *Sex at the Margins: Migration, Labour, Markets and the Rescue Industry*. London: Zed Books.

Ahern, E. M. 1978. "Sacred and Secular Medicine in a Taiwan Village: A Study of Cosmological Disorders." In *Culture and Healing in Asian Societies*, edited by

A. Kleinman et al., P. Kunstadter, E. R. Alexander, and J. L. Gale, 17–39. Cambridge, MA: Schenkman Publishing.

Alinsky, S. 1971. *Rules for Radicals: A Pragmatic Primer for Realistic Radicals*. New York: Random House.

Almeida, V. 1997. *Cabaret Prevenção*. Rio de Janeiro: ABIA.

Almeida, V., and R. Parker. 1989. "The Use of Theatre in AIDS Education." Paper presented at the Second International Symposium on AIDS Information and Education, Yaoundé, Cameroon.

Almeida, V., V. Terto Jr., J. C. Rexach, J. Galvão, and R. Parker. 1998. *Cultural Activism and Community Mobilization: Rethinking Models of HIV/AIDS Prevention for Gay and Bisexual Men*. International Conference on AIDS, Geneva, Switzerland, Abstract No. 43178.

Almqvist, E., S. Adam, M. Bloch, A. Fuller, P. Welch, D. Eisenberg, D. Whelan, D. Macgregor, W. Meschino, and M. R. Hayden. 1997. "Risk Reversals in Predictive Testing of Huntington Disease." *American Journal of Human Genetics* 61(4): 945–52.

Alter, J. S. 1992. *The Wrestler's Body: Identity and Ideology in North India*. Berkeley: University of California Press.

———. 2000. *Gandhi's Body: Sex, Diet, and the Politics of Nationalism*. Philadelphia: University of Pennsylvania Press.

———. 2004. *Yoga in Modern India: The Body between Science and Philosophy*. Princeton: Princeton University Press.

American Anthropologist. 1909. Vol. 2. Report of meeting of January 19, 1909, 482–83.

Amuchástegui, A. 2001. *Virgindad e Iniciación Sexual en México: Experiencias y Significados*. México, D.F.: Edamex S.A.

Anagnost, A. 1995. "A Surfeit of Bodies: Population and the Rationality of the State in Post-Mao China." In *Conceiving the New World Order: The Global Politics of Reproduction*, edited by F. Ginsburg and R. Rapp, 22–41. Berkeley: University of California Press.

———. 2004. "Maternal Labor in a Transnational Circuit." In *Consuming Motherhood*, edited by J. S. Taylor, L. L. Layne, and D. F. Wozniak, 139–67. New Brunswick: Rutgers University Press.

Anderson, P. G. n.d. *Paul H. Stevenson, 1890–1971*. http://beckerexhibits.wustl.edu/mig/bios/stevenson.html.

———. 1983. "Bandits, Bodies, and Bones." *Outlook Magazine* 20 (1–2): 14–19, 24–31.

Anderson, W. 2000. "The Possession of Kuru: Medical Science and Biocolonial Exchange." *Comparative Studies in Society and History* 42: 713–44.

———. 2006. *Colonial Pathologies: American Tropical Medicine, Race, and Hygiene in the Philippines*. Durham: Duke University Press.

———. 2008. *The Collectors of Lost Souls: Kuru, Moral Peril, and the Creation of Value in Science*. Baltimore: Johns Hopkins University Press.

Appadurai, A. 1988. "Putting Hierarchy in Its Place." *American Ethnologist* 3 (1): 36–49.

———. 2001. "Grassroots Globalization and the Research Imagination." In *Globalization*, edited by A. Appadurai, 1–21. Durham: Duke University Press.

Apse, K. A., B. B. Biesecker, F. M. Giardiello, B. P. Fuller, and B. A. Bernhardt. 2004. "Perceptions of Genetic Discrimination among At-Risk Relatives of Colorectal Cancer Patients." *Genetics in Medicine* 6 (6): 510–16.

Arendt, H. 1976. *The Origins of Totalitarianism*. 1st English ed. New York: Harcourt Brace Jovanovich.

Armelagos, G. J., T. Leatherman, M. Ryan, and L. Sibley. 1992. "Biocultural Synthesis in Medical Anthropology." *Medical Anthropology: Cross-Cultural Studies in Health and Illness* 14 (1): 35–52.

Arnold, D. 1987. "Touching the Body: Perspectives on the Indian Plague, 1896–1900." In *Subaltern Studies V*, edited by Ranajit Guha, 55–90. New Delhi: Oxford University Press.

Asad, T., ed. 1973. *Anthropology and the Colonial Encounter*. London: Ithaca Press.

Associated Press. 2009. "Cannibal Mom 911 Call: 'I Didn't Mean to Do It. He Told Me To!'" July 30. http://www.cbsnews.com/blogs/2009/07/30/crimesider/entry5197361.shtml.

Axel, B. K., ed. 2002. *From the Margins: Historical Anthropology and Its Futures*. Durham: Duke University Press.

Ayres, J. R. C. M., I. França Jr., and G. Calazans. 1997. "AIDS, Vulnerabilidade e Prevenção." In *Saúde Reprodutiva em Tempos de AIDS*, 20–37. Rio de Janeiro: ABIA e IMS/UERJ.

Ayres, J. R. C. M., V. Paiva, I. França Jr., N. Gravato, R. Lacerda, M. Della Negra, H. H. S. Marques, E. Galano, P. Lecussan, A. C. Segurado, and M. H. Silva. 2006. "Vulnerability, Human Rights, and Comprehensive Health Care Needs of Young People Living with HIV/AIDS." *American Journal of Public Health* 96 (6): 1001–6.

Baer, H. A. 1986. "Sociological Contributions to the Political Economy of Health: Lessons for Medical Anthropologists." *Medical Anthropology Quarterly* 17 (5): 129–31.

Baer, H. A., M. Singer, and I. Susser. 2003. *Medical Anthropology and the World System*. Westport: Greenwood Publishing Group.

Balsham, M. 1993. *Cancer in the Community: Class and Medical Authority*. Washington, D.C.: Smithsonian Institution Press.

Banner, L. W. 2003. "Mannish Women, Passive Men, and Constitutional Types: Margaret Mead's *Sex and Temperament in Three Primitive Societies* as a Response to Ruth Benedict's *Patterns of Culture*." *Signs* 28 (3): 833–58.

Barnes, A., and S. Jentoft. 2009. "Building Bridges: Institutional Perspectives on Interdisciplinarity." *Futures* 41: 446–54.

Barnes, B., and J. Dupré. 2008. *Genomes and What to Make of Them*. Chicago: University of Chicago Press.

Bastos, C. 1999. *Global Responses to AIDS: Science in Emergency*. Bloomington: Indiana University Press.

Bates, D., ed. 1995. *Knowledge and the Scholarly Medical Traditions*. Cambridge: Cambridge University Press.

Bauman, Z. 2004. *Wasted Lives. Modernity and Its Outcasts*. Cambridge: Polity Press.

Beck, S., and J. Niewöhner. 2009. "Localizing Genetic Testing and Screening in Cyprus and Germany: Contingencies, Continuities, Ordering Effects and Bio-Cultural Intimacy." In *Handbook of Genetics and Society: Mapping the New Genomic Era*, edited by P. Atkinson, P. Glasner, and M. Lock, 76–93. London: Routledge.

Becker, A. E. 1995. *Body, Self, and Society: The View from Fiji*. Philadelphia: University of Pennsylvania Press.

Becker, G. 1983. *Growing Old in Silence*. Berkeley: University of California Press.

———. 2000. *The Elusive Embryo: How Men and Women Approach New Reproductive Technologies*. Berkeley: University of California Press.

Beeson, D., and T. Doksum. 2001. "Family Values and Resistance to Genetic Testing." In *Bioethics in Social Context*, edited by B. Hoffmaster, 153–79. Philadelphia: Temple University Press.

Bendix, R. 1960. *Max Weber: An Intellectual Portrait*. Garden City: Doubleday.

Benedict, B. 1961. "Review: Mauritius at the Crossroads." *British Journal of Sociology* 12 (4): 387–92.

Benedict, R. 1934. *Patterns of Culture*. Boston: Houghton Mifflin.

Benjamin, W. 1978. "Critique of Violence." In *Reflections*, 1st German ed., 1921, 299–300. New York: Schocken Books.

Bennett, B. 1918. "Giving China's Babies a Square Deal." *World Outlook* 4 (May): 24.

Benyshek, D. C., and J. T. Watson. 2006. "Exploring the Thrifty Genotype's Food-Shortage Assumptions: A Cross-Cultural Comparison of Ethnographic Accounts of Food Security among Foraging and Agricultural Societies." *American Journal of Physical Anthropology* 131 (1): 120–26.

Berg, M., and A. Mol, eds. 1998. *Differences in Medicine: Unraveling Practices, Techniques, and Bodies*. Durham: Duke University Press.

Berkman, A., J. García, M. Muñoz-Laboy, V. Paiva, and R. Parker. 2005. "A Critical Analysis of the Brazilian Response to HIV/AIDS: Lessons Learned for Controlling and Mitigating the Epidemic in Developing Countries." *American Journal of Public Health* 95 (7): 1162–72.

Bertram, L., M. B. McQueen, K. Mullin, D. Blacker, and R. E. Tanzi. 2007. "Systematic Meta-Analyses of Alzheimer Disease Genetic Association Studies: The AlzGene Database." *Nature Genetics* 39: 17–23.

Bertram, L., and R. Tanzi. 2009. "Genome-Wide Association Studies in Alzheimer's Disease." *Human Molecular Genetics* 18 (2): R137–45.

Bhabha, H. 1994. *The Location of Culture*. London: Routledge.

Bibeau, G. 1982. "Systems Approach to Ngbandi Medicine." In *African Health and Healing Systems*, edited by P. Stanley Yoder, 43–84. Los Angeles: African Studies Center.

Biehl, J. 2004. "The Activist State: Global Pharmaceuticals, AIDS, and Citizenship in Brazil." *Social Text* 22 (3): 105–32.

———. 2005. *Vita: Life in a Zone of Social Abandonment*. Berkeley: University of California Press.

———. 2006. "Pharmaceutical Governance." In *Global Pharmaceuticals: Ethics, Markets, Practices*, edited by A. Petryna, A. Lakoff, and A. Kleinman, 206–39. Durham: Duke University Press.

———. 2007. "Pharmaceuticalization: AIDS Treatment and Global Health Politics." *Anthropological Quarterly* 80 (4): 1083–126.

———. 2009. *Will to Live: AIDS Therapies and the Politics of Survival*. Princeton: Princeton University Press.

Biehl, J., B. Good, and A. Kleinman, eds. 2007. *Subjectivity: Ethnographic Investigations*. Berkeley: University of California Press.

Birenbaum-Carmeli, D., and M. C. Inhorn, eds. 2009. *Assisting Reproduction, Testing Genes: Global Encounters with New Biotechnologies*. New York: Berghahn.

Black, D. 1919a. Letter to E. V. Cowdry, April 14. Davidson Black folder, E. V. Cowdry Papers, Becker Medical Library, Washington University School of Medicine.

———. 1919b. Letter to E. V. Cowdry, March 27. Davidson Black folder, E. V. Cowdry Papers, Becker Medical Library, Washington University School of Medicine.

Blackwood, E., ed. 1986. *Anthropology and Homosexual Behavior*. New York: Haworth.

Blackwood, E., and S. E. Wieringa, eds. 1999. *Female Desires: Same-Sex Relations and Transgender Practices across Cultures*. New York: Columbia University Press.

Blakey, M. L. 1987. "Skull Doctors: Intrinsic Social and Political Bias in the History of American Physical Anthropology." *Critique of Anthropology* 7 (2): 7–35.

Bledsoe, C., B. Fatoumatta, and A. G. Hill. 1998. "Reproductive Mishaps and Western Contraception: An African Challenge to Fertility Theory." *Population and Development Review* 24 (1): 15–57.

Bloch, E. 1986. *The Principle of Hope*. Vols. 1–3. Translated by N. Plaice, S. Plaice, and P. Knight. Cambridge: MIT Press.

Boaz, F. 1982. *Race, Language, and Culture*. Chicago: University of Chicago Press.

Boaz, N. T., and R. L. Ciochon. 2004. *Dragon Bone Hill: An Ice-Age Saga of Homo erectus*. Oxford: Oxford University Press.

Boddy, J. 1982. "Womb as Oasis: The Symbolic Context of Pharaonic Circumcision in Rural Northern Sudan." *American Ethnologist* 9 (4): 682–98.

———. 1989. *Wombs and Alien Spirits: Men, Women, and the Zar in Northern Sudan*. Madison: University of Wisconsin Press.

———. 2007. *Civilizing Women: British Crusades in Colonial Sudan*. Princeton: Princeton University Press.

Bolton, R., and M. Singer, eds. 1992. *Rethinking AIDS Prevention: Cultural Approaches*. Philadelphia: Gordon and Breach.

Borofsky, R. 2008. "Public Anthropology: A Personal Perspective." http://www.publicanthropology.org/Defining/publicanth-07Oct10.htm.

Bosk, C. 1979. *Forgive and Remember: Managing Medical Failure*. Chicago: University of Chicago Press.

Bourgois, P. I. 2002. *In Search of Respect: Selling Crack in El Barrio*. Cambridge: Cambridge University Press.

Bourgois, P., and J. Schonberg. 2009. *Righteous Dopefiend*. Berkeley: University of California Press.

Bowker, G., and S. Star. 2000. *Sorting Things Out: Classification and Its Consequences*. Cambridge: MIT Press.

Brager, G., H. Specht, and J. Torczyner. 1987. *Community Organizing*. New York: Columbia University Press.

Bribiescas, R. G. 2008. *Men: Evolutionary and Life History*. Cambridge: Harvard University Press.

Brieger, G. 2004. "Bodies and Borders: A New Cultural History of Medicine." *Perspectives in Biology and Medicine* 47 (3): 402–21.

Brier, J. 2009. *Infectious Ideas: U.S. Political Responses to the AIDS Crisis*. Chapel Hill: University of North Carolina Press.

Briggs, L. 2003. *Reproducing Empire: Race, Sex, Science, and U.S. Imperialism in Puerto Rico*. Berkeley: University of California Press.

Briggs, C. L., and C. Mantini-Briggs. 2003. *Stories in the Time of Cholera: Racial Profiling During a Medical Nightmare*. Berkeley: University of California Press.

Brodey, D. 2007. *The Elephant in the Playroom: Ordinary Parents Write Intimately and Honestly about the Extraordinary Highs and Heartbreaking Lows of Raising Kids with Special Needs*. New York: Hudson Street Press.

Brodwin, P. E. 1996. *Medicine and Morality in Haiti*. Cambridge: Cambridge University Press.

———, ed. 2000. *Biotechnology and Culture: Bodies, Anxieties, Ethics*. Bloomington: Indiana University Press.

Brown, P. J. 1998. *Understanding and Applying Medical Anthropology*. Mountain View: Mayfield.

Brown, T., and M. Bell. 2008. "Imperial or Postcolonial Governance? Dissecting the Genealogy of a Global Public Health Governance." *Social Science & Medicine* 67: 1571–79.

Brown T., M. Cueto, and E. Fee. 2006. "The World Health Organization and the Transition from International to Global Public Health." *American Journal of Public Health* 96: 62–72.

Browner, C. H. 2000. "Situating Women's Reproductive Activities." *American Anthropologist* 102 (4): 773–88.

———. 2007. "Can Gender 'Equity' in Prenatal Genetic Services Unintentionally Reinforce Male Authority?" In *Reproductive Disruptions: Gender, Technology, and Biopolitics in the New Millennium*, edited by M. C. Inhorn, 147–64. New York: Berghahn.

Browner, C. H., H. M. Preloran, M. C. Casado, H. N. Bass, and A. P. Walker. 2003. "Genetic Counseling Gone Awry: Miscommunication between Prenatal Genetic Service Providers and Mexican-Origin Clients." *Social Science & Medicine* 56 (9): 1933–46.

Browner, C. H., and C. F. Sargent. 1990. "Anthropology and Studies of Human Reproduction." In *Medical Anthropology: A Handbook of Theory and Method*, edited by T. M. Johnson and C. F. Sargent, 215–29. New York: Greenwood Press.

Brummelhuis, H., and G. Herdt, eds. 1995. *Culture and Sexual Risk: Anthropological Perspectives on AIDS*. Amsterdam: Gordon and Breach.

Buckley, T., and A. Gottlieb, eds. 1988. *Blood Magic: The Anthropology of Menstruation*. Berkeley: University of California Press.

Buck-Morss, S. 2000. *Dreamworld and Catastrophe: The Passing of Mass Utopia in East and West*. Cambridge: MIT Press.

Bullock, M. B. 1980. *An American Transplant: The Rockefeller Foundation and Peking Union Medical Foundation.* Berkeley: University of California Press.

Bureau of American Ethnology (BAE). 1880–81. *Second Report of the Bureau of American Ethnology to the Secretary of the Smithsonian Institution.* Washington, D.C.: U.S. Government Printing Office.

———. 1908–9. *Thirteenth Report of the Bureau of American Ethnology to the Secretary of the Smithsonian Institution.* Washington, D.C.: U.S. Government Printing Office.

Burghart, R. 1990. "Ethnographers and Their Local Counterparts in India." In *Localizing Strategies: Regional Traditions of Ethnographic Writing,* edited by R. Fardon, 260–79. Edinburgh: Scottish Academic Press.

Burns, A. 2008. "ACORN Gives GOP New Line of Attack." *Politico.* October 10. http://www.politico.com/news/stories/1008/14492.html.

Burri, R. V., and J. Dumit. 2007. *Biomedicine as Culture: Instrumental Practices, Technoscientific Knowledge, and New Modes of Life.* Hoboken: Taylor and Francis.

Butler, J. 1993. *Bodies That Matter: On the Discursive Limits of Sex.* New York: Routledge.

———. 1999. *Gender Trouble: Feminism and the Subversion of Identity.* New York: Routledge.

Butler, R. N. 2008. *The Longevity Revolution.* New York: Perseus Public Affairs.

Butt, L. 2002. "The Suffering Stranger: Medical Anthropology and International Morality." *Medical Anthropology Quarterly* 21 (1): 1–24.

Cabral, M., and G. Benzur. 2006. "Cuando Digo Intersex: Un Diálogo Introductorio a la Intersexualidad." *Cadernos Pagu* 24: 283–304.

Callon, M. 1986. "Some Elements of a Sociology of Translation: Domestication of the Scallops and the Fishermen of St. Brieuc Bay." In *Power, Action, and Belief,* edited by J. Law, 196–233. New York: Routledge and Kegan Paul.

Callon, M., and V. Rabeharisoa. 2004. "Gino's Lesson on Humanity: Genetics, Mutual Entanglements and the Sociologist's Role." *Economy and Society* 33 (1): 1–27.

Canguilhem, G. 1989. *The Normal and the Pathological.* 1st French ed., 1943. New York: Zone Books.

———. 1991. *The Normal and the Pathological.* Translated by C. Fawcett. Cambridge: Zone Books.

Carpenter-Song, E. A., M. Nordquest, M. A. Schwallie, and J. Longhofer. 2007. "Cultural Competence Reexamined: Critique and Directions for the Future." *Psychiatric Services* 58: 1362–65.

Carrier, J. 1995. *De Los Otros: Intimacy and Homosexuality among Mexican Men.* New York: Columbia University Press.

———. 2001. "Some Reflections on Ethnographic Research on Latino and Southeast Asian Male Homosexuality and HIV/AIDS." *AIDS and Behavior* 5 (2): 183–91.

Carstairs, G. M. 1956. "Hijra and Jiryan: Two Derivatives of Hindu Attitudes to Sexuality." *British Journal of Medical Psychology* 29: 128–38.

———. 1957. *The Twice-Born: A Study of a Community of High-Caste Hindus.* London: Hogarth.

Casper, M. J. 1998. *The Making of the Unborn Patient: A Social Anatomy of Fetal Surgery.* New Brunswick: Rutgers University Press.

Castel, R. 1991. "From Dangerousness to Risk." In *The Foucault Effect: Studies in Governmentality,* edited by G. Burchell, C. Gordon, and P. Miller, 281–98. Chicago: University of Chicago Press.

Castro, A., and M. Singer, eds. 2004. *Unhealthy Health Policy: A Critical Anthropological Examination.* Lanham: AltaMira Press.

Caton, H. 2005. "The Exalted Self: Derek Freeman's Quest for the Perfect Identity." *Identity* 5 (4): 359–84.

Cecil, R., ed. 1996. *The Anthropology of Pregnancy Loss: Comparative Studies in Miscarriage, Stillbirth, and Neonatal Death.* New York: Berg.

Center for Constitutional Rights. 2009. "Association of Community Organizations for Reform Now (ACORN) v. USA." http://www.ccrjustice.org/acorn-v-usa.

Champagne, F., and M. J. Meaney. 2001. "Like Mother, Like Daughter: Evidence for Non-Genomic Transmission of Parental Behavior and Stress Responsivity." *Progress in Brain Research* 133: 287–302.

Charlton, J., ed. 1998. *Nothing about Us without Us: Disability Oppression and Empowerment.* Berkeley: University of California Press.

Chen, N. 2003. *Breathing Spaces: Qigong, Psychiatry, and Healing in China.* New York: Columbia University Press.

Chilibeck, G., M. Lock, and M. Sedhev. 2011. "Postgenomics, Uncertain Futures, and the Familiarization of Susceptibility Genes." *Social Science & Medicine* 72 (11): 1768–75.

Clark, F. E. 1895. "World Wide Endeavor." *Junior Christian Endeavor Society Newsletter* 57 (642): 415.

Clarke, A. 1987. "Research Materials and Reproductive Science in the United States, 1910–1940." In *Physiology in the American Context, 1850–1940,* edited by G. L. Geison, 323–50. Baltimore: American Physiological Society and Williams and Wilkins.

———. 1991. "Embryology and the Rise of American Reproductive Sciences, circa 1910–1940." In *The Expansion of American Biology,* edited by K. R. Benson, J. Maienschein, and R. Rainger, 107–32. New Brunswick: Rutgers University Press.

———. 1998. *Disciplining Reproduction: Modernity, American Life Sciences, and "The Problems of Sex."* Berkeley: University of California Press.

———. 2009. "Musings on Genome Medicine: The Value of Family History." *Genome Medicine* 1: 1–3.

Clatts, M. C. 1995. "Disembodied Acts: On the Perverse Use of Sexual Categories in the Study of High-Risk Behaviour." In *Culture and Sexual Risk: Anthropological Perspectives on AIDS*, edited by H. Brummelhuis and G. Herdt, 241–55. Amsterdam: Gordon and Breach.

Clifford, J. 1988. *The Predicament of Culture: Twentieth-Century Ethnography, Literature, and Art.* Cambridge: Harvard University Press.

Cohen, L. 1998. *No Aging in India: Alzheimers, the Bad Family, and Other Modern Things.* Berkeley: University of California Press.

———. 1999. "Where It Hurts: Indian Material for an Ethics of Organ Transplantation." *Daedalus* 128 (4): 135–65.

———. 2001. "The Other Kidney: Biopolitics beyond Recognition." *Body and Society* 7 (2–3): 9–29.

———. 2004a. "Operability, Bioavailability, and Exception." In *Global Assemblages: Technology, Politics, and Ethics as Anthropological Problems*, edited by A. Ong and S. J. Collier, 79–90. Oxford: Blackwell.

———. 2004b. "Operability: Surgery at the Margins of the State." In *Anthropology in the Margins of the State*, edited by V. Das and D. Poole, 165–90. Santa Fe: School of American Research Press.

Comaroff, J. 1985. *Body of Power, Spirit of Resistance: The Culture and History of a South African People.* Chicago: University of Chicago Press.

Connell, R. W. 1995. *Masculinities.* Berkeley: University of California Press.

Connelly, M. J. 2008. *Fatal Misconception: The Struggle to Control World Population.* Cambridge: Harvard University Press.

Cooke, G. W. 1858. *China.* London: Routledge.

Cooper, M. 2008. *Life as Surplus: Biotechnology and Capitalism in the Neoliberal Era.* Seattle: University of Washington Press.

Copeman, J. 2009. *Veins of Devotion: Blood Donation and Religious Experience in North India.* New Brunswick: Rutgers University Press.

Corbo, R. M., and R. Scacchi. 1999. "Apolipoprotein E (APOE) Allele Distribution in the World: Is APOE*4 a 'Thrifty' Allele?" *Annals of Human Genetics* 63 (4): 301–10.

Corder, E. H., A. M. Saunders, W. J. Strittmatter, D. E. Schmechel, P. C. Gaskell, G. W. Small, A. D. Roses, J. L. Haines, and M. A. Pericak-Vance. 1993. "Gene Dose of Apolipoprotein E Type 4 Allele and the Risk of Alzheimer's Disease in Late Onset Families." *Science* 261 (5123): 921–23.

Corin, E. 1979. "A Possession Psychotherapy in an Urban Setting: Zebola in Kinshasa." *Social Science & Medicine* 13B (4): 327–38.

Corin, E., and G. Bibeau. 1975. "De la forme culturelle au vecu des troubles psychiques en Afrique: Propositions méthodologiques pour une étude interculturelle du champ des maladies mentales." *Africa* 45 (3): 280–315.

Corker, M., and T. Shakespeare, eds. 2002. *Disability/Postmodernity: Embodying Disability Theory*. London: Continuum.

Cornwall, A., and N. Lindisfarne, eds. 1994. *Dislocating Masculinity: Comparative Ethnographies*. London: Routledge.

Corrêa, S., with Reichmann, R. 1994. *Population and Reproductive Rights: Feminist Perspectives from the South*. London: Zed Books.

Corrêa, S., R. Petchesky, and R. Parker. 2008. *Sexuality, Health and Human Rights*. London and New York: Routledge.

Cowdry, E. V. 1919a. Letter to George L. Streeter, July 18. George L. Streeter folder, E. V. Cowdry Papers, Becker Medical Library, Washington University School of Medicine.

———. 1919b. Letter to George L. Streeter, October 24. George L. Streeter folder, E. V. Cowdry Papers, Becker Medical Library, Washington University School of Medicine.

———. 1920a. Letter to George L. Streeter, August 25. George L. Streeter folder, E. V. Cowdry Papers, Becker Medical Library, Washington University School of Medicine.

———. 1920b. Letter to Paul H. Stevenson, August 14. Paul H. Stevenson folder, E. V. Cowdry Papers, Becker Medical Library, Washington University School of Medicine.

———. 1920c. "Anatomy in China." *Anatomical Record* 20: 32–60.

———. 1925. "Medical Research in China." *Science* 62 (Oct. 23): 374–77.

Cox, S., and W. McKellin. 1999. "'There's This Thing in Our Family': Predictive Testing and the Construction of Risk for Huntington Disease." In *Sociological Perspectives on the New Genetics*, edited by P. Conrad and J. Gabe, 121–48. London: Blackwell.

Crandon-Malamud, L. 1991. *From the Fat of Our Souls: Social Change, Political Process, and Medical Pluralism in Bolivia*. Berkeley: University of California Press.

Crapanzano, V. 1980. *Tuhami: Portrait of a Moroccan*. Chicago: University of Chicago Press.

Crenshaw, K. W. 1991. "Mapping the Margins: Intersectionality, Identity Politics, and Violence against Women of Color." *Stanford Law Review* 43 (6): 1241–99.

Croll, E. 2001. *Endangered Daughters: Discrimination and Development in Asia*. London: Routledge.

Crozier, R. C. 1968. *Traditional Medicine in Modern China: Science, Nationalism, and the Tensions of Cultural Change*. Cambridge: Harvard University Press.

Csordas, T. 1990. "Embodiment as a Paradigm for Anthropology." *Ethos* 18 (1): 5–47.

———. 1993. "Somatic Modes of Attention." *Cultural Anthropology* 8 (2): 135–56.

Cupples, A. L., L. A. Farrer, D. A. Sadovnick, N. Relkin, P. Whitehouse, and R. C. Green. 2004. "Estimating Risk Curves for First-Degree Relatives of Patients with Alzheimer's Disease: The REVEAL Study." *Genetics in Medicine* 6 (4): 192–96.

Currah, P., R. M. Juang, and S. Price Minter, eds. 2006. *Transgender Rights*. Minneapolis: University of Minnesota Press.

Daniel, H. 1989. *Vida Antes da Morte/Life Before Death*. Rio de Janeiro: Jaboti.

Daniel, H., and R. Parker. 1993. *Sexuality, Politics and AIDS in Brazil*. London: Falmer Press.

Das, V. 1995. *Critical Events: An Anthropological Perspective on Contemporary India*. Delhi: Oxford University Press.

———. 2002. "Stigma, Contagion, Defect: Issues in the Anthropology of Public Health." Paper presented at U.S. NIH Conference on Stigma and Global Health: Developing a Research Agenda. Bethesda, Maryland, 2001.

———. 2004. "The Signature of the State: The Paradox of Illegibility." In *Anthropology in the Margins of the State*, edited by V. Das and D. Poole, 225–52. Santa Fe: School of American Research Press.

———. 2007. *Life and Words: Violence and the Descent into the Ordinary*. Berkeley: University of California Press.

Das, V., and R. Addlakha. 2001. "Disability and Domestic Citizenship: Voice Gender, and the Making of the Subject." *Public Culture* 13 (3): 511–32.

Das, V., and R. K. Das. 2005. "Urban Health and Pharmaceutical Consumption in Delhi, India." *Journal of Biosocial Science* 38 (2): 69–82.

Das, V., and D. Poole, eds. 2004. *Anthropology at the Margins of the State*. Santa Fe: School of American Research.

Daston, L. 2004. *Things That Talk: Object Lessons from Art and Science*. New York: Zone Books.

Daston, L., and P. Gailson. 2007. *Objectivity*. New York: Zone Books.

Davis, L. 2010. *The Disability Studies Reader*. New York, Routledge.

Davis, S., and R. Matthews. 1999. "Public Interest Anthropology: Beyond the Bureaucratic Ethos." In *Classics of Practicing Anthropology*, edited by P. J. Higgins and A. Paredes, 37–42. Oklahoma City: Society for Applied Anthropology.

Davis-Floyd, R. E. 1993. *Birth as an American Rite of Passage*. Berkeley: University of California Press.

Davis-Floyd, R., and J. Dumit. 1998. *Cyborg Babies: From Techno-Sex to Techno-Tots*. New York: Routledge.

de Groot, J. J. M. 1897. *The Religious System of China, Volume III*. Leiden: E. J. Brill.

de Souza, H. 1994. *A Cura da AIDS/The Cure of AIDS*. Bilingual ed. Edited by R. Parker. Rio de Janeiro: Editora Relume-Dumará.

De Vos, P., W. De Ceukelaire, G. Malaise, D. Pérez, D. Lefèvre, and P. Van der Stuyft. 2009. "Health through People's Empowerment: A Rights-based Approach to Participation." *Health and Human Rights* 11 (1): 23–35.

de Zalduondo, B. O. 1991. "Prostitution Viewed Cross-Culturally: Toward Re-Contextualizing Sex Work in AIDS Research." *Journal of Sex Research* 22 (2): 223–48.

Defoe, W. 2007 [1719]. *Robinson Crusoe*. Digireads.com Publishing.

Dehavenon, A. L., ed. 1999. *There's No Place Like Home: Anthropological Perspectives on Housing and Homelessness in the United States*. Santa Barbara: Praeger Publishers.

Desjarlais, R. R. 1992. *Body and Emotion: The Aesthetics of Illness and Healing in the Nepal Himalayas*. Philadelphia: University of Pennsylvania Press.

———. 1997. *Shelter Blues: Sanity and Selfhood among the Homeless*. Philadelphia: University of Pennsylvania Press.

Desjarlais, R., L. Eisenberg, B. Good, and A. Kleinman, eds. 1995. *World Mental Health: Problems, Priorities, and Policies in Low-Income Countries*. New York: Oxford University Press.

Desrosières, A. 1993. *La politique des grands nombres. Histoire de la raison statistique*. Paris: La Découverte.

Devereux, G. 1961. "Shamans as Neurotics." *American Anthropologist* 63: 1088–90.

———. 1967. *From Anxiety to Method in the Behavioral Sciences*. The Hague: Mouton.

Devisch, R. 1983. "Beyond a Structural Approach to Therapeutic Efficacy." In *The Future of Structuralism*, edited by J. Oosten and A. de Ruijter, 403–21. Göttingen: Edition Herodot.

Dezeimeris, J. E. 1983. *Lettres sur l'histoire de la médecine*. Paris: Chez l'auteur.

Diggins, J. P. 1996. *Max Weber: Politics and the Spirit of America*. New York: Basic Books.

Dikötter, F. 1995. *Sex, Culture, and Modernity in China: Medical Science and the Construction of Sexual Identities in the Early Republican Period*. Honolulu: University of Hawaii Press.

———, ed. 1997. *The Construction of Racial Identities in China and Japan*. London: C. Hurst.

Dirks, N. 1987. *The Hollow Crown: An Ethnohistory of an Indian Kingdom*. Cambridge: Cambridge University Press.

Dixon, P. 2000. "Eating Fetuses: The Lurid Christian Fantasy of Godless Chinese Eating 'Unborn Children.'" http://www.jesus21.com/poppydixon/sex/chinese_eating_fetuses.html.

Dorow, S. K. 2006. *Transnational Adoption: A Cultural Economy of Race, Gender, and Kinship*. New York: New York University Press.

Douglas, M. 1966. "Population Control in Primitive Groups." *British Journal of Sociology* 17 (3): 263–73.

———. 1990. "Risk as a Forensic Resource." *Daedelus* 119 (4): 1–16.

———. 1991. *Purity and Danger*. London: Routledge.

Downey, G. L, and J. Dumit. 1997. *Cyborgs and Citadels: Anthropological Interventions in Emerging Sciences and Technologies*. Santa Fe: School of American Research Press.

Doyal, L. 1979. *The Political Economy of Health*. Boston: South End Press.

Dressler, W. W., M. C. Balieiro, R. P. Ribeiro, and J. E. Dos-Santos. 2006. "Depressive Symptoms and C-reactive Protein in a Brazilian Urban Community." *Brazilian Journal of Medical and Biological Research* 39: 1013–19.

Dressler, W. W., K. S. Oths, and C. C. Gravlee. 2005. "Race and Ethnicity in Public Health Research: Models to Explain Health Disparities." *Annual Review of Anthropology* 34: 231–52.

Duden, B. 1993. *Disembodying Women: Perspectives on Pregnancy and the Unborn*. 1st German ed., 1991. Cambridge: Harvard University Press.

Dumit, J. 2003. *Picturing Personhood: Brain Scans and Biomedical Identity*. Princeton: Princeton University Press.

———. 2005. "The Depsychiatrisation of Mental Illness." *Journal of Public Mental Health* 4 (3): 8–13.

Dumont, L. 1980 [1966]. *Homo Hierarchicus: The Caste System and Its Implications*. Translated by Mark Sainsbury, Louis Dumont, and Basia Gulati. Chicago: University of Chicago Press.

Durkheim, E. 1966 [1893]. *The Division of Labor in Society*. Translated by George Simpson. New York: Free Press.

———. 1979 [1897]. *Suicide: A Study in Sociology*. Translated by John A. Spaulding and George Simpson. New York: Free Press.

Eberhard, W. 1982. *China's Minorities: Yesterday and Today*. Belmont: Wadsworth.

Ecks, S. 2005. "Pharmaceutical Citizenship: Antidepressant Marketing and the Promise of Demarginalization in India." *Anthropology and Medicine* 12 (3): 239–54.

Edgerton, R. 1993 [1967]. *The Cloak of Competence: Stigma in the Lives of the Mentally Retarded*. 2nd ed. Berkeley: University of California Press.

Eisenberg, M. 2010. "The State and Disability: How Participant Observation Led to Legislative and Administrative Policy Change." Paper presented at the Society for Applied Anthropology, Merida, Mexico.

Eitel, E. J. 1885. "Review of Mrs. Bryson's *Child Life in Chinese Homes.*" *China Review* 13 (May–June), 423–24.

Elegant, S. 2007. "Why Forced Abortion Persists in China." *Time* (April 30). http://www.time.com/time/world/article/0,8599,1615936,00.html.

Elias, N. 1987. *Involvement and Detachment.* Malden: Blackwell.

Engels, F., and E. B. Leacock. 1972. *The Origin of the Family, Private Property, and the State, in the Light of the Researches of Lewis H. Morgan.* New York: International Publishers Co.

Epprecht, M. 2004. *Hungochani: The History of a Dissident Sexuality in Southern Africa.* Montreal: McGill-Queen's University Press.

Epstein, S. 2007. *Inclusion: The Politics of Difference in Medical Research.* Chicago: University of Chicago Press.

Erickson, P. 2003. "Medical Anthropology and Global Health." *Medical Anthropology Quarterly* 17 (1): 3–4.

Erikson, S. L. 2011. "Global Ethnography: Problems of Theory and Method." In *Reproduction, Globalization, and the State: New Theoretical and Ethnographic Perspectives*, edited by C. H. Browner and C. F. Sargent, 23–37. Durham: Duke University Press.

Errington, F., and D. Gewertz. 2004. *Yali's Question: Sugar, Culture, and History.* Chicago: University of Chicago Press.

Escobar, A. 1995. *Encountering Development: The Making and Unmaking of the Third World.* Princeton: Princeton University Press.

Estroff, S. 1985. *Making It Crazy: An Ethnography of Psychiatric Clients in an American Community.* Berkeley: University of California Press.

Evans-Pritchard, E. E. 1937. *Witchcraft, Oracles and Magic among the Azande.* Oxford: Clarendon Press.

Ewald, F. 1991. "Insurance and Risk." In *The Foucault Effect: Studies in Governmentality*, edited by G. Burchell, C. Gordon, and P. Miller, 197–210. Chicago: University of Chicago Press.

Fabian, J. 1983. *Time and the Other: How Anthropology Makes Its Object.* New York: Columbia University Press.

Fahs, A. 2002. "Newspaper Women and the Making of the Modern, 1885–1910." *Prospects* 27: 303–39.

Fardon, R., ed. 1990. *Localizing Strategies: Regional Traditions of Ethnographic Writing.* Edinburgh: Scottish Academic Press.

Farmer, P. 1992. *AIDS and Accusation: Haiti and the Geography of Blame.* Berkeley: University of California Press.

———. 1997. "AIDS and Anthropologists: Ten Years Later." *Medical Anthropology Quarterly* 11 (4): 516–25.

———. 1999. *Infections and Inequalities: The Modern Plagues.* Berkeley: University of California Press.

———. 2003. *Pathologies of Power: Health, Human Rights, and the New War on the Poor.* Berkeley: University of California Press.

———. 2004. "An Anthropology of Structural Violence." *Current Anthropology* 45 (3): 304–24.

Farmer, P., M. Connors, and J. Simmons, eds. 1996. *Women, Poverty, and AIDS: Sex, Drugs and Structural Violence.* Monroe: Common Courage Press.

Farmer, P., H. Saussy, and T. Kidder. 2010. *Partner to the Poor: A Paul Farmer Reader.* Berkeley: University of California Press.

Farquhar, J. 1994a. "Eating Chinese Medicine." *Cultural Anthropology* 9 (4): 471–97.

———. 1994b. *Knowing Practice: The Clinical Encounter of Chinese Medicine.* Boulder: Westview.

———. 2002. *Appetites: Food and Sex in Post-Socialist China.* Durham: Duke University Press.

Farrer, L. A. 2000. "Familial Risk for Alzheimer's Disease in Ethnic Minorities: Nondiscriminating Genes." *Archives of Neurology* 57 (1): 28–29.

Farrer, L. A., L. A. Cupples, J. L. Haines, B. Hyman, W. A. Kukull, R. Mayeux, M. A. Pericak-Vance, N. Risch, and C. M. van Dujin. 1997. "Effects of Age, Sex, and Ethnicity on the Association between Apolipoprotein E Genotype and Alzheimer's Disease: A Meta-analysis." *Journal of the American Medical Association* 278: 1349–56.

Fassin, D. 2005. "Compassion and Repression. The Moral Economy of Immigration Policies in France." *Cultural Anthropology* 20, 362–87.

———. 2007. *When Bodies Remember: Experience and Politics of AIDS in South Africa.* Berkeley: University of California Press.

———. 2008. "The Humanitarian Politics of Testimony: Subjectification through Trauma in the Israeli-Palestinian Conflict." *Cultural Anthropology* 23: 531–58.

———. 2009. "Another Politics of Life Is Possible." *Theory, Culture, and Society* 26 (5): 44–60.

———. 2011a. *Humanitarian Reason: A Moral History of the Present.* Berkeley: University of California Press.

———. 2011b. "Noli Me Tangere: The Moral Untouchability of Humanitarianism." In *Forces of Compassion: Humanitarianism Between Ethics and Politics,* edited by E. Bornstein and P. Redfield, 35–52. Santa Fe: School of Advanced Research Press.

Fassin, D., and M. Pandolfi, eds. 2010. *Contemporary States of Emergency: The Politics of Military and Humanitarian Interventions.* New York: Zone Books.

Fassin, D., and R. Rechtman. 2009. *The Empire of Trauma. An Inquiry into the Condition of Victimhood.* Princeton: Princeton University Press.

Favret-Saada, J. 1977. *Les mots, la mort, et les sorts: La sorcellerie dans le bocage.* Paris: Gallimard.

Fee, E. 1973. "The Sexual Politics of Victorian Social Anthropology." *Feminist Studies* 1 (3–4): 23–39.

Ferguson, J. 1994. *The Anti-Politics Machine: "Development," De-politicization and Bureaucratic Power in Lesotho.* Minneapolis: University of Minnesota Press.

———. 2006. *Global Shadows: Africa in the Neoliberal World Order.* Durham: Duke University Press.

Finkler, K. 2000. *Experiencing the New Genetics: Family and Kinship on the Medical Frontier.* Philadelphia: University of Pennsylvania Press.

———. 2001. "The Kin in the Gene: The Medicalization of Family and Kinship in American Society." *Current Anthropology* 42 (2): 235–63.

Finkler, K., C. Skrzynia, and J. P. Evans. 2003. "The New Genetics and Its Consequences for Family, Kinship, Medicine, and Medical Genetics." *Social Science & Medicine* 57 (3): 403–12.

Firth, R. 1963. *We, the Tikopia.* Boston: Beacon Press.

Fischer, M. M. J. 2003. *Emergent Forms of Life and the Anthropological Voice.* Durham: Duke University Press.

Fisher, K. 2000. "The Accidental Advocate: Two Decades of Studying Homelessness." *Reed Magazine* (February). http://www.reed.edu/reed_magazine/feb2000/a_accidental/index.html.

Fong, V. L. 2004. *Only Hope: Coming of Age under China's One-Child Policy.* Stanford: Stanford University Press.

Ford Foundation. 1991. "Reproductive Health: A Strategy for the 1990s." Program paper, New York, Ford Foundation. http://www.fordfound.org/elibrary/documents/0148/normal/low/0148norm-low.pdf.

Fortes, M. 1949. *The Web of Kinship among the Tallensi.* Oxford: Oxford University Press.

Fortun, K. 2001. *Advocacy after Bhopal: Environmentalism, Disaster, New Global Orders.* Chicago: University of Chicago Press.

Foster, G. M., and B. G. Anderson. 1978. *Medical Anthropology.* New York: John Wiley and Sons.

Foucault, M. 1980. *Power/Knowledge: Selected Interviews and Other Writings, 1972–1977.* Edited by Colin Gordon. New York: Pantheon.

———. 1994 [1973]. *The Birth of the Clinic: An Archaeology of Medical Perception.* New York: Vintage Books.

———. 1998a. *Madness and Civilization: A History of Insanity in the Age of Reason.* New York: Routledge.

———. 1998b. *Ethics: Subjectivity and Truth*, edited by P. Rabinow. New York: New Press.

———. 2003a. "Abnormal: Lectures at the College de France, 1974–75." Edited by V. Marchetti and A. Salomoni. New York: Picador.

———. 2003b. "The Subject and Power." In *The Essential Foucault*. 1st ed., 1982. Edited by P. Rabinow and N. Rose, 126–44. New York: New Press.

———. 2008. *The Birth of Biopolitics: Lectures at the Collège de France, 1978–1979*. New York: Palgrave Macmillan.

———. 2009 [1984]. "Le souci de la vérité." In *Dits et ecrits II, 1976–1988*, 1487–97. Paris: Gallimard.

Frank, G. 2000. *Venus on Wheels: Two Decades of Dialogue on Disability, Biography, and Being Female in America*. Berkeley: University of California Press.

Frankel, S. 1986. *Huli Response to Illness*. Cambridge: Cambridge University Press.

Frankenberg, R. 1976. "Disease, Illness and Sickness: Social Aspects of the Choice of Healer in a Lusaka Suburb." In *Social Anthropology and Medicine*, edited by J. B. Loudon, 223–58. London: Academic Press.

———. 1980. "Medical Anthropology and Development: A Theoretical Perspective." *Social Science & Medicine. Part B: Medical Anthropology* 14 (4): 197–207.

Franklin, S. 1991. "Fetal Fascinations: New Dimensions to the Medical-Scientific Construction of Fetal Personhood." In *Off-Centre: Feminism and Cultural Studies*, edited by S. Franklin, C. Lury, and J. Stacey, 190–205. London: Harper Collins.

———. 1995. "Science as Culture, Cultures of Science." *Annual Review of Anthropology* 24: 163–84.

———. 1997. *Embodied Progress: A Cultural Account of Assisted Conception*. New York: Routledge.

———. 2001. "Sheepwatching." *Anthropology Today* 17 (3): 3–9.

———. 2007. *Dolly Mixtures: The Remaking of Genealogy*. Durham: Duke University Press.

Franklin, S., and C. Roberts. 2006. *Born and Made: An Ethnography of Preimplantation Genetic Diagnosis*. Princeton: Princeton University Press.

Freeman, D. 1983. *Margaret Mead and Samoa: The Making and Unmaking of an Anthropological Myth*. Cambridge: Harvard University Press.

French, L. 1994. "The Political Economy of Injury and Compassion: Amputees on the Thai-Cambodia Border." In *Embodiment and Experience: The Existential Ground of Culture and Self*, edited by T. J. Csordas, 69–99. Cambridge: Cambridge University Press.

Freud, S. 1963 [1930]. *Civilization and Its Discontents*. Translated by James Strachey. New York: W. W. Norton and Company.

Fry, P. 1982. *Para Inglês Ver: Identidade e Política na Cultura Brasileira*. Rio de Janeiro: Zahar Editores.

Fullwiley, D. 2004. "Discriminate Biopower and Everyday Biopolitics: Views on Sickle Cell Testing in Dakar." *Medical Anthropology* 23 (2): 157–94.

———. 2007. "The Molecularization of Race: Institutionalizing Human Difference in Pharmacogenetics Practice." *Science as Culture* 16 (1): 1–30.

Gaines, A. D. 1982. "Knowledge and Practice: Anthropological Ideas and Psychiatric Practice." In *Clinically Applied Anthropology*, edited by N. J. Chrisman and T. W. Maretzki, 243–73. New York: Springer.

Galison, P., and D. J. Stump, eds. 1996. *The Disunity of Science: Boundaries, Contexts, and Power*. Stanford: Stanford University Press.

Gallagher, G., and P. Konjoian. 2010. *Shut Up About Your Perfect Kid: A Survival Guide for Ordinary Parents of Special Children*. New York: Three Rivers Press.

Galvão, J. 2000. *AIDS No Brasil: A Agenda de Construção de uma Epidemia*. São Paulo: Editora 34.

———. 2008. "Betinho: Celebration of a Life in Brazil." In *The Practice of International Health*, edited by D. Perlman and A. Roy, 231–44. New York: Oxford University Press.

Garcia, A. 2010. *The Pastoral Clinic: Addiction and Dispossession along the Rio Grande*. Berkeley: University of California Press.

García, J., M. Muñoz-Laboy, V. de Almeida, and R. Parker. 2009. "Local Impacts of Religious Discourses on Rights to Express Same-sex Sexual Desires in Periurban Rio de Janeiro." *Sexuality Research and Social Policy* 6 (3): 44–60.

Garland-Thomson, R. 2009. *Staring: How We Look*. New York: Oxford University Press.

Garrett, L. 2005. *HIV and National Security. Where Are the Links?* New York: Council on Foreign Affairs.

Geertz, C. 1973. *The Interpretation of Cultures: Selected Essays*. New York: Basic Books.

Gell, A. 1996. "Vogel's Net." *Journal of Material Culture* 1 (1): 15–38.

Gibbon, S. 2007. *Breast Cancer Genes and the Gendering of Knowledge: Science and Citizenship in the Context of the "New" Genetics*. London: Palgrave Macmillan.

Gibbon, S., and C. Novas, eds. 2007. *Biosocialities, Genetics and the Social Sciences: Making Biologies and Identities*. London: Routledge.

Gibbons, J. 1995. "Reveille For Radicals: Lessons from the Life of Saul Alinsky, A Sermon." http://www.uubedford.org/sermons/19950226.htm.

Gibbs, W. W. 2003. "The Unseen Genome: Gems among the Junk." *Scientific American* 289 (5): 47–53.

Gilbert, S. F. 2002. "The Genome in Its Ecological Context: Philosophical Perspectives on Interspecies Epigenesis." *Annals of the New York Academy of Sciences* 981: 202–18.

Gillette, H. 2006. *Between Justice and Beauty: Race, Planning, and the Failure of Urban Policy in Washington, D.C.* Philadelphia: University of Pennsylvania Press.

Ginsburg, F. D. 1987. "Procreation Stories: Reproduction, Nurturance, and Procreation in Life Narratives of Abortion Activists." *American Ethnologist* 14 (4): 623–36.

———. 1989.*Contested Lives: The Abortion Debate in an American Community.* Berkeley: University of California Press.

Ginsburg, F. D., L. Abu-Lughod, and B. Larkin, eds. 2002. *Media Worlds: Anthropology on New Terrain.* Berkeley: University of California Press.

Ginsburg, F. D., and R. Rapp. 1991. "The Politics of Reproduction." *Annual Review of Anthropology* 20: 311–43.

———, eds. 1995. *Conceiving the New World Order: The Global Politics of Reproduction.* Berkeley: University of California Press.

Gonzalez, R. 2009. *American Counterinsurgency: Human Science and the Human Terrain.* Chicago: University of Chicago Press, Prickly Paradigm Press.

Good, B. 1977. "The Heart of What's the Matter: The Semantics of Illness in Iran." *Culture, Medicine, and Psychiatry* 1 (1): 25–58.

———. 1994. *Medicine, Rationality and Experience.* Cambridge: Cambridge University Press.

Good, B., M. M. J. Fischer, S. S. Willen, and M.-J. D. Good, eds. 2010. *A Reader in Medical Anthropology: Theoretical Trajectories, Emergent Realities.* Malden: Wiley-Blackwell.

Good, B., and M.-J. Delvecchio Good. 1981. "The Meaning of Symptoms: A Cultural Hermeneutic Model for Clinical Practice." In *The Relevance of Social Science for Medicine*, edited by L. Eisenberg and A. Kleinman, 165–96. Dordrecht: D. Reidel.

———. 2008. "Postcolonial Disorders: Reflections on Subjectivity in the Contemporary World." In *Postcolonial Disorders*, edited by M.-J. D. Good, S. T. Hyde, S. Pinto, and B. J. Good, 1–41. Berkeley: University of California Press.

Good, B., M.-J. Good, and J. H. Grayman. 2009. "Conflict Nightmares and Trauma in Aceh." *Culture, Medicine, and Psychiatry* 33 (2): 290–312.

Good, M.-J. D., S. S. Willen, S. D. Hannah, K. Vickory, and L. T. Park, eds. 2011. *Shattering Culture: American Medicine Responds to Cultural Diversity.* New York: Russell Sage Foundation.

Goodman, A. H., and T. L. Leatherman, eds. 1998. *Building a New Biocultural Synthesis: Political-Economic Perspectives on Human Biology*. Ann Arbor: University of Michigan Press.

Gottweis, H., B. Salter, and C. Waldby. 2009. *The Global Politics of Human Embryonic Stem Cell Science: Regenerative Medicine in Transition*. Basingstoke: Palgrave Macmillan.

Grace, V. M. 2008. "Human Genome Epidemiology: Reviewing the Stakes." *International Journal of Health Services* 38 (1): 143–59.

Gravlee, C. C. 2009. "How Race Becomes Biology: Embodiment of Social Inequality." *American Journal of Physical Anthropology* 139 (1): 47–57.

Green, E. C. 2003. *Rethinking AIDS Prevention: Learning from Success in Developing Countries*. Westport: Praeger.

Green, L. 1999. *Fear as a Way of Life: Mayan Widows in Rural Guatemala*. New York: Columbia University Press.

Greenhalgh, S. 1995. "Anthropology Theorizes Reproduction: Integrating Practice, Political Economic, and Feminist Perspectives." In *Situating Fertility: Anthropology and Demographic Inquiry*, edited by S. Greenhalgh, 3–28. Cambridge: Cambridge University Press.

———. 1996. "The Social Construction of Population Science: An Intellectual, Institutional, and Political History of 20th Century Demography." *Comparative Studies in Society and History* 38 (1): 26–66.

———. 2001. *Under the Medical Gaze: Facts and Fictions of Chronic Pain*. Berkeley: University of California Press.

———. 2005. "Globalization and Population Governance in China." In *Global Assemblages: Technology, Politics, and Ethics as Anthropological Problems*, edited by A. Ong and S. J. Collier, 354–72. Malden: Wiley-Blackwell.

———. 2008. *Just One Child: Science and Policy in Deng's China*. Berkeley: University of California Press.

Greenhalgh, S., and E. Winckler. 2005. *Governing China's Population: From Leninist to Neoliberal Politics*. Stanford: Stanford University Press.

Grezemkovsky, U. 2005. "Happiness Is the Cure: Self-Improvement and Authenticity in Contemporary American Life." PhD dissertation, Department of Anthropology, University of California, Berkeley.

Grinker, R. R. 2007. *Unstrange Minds: Remapping the World of Autism*. New York: Basic Books.

Groce, N. 1985. *Everyone Here Spoke Sign Language: Hereditary Deafness on Martha's Vineyard*. Cambridge: Harvard University Press.

Gruenbaum, E. 2001. *The Female Circumcision Controversy: An Anthropological Perspective*. Philadelphia: University of Pennsylvania Press.

Guarnaccia, P. J. 1993. "Ataques De Nervios in Puerto Rico: Culture-Bound Syndrome or Popular Illness?" *Medical Anthropology* 15 (2): 157–70.

Gudding, G. 1996. "The Phenotype/Genotype Distinction and the Disappearance of the Body." *Journal of the History of Ideas* 57 (3): 525–45.

Guo, J. H. 2008. "Stigma: Social Suffering for Social Exclusion and Social Insecurity." PhD dissertation, Department of Anthropology, Harvard University.

Gutmann, M. C. 1996. *The Meanings of Macho: Being a Man in Mexico City.* Berkeley: University of California Press.

———. 1997. "Trafficking in Men: The Anthropology of Masculinity." *Annual Review of Anthropology* 26: 385–409.

———, ed. 2003. *Changing Men and Masculinities in Latin America.* Durham: Duke University Press.

———. 2007. *Fixing Men: Sex, Birth Control, and AIDS in Mexico.* Berkeley: University of California Press.

Guyer, J. I. 2007. "Prophecy and the Near Future: Thoughts on Macroeconomic, Evangelical, and Punctuated Time." *American Ethnologist* 34 (3): 409–21.

Gwaltney, J. L. 1980. *Drylongso: A Self-Portrait of Black America.* New York: Random House.

Hacking, I. 1995. "The Looping Effects of Human Kinds." In *Causal Cognition: A Multidisciplinary Approach*, edited by D. Sperber, D. Premack, and A. J. Premack, 351–83. Oxford: Oxford University Press.

———. 2007. "Making Up People." In *Beyond the Body Proper: Reading the Anthropology of Material Life*, edited by M. Lock and J. Farquhar, 150–63. Durham: Duke University Press.

Hahn, R. A. 1995. *Sickness and Healing: An Anthropological Perspective.* New Haven: Yale University Press.

Hahn, R. A., and M. C. Inhorn, eds. 2009. *Anthropology and Public Health: Bridging Differences in Culture and Society.* 2nd ed. New York: Oxford University Press.

Hallowell, A. I. 1955. *Culture and Experience.* Philadelphia: University of Pennsylvania Press.

Hallowell, N. 1999. "Doing the Right Thing: Genetic Risk and Responsibility." *Sociology of Health and Illness* 21 (5): 597–621.

Hamann, E., K. Anderson, B. Levinson, C. Cannella, M. Pollock, and S. Wright. 2007. "Educational Policy as a Matter for Anthropologists' Scholarly and Applied Engagement." Unpublished manuscript, Council on Anthropology and Education, American Anthropological Association.

Han, C. 2007. "Life in Debt: Depression and Survival in Chile's Market Democracy." PhD dissertation, Department of Anthropology, Harvard University.

Hansen, T. B. 1999. *The Saffron Wave: Democracy and Hindu Nationalism in Modern India*. Princeton: Princeton University Press.

Haraway, D. J. 1985. "A Manifesto for Cyborgs: Science, Technology, and Socialist Feminism in the 1980s." *Socialist Review* 80: 65–107.

———. 1988. "Situated Knowledges: The Science Question in Feminism and the Privilege of Partial Perspective." *Feminist Studies* 14: 575–99.

———. 1989. *Primate Visions: Gender, Race, and Nature in the World of Modern Science*. New York: Routledge.

Harding, J. E. 2001. "The Nutritional Basis of the Fetal Origins of Adult Disease." *International Journal of Epidemiology* 30: 15–23.

Harding, S. F. 2000. *The Book of Jerry Falwell: Fundamentalist Language and Politics*. Princeton: Princeton University Press.

Harmon, A. 2007. "After DNA Diagnosis: 'Hello, 16p11.2. Are You Just Like Me?'" *New York Times*, December 28.

Harold, D., A. Richard, P. Hollingworth et al. 2009. "Genome-wide Association Study Identifies Variants at CLU and PICALM Associated with Alzheimer's Disease." *Nature Genetics* 41: 1088–93. doi:10.1038/ng.440.

Harper, I. 2005. "Anthropology, DOTS, and Understanding Tuberculosis Control in Nepal." *Journal of Biosocial Science* 38 (2): 57–67.

Harrison, F. V. 1994. "Racial and Gender Inequalities in Health Care." *Medical Anthropology Quarterly* 8 (1): 90–95.

Hartsock, N. 2004. "The Feminist Standpoint: Developing the Ground for a Specifically Feminist Historical Materialism." In *Discovering Reality: Feminist Perspectives on Epistemology, Metaphysics, Methodology, and Philosophy of Science*, edited by S. Harding and M. Hintikka, 283–310. Amsterdam: D. Reidel.

Harvey, D. 1985. *Consciousness and the Urban Experience: Studies in the History and Theory of Capitalist Urbanization*. Baltimore: Johns Hopkins University Press.

Harwood, A., ed. 1981. *Ethnicity and Medical Care*. Cambridge: Harvard University Press.

Hawkeswood, W. G. 1996. *One of the Children: Gay Black Men in Harlem*. Berkeley: University of California Press.

Hayden, C. 2003. *When Nature Goes Public: The Making and Unmaking of Bioprospecting in Mexico*. Princeton: Princeton University Press.

———. 2007. "A Generic Solution? Pharmaceuticals and the Politics of the Similar in Mexico." *Current Anthropology* 48 (4): 475–95.

Head, C. 2008. "Lost in Translation and Political Will: Research and Policy as a Means to Advance Human Rights." *Entrepreneur* (Fall). http://www.entrepreneur.com/tradejournals/article/191854972.html.

Heath, D., R. Rapp, and K. S. Taussig. 2004. "Genetic Citizenship." In *A Companion to the Anthropology of Politics*, edited by D. Nugent and J. Vincent, 152–67. London: Blackwell.

Heilborn, M. L., E. M. L. Aquino, M. Bozon, and D. R. Knauth, eds. 2006. *O aprendizado da sexualidade: Reprodução e trajetórias sociais de jovens Brasileiros.* Rio de Janeiro: Editora Fiocruz and Editora Garamond.

Heimer, R., S. Clair, W. Teng, L. Grau, K. Khoshnood, and M. Singer. 2002. "Effects of Increasing Syringe Availability on Syringe-Exchange Use and HIV Risk: Connecticut, 1990–2001." *Journal of Urban Health* 79 (4): 556–70.

Heinemann, L. L. 2011. "Transplanting Kinship: Transplantation, Kin Relatedness, and Daily Home Life in the Midwest U.S." PhD dissertation, University of Michigan.

Helman, C. G. 1982. "Prevailing Beliefs and Attitudes of British Patients in General Practice: Some Examples and Their Clinical Implications." In *Folk Medicine and Health Culture: Role of Folk Medicine in Modern Health Care*, edited by T. Vaskilampi and C. MacCormack, 143–63. Kuopio: University of Kuopio.

———. 1992. *Culture, Health, and Society.* 2nd ed. Boston: Wright.

———. 2007. *Culture, Health, and Illness.* London: Hodder Arnold.

Hemminki, E., Z. Wu, G. Cao, and K. Viisainen. 2005. "Illegal Births and Legal Abortions—the Case of China." *Reproductive Health* 11 (2): 5.

Herdt, G. 1987. "AIDS and Anthropology." *Anthropology Today* 3 (2): 1–3.

———. 1997. "Sexual Culture and Population Movement: Implications for AIDS/STDs." In *Sexual Cultures and Migration in the Era of AIDS: Anthropological and Demographic Perspectives*, edited by G. Herdt, 3–22. Oxford: Clarendon Press.

Herle, A. 1998. "The Life Histories of Objects: Collections of the Cambridge Anthropological Expedition to the Torres Strait." In *Cambridge and the Torres Strait: Centenary Essays on the 1898 Anthropological Expedition*, edited by A. Herle and S. Rouse, 77–105. Cambridge: Cambridge University Press.

Herle, A., and S. Rouse, eds. 1998. *Cambridge and the Torres Strait: Centenary Essays on the 1898 Anthropological Expedition.* Cambridge: Cambridge University Press.

Hill, S. A. 1994. *Managing Sickle Cell Disease in Low-Income Families.* Philadelphia: Temple University Press.

Hilzenrath, D. 2009. "Health Insurance Industry Spins Data in Fight against Public Plan." *Washington Post*, July 22. http://www.washingtonpost.com/wp-dyn/content/article/2009/07/21/AR2009072101677.html.

Hirsch, J. S. 2003. *A Courtship after Marriage: Sexuality and Love in Mexican Transnational Families.* Berkeley: University of California Press.

Hirsch, J. S., H. Wardlow, D. Jordan Smith, H. Phinney, S. Parikh, and C. A.

Nathanson. 2010. *The Secret: Love, Marriage, and HIV.* Nashville: Vanderbilt University Press.

Hodges, S. 2008. *Contraception, Colonialism, and Commerce: Birth Control in South India, 1920–1940.* Aldershot: Ashgate.

Hogle, L. F. 1999. *Recovering the Nation's Body: Cultural Memory, Medicine, and the Politics of Redemption.* New Brunswick: Rutgers University Press.

Holmes, D. R., and G. E. Marcus. 2006. "Fast Capitalism: Para-Ethnography and the Rise of the Symbolic Analyst." In *Frontiers of Capital*, edited by M. S. Fisher and G. Downey, 33–57. Durham: Duke University Press.

Hood, D. 1964. *Davidson Black, A Biography.* Toronto: University of Toronto Press.

Hopper, K. 1988. "More Than Passing Strange: Homelessness and Mental Illness in New York City." *American Ethnologist* 15 (1): 155–67.

———. 2003. *Reckoning with Homelessness.* Ithaca: Cornell University Press.

Horowitz, I. L. 1983. "Struggling for the Soul of Social Science." *Society* 20 (5): 4–15.

Horton, S., and L. Lamphere. 2006. "A Call to an Anthropology of Health Policy." *Anthropology News* 47 (1): 33–36.

Horwitz, A., and J. Wakefield. 2007. *The Loss of Sadness: How Psychiatry Transformed Normal Sorrow into Depressive Disorder.* New York: Oxford University Press.

Houppert, K. 2009. "How Could a Mother Eat Her Own Baby?" *Salon.com.* http://www.salon.com/mwt/feature/2009/08/01/otty_sanchez/.

Howes, R. 2001. "Herbert Daniel." In *Who's Who in Contemporary Gay and Lesbian History: From World War II to the Present Day*, edited by R. Aldrich and G. Witherspoon, 102–4. New York and London: Routledge.

Hugo, G. 1996. "Environmental Concerns and International Migration." *International Migration Review* 30 (1): 105–31.

Hunt, N. R. 1999. *A Colonial Lexicon of Birth Ritual, Medicalization, and Mobility in the Congo.* Durham: Duke University Press.

Hunter, M. 2002. "The Materiality of Everyday Sex: Thinking Beyond 'Prostitution.'" *African Studies* 61 (1): 99–120.

———. 2005. "Cultural Politics and Masculinities: Multiple-Partners in Historical Perspective in KwaZulu-Natal." *Culture, Health and Sexuality* 7 (4): 389–403.

Hyde, S. 2007. *Eating Spring Rice: The Cultural Politics of AIDS in Southwest China.* Berkeley: University of California Press.

Illich, I. 1976. *Medical Nemesis: The Expropriation of Health.* New York: Pantheon.

Inciardi, J. A., H. L. Surratt, and P. R. Telles. 2000. *Sex, Drugs, and HIV/AIDS in Brazil.* Boulder: Westview Press.

Inden, R. 1990. *Imagining India*. London: Basil Blackwell.

Ingstad, B. 1992. "Care for the Elderly, Care by the Elderly: The Role of Elderly Women in a Changing Tswana Society." *Journal of Cross-Cultural Gerontology* 7: 379–98.

Ingstad, B., and S. R. Whyte, eds. 1995. *Disability and Culture*. Berkeley: University of California Press.

———. 2007. *Disability in Local and Global Worlds*. Berkeley: University of California Press.

Inhorn, M. C. 1994. *Quest for Conception: Gender, Infertility, and Egyptian Medical Traditions*. Philadelphia: University of Pennsylvania Press.

———. 1996. *Infertility and Patriarchy: The Cultural Politics of Gender and Family Life in Egypt*. Philadelphia: University of Pennsylvania Press.

———. 2003a. *Local Babies, Global Science: Gender, Religion, and In Vitro Fertilization in Egypt*. New York: Routledge.

———. 2003b. "Global Infertility and the Globalization of New Reproductive Technologies: Illustrations from Egypt." *Social Science & Medicine* 56: 1837–51.

———. 2006. "Defining Women's Health: A Dozen Messages from More Than 150 Ethnographies." *Medical Anthropology Quarterly* 20 (3): 345–78.

———. 2007a. "Medical Anthropology at the Intersections." *Medical Anthropology Quarterly* 21 (3): 249–55.

———, ed. 2007b. *Reproductive Disruptions: Gender, Technology, and Biopolitics in the New Millennium*. New York: Berghahn.

———. 2012. *The New Arab Man: Emergent Masculinities, Technologies, and Islam in the Middle East*. Princeton: Princeton University Press.

Inhorn, M. C., and P. J. Brown. 1990. "The Anthropology of Infectious Disease." *Annual Review of Anthropology* 19: 89–117.

Inhorn, M. C., T. Tjørnhøj-Thomsen, H. Goldberg, and M. L. Mosegaard, eds. 2009. *Reconceiving the Second Sex: Men, Masculinity and Reproduction*. New York: Berghahn.

Inhorn, M. C., and S. Tremayne, eds. 2012. *Islam and Assisted Reproductive Technologies: Sunni and Shia Perspectives*. New York: Berghahn.

Jablonka, E., and M. J. Lamb. 1995. *Epigenetic Inheritance and Evolution: The Lamarckian Dimension*. Oxford: Oxford University Press.

———. 2005. *Evolution in Four Dimensions: Genetic, Epigenetic, Behavioral, and Symbolic Variation in the History of Life*. Cambridge: MIT Press.

Jackson, J. 1999. *Camp Pain: Talking with Chronic Pain Patients*. Philadelphia: University of Pennsylvania.

Jackson, M. 1998. *Minima Ethnographica: Intersubjectivity and the Anthropological Project*. Chicago: University of Chicago Press.

Jain, S. S. L. 2006. *Injury: The Politics of Product Design and Safety Law in the United States*. Princeton: Princeton University Press.

Jameson, F. 1998. "Preface." In *The Cultures of Globalization*, edited by F. Jameson and M. Miyoshi, xi-xvi. Durham: Duke University Press.

Janes, C. R., O. Chuluundorj, C. E. Hilliard, K. Rak, and K. Janchiv. 2006. "Poor Medicine for Poor People? Assessing the Impact of Neoliberal Reform on Health Care Equity in a Post-Socialist Context." *Global Public Health* 1 (1): 5–30.

Janes, C., and K. Corbett. 2009. "Anthropology and Global Health." *Annual Review of Anthropology* 38: 167–83.

———. 2011. "Global Health." In *A Companion to Medical Anthropology*, edited by M. Singer and P. I. Erickson, 135–58. Malden: Wiley.

Janzen, J. 1978a. "The Comparative Study of Medical Systems as Changing Social Systems." *Social Science & Medicine* 12 (2B): 121–29.

———. 1978b. *The Quest for Therapy in Lower Zaire*. Berkeley: University of California Press.

———. 1992. *Ngoma: Discourses of Healing in Central and Southern Africa*. Berkeley: University of California Press.

Jasen, P. 2002. "Breast Cancer and the Language of Risk, 1750–1950." *Social History of Medicine* 15 (1): 17–43.

Jenkins, J. H. 2004. "Schizophrenia as a Paradigm Case for Understanding Fundamental Human Processes." In *Schizophrenia, Culture, and Subjectivity: The Edge of Experience*, edited by J. H. Jenkins and R. J. Barrett, 29–61. Cambridge: Cambridge University Press.

Jenkins, J. H., and R. J. Barrett. 2004. *Schizophrenia, Culture, and Subjectivity: The Edge of Experience*. Cambridge: Cambridge University Press.

Jenks, A. C. 2010. "What's the Use of Culture? Health Disparities and the Development of Culturally Competent Health Care." In *What's the Use of Race? Modern Governance and the Biology of Difference*, edited by I. Whitmarsh and D. S. Jones, 207–24. Cambridge: MIT Press.

Johnson, K. 2002. "Politics of International and Domestic Adoption in China." *Law and Society Review* 36 (2): 379–96.

Johnston, B. R., ed. 2007. *Half Lives and Half Truths: Confronting the Radioactive Legacies of the Cold War*. Santa Fe: School for Advanced Research Press.

———. 2011. *Life and Death Matters: Human Rights, Environment, and Social Justice*. 2nd ed. New York: Left Coast Press.

Jones, A., ed. 2006. *Men of the Global South: A Reader*. London: Zed Books.

Jordan, B. 1978. *Birth in Four Cultures: A Cross-cultural Investigation of Childbirth in Yucatan, Holland, Sweden, and the United States*. Montreal: Eden Press.

Joyce, K. A. 2008. *Magnetic Appeal: MRI and the Myth of Transparency*. Ithaca: Cornell University Press

Kahn, S. M. 2000. *Reproducing Jews: A Cultural Account of Assisted Conception in Israel*. Durham: Duke University Press.

Kaiser, R. 2009. "Stuck in the Revolving Door." *Washington Post*, January 30. http://www.washingtonpost.com/wp-dyn/content/story/2009/01/30/ ST2009013002643.html.

Kalb, D., and H. Tak. 2005. *Critical Junctions: Anthropology and History beyond the Cultural Turn*. New York: Berghahn.

Kane, S., and T. Mason. 1992. "'IV Drug Users' and 'Sex Partners': The Limits of Epidemiological Categories and the Ethnography of Risk." In *The Time of AIDS: Social Analysis, Theory, and Method*, edited by G. Herdt and S. Lindenbaum, 199–222. Newbury Park: Sage.

Kapferer, B. 1983. *A Celebration of Demons: Exorcism and the Aesthetics of Healing in Sri Lanka*. Bloomington: Indiana University Press.

Karsh, J., dir. 2003. *My Flesh and Blood*. Chaiken Films: 83 minutes.

Kasnitz, D., and R. P. Shuttleworth. 2001. "Introduction: Anthropology in Disability Studies." *Disability Studies Quarterly* 21 (3): 2–17.

Katsulis, Y. 2009. *Sex Work and the City: The Social Geography of Health and Safety in Tijuana, Mexico*. Austin: University of Texas Press.

Kaufman, S. R. 1986. *The Ageless Self: Sources of Meaning in Late Life*. Madison: University of Wisconsin Press.

———. 2005. *...And a Time to Die: How American Hospitals Shape the End of Life*. New York: Scribner.

Kavanagh, A. M., and D. H. Broom. 1998. "Embodied Risk: My Body, Myself?" *Social Science & Medicine* 46 (3): 437–44.

Keller, E. F. 2000. "Is There an Organism in This Text?" In *Controlling Our Destinies: Historical, Philosophical, Ethical, and Theological Perspectives on HGP*, edited by P. Sloan, 273–90. South Bend: Notre Dame University Press.

Kempadoo, K., and J. Doezema. 1999. *Global Sex Workers: Rights, Resistance, and Redefinition*. London: Routledge.

Kertzer, D. I. 2009. "Social Anthropology and Social Science History." Presidential address, Social Science History Association. http://ssh.dukejournals.org/cgi/ reprint/33/1/1.pdf.

Kim, J. Y., J. V. Millen, A. Irwin, and J. Gershman. 2000. *Dying for Growth: Global Inequality and the Health of the Poor*. Monroe: Common Courage Press.

King, M. C., J. H. Marks, J. B. Mandell, and the New York Breast Cancer Study Group. 2003. "Breast and Ovarian Cancer Risks Due to Inherited Mutations in BRCA1 and BRCA2." *Science* 302 (5645): 643–46.

King, M. L. 1967. "Beyond Vietnam—A Time to Break Silence." Delivered April 4 at a meeting of Clergy and Laity Concerned at Riverside Church, New York City. http://www.writespirit.net/inspirational_talks/political/martin_luther_king_talks/beyond_vietnam/.

Kirk, S. 1962. *Educating Exceptional Children*. Boston: Houghton Mifflin.

———. 1963. *Behavioral Diagnosis and Remediation of Learning Disabilities*. In *Proceedings from the Conference on the Exploration into the Problems of the Perceptually Handicapped Child*, 1–7. Evanston: n.p.

Klein, J. T. 1991. *Interdisciplinarity: History, Theory, and Practice*. Detroit: Wayne State University Press.

Kleinman, A. 1980. *Patients and Healers in the Context of Culture: An Exploration of the Borderland between Anthropology, Medicine, and Psychiatry*. Berkeley: University of California Press.

———. 1985. "Interpreting Illness Experience and Clinical Meanings: How I See Clinically Applied Anthropology." *Medical Anthropology Quarterly* 16 (3): 69–71.

———. 1988. *The Illness Narratives*. New York: Basic Books.

———. 1995. *Writing at the Margin: Discourse between Anthropology and Medicine*. Berkeley: University of California Press.

———. 2007. "Today's Biomedicine and Caregiving: Are They Incompatible to the Point of Divorce?" Cleveringa Address delivered at the University of Leiden, November 26, University of Leiden, The Netherlands.

———. 2008. "Catastrophe and Caregiving: The Failure of Medicine as an Art." *The Lancet* 371: 22–23.

———. 2009a. "Global Mental Health: A Failure of Humanity." *The Lancet* 374: 1–2.

———. 2009b. "Caregiving: The Odyssey of Becoming More Human." *The Lancet* 373: 292–93.

Kleinman, A., and P. Benson. 2006. "Anthropology in the Clinic: The Problem of Cultural Competency and How to Fix It." *PLOS Medicine* 3 (10): e294. doi: 10.1371/journal.pmed.0030294.

Kleinman, A., W. Fei, J. Jing, G. Jinhua, S. Lee, T. Pan, and E. Zhang. 2011. *Deep China: The Moral Life of the Person*. Berkeley: University of California Press.

Kleinman, A., and B. Good, eds. 1985. *Culture and Depression: Studies in the Anthropology and Cross-cultural Psychiatry of Affect and Disorder*. Berkeley: University of California Press.

Kleinman, A., and J. Kleinman. 1994. "How Bodies Remember: Social Memory and Bodily Experiences of Criticism, Resistance, and Delegitimation Following China's Cultural Revolution." *New Literary History* 25: 707–23.

———. 1996. "The Appeal of Experience: The Dismay of Images: Cultural Appropriations of Suffering in Our Times." *Daedalus* 125 (1): 1–23.

Kleinman, A., M. Lock, and V. Das, eds. 1997. *Social Suffering*. Berkeley: University of California Press.

Kligman, G. 1998. *The Politics of Duplicity: Controlling Reproduction in Ceausescu's Romania*. Berkeley: University of California Press.

Kober, G. 1899. *Report on the Housing of the Laboring Classes in the City of Washington, D.C.* District of Columbia: Health Office.

———. 1908. *Report of the Committee on Social Benefit*. Washington, D.C.: President's Homes Commission.

Kohrman, M. 2005. *Bodies of Difference: Experiences of Disability and Institutional Advocacy in the Making of Modern China*. Berkeley: University of California Press.

Konrad, M. 2005. *Nameless Relations: Anonymity, Melanesia and Reproductive Gift Exchange Between British Ova Donors and Recipients*. New York: Berghahn.

Kranish, M. 2008. "A Defining Time of Advocacy: Obama Shaped by Chicago Activism." *Boston Globe, January 22*. http://www.boston.com/news/nation/articles/2008/01/22/a_defining_time_of_advocacy/.

Kristof, N. D., and S. WuDunn. 2009. "The Women's Crusade." *New York Times Magazine*, August 23.

Kuklick, H. 1998. "Fieldworkers and Physiologists." In *Cambridge and the Torres Strait: Centenary Essays on the 1898 Anthropological Expedition*, edited by A. Herle and S. Rouse, 158–80. Cambridge: Cambridge University Press.

Kulick, D. 1998. *Travestí: Sex, Gender, and Culture among Brazilian Transgendered Prostitutes*. Chicago: University of Chicago Press.

Kuriyama, S. 1994. "On Knowledge and the Diversity of Cultures: Comment on Harding." *Configurations* 2 (2): 337–42.

———. 1999. *The Expressiveness of the Body and the Divergence of Greek and Chinese Medicine*. New York: Zone.

Labonte, R. 1996. "Community Development in the Public Health Sector: The Possibilities of an Empowering Relationship between State and Civil Society." PhD dissertation, York University.

Laderman, C. 1991. *Taming the Wind of Desire: Psychology, Medicine, and Aesthetics in Malay Shamanistic Performance*. Berkeley: University of California Press.

Lakoff, A. 2005. *Pharmaceutical Reason: Knowledge and Value in Global Psychiatry*. Cambridge: Cambridge University Press.

Lakoff, A., and S. J. Collier, eds. 2008. *Biosecurity Interventions: Global Health and Security in Question*. New York: Columbia University Press.

Lambek, M. 1993. *Knowledge and Practice in Mayotte: Local Discourses of Islam, Sorcery, and Spirit Possession*. Toronto: University of Toronto Press.

Lampland, M., and S. Star, eds. 2009. *Standards and Their Stories*. Ithaca: Cornell University Press.

Lancaster, R. N. 1988. "Subject Honor and Object Shame: The Construction of Male Homosexuality and Stigma in Nicaragua." *Ethnology* 27 (2): 111–25.

———. 1992. *Life Is Hard: Machismo, Danger, and Intimacy of Power in Nicaragua*. Berkeley: University of California Press.

———. 1995. "'That We Should All Turn Queer?': Homosexual Stigma in the Making of Manhood and the Breaking of a Revolution in Nicaragua." In *Conceiving Sexuality: Approaches to Sex Research in a Postmodern World*, edited by R. Parker and J. Gagnon, 135–56. London: Routledge.

Landecker, H. 2007. *Culturing Life: How Cells Became Technologies*. Cambridge: Harvard University Press.

Landsman, G. 2009. *Reconstructing Motherhood and Disability in the Age of Perfect Babies*. New York: Routledge.

Lane, S. D. 1994. "From Population Control to Reproductive Health: An Emerging Policy Agenda." *Social Science & Medicine* 39 (9): 1303–14.

Langbehn, D. R., R. R. Brinkman, D. Falush, J. S. Paulsen, and M. R. Hayden. 2004. "A New Model for Prediction of the Age of Onset and Penetrance for Huntington Disease Based on CAG Length." *Clinical Genetics* 65 (4): 267–77.

Langford, J. M. 2002. *Fluent Bodies: Ayurvedic Remedies for Postcolonial Imbalance*. Durham: Duke University Press.

Last, M. 1976. "The Presentation of Sickness in a Community of Non-Muslim Hausa." In *Social Anthropology and Medicine*, edited by J. B. Loudon, 104–49. London: Academic Press.

Latour, B., and M. Biezunski. 1994. *Science in Action*. Cambridge: Harvard University Press.

Laufer, B. 1920. "Multiple Births among the Chinese." *New China Review* 2 (2): 109–36.

Layne, L. 1990. "Motherhood Lost: Cultural Dimensions of Miscarriage and Stillbirth in America." *Women and Health* 16 (3): 75–104.

Leach, E. 1961. *Rethinking Anthropology*. London: Athlone Press.

———. 1964. "Anthropological Aspects of Language: Animal Categories and Verbal Abuse." In *New Directions in the Study of Language*, edited by E. Linnenburg, 23–63. Cambridge: MIT Press.

Leatherman, T. 2005. "A Space of Vulnerability in Poverty and Health: Political-Ecology and Biocultural Analysis." *Ethos* 33 (1): 46–70.

Lee, K., and H. Goodman. 2002. "Global Policy Networks: The Propagation of Health Care Financing Reform since the 1980s." In *Health Policy in a Global-*

izing World, edited by K. Lee, K. Buse, and S. Fustukian, 97–119. Cambridge: Cambridge University Press.

Leibing, A., and L. Cohen, eds. 2006. *Thinking about Dementia: Culture, Loss, and the Anthropology of Senility.* New Brunswick: Rutgers University Press.

Leng, C. H., and A. Whittaker, eds. 2010. Special issue on medical travel. *Global Social Policy* 10 (3).

Leslie, C. M., ed. 1976. *Asian Medical Systems: A Comparative Study.* Berkeley: University of California Press.

Leslie, C. M., and A. Young, eds. 1992. *Paths to Asian Medical Knowledge.* Berkeley: University of California Press.

Leung, T. N., M. W. Pang, S. S. Daljit, T. Y. Leung, C. F. Poon, S. M. Wong, and T. K. Lau. 2008. "Fetal Biometry in Ethnic Chinese: Biparietal Diameter, Head Circumference, Abdominal Circumference and Femur Length." *Ultrasound in Obstetrics and Gynecology* 31 (3): 321–27.

Lévi-Strauss, C. 1963. *Structural Anthropology.* New York: Basic Books.

Levin, B. W. 1990. "International Perspectives on Treatment Choice in Neonatal Intensive Care Units." *Social Science & Medicine* 30 (8): 901–12.

Levine, M. 1992. *All Kinds of Minds: A Young Student's Book about Learning Disabilities and Learning Disorders.* Cambridge: Educator's Publishing Service.

Levine, N. E. 2008. "Alternative Kinship, Marriage, and Reproduction." *Annual Review of Anthropology* 37 (1): 375–89.

Levy, R. I., and D. Hollan. 1998. "Person-Centered Interviewing and Observation in Anthropology." In *Handbook of Methods in Cultural Anthropology*, edited by H. R. Bernard, 333–64. Walnut Creek: Altamira Press.

Lewin, E., and W. Leap, eds. 2002. *Out in Theory: The Emergence of Lesbian and Gay Anthropology.* Chicago: University of Illinois Press.

Lewis, W. H. 1920. Letter to E. V. Cowdry, September 27. Warren H. Lewis folder, E. V. Cowdry Papers, Becker Medical Library, Washington University School of Medicine.

Lewontin, R. 2000. *It Ain't Necessarily So: The Dream of the Human Genome and Other Illusions.* 2nd ed. New York: New York Review of Books.

Li, V. 2001. "Marshall Sahlins and the Apotheosis of Culture." *CR: The New Centennial Review* 1 (3): 201–87.

Lieberman, E. S. 2009. *Boundaries of Contagion: How Ethnic Politics Have Shaped Government Responses to AIDS.* Princeton: Princeton University Press.

Lindenbaum, S., and M. Lock, eds. 1993. *Power and Practice: The Anthropology of Medicine and Everyday Life.* Berkeley: University of California Press.

Linton, S. 1998. *Claiming Disability: Knowledge and Identity.* New York: New York University Press.

Lippman, A. 1992. "Led (Astray) by Genetic Maps: The Cartography of the Human Genome and Human Care." *Social Science and Medicine* 35 (12): 1469–76.

Littlewood, R. 1986. "Anthropology and British Psychiatry." *Anthropology Today* 2 (1): 8–11.

Livingston, J. 2009. *Debility and the Moral Imagination in Botswana*. Bloomington: Indiana University Press.

Lock, M. 1980. *East Asian Medicine in Urban Japan: Varieties of Medical Experience*. Berkeley: University of California Press.

———. 1981. "Japanese Psychotherapeutic Systems: On Acceptance and Responsibility." *Culture, Medicine, and Psychiatry* 5 (3): 303–12.

———. 1995. *Encounters with Aging: Mythologies of Menopause in Japan and North America*. Berkeley: University of California Press.

———. 2001. "The Tempering of Medical Anthropology: Toward Troubling Natural Categories." *Medical Anthropology Quarterly* 15 (4): 478–92.

———. 2002. *Twice Dead: Organ Transplants and the Reinvention of Death*. Berkeley: University of California Press.

———. 2007. "The Future Is Now: Locating Biomarkers for Dementia." In *Biomedicine as Culture: Instrumental Practices, Technoscientific Knowledge, and New Modes of Life*, edited by R. V. Burri and J. Dumit, 61–86. New York: Routledge.

———. 2009. "Demoting the Genetic Body." *Anthropologica* 51: 159–72.

———. 2011. "Dementia Entanglements in a Postgenomic Era." *Science, Technology, and Human Values* 36 (5): 685–703.

Lock, M., J. Freeman, G. Chilibeck, B. Beveridge, and M. Padolsky. 2007. "Susceptibility Genes and the Question of Embodied Identity." *Medical Anthropology Quarterly* 21 (3): 256–76.

Lock, M., J. Freeman, R. Sharples, and S. Lloyd. 2006. "When It Runs in the Family: Putting Susceptibility Genes in Perspective." *Public Understanding of Science* 15: 277–300.

Lock, M., and D. R. Gordon, eds. 1988. *Biomedicine Examined*. New York: Springer-Verlag.

Lock, M., and V. K. Nguyen. 2010. *An Anthropology of Biomedicine*. Boston: Wiley-Blackwell.

Longmore, P. 2003. *Why I Burned My Book and Other Essays on Disability*. Philadelphia: Temple University Press.

Lorway, R. 2006. "Dispelling 'Heterosexual African AIDS' in Namibia: Same-Sex Sexuality in the Township of Katutura." *Culture, Health, and Sexuality* 8 (5): 435–49.

———. 2008a. "Beyond the New Geography of Dissident Gender-Sexual Identity Categories: Masculinities, Homosexualities, and Intimate Partner Violence in

Namibia." Working paper in the Fourth Wave online forum, UNESCO and the SSRC. http://blogs.ssrc.org/fourthwave/files/2008/10/lorway1.pdf.

———. 2008b. "Pursuing Sexual Freedom in a Time of AIDS: Exploring the HIV Vulnerability of Lesbian Women in a Namibian Township." *EthnoScripts* 10 (1): 65–82.

Lorway, R., R. P. Sushena, and A. Pasha. 2009. "On Becoming a Male Sex Worker in Mysore: Sexual Subjectivity, 'Empowerment,' and Community-Based HIV Prevention Research." *Medical Anthropology Quarterly* 23 (2): 142–60.

Louie, K. 2002. *Theorising Chinese Masculinity: Society and Gender in China.* Cambridge: Cambridge University Press.

Luhrmann, T. M. 2000. *Of Two Minds: The Growing Disorder in American Psychiatry.* New York: Knopf.

Luker, K. 1985. *Abortion and the Politics of Motherhood.* Berkeley: University of California Press.

Lumey, L. H. 1992. "Decreased Birthweights in Infants after Maternal In Utero Exposure to the Dutch Famine of 1944–1945." *Paediatric Perinatal Epidemiology* 6 (2): 240–53.

Lyttleton, C. 2000. *Endangered Relations: Negotiating Sex and AIDS in Thailand.* Amsterdam: Harwood Academic.

MacCormack, C. 1992. "Health Care and the Concept of Legitimacy in Sierra Leone." In *The Social Basis of Health and Healing in Africa,* edited by S. Feierman and J. Janzen, 426–36. Berkeley: University of California Press.

Macfarlane, A. 1968. "Population Crisis: Anthropology's Failure." *New Society* 315. http://www.alanmacfarlane.com/TEXTS/crisis.pdf.

Macfarlane, S., M. Jacobs, and E. Kaaya. 2008. "In the Name of Global Health: Trends in the Academic Institutions." *Journal of Public Health Policy* 29: 383–401.

Machado, P. 2009. "Intersexuality and Sexual Rights in Southern Brazil." *Culture, Health, and Sexuality* 11 (3): 237–50.

Madan, T. N. 1980. *Doctors and Society: Three Asian Case Studies.* Sahabadad: Vikas.

Maddow, R. 2009. "How Did ACORN Become a Target?" *Msnbc.com.* http://www.msnbc.msn.com/id/26315908/#33027963.msnbc.msn.com/id/26315908/#33027963.

Maher, B. 2009. "New Rule: Not Everything in America Has to Make a Profit." *Huffington Post,* May 30. http://www.huffingtonpost.com/bill-maher/new-rule-not-everything-i_b_244050.html.

Malkki, L. 1996. "Speechless Emissaries: Refugees, Humanitarianism, and Dehistoricization." *Cultural Anthropology* 11: 377–404.

Mamdani, M. 1972. *The Myth of Population Control: Family, Caste, and Class in an Indian Village.* New York: Monthly Review Press.

Manderson, L., and M. Jolly, eds. 1997. *Sites of Desire/Economies of Pleasure: Sexualities in Asia and the Pacific.* Chicago: University of Chicago Press.

Manderson, L., and C. Smith-Morris, eds. 2010. *Chronic Conditions, Fluid States: Chronicity and the Anthropology of Illness.* New Brunswick: Rutgers University Press.

Marcus, G. E. 1995. "Ethnography in/of the World System: The Emergence of Multi-sited Ethnography." *Annual Review of Anthropology* 24: 95–117.

Marcus, G. E., and M. M. J. Fischer. 1986. *Anthropology as Cultural Critique: An Experimental Moment in the Human Sciences.* Chicago: University of Chicago Press.

Marriott, M. K. 1976. "Hindu Transactions: Diversity without Dualism." In *Transaction and Meaning: Directions in the Anthropology of Exchange and Symbolic Behavior,* edited by B. Kapferer, 109–42. Philadelphia: Institute for the Study of Human Issues.

Marshall, P. L., M. Singer, and M. C. Clatts. 1999. *Integrating Cultural, Observational, and Epidemiological Approaches in the Prevention of Drug Abuse and HIV/ AIDS.* DHHS Publication, No. (NIH) 99-4565. Bethesda: U.S. Dept. of Health and Human Services National Institute on Drug Abuse Division of Epidemiology and Prevention Research.

Martin, E. 1987. *The Woman in the Body: A Cultural Analysis of Reproduction.* Boston: Beacon Press.

———. 1989. "The Cultural Construction of Gendered Bodies: Biology and Metaphors of Production and Destruction." *Ethos* 54 (3–4): 143–60.

———. 1994. *Flexible Bodies: Tracking Immunity in American Culture: From the Days of Polio to the Age of AIDS.* Boston: Beacon Press.

———. 1999. "The Woman in the Flexible Body." In *Revisioning Women, Health, and Healing: Feminist, Cultural, and Technoscience Perspectives,* edited by A. Clarke and V. L. Olesen, 97–118. New York: Routledge.

———. 2007. *Bipolar Expeditions: Mania and Depression in American Culture.* Princeton: Princeton University Press.

Maternowska, M. C. 2006. *Reproducing Inequalities: Poverty and the Politics of Population in Haiti.* New Brunswick: Rutgers University Press.

Mather, A. S. 1910. *Extracts from the Letters, Diary, and Note Books of Amasa Stone Mather: June 1907 to December 1908.* Vol. 2. Arthur H. Clark Co. (privately printed).

Mattick, J. S. 2003. "Challenging the Dogma: The Hidden Layer of Non-Protein-Coding RNAs in Complex Organisms." *Bioessays* 25 (10): 930–39.

———. 2004. "The Hidden Genetic Program of Complex Organisms." *Scientific American* 291: 60–67.

Mattingly, C., and L. C. Garro. 2000. *Narrative and the Cultural Construction of Illness and Healing.* Berkeley: University of California Press.

Maugham, W. S. 1922. *On a Chinese Screen.* New York: George H. Doran Company.

Mauss, M. 1954. *The Gift: Forms and Functions of Exchange in Archaic Societies.* London: Cohen and West.

———. 1973. "Techniques of the Body." *Economy and Society* 2 (1): 70–88.

Mauss, M., and N. Schlanger. 2006. *Techniques, Technology, and Civilization.* New York: Berghahn.

Mayer, A. 2006. "Lost Objects: From the Laboratories of Hypnosis to the Psycho-analytic Setting." *Science in Context* 19 (1): 37–64.

Mazzaschi, A., and E. A. McDonald, eds. 2011. "Comparative Perspectives Symposium: Gender and Medical Tourism." Special issue, *Signs* 36 (2).

McClelland, D. C. 1961. *The Achieving Society.* Princeton: Princeton University Press.

McCord, C., and H. Freeman. 1990. "Excess Mortality in Harlem." *New England Journal of Medicine* 322: 173–77.

McElroy, A., and P. K. Townsend. 2004. *Medical Anthropology in Ecological Perspective.* Boulder: Westview Press.

McGowan, P. O., A. Sasaki, A. C. D'Alessio, S. Dymov, B. Labonté, M. Szyf, G. Turecki, and M. Meaney. 2009. "Epigenetic Regulation of the Glucocorticoid Receptor in Human Associates with Childhood Abuse." *Nature Neuroscience* 12: 342–48.

McGuire, M. 1988. *Ritual Healing in Suburban America.* New Brunswick: Rutgers University Press.

McLean, A. 2006. *The Person in Dementia: A Study of Nursing Home Care in the U.S.* Toronto: University of Toronto Press.

McLean, M. 2005. "Controversial Art Exhibit to Go on Show Again." *SwissInfo.ch.* http://www.swissinfo.ch/eng/index.html?siteSect=106andsid=6054757andcKey=1125591308000.

Mead, M. 1928. *Coming of Age in Samoa: A Psychological Study of Primitive Youth for Western Civilization.* New York: Morrow.

———. 1935. *Sex and Temperament in Three Primitive Societies.* New York: Mentor Books.

Miller, G. 2010. "The Seductive Allure of Behavioral Epigenetics." *Science* 329: 24–27.

Mirsepassi, A., A. Basu, and F. S. Weaver, eds. 2003. *Localizing Knowledge in a Globalizing World: Recasting the Area Studies Debate.* Syracuse: Syracuse University Press.

Mitchell, D., and S. Snyder, eds. 1997. *The Body and Physical Difference: Discourses of Disability*. Ann Arbor: University of Michigan Press.

Mitchell, T. 2003. "Deterritorialization and the Crisis of Social Science." In *Localizing Knowledge in a Globalizing World: Recasting the Area Studies Debate*, edited by A. Mirsepassi, A. Basu, and F. S. Weaver, 148–70. Syracuse: Syracuse University Press.

Miyazaki, H. 2003. "The Temporalities of the Market." *American Anthropologist* 105 (2): 255–65.

———. 2004. *The Method of Hope: Anthropology, Philosophy, and Fijian Knowledge*. Stanford: Stanford University Press.

Moberg, D. 2007. "Obama's Community Roots." *Nation*. http://www.thenation.com/doc/20070416/moberg.

Moerman, D. E. 2002. *Meaning, Medicine, and the "Placebo Effect."* Cambridge: Cambridge University Press.

Mol, A. 2002. *The Body Multiple: Ontology in Medical Practice*. Durham: Duke University Press.

———. 2008. *The Logic of Care: Health and the Problem of Patient Choice*. New York: Routledge.

Montoya, M. J. 2007. "Bioethnic Conscription: Genes, Race, and Mexicana/o Ethnicity in Diabetes Research." *Cultural Anthropology* 22 (1): 94–128.

Morgan, L. M. 1993. *Community Participation in Health: The Politics of Primary Care in Costa Rica*. Cambridge: Cambridge University Press.

———. 2009. *Icons of Life: A Cultural History of Human Embryos*. Berkeley: University of California Press.

Morrell, R. 2001. *Changing Men in Southern Africa*. London: Zed Books.

Morsy, S. 1979. "The Missing Link in Medical Anthropology: The Political Economy of Health." *Reviews in Anthropology* 6 (3): 349–63.

Moshe, S., P. McGowan, and M. J. Meaney. 2008. "The Social Environment and the Epigenome." *Environmental and Molecular Mutagenesis* 49: 46–60.

Müller-Wille, S., and H.-J. Rheinberger. 2007. *Heredity Produced: At the Crossroads of Biology, Politics, and Culture, 1500–1870*. Cambridge: MIT Press.

Mullings, L. 1997. *On Our Own Terms: Race, Class, and Gender in the Lives of African American Women*. London: Routledge.

Mungello, D. E. 2008. *Drowning Girls in China: Female Infanticide since 1650*. Lanham: Rowman and Littlefield.

Muraskin, W. 2005. *Crusade to Immunize the World's Children*. Los Angeles: USC Marshall Global Bio Business.

Murphy, R. F. 1987. *The Body Silent*. New York: Henry Holt.

———. 2001. *The Body Silent: The Different World of the Disabled*. New York: W. W. Norton and Company.

Murray, S. O. 1992. "The 'Underdevelopment' of Modern/Gay Homosexuality in Mesoamerica." In *Modern Homosexualities*, edited by K. Plummer, 29–38. London: Routledge.

Myers, R. H., E. J. Schaefer, P. W. Wilson, R. D'Agostino, J. M. Ordovas, A. Espino, R. Au, R. F. White, J. E. Knoefel, J. L. Cobb, K. A. McNulty, A. Beiser, and P. A. Wolf. 1996. "Apolipoprotein E Epsilon 4 Association with Dementia in a Population-Based Study: The Framingham Study." *Neurology* 46 (3): 673–77.

Nader, L. 2001. "Anthropology!" *American Anthropologist* 103 (3): 609–20.

Nakamura, K. 2007. *Deaf in Japan: Signing and the Politics of Identity*. Ithaca: Cornell University Press.

Nanda, S. 1990. *Neither Man nor Woman: The Hijras of India*. Belmont: Wadsworth Publishing.

Naraindas, H. 2006. "Of Spineless Babies and Folic Acid: Evidence and Efficacy in Biomedicine and Ayurvedic Medicine." *Social Science & Medicine* 62 (11): 2658–69.

Nations, M., and L. A. Rebhun. 1988. "Angels with Wet Wings Won't Fly: Maternal Sentiment in Brazil and the Image of Neglect." *Culture, Medicine, and Psychiatry* 12 (2): 141–200.

Navarro, V. 2009. "Obama's Mistakes in Health Care Reform." *Counterpunch*, September 7. http://www.counterpunch.org/navarro09072009.html.

Network of Concerned Anthropologists. 2009. *The Counter-Counterinsurgency Manual*. Chicago: University of Chicago Press, Prickly Paradigm Press.

Neumann-Held, E. M., and C. Rehmann-Sutter. 2006. *Genes in Development: Rereading the Molecular Paradigm*. Durham: Duke University Press.

New York Times. 1987. "Brazilians Break Down Taboo of Silence on AIDS." October 26.

———. 1993. "AIDS in Latin America—A special report; In Deception and Denial, an Epidemic Looms." January 25.

———. 1997. "Herbert Jose De Souza, Brazilian Sociologist." April 11.

Nguyen, V. K. 2005. "Antiretroviral Globalism, Biopolitics, and Therapeutic Citizenship." In *Global Assemblages: Technology, Politics, and Ethics as Anthropological Problems*, edited by A. Ong and S. J. Collier, 124–44. Malden: Blackwell.

Nguyen, V. K., C. Y. Ako, P. Niamba, A. Sylla, and I. Tiendrébéogo. 2007. "Adherence as Therapeutic Citizenship: Impact of the History of Access to Antiretroviral Drugs on Adherence to Treatment." *AIDS* 21 (suppl. 5): S31–S35.

Nichter, M. 1985. "Drink Boiled Water: A Cultural Analysis of a Health Education Message." *Social Science & Medicine* 21 (6): 667–69.

———. 1987. "Cultural Dimensions of Hot, Cold and Sema in Sinhalese Health Culture." *Social Science & Medicine* 25 (4): 377–87.

———. 1989. *Anthropology and International Health: South Asian Case Studies.* Dordrecht: Kluwer Academic.

———. 1992. *Anthropological Approaches to the Study of Ethnomedicine.* New York: Routledge.

———. 2008. *Global Health: Why Cultural Perceptions, Social Representations, and Biopolitics Matter.* Tucson: University of Arizona Press.

Nie, J. B. 2009. "Limits of State Intervention in Sex-Selective Abortion: The Case of China." *Culture, Health, and Sexuality* 4 (1): 205–19.

Nie, J. B., N. Guo, M. Selden, and A. Kleinman, eds. 2010. *Japan's Wartime Medical Atrocities: Comparative Inquiries in Science, History, and Ethics.* New York: Routledge.

Nietzsche, F. 1979. *Philosophy and Truth: Selections from Nietzsche's Notebooks of the Early 1870s,* edited and translated by D. Breazeale. New Jersey: Humanitarian Press.

———. 1997. *Philosophical Writings, Vol. 48.* New York: Continuum Publishing Company.

NIH Common Fund. 2009. "Translation Research." http://commonfund.nih.gov/clinicalresearch/overview-translational.asp.

Nissani, M. 1997. "Ten Cheers for Interdisciplinarity: The Case for Interdisciplinary Knowledge and Research." *Social Science Journal* 34: 201–16.

Norton, E. 1972. "Interview with Saul Alinsky." *Playboy Magazine* 19 (3): 59–79. Available online at *Progress Report*: http://www.progress.org/2003/alinsky2.htm.

Nunn, A. 2009. *The Politics and History of AIDS Treatment in Brazil.* New York: Springer.

Oaks, L. 2001. *Smoking and Pregnancy: The Politics of Fetal Protection.* New Brunswick: Rutgers University Press.

Obama, B. 1990. "Why Organize? Problems and Promise in the Inner City." In *After Alinsky: Community Organizing in Illinois,* edited by Peg Knoepfle, 35–40. Springfield: University of Illinois Press.

———. 2004. *Dreams from My Father: A Story of Race and Inheritance.* New York: Three Rivers Press.

———. 2008. "Barack Obama on Community Organizing." *YouTube.* http://www.youtube.com/watch?v=htnL6QRCqKo.

Obermeyer, C. M. 1999. "The Cultural Context of Reproductive Health: Implications for Monitoring the Cairo Agenda." *International Family Planning Perspectives* 25 (suppl.): S50–S55.

Obeyesekere, G. 1981. *Medusa's Hair: An Essay on Personal Symbols and Religious Experience.* Chicago: University of Chicago Press.

Okongwu, A., and J. Mencher. 2000. "The Anthropology of Public Policy: Shifting Terrains." *Annual Review of Anthropology* 29: 107–24.

Oldani, M. J. 2004. "Thick Prescriptions: Toward an Interpretation of Pharmaceutical Sales Practices." *Medical Anthropology Quarterly* 18 (3): 325–56.

———. 2006. "Filling Scripts: A Multi-sited Ethnography of Pharmaceutical Sales Practices, Psychiatric Prescribing, and Phamily Life in North America." PhD dissertation, Princeton University.

Ong, A. 1987. *Spirits of Resistance and Capitalist Discipline: Factory Women in Malaysia*. Albany: State University of New York Press.

Ong, A., and S. Collier, eds. 2005. *Global Assemblages: Technology, Politics, and Ethics as Anthropological Problems*. Malden: Blackwell.

OpenSecrets.Org. 2009. "Annual Lobbying by America's Health Insurance Plans." http://www.opensecrets.org/lobby/clientsum.php?lname=America%27s+Health+Insurance+Plansandyear=2009.

Orr, J. 1990. "Theory on the Market: Panic, Incorporating." *Social Problems* 37 (4): 460–84.

———. 2006. *Panic Diaries: A Genealogy of Panic Disorder*. Durham: Duke University Press.

Osella, C., and F. Osella. 2006. *Men and Masculinities in India*. London: Anthem Press.

Ouzgane, L., and R. Morrell, eds. 2005. *African Masculinities: Men in Africa from the Late 19th Century to the Present*. New York: Palgrave Macmillan.

Oxfam. 2009. "Oxfam Australia: How We Work." http://www.oxfam.org.au/about-us/how-we-work.

Oyama, S. 2001. "Terms in Tension: What Do You Do When All the Good Words Are Taken?" In *Cycles of Contingency: Developmental Systems and Evolution*, edited by S. Oyama, P. E. Griffiths, and R. D. Gray, 177–94. Cambridge: MIT Press.

Packard, R. 1996. "Visions of Postwar Health and Development and Their Impact on Public Health Interventions in the Developing World." In *International Development and the Social Sciences*, edited by F. Cooper and R. Packard, 93–115. Berkeley: University of California Press.

Palladino, P. 2002. "Between Knowledge and Practice: On Medical Professionals, Patients, and the Making of the Genetics of Cancer." *Social Studies of Science* 32 (1): 137–65.

Palmer, S. 2010. *Launching Global Health. The Caribbean Odyssey of the Rockefeller Foundation*. Ann Arbor: University of Michigan Press.

Pandolfi, M. 1986. "Dall'antropologia medica all'antropologia della malattia." *Antropologia Medica* 1: 43–47.

Pandolfo, S. 1989. "Detours of Life: Space and Bodies in a Moroccan Village." *American Ethnologist* 16 (1): 3–23.

Panos. 1990. *Triple Jeopardy: Women and AIDS*. London: Panos Institute.

———. 1993. *Tripla ameaça: Mulheres e AIDS*. Rio de Janeiro: ABIA e SOS Corpo.

Panter-Brick, C., and A. Fuentes, eds. 2010. *Health, Risk, and Adversity*. New York: Berghahn.

Panter-Brick, C., and C. M. Worthman, eds. 2008. *Hormones, Health and Behaviour: A Socio-ecological and Lifespan Perspective*. Cambridge: Cambridge University Press.

Parker, R. 1987. "Acquired Immunodeficiency Syndrome in Urban Brazil." *Medical Anthropology Quarterly* 1 (2): 155–75.

———. 1991. *Bodies, Pleasures, and Passions: Sexual Culture in Contemporary Brazil*. Boston: Beacon Press.

———. 1994. *A construção da solidariedade: AIDS, sexualidade e política no Brasil*. Rio de Janeiro: Editora Relume-Dumará.

———. 1996. "Empowerment, Community Mobilization, and Social Change in the Face of HIV/AIDS." *AIDS* 10 (suppl. 3): S27–S31.

———. 1997. "Sexual Rights: Concepts and Action." *Health and Human Rights* 2 (3): 31–37.

———. 1999. *Beneath the Equator: Cultures of Desire, Male Homosexuality, and Emerging Gay Communities in Brazil*. New York: Routledge.

———. 2000a. "Administering the Epidemic: HIV/AIDS Policy, Models of Development and International Health in the Late-Twentieth Century." In *Globalization, Health and Identity: The Fallacy of the Level Playing Field*, edited by L. M. Whiteford and L. Manderson, 39–55. Boulder: Lynne Rienner.

———. 2000b. *Na contramão da AIDS: Sexualidade, intervenção, política*. São Paulo: Editora 34.

———. 2001. "Sexuality, Culture and Power in HIV/AIDS Research." *Annual Review of Anthropology* 30: 163–79.

———. 2003. "Building the Foundations for the Response to HIV/AIDS in Brazil: The Development of HIV/AIDS Policy, 1982–1996." *Divulgação em Saúde para Debate* 27: 143–83.

———. 2009. "Preface." *Bodies, Pleasures, and Passions: Sexual Culture in Contemporary Brazil*. 2nd ed. Nashville: Vanderbilt University Press.

Parker, R., and P. Aggleton. 2003. "HIV and AIDS-Related Stigma and Discrimination: A Conceptual Framework and Implications for Action." *Social Science & Medicine* 57 (1): 13–24.

Parker, R., R. M. Barbosa, and P. Aggleton, eds. 2000. *Framing the Sexual Subject: The Politics of Gender, Sexuality, and Power*. Berkeley: University of California Press.

Parker, R., and J. Gagnon, eds. 1995. *Conceiving Sexuality: Approaches to Sex Research in a Postmodern World*. New York: Routledge.

Parker, R., and V. Terto Jr., eds. 1997. *Entre homens: Homossexualidade e AIDS no Brasil*. Rio de Janeiro: ABIA.

———. 2001. *Solidariedade: A ABIA na virada do milênio*. Rio de Janeiro: ABIA.

Parker, R., V. Terto Jr., and M. C. Pimenta, eds. 2002. *Solidariedade e cidadania: Princípios possíveis para as respostas ao HIV/AIDS? Anais*. Rio de Janeiro: ABIA.

Parsons, T. 1951. *The Social System*. Glencoe: Free Press.

Patel, V., and A. Kleinman. 2003. "Poverty and Common Mental Disorders in Developing Countries." *Bulletin of the World Health Organization* 81 (8): 609–15.

Patel, V., B. Saraceno, and A. Kleinman. 2006. "Beyond Evidence: The Moral Case for International Mental Health." *American Journal of Psychiatry* 163 (8): 1312–15.

Paul, B. D., ed. 1955. *Health, Culture, and Community: Case Studies of Public Reactions to Health Programs*. New York: Russell Sage Foundation.

Perlongher, N. 1987. *O negócio do michê: A prostituição viril*. São Paulo: Editora Brasiliense.

Petchesky, R. P. 1987. "Fetal Images: The Power of Visual Culture in the Politics of Reproduction." *Feminist Studies* 13 (2): 263–92.

———. 2000. "Sexual Rights: Inventing a Concept, Mapping an International Practice." In *Framing the Sexual Subject*, edited by R. Parker, R. M. Barbosa, and P. Aggleton, 81–103. Berkeley: University of California Press.

———. 2003. *Global Prescriptions: Gendering Health and Human Rights*. London: Zed Books.

Petchesky, R. P., and K. Judd. 1998. *Negotiating Reproductive Rights: Women's Perspectives across Countries and Cultures*. London: Zed Books.

Peterson, E. A., K. J. Milliron, K. E. Lewis, S. D. Goold, and S. D. Merajver. 2002. "Health Insurance and Discrimination Concerns and BRCA1/2 Testing in a Clinic Population." *Cancer Epidemiology, Biomarkers, and Prevention* 11: 79–87.

Petryna, A. 2002. *Life Exposed: Biological Citizens after Chernobyl*. Princeton: Princeton University Press.

———. 2009. *When Experiments Travel: Clinical Trials and the Global Search for Human Subjects*. Princeton: Princeton University Press.

Petryna, A., A. Lakoff, and A. Kleinman, eds. 2006. *Global Pharmaceuticals: Ethics, Markets, Practices*. Durham: Duke University Press.

Pfeffer, N., and J. Kent. 2007. "Framing Women, Framing Fetuses: How Britain Regulates Arrangements for the Collection and Use of Aborted Fetuses in Stem Cell Research and Therapies." *BioSocieties* 2 (4): 429–47.

Pfeiffer, J., and M. Nichter. 2008. "What Can Critical Medical Anthropology Contribute to Global Health?" *Medical Anthropology Quarterly* 22: 410–15.

Pigg, S. L. 1992. "Inventing Social Categories through Place: Social Representations and Development in Nepal." *Comparative Studies in Society and History* 34 (3): 491–513.

———. 1997. "Authority in Translation: Finding, Knowing, Naming, and Training 'Traditional Birth Attendants' in Nepal." In *Childbirth and Authoritative Knowledge: Cross-Cultural Perspectives*, edited by R. Davis-Floyd and C. F. Sargent, 233–62. Berkeley: University of California Press.

Pimenta, M. C., J. C. Raxach, and V. Terto Jr., eds. 2010. *Prevenção das DST/AIDS: Novos desafios*. Anais. Rio de Janeiro: ABIA.

Pinto, S. 2008. *Where There Is No Midwife: Birth and Loss in Rural India*. New York: Berghahn.

Plummer, K. 1975. *Sexual Stigma: An Interactionist Account*. London: Routledge and Kegan Paul.

Polanyi, K. 2001 [1944]. *The Great Transformation: The Political and Economic Origins of Our Time*. Boston: Beacon Press.

Polgar, S. 1972. "Population History and Population Policies from an Anthropological Perspective." *Current Anthropology* 13 (2): 203–11.

Povinelli, E. A. 2006. *The Empire of Love: Toward a Theory of Intimacy, Genealogy, and Carnality*. Durham: Duke University Press.

Prainsack, B., and G. Siegal. 2006. "The Rise of Genetic Couplehood? A Comparative View of Premarital Genetic Testing." *BioSocieties* 1: 17–36.

Prakash, G. 1999. *Another Reason: Science and the Imagination of Modern India*. Princeton: Princeton University Press.

Prasad, A. 2009. "Capitalizing Disease: Biopolitics of Drug Trials in India." *Theory, Culture, and Society* 26: 1–29.

Prieur, A. 1998. *Mema's House, Mexico City: On Transvestites, Queens, and Machos*. Chicago: University of Chicago Press.

Proschan, F. 2002. "'Syphilis, Opiomania, and Pederasty': Colonial Constructions of Vietnamese (and French) Social Diseases." *Journal of the History of Sexuality* 11 (4): 610–36.

Quaid, K. A., and M. Morris. 1993. "Reluctance to Undergo Predictive Testing: The Case of Huntington Disease." *American Journal of Medical Genetics* 45 (1): 41–45.

Quote Garden. 2009. Daily Harvest. http://www.quotegarden.com/friendship .html.quotegarden.com/friendship.html.

Rabinow, P. 1977. *Reflections on Fieldwork in Morocco*. Berkeley: University of California Press.

———. 1992. "Studies in the Anthropology of Reason." *Anthropology Today* 8 (5): 7–10.

———. 1996a. *Essays on the Anthropology of Reason*. Princeton: Princeton University Press.

———. 1996b. *Making PCR: A Story of Biotechnology*. Chicago: University of Chicago Press.

———. 1999. *French DNA: Trouble in Purgatory*. Chicago: University of Chicago Press.

Rabinow, P., and N. Rose. 2006. "Biopower Today." *BioSocieties* 1: 195–217.

Raeburn, P. 2005. "The Therapeutic Mind Scan." *New York Times Magazine*, February 20.

Ragoné, H. 1994. *Surrogate Motherhood: Conception in the Heart*. Boulder: Westview Press.

Raphael, D., M. Salovesh, and M. Laclave. 2001. "The World in 3-D: Dyslexia, Dysgraphia, Dysnumia." *Disability Studies Quarterly* 21 (2): 152–60.

Rapp, R. 1988. "Chromosomes and Communication: The Discourse of Genetic Counseling." *Medical Anthropology Quarterly* 2 (2): 143–157.

———. 2000. *Testing Women, Testing the Fetus: The Social Impact of Amniocentesis in America*. New York: Routledge.

———. 2003. "Cell Life and Death, Child Life and Death: Genomic Horizons, Genetic Diseases, Family Stories." In *Remaking Life and Death: Toward an Anthropology of the Biosciences*, edited by S. Franklin and M. Lock, 23–60. Santa Fe: School of American Research Press.

Rapp, R., and F. Ginsburg. 2001. "Enabling Disability: Rewriting Kinship, Reimagining Citizenship." *Public Culture* 13 (3): 533–56.

Rapp, R., D. Heath, and K. S. Taussig. 2001. "Genealogical Disease: Where Hereditary Abnormality, Biomedical Explanation, and Family Responsibility Meet." In *Relative Matters: New Directions in the Study of Kinship*, edited by S. Franklin and S. MacKinnon, 384–412. Durham: Duke University Press.

Raspberry, K., and D. Skinner. 2007. "Experiencing the Genetic Body: Parents' Encounters with Pediatric Clinical Genetics." *Medical Anthropology* 26 (4): 355–91.

Reagan, T., dir. 2007. *Autism: The Musical*. HBO.

Reardon, J. 2005. *Race to the Finish: Identity and Governance in an Age of Genomics*. Princeton: Princeton University Press.

Redfield, P. 2005. "Doctors, Borders, and Life in Crisis." *Cultural Anthropology* 20 (3): 328–61.

———. 2008. "Vital Mobility and the Humanitarian Kit." In *Biosecurity Interventions: Global Health and Security in Question*, edited by A. Lakoff and S. J. Collier, 147–71. New York: Columbia University Press.

Redfield, R. 1953. *The Primitive World and Its Transformations*. Ithaca: Cornell University Press.

———. 1957. *A Village That Chose Progress: Chan Kom Revisited*. Chicago: University of Chicago Press.

Reid, J. 1983. *Sorcerers and Healing Spirits*. Canberra: Australian National University Press.

Reid, R., and S. Traweek. 2000. *Doing Science + Culture*. New York: Routledge.

Reis, R., V. Terto Jr., and M. C. Pimenta, eds. *Intellectual Property Rights and Access to ARV Medicines: Civil Society Resistance in the Global South*. Rio de Janeiro: ABIA.

Reiter, R., ed. 1975. *Toward an Anthropology of Women*. New York: Monthly Review Press.

Rhodes, L. A. 1991. *Emptying Beds: The Work of an Emergency Psychiatric Unit*. Berkeley: University of California Press.

———. 2004. *Total Confinement: Madness and Reason in the Maximum Security Prison*. Berkeley: University of California Press.

Richards, G. 1998. "Getting a Result: The Expeditions' Psychological Research, 1898–1913." In *Cambridge and the Torres Strait: Centenary Essays on the 1898 Anthropological Expedition*, edited by A. Herle and S. Rouse, 136–57. Cambridge: Cambridge University Press.

Richards, M. 1996. "Lay and Professional Knowledge of Genetics and Inheritance." *Public Understanding of Science* 5 (3): 217–30.

Rigdon, S. M. 1996. "Abortion Law and Practice in China: An Overview with Comparisons to the United States." *Social Science & Medicine* 42 (4): 543–60.

Rios, L. F., V. Almeida, R. Parker, M. C. Pimenta, and V. Terto Jr., eds. 2004. *Homossexualidades: Produção cultural, cidadania e saúde*. Rio de Janeiro: ABIA.

Rivkin-Fish, M. 2005. *Women's Health in Post-Soviet Russia: The Politics of Intervention*. Bloomington: Indiana University Press.

Robben, A. C. G. M., and M. Suárez-Orozco, eds. 2000. *Cultures under Siege: Collective Violence and Trauma*. New York: Cambridge University Press.

Roberts, E. 2007. "Extra Embryos: The Ethics of Cryopreservation in Ecuador and Elsewhere." *American Ethnologist* 34 (1): 181–99.

Roberts, J., L. Scott, A. Cupples, N. R. Relkin, P. J. Whitehouse, and R. C. Green. 2005. "Genetic Risk Assessment for Adult Children of People with Alzheimer's Disease: The Risk Evaluation and Education for Alzheimer's Disease (REVEAL) Study." *Journal of Geriatric Psychiatry and Neurology* 18 (4): 250–55.

Robins, S. 2004. "'Long Live Zackie, Long Live': AIDS Activism, Science, and Citizenship after Apartheid." *Journal of Southern African Studies* 30 (3) 651–72.

———. 2006. "From 'Rights' to 'Ritual': AIDS Activism and Treatment Testimonies in South Africa." *American Anthropologist* 108 (2): 312–23.

———. 2009. "Foot Soldiers of Global Health: Teaching and Preaching AIDS Science and Modern Medicine on the Frontline." *Medical Anthropology* 28: 81–107.

Robins, S., and B. von Lieres. 2005. "Remaking Citizenship, Unmaking Marginalization: The Treatment Action Campaign in Post-Apartheid South Africa." *Canadian Journal of African Studies* 38 (3): 575–86.

Rogaski, R. 2004. *Hygienic Modernity: The Meanings of Health in Treaty-Port China.* Berkeley: University of California Press.

Roney, J. C. 1959. "Medical Anthropology: A Synthetic Discipline." *New Physician* 8: 32–81.

Rose, N. 1998. *Inventing Ourselves: Psychology, Power, and Personhood.* Cambridge: Cambridge University Press.

———. 2007. *The Politics of Life Itself: Biomedicine, Power, and Subjectivity in the Twenty-First Century.* Princeton: Princeton University Press.

Roseman, M. 1991. *Healing Sounds from the Malaysian Rainforest: Temiar Music and Medicine.* Berkeley: University of California Press.

Rosner, G., S. Rosner, and A. Orr-Urtreger. 2009. "Genetic Testing in Israel: An Overview." *Annual Review of Genomics and Human Genetics* 10: 175–92.

Rostow, W. W. 1960. *The Stages of Economic Growth: A Non-Communist Manifesto.* Cambridge: Cambridge University Press.

Rothman, J. 1974. *Planning and Organizing for Social Change.* New York: Columbia University Press.

Rothstein, E. 2009. "Claude Levi-Strauss, 100, Dies; Altered Western Views of the 'Primitive.'" *New York Times*, November 4, A28.

Rousseau, J. J. 1994 [1754]. *Discourse on Inequality.* Oxford: Oxford University Press.

Rubel, A. J., C. W. O'Neil, and R. Collado-Ardon. 1991. *Susto: A Folk Illness.* Berkeley: University of California Press.

Rubin, G. 1975. "The Traffic in Women: Notes on the 'Political Economy' of Sex." In *Toward an Anthropology of Women*, edited by R. Reiter, 157–210. New York: Monthly Review Press.

———. 1984. "Thinking Sex: Notes for a Radical Theory of the Politics of Sexuality." In *Pleasure and Danger: Exploring Female Sexuality*, edited by C. Vance, 267–319. Boston: Routledge and Kegan Paul.

Rylko-Bauer, B., M. Singer, and J. Van Willigen. 2006. "Reclaiming Applied Anthropology: Its Past, Present, and Future." *American Anthropologist* 108 (1): 178–90.

Rylko-Bauer, B., L. Whiteford, and P. Farmer, eds. 2009. *Global Health in Times of Violence.* Santa Fe: School for Advanced Research Press.

Sahlins, M. D. 1976. *The Use and Abuse of Biology: An Anthropological Critique of Sociobiology.* Ann Arbor: University of Michigan Press.

———. 1995. *How "Natives" Think: About Captain Cook, for Example.* Chicago: University of Chicago Press.

———. 2008. *The Western View of Human Nature*. Chicago: University of Chicago, Prickly Paradigm Press.

Said, E. W. 1979. *Orientalism*. New York: Vintage.

———. 1993. *Culture and Imperialism*. New York: Alfred Knopf.

Sandelowski, M. 1993. *With Child in Mind: Studies of the Personal Encounter with Infertility*. Philadelphia: University of Pennsylvania Press.

Sapp, J. 1983. "The Struggle for Authority in the Field of Heredity, 1900–1932: New Perspectives on the Rise of Genetics." *Journal of the History of Biology* 16 (3): 311–42.

Sappol, M. 2002. *A Traffic of Dead Bodies: Anatomy and Embodied Social Identity in Nineteenth-Century America*. Princeton: Princeton University Press.

Sargent, C. F. 1989. *Maternity, Medicine, and Power: Reproductive Decisions in Urban Benin*. Berkeley: University of California Press.

———. 2009. "President, Society for Medical Anthropology, Speaking to the National Health Crisis." *Medical Anthropology Quarterly* 23 (3): 342–49.

Sawchuck, J. 1993. "Anthropology and Canadian Native Political Organizations: Past and Future Trends." In *Anthropology, Public Policy, and Native Peoples in Canada*, edited by N. Dyck and J. Waldram, 271–92. Montreal: McGill-Queen's University Press.

Scammon, R. E., and L. A. Calkins. 1929. *The Development and Growth of the External Dimensions of the Human Body in the Fetal Period*. Minneapolis: University of Minnesota Press.

Scheff, T. 1975. *Labeling Madness*. Englewood Cliffs: Prentice Hall.

Schensul, S. L., and J. J. Schensul. 1978. "Advocacy and Applied Anthropology." In *Social Scientists as Advocates: Views from the Applied Disciplines*, edited by G. H. Weber and G. J. McCall, 121–64. Beverly Hills: Sage.

Scheper-Hughes, N. 1978. "Saints, Scholars and Schizophrenics: Madness and Badness in Western Ireland." *Medical Anthropology* 2 (3): 59–93.

———. 1985. "Culture, Scarcity, and Maternal Thinking: Maternal Detachment and Infant Survival in a Brazilian Shantytown." *Ethos* 13 (4): 291–317.

———. 1990. "Three Propositions for a Critically Applied Medical Anthropology." *Social Science & Medicine* 30 (2): 189–97.

———. 1992. *Death without Weeping: The Violence of Everyday Life in Brazil*. Berkeley: University of California Press.

———. 2000. "The Global Traffic in Human Organs." *Current Anthropology* 41 (2): 191–211.

———. 2002. "Min(d)ing the Body: On the Trail of Organ-Stealing Rumors." In *Exotic No More: Anthropology on the Front Lines*, edited by J. MacLancy, 33–63. Chicago: University of Chicago Press.

———. 2004. "Parts Unknown: Undercover Ethnography of the Organs-trafficking Underworld." *Ethnography* 5 (1): 29–73.

Scheper-Hughes, N., and M. Lock. 1987. "The Mindful Body: A Prolegomenon to Future Work in Medical Anthropology." *Medical Anthropology Quarterly* 1 (1): 6–41.

Scheper-Hughes, N., and L. Wacquant, eds. 2002. *Commodifying Bodies*. London: Sage Publications.

Schmalzer, S. 2008. *The People's Peking Man: Popular Science and Human Identity in Twentieth-Century China*. Chicago: University of Chicago Press.

Schoepf, B. G. 1991. "Ethical, Methodological, and Political Issues of AIDS Research in Central Africa." *Social Science & Medicine* 33 (7): 749–63.

———. 2001. "International AIDS Research in Anthropology: Take a Critical Perspective on the Crisis." *Annual Review of Anthropology* 30 (1): 335–61.

Schull, N. 2010. *Machine Life: Design and Dependency in Las Vegas*. Princeton: Princeton University Press.

Schultz, A. H. 1923. "Fetal Growth in Man." *American Journal of Physical Anthropology* 6 (4): 389–99.

———. 1945. *Aleš Hrdlička, 1869–1943. Biographical Memoirs Vol. XXIII*. Washington: National Academy of Sciences.

Schulz, A. J., and L. Mullings, eds. 2006. *Gender, Race, Class, and Health: Intersectional Approaches*. San Francisco: Jossey-Bass.

Schweik, S. 2009. *The Ugly Laws: Disability in Public*. New York: New York University Press.

Segal, D. A., and S. J. Yanagisaki, eds. 2005. *Unwrapping the Sacred Bundle: Reflections on the Disciplining of Anthropology*. Durham: Duke University Press.

Setel, P. 1999. *A Plague of Paradoxes: AIDS, Culture, and Demography in Northern Tanzania*. Chicago: University of Chicago Press.

Shapiro, J. 1993. *No Pity: How the Disability Rights Movement Is Changing America*. New York: New York Times Book.

Sharp, L. A. 2006. *Strange Harvest: Organ Transplants, Denatured Bodies, and the Transformed Self*. Berkeley: University of California Press.

Shaw, G. B. 1949. *Back to Methuselah: Selected Plays with Prefaces*, vol. 2. New York: Dodd, Mead.

———. 2006. *The Shrewing Up of Blanco Postnet*. Fairford, UK: Echo Library.

Shaw, S. 2005. "The Politics of Recognition in Culturally Appropriate Care." *Medical Anthropology Quarterly* 19 (3): 290–309.

Shils, E. 1960. "Political Development in the New States." *Comparative Studies in Society and History* 2 (3): 265–92.

Shipman, P. 2002. *The Evolution of Racism*. Cambridge: Harvard University Press.

Shore, C., and S. Wright. 1997. *Anthropology of Policy: Critical Perspectives on Governance and Power*. London: Routledge.

Sider, G. M., and G. A. Smith, eds. 1997. *Between History and Histories: The Making of Silences and Commemorations*. Toronto: University of Toronto Press.

Siebers, T. A. 2006. *Disability Theory*. Ann Arbor: University of Michigan Press.

Simons, R. C., and C. C. Hughes, eds. 1985. *The Culture-Bound Syndromes*. Boston: D. Reidel.

Singer, M. 1986. "Developing a Critical Perspective in Medical Anthropology." *Medical Anthropology Quarterly* 17 (5): 128–29.

———, ed. 1998. *The Political Economy of AIDS*. Amityville: Baywood Publishing Company.

———. 2008. "Applied Anthropology." In *A New History of Anthropology*, edited by H. Kuklick, 326–40. Malden: Blackwell Press.

———. 2010. "Entering the Troubled Policy Process." *Anthropology Newsletter* 51 (5): 27–28.

Singer, M., and H. A. Baer. 1995. *Critical Medical Anthropology*. Amityville: Baywood.

———. 2007. *Introducing Medical Anthropology: A Discipline in Action*. Lanham: AltaMira.

Singer, M., and A. Castro. 2004. "Anthropology and Health Policy: A Critical Perspective." In *Unhealthy Health Policy: A Critical Anthropological Examination*, edited by A. Castro and M. Singer, xi–xx. Walnut Creek: Altamira Press.

Singer, M., and S. Clair. 2003. "Syndemics and Public Health: Reconceptualizing Disease in Bio-social Context." *Medical Anthropology Quarterly* 17 (4): 423–41.

Singer, M., P. Erickson, L. Badiane, R. Diaz, D. Ortiz, T. Abraham, and A. M. Nicolaysen. 2006. "Syndemics, Sex, and the City: Understanding Sexually Transmitted Disease in Social and Cultural Context." *Social Science & Medicine* 63 (8): 2010–21.

Singer, M., Z. Jia, J. Schensul, M. Weeks, and B. Page. 1992. "AIDS and the IV Drug User: The Local Context in Prevention Efforts." *Medical Anthropology* 14 (2–4): 285–306.

Smith, D. J. 2004. "Youth, Sin, and Sex in Nigeria: Christianity and HIV/AIDS-Related Beliefs and Behavior among Rural-Urban Migrants." *Culture, Health, and Sexuality* 6 (5): 425–37.

Snyder, S. L., and D. T. Mitchell. 2006. *Cultural Locations of Disability*. Chicago: University of Chicago Press.

Sobo, E. J. 1995. *Choosing Unsafe Sex: AIDS-Risk Denial among Disadvantaged Women*. Philadelphia: University of Pennsylvania Press.

Society for Medical Anthropology Alcohol, Drug, and Tobacco Study Group.

2007. "Alcohol, Drug and Tobacco Study Group Takes a Stand." *Medical Anthropology Quarterly* 21 (3): 343–47.

Society for Medical Anthropology Council on Infant and Child Health and Welfare (CICH) Policy Statement Task Force. 2006. "The Rights of Children." http://www.medanthro.net/stand/rights.html.

Solinger, R. 1998. *Abortion Wars: A Half-Century of Struggle, 1950–2000*. Berkeley: University of California Press.

Song, P. 2010. "Biotech Pilgrims and the Transnational Quest for Stem Cell Cures." *Medical Anthropology* 29 (4): 384–402.

Sontag, S. 1963. "A Hero of Our Time." *New York Review of Books*. http://www.nybooks.com/articles/archives/1963/nov/28/a-hero-of-our-time/.

Spencer, F. 1997. *History of Physical Anthropology: An Encyclopedia, Volume 1*. New York: Garland.

Star, S. L., and J. R. Griesemer. 1989. "Institutional Ecology, 'Translations,' and Boundary Objects: Amateurs and Professionals in Berkeley's Museum of Comparative Zoology." *Social Studies of Science* 19: 387–420.

Stark, W. 1958. *The Sociology of Knowledge: An Essay in Aid of a Deeper Understanding of the History of Ideas*. Glencoe: Free Press.

Starn, O. 2004. *Ishi's Brain: In Search of America's Last 'Wild' Indian*. New York: Norton.

Stassinos, E. 2009. "An Early Case of Personality: Ruth Benedict's Autobiographical Fragment and the Case of the Biblical 'Boaz.'" *Histories of Anthropology Annual* 5: 28–51.

Sterk, C. 1999. *Fast Lives: Women Who Use Crack Cocaine*. Philadelphia: Temple University Press.

Stevenson, P. H. 1921. "A Collection of Chinese Embryos." *China Medical Journal* 35: 503–20.

St. George-Hyslop, P. H. 2000. "Molecular Genetics of Alzheimer's Disease." *Biological Psychiatry* 47 (3): 183–99.

Stocking, G. 1968. "Franz Boas and the Culture Concept." *Race, Culture, and Evolution: Essays in the History of Anthropology*, 214–19. New York: Free Press.

Stoler, A. L. 1995. *Race and the Education of Desire: Foucault's History of Sexuality and the Colonial Order of Things*. Durham: Duke University Press.

———. 2002. *Carnal Knowledge and Imperial Power: Race and the Intimate in Colonial Rule*. Berkeley: University of California Press.

Stotz, K., A. Bostanci, and P. Griffiths. 2006. "Tracking the Shift to 'Postgenomics.'" *Community Genetics* 9 (3): 190–96.

Strathern, A., and P. Stewart. 1999. *Curing and Healing: Medical Anthropology in Global Perspective*. Columbia: Carolina Academic Press.

Strathern, M. 1985. "Kinship and Economy: Constitutive Orders of a Provisional Kind." *American Ethnologist* 12 (2): 191–209.

———. 1992a. *After Nature: English Kinship in the Late Twentieth Century*. Cambridge: Cambridge University Press.

———. 1992b. *Reproducing the Future*. New York: Routledge.

Strohman, R. C. 2001. "A New Paradigm for Life: Beyond Genetic Determinism." *California Monthly* 111: 4–27.

Stull, D. D., and F. Moos. 1981. "A Brief Overview of the Role of Anthropology in Public Policy." *Policy Studies Review* 1 (1): 19–27.

Sun, M. 1983. "The Mysterious Expulsion of Steven Mosher." *Science* 220 (4598): 692–94.

Sunder Rajan, K. 2006. *Biocapital: The Constitution of Postgenomic Life*. Durham: Duke University Press.

———. 2007. "Experimental Values: Indian Clinical Trials and Surplus Health." *New Left Review* 45: 67–88.

Susser, I. 2009. *AIDS, Sex, and Culture: Global Politics and Survival in Southern Africa*. Malden: Wiley-Blackwell.

Szyf, M., P. McGowan, and M. J. Meaney. 2008. "The Social Environment and the Epigenome." *Environmental and Molecular Mutagenesis* 49: 46–60.

Tan, M. L. 1995. "From *Bakla* to Gay: Shifting Gender Identities and Sexual Behaviors in the Philippines." In *Conceiving Sexuality: Approaches to Sex Research in a Postmodern World*, edited by R. Parker and J. Gagnon, 85–96. New York: Routledge.

———. 1996. "*Silahis*: Looking for the Missing Filipino Bisexual Male." In *Bisexualities and AIDS: International Perspectives*, edited by P. Aggleton, 207–25. London: Taylor and Francis.

———. 2001. "Survival through Pluralism: Emerging Gay Communities in the Philippines." *Journal of Homosexuality* 40 (3–4): 117–42.

Tarlo, E. 2001. *Unsettling Memories: Narratives of the Emergency in Delhi*. Berkeley: University of California Press.

Taussig, K. S. 2009. *Ordinary Genomes: Science, Citizenship, and Genetic Identities*. Durham: Duke University Press.

Taussig, K.S., R. Rapp, and D. Heath. 2003. "Flexible Eugenics: Technologies of the Self in the Age of Genetics." In *Genetic Nature/Culture: Anthropology and Science beyond the Two Culture Divide*, edited by A. H. Goodman, D. Heath, and M. S. Lindee, 58–76. Berkeley: University of California Press.

Taussig, M. T. 1980. "Reification and the Consciousness of the Patient." *Social Science and Medicine* 14B (1): 3–13.

———. 1987. *Shamanism, Colonialism, and the Wild Man: A Study in Terror and Healing*. Chicago: University of Chicago Press.

Taylor, C. 1985. "Mexican Male Homosexual Interaction in Public Contexts." *Journal of Homosexuality* 11 (3–4): 117–36.

Taylor, J. S. 2001. "Revisioning Women, Health, and Healing: Feminist, Cultural, and Technoscience Perspectives." *Medical Anthropology Quarterly* 15 (3): 410–11.

———. 2003. "The Story Catches You and You Fall Down: Tragedy, Ethnography, and 'Cultural Competence.'" *Medical Anthropology Quarterly* 17 (2): 159–81.

———. 2004. "Introduction." In *Consuming Motherhood*, edited by J. S. Taylor, L. L. Layne, and D. F. Wozniak, 1–16. New Brunswick: Rutgers University Press.

———. 2005. "Surfacing the Body Interior." *Annual Review of Anthropology* 34: 741–56.

Terto Jr., V. 1999. "Seropositivity, Homosexuality, and Identity Politics in Brazil." *Culture, Health, and Sexuality* 1 (4): 329–46.

———. 2000. "Male Homosexuality and Seropositivity: The Construction of Social Identities in Brazil." In *Framing the Sexual Subject: The Politics of Gender, Sexuality, and Power*, edited by R. Parker, R. M. Barbosa, and P. Aggleton, 60–78. Berkeley: University of California Press.

Terto Jr., V., and J. García. 2008. "Mechanisms of Representation and Coordination of the Brazilian AIDS Responses: A Perspective from Civil Society." In *The Politics of AIDS: Globalization, the State, and Civil Society*, edited by M. L. Follér and H. Thörn, 242–54. Basingstoke: Palgrave Macmillan.

Terto Jr., V., C. G. Victora, and D. Knauth, eds. 2004. "Direitos sexuais e reprodutivos como direitos humanos." Special issue, *Corpus* 1.

Thornton, R. 2008. *Unimagined Community: Sex, Networks, and AIDS in Uganda and South Africa*. Berkeley: University of California Press.

Tilley, L., K. Morgan, and N. Kalsheker. 1998. "Genetic Risk Factors in Alzheimer's Disease." *Journal of Clinical Pathology: Molecular Pathology* 51: 293–304.

Titmuss, R., and B. Abel-Smith. 1961. *Social Policies and Population Growth in Mauritius*. London: Methuen.

Trachtman, I., dir. 2008. *Praying with Lior*. USA. Ruby Pictures.

Traweek, S. 1992. *Beamtimes and Lifetimes: The World of High Energy Physicists*. Boston: Harvard University Press.

———. 1993. "An Introduction to Cultural, Gender, and Social Studies of Science and Technology." *Journal of Culture, Medicine, and Psychiatry* 17: 3–25.

Treichler, P. A. 1987. "AIDS, Homophobia, and Biomedical Discourse: An Epidemic of Signification." *AIDS: Cultural Analysis/Cultural Activism* 43: 31–70.

———. 1999. *How to Have Theory in an Epidemic: Cultural Chronicles of AIDS*. Durham: Duke University Press.

Trouillot, M. R. 1991. "Anthropology and the Savage Slot: The Poetics and Politics of Otherness." In *Recapturing Anthropology*, edited by R. G. Fox, 17–44. Santa Fe: School of American Research Press.

Turner, C. F., H. G. Miller, and L. E. Moses, eds. 1989. *AIDS: Sexual Behavior and Intravenous Drug Use*. Washington, D.C.: National Academy Press.

Turner, V. W. 1967. *The Forest of Symbols: Aspects of Ndembu Ritual*. Ithaca: Cornell University Press.

———. 1979. *The Ritual Process: Structure and Anti-Structure*. Chicago: Aldine.

Turney, J. 1995. "The Public Understanding of Science—Where Next?" *European Journal of Genetics in Society* 1 (2): 5–22.

Turshen, M. 1984. *The Political Ecology of Disease in Tanzania*. New Brunswick: Rutgers University Press.

———. 1989. *The Politics of Public Health*. New Brunswick: Rutgers University Press.

———. 2007. *Women's Health Movements: A Global Force for Change*. New York: Palgrave Macmillan.

Umansky, L., and P. Longmore, eds. 2001. *The New Disability History: American Perspectives*. New York: New York University Press.

United States Code. 1978. Public Law 95–341, American Indian Religious Freedom Act. Washington, D.C.: Office of the Law Revision Counsel.

Valdés, T., and J. Olavarria, eds. 1998. *Masculinidades y equidad de género en América Latina*. Santiago: FLASCO-Chile.

Valentine, D. 2007. *Imagining Transgender: An Ethnography of a Category*. Durham: Duke University Press.

Van Hollen, C. C. 2003. *Birth on the Threshold: Childbirth and Modernity in South India*. Berkeley: University of California Press.

Van Willigen, J. 2002. "Anthropology as a Policy Research." In *Applied Anthropology*, edited by John Van Willigen, 165–74. Santa Barbara: Praeger.

Varenne, H., and R. McDermott. 1998. *Successful Failure: The School America Builds*. Boulder: Westview Press.

Verdery, K. 1999. *The Political Lives of Dead Bodies: Reburial and Postsocialist Change*. New York: Columbia University Press.

Visweswaran, K. 1999. "Affective States." *Topoi* 18: 81–86.

Viveros Vigoya, M. 2001. "Contemporary Latin American Perspectives on Masculinity." *Men and Masculinities* 3 (3): 237–60.

———. 2002. "Dionysian Blacks: Sexuality, Body, and Racial Order in Colombia." *Latin American Perspectives* 29 (2): 60–77.

Volkman, T. A., ed. 2005. *Cultures of Transnational Adoption*. Durham: Duke University Press.

Waldby, C., and R. Mitchell. 2006. *Tissue Economies: Blood, Organs, and Cell Lines in Late Capitalism*. Durham: Duke University Press.

Wallerstein, I. 1974. *The Modern World-System. Capitalist Agriculture and the Origins of the European World Economy in the Sixteenth Century*. New York: Academic Press.

Walsh, K. 2007. "On the Streets of Chicago, a Candidate Comes of Age." *U.S. News and World Report*. http://www.usnews.com/usnews/news/articles/070826/30bama.htm.

Walton, S. M. 1981. "Ethnic Considerations in Ultrasonic Scanning of Fetal Biparietal Diameters." *Australian and New Zealand Journal of Obstetrics and Gynecology* 21 (2): 82–84.

Ware, N., H. Hopper, T. Tugenberg, B. Dickey, and D. Fisher. 2007. "Connectedness and Citizenship: Re-defining Social Integration." *Psychiatric Services* 58 (4): 469–74.

Watson, J. L. 1988. "Of Flesh and Bones: The Management of Death Pollution in Cantonese Society." In *Death and the Regeneration of Life*, edited by M. Bloch and J. Parry, 155–86.

Weber, M. 1978 [1914]. *Economy and Society: An Outline of Interpretive Sociology*. Berkeley: University of California Press.

———. 2003 [1905]. *The Protestant Ethic and the Spirit of Capitalism*. Dover: Mineola.

Wellin, E. 1955. "Water Boiling in a Peruvian Town." In *Health, Culture and Community: Public Reactions to Health Programs*, edited by B. D. Paul, 71–102. New York: Russell Sage Foundation.

Wexler, N. 1992. "Clairvoyance and Caution: Repercussions from the Human Genome Project." In *The Code of Codes: Scientific and Social Issues in the Human Genome Project*, edited by D. J. Kevles and L. Hood, 211–43. Cambridge: Harvard University Press.

White, R. 1999. *Putting Risk in Perspective: Black Teenage Lives in the Era of AIDS*. Lanham: Rowman and Littlefield.

Whiteford, L. M., and L. G. Branch. 2008. *Primary Health Care in Cuba: The Other Revolution*. Lanham: Rowman and Littlefield.

Whiteford, L., and L. Manderson, eds. 2000. *Global Health Policy, Local Realities: The Fallacy of the Level Playing Field*. Boulder: Lynne Rienner.

Whiteford, L., and C. Vindrola Padros. 2011. "The Medical Anthropology of Water." In *A Companion to Medical Anthropology*, edited by M. Singer and P. Erickson, 197–218. Hoboken: Wiley.

Whitehead, H. 1987. *Renunciation and Reformulation: A Study of Conversion in an American Sect*. Ithaca: Cornell University Press.

Whitington, J. 2008. "The Simulation of Politics: Developmental Natures in Lao

Hydropower." PhD dissertation, Department of Anthropology, University of California, Berkeley.

Whitmarsh, I. 2008a. "Biomedical Ambivalence: Asthma Diagnosis, the Pharmaceutical, and Other Contradictions in Barbados." *American Ethnologist* 35 (1): 49–63.

———. 2008b. *Biomedical Ambiguity: Race, Asthma, and the Contested Meaning of Genetic Research in the Caribbean*. Ithaca: Cornell University Press.

Whittaker, A. M. 1992. "Living with HIV: Resistance by Positive People." *Medical Anthropology Quarterly* 6 (4): 385–90.

Whittaker, A., L. Manderson, and E. Cartwright, eds. 2010. Special issue on "Patients without Borders: Understanding Medical Travel." *Medical Anthropology* 29 (4).

Whyte, M. K. 1984. "Rural Chinese and Stephen Mosher." *Peasant Studies* 11 (2): 111–18.

Whyte, S. R. 1997. *Questioning Misfortune: The Pragmatics of Uncertainty in Eastern Uganda*. Cambridge: Cambridge University Press.

Wikan, U. 1990. *Managing Turbulent Hearts: A Balinese Formula for Living*. Chicago: University of Chicago Press.

Wiley, A. S., and J. S. Allen. 2008. *Medical Anthropology: A Biocultural Approach*. New York: Oxford University Press.

Willen, S., and H. Castañeda. 2008. "Unauthorized Im/migration and Health." Presented at the American Anthropological Association meeting, San Francisco.

Wilson, M. 2008. "'Bodies' Exhibitors Admit Corpse Origins Are Murky." *New York Times*, May 30. http://www.nytimes.com/2008/05/30/nyregion/30bodies .html.

Wohl, I., dir. 1979. *Best Boy*. Australia: Only Child Pictures.

Wolf, E. R. 1982. *Europe and the People without History*. Berkeley: University of California Press.

Wolpoff, M., and R. Caspari. 1998. *Race and Human Evolution: A Fatal Attraction*. New York: Basic.

World Health Organization. 2006. "Working Definitions." In *Defining Sexual Health: Report of a Technical Consultation on Sexual Health, 28–31 January 2002, Geneva* (2–4). Sexual Health Document Series. Geneva: World Health Organization. http://www.who.int/reproductivehealth/topics/gender_rights/ defining_sexual_health.pdf.

Wu, R., and X. Wu. 1997. *China*. In *History of Physical Anthropology: An Encyclopedia, Volume 1*, edited by F. Spencer, 273–82. New York: Garland.

X, Jacobus [as "A French Army Surgeon"]. 1898 [1893]. *Untrodden Fields of*

Anthropology: Observations on the Esoteric Manners and Customs of Semi-Civilized Peoples; Being a Record of Thirty Years Experience in Asia, Africa, America, and Oceania. 2 vols. Paris: Librarie de Médecine, Folklore, et Anthropologie.

Yang, L. H., and A. Kleinman. 2008. "'Face' and the Embodiment of Stigma in China: The Cases of Schizophrenia and AIDS." *Social Science & Medicine* 67: 398–408.

Yang, L. H., A. Kleinman, B. G. Link, J. C. Phelan, S. Lee, and B. Good. 2007. "Culture and Stigma: Adding Moral Experience to Stigma Theory." *Social Science & Medicine* 64 (7): 1524–35.

Young, A. 1981. "When Rational Men Fall Sick." *Culture, Medicine, and Psychiatry,* 5, 317–335.

———. 1982. "The Anthropologies of Illness and Sickness." *Annual Review of Anthropology* 11: 257–87.

———. 1995. *The Harmony of Illusions: Inventing Post Traumatic Stress Disorder.* Princeton: Princeton University Press.

Yoxen, E. J. 1982. "Constructing Genetic Diseases." In *The Problem of Medical Knowledge: Examining the Social Construction of Medicine,* edited by P. Wright and A. Treacher, 144–61. Edinburgh: University of Edinburgh Press.

LAWRENCE COHEN is Professor of Anthropology and South and Southeast Asian Studies at the University of California, Berkeley. His work focuses on the study of medicine, health, and the body in contemporary India. His first book, *No Aging in India: Alzheimer's, the Bad Family, and Other Modern Things* (1998), won the J. I. Staley Prize, the Victor Turner Prize, and the American Ethnological Society's First Book Prize. With Annette Leibing, he is the coeditor of *Thinking about Dementia: Culture, Loss, and the Anthropology of Senility.* He has written extensively on the politics of AIDS prevention and of sexuality in small-town India and on the science and regulation of organ transplantation.

DIDIER FASSIN is James D. Wolfensohn Professor of Social Science at the Institute for Advanced Study, Princeton, and Director of Studies at the École des Hautes Études en Sciences Sociales, Paris. He directs the Interdisciplinary Research Institute for Social Sciences (CNRS—Inserm—EHESS—University Paris North). Trained as a medical doctor, he has been vice president of Médecins sans Frontières and is currently president of the Comité Médical pour les Exilés. His field of interest is political and moral anthropology. He has conducted research on maternal health in Ecuador, the experience of AIDS in South Africa, the politics of trauma in Palestine, and the anthropology of the state in France. His recent publications include, as author, *The Empire of Trauma: An Inquiry into the Condition of Victimhood* (with Richard Rechtman), *Humanitarian Reason: A Moral History of the Present*, and *La Force de l'Ordre: Une Anthropologie de la Police des Quartiers*; and, as editor, *Contemporary States of Emergency* (with Mariella Pandolfi), *Les Nouvelles Frontières de la Société Française*, and *A Companion to Moral Anthropology.*

FAYE GINSBURG is the director of the Center for Media, Culture, and History at NYU, where she is David Kriser Professor of Anthropology. She is also a codirector of the Center for Religion and Media and of the Council for the Study of Disability. Ginsburg has written or edited four books, from her first work, *Contested Lives: The Abortion Debate in an American Community* (winner of four awards), to her most recent book, *Media Worlds: Anthropology on New Terrain.* She has received numerous awards, including a MacArthur, a Guggenheim, and grants for her work from Ford, Rockefeller, Wenner Gren, and the Spencer Foundations. She is working with Rayna Rapp on a project titled "Cultural Innovation and Learning Disabilities."

MARCIA C. INHORN is the William K. Lanman Jr. Professor of Anthropology and International Affairs at Yale University, where she has also served as the chair of the Council on Middle East Studies. In Fall 2010 she was the inaugural Diane Middlebrook and Carl Djerassi Visiting Professor at the University of Cambridge's Centre for Gender Studies. A scholar of Middle Eastern gender, religion, and health, she has conducted multi-sited research on the social impact of infertility and assisted reproductive technologies in Egypt, Lebanon, the United Arab Emirates, and Arab America. She has written four books on this subject, including her latest, *The New Arab Man: Emergent Masculinities, Technologies, and Islam in the Middle East* (2012), which have won the American Anthropological Association's Eileen Basker Prize and Diana Forsythe Prize for outstanding feminist anthropological research in the areas of gender, health, science, technology, and biomedicine. Inhorn is also the primary editor or coeditor of eight volumes and the founding editor of the *Journal of Middle East Women's Studies*. As past president of the Society for Medical Anthropology (SMA), she was the chief organizer and program chair of the Yale SMA conference on which this book is based.

ARTHUR KLEINMAN is the Esther and Sidney Rabb Professor of Anthropology in the Department of Anthropology, Harvard University, and Professor of Medical Anthropology and Professor of Psychiatry at Harvard Medical School. He is also the Victor and William Fung Director of Harvard's Asia Center. An anthropologist-physician, he has conducted research on Chinese society since 1968. He has studied the experience of serious illness, caregiving, social suffering, and the person in the moral context. He also has worked extensively on global mental health policies and programs, the medical humanities, and the culture of medicine. He is the author of 229 articles, 6 books, and coeditor of more than 30 volumes and special issues of journals. His honors include the Wellcome Medal for Medical Anthropology; the Franz Boas Award from the American Anthropological Association; and both the Career Achievement Award and the George Foster Practicing Medical Anthropology Award from the SMA. He is a member of the Institute of Medicine in the National Academies and of the American Academy of Arts and Sciences.

MARGARET LOCK is Marjorie Bronfman Professor Emerita affiliated with the Department of Social Studies of Medicine and the Department of Anthropology at McGill University. Among her research interests are comparative epistemologies of medical knowledge, the global impact of emerging biomedical technologies, and an anthropology of the body. She is past president of the SMA, is the author and/or coeditor of fourteen books, and has published over two hundred articles. Her monograph *Encounters with Aging: Mythologies of Menopause in Japan and North America* (1993) won six prizes, including the J. R. Staley Prize of the School of American

Research and the Wellcome Medal of the Royal Anthropological Institute of Great Britain, and *Twice Dead: Organ Transplants and the Reinvention of Death* (2002) is also a prize-winning monograph. Lock's most recent coauthored book is *An Anthropology of Biomedicine* (2010), and she is working on a book tentatively titled *The Eclipse of the Gene and the Return of Divination.* Among other major career awards, Lock was named a fellow of the Royal Society of Canada and an Officier de L'Ordre National du Québec, awarded the Gold Medal for Research by the Social Sciences and Humanities Research Council of Canada (SSHRC), and the Career Achievement Award of the SMA. In 2010 she was appointed an Officer of the Order of Canada.

EMILY MARTIN is Professor in the Department of Anthropology at New York University. Her work has combined feminist analysis with ethnographic investigation to shed light on the gendered meanings encoded in medical texts, and the ways that these medical models in turn shape individuals' understandings of their gendered and social bodies. Martin has taught cultural anthropology at the University of California, Irvine, Yale University, Johns Hopkins University, Princeton University, and currently at New York University. She has served on the board of directors of the Social Science Research Council and as president of the American Ethnological Society. Dr. Martin's early book, *The Woman in the Body: A Cultural Analysis of Reproduction* (1987), was a pathbreaking example of feminist technoscience studies, critically examining medical and scientific representations of female bodies, from menarche to menopause. The book was awarded the SMA's Eileen Basker Prize for outstanding research in gender and health. Since then, Dr. Martin has gone on to publish seminal ethnographies on cultural representations of the immune system and depression.

LYNN M. MORGAN is Mary E. Woolley Professor of Anthropology at Mount Holyoke College. She is the author of *Icons of Life: A Cultural History of Human Embryos* (2009), which focuses on the history of human embryo collecting in the early twentieth century and its relation to contemporary fetal politics. She is also the author of *Community Participation in Health: The Politics of Primary Care in Costa Rica* (1993), and coeditor of *Fetal Subjects, Feminist Positions* (1999). She recently completed a Weatherhead Resident Scholarship at the School for Advanced Research, where she was writing about recent reproductive governance in Costa Rica, Nicaragua, and Mexico.

RICHARD PARKER is Professor of Anthropology and Sociomedical Sciences, and Director of the Center for Gender, Sexuality, and Health at the Mailman School of Public Health, Columbia University, in New York City. He is also the director and president of the Brazilian Interdisciplinary AIDS Association (ABIA) in Rio de Janeiro, Brazil. His research focuses on the social and cultural construction of gender and sexuality, the social aspects of HIV/AIDS, and the relationships among social inequality, health, and disease. He has also served on numerous commissions and held a range of positions in program and advocacy work, including leadership roles in the prevention unit for the Brazilian National AIDS Program, the Commission on Citizenship and Reproduction (CCR), the International Council of AIDS Service Organizations (ICASO), the International Planned Parenthood Federation-Western Hemisphere Region (IPPF-WHR), and Sexuality Policy Watch (SPW). He is the editor in chief of the journal *Global Public Health* and the founding editor of *Culture, Health, and Sexuality*.

RAYNA RAPP is Professor in the Department of Anthropology at New York University, where she is also an affiliated faculty member in the Center for Bioethics and the Center for the Study of Gender and Sexuality. As one of the founders of the field of feminist anthropology, Rapp is the editor of several key works, including *Toward an Anthropology of Women* (1975), *Conceiving the New World Order* (Ginsburg and Rapp 1995), and *Articulating Hidden Histories* (Rapp and Schneider 1995). Her research has focused on gender and reproduction, particularly the use of prenatal genetic testing, and has explored the genetics of disability, eugenic discourses in American society, and the notion of "genetic citizenship." Her book *Testing Women, Testing the Fetus: The Social Impact of Amniocentesis in America* (1999) has won numerous awards, including the Eileen Basker Prize, the Diana Forsythe Prize, and the J. I. Staley Prize of the School of American Research. Rapp's and Faye Ginsburg's current collaborative research on the familial impacts of learning disability diagnosis and treatment links medical anthropological analysis with key themes from disability studies.

MERRILL SINGER is Professor in the Department of Anthropology and a Senior Research Fellow at the Center for Health, Intervention, and Prevention, University of Connecticut, as well as a research affiliate at the Center for Interdisciplinary Research on AIDS (CIRA) at Yale University. He is best known for his research on substance abuse, HIV/AIDS, health disparities, and minority health, but he has recently begun new work in the area of environmental health. As the director of the Center for Community Health Research at the Hispanic Health Council in Hartford, Connecticut, Dr. Singer helped to develop the theoretical perspective within medical anthropology known as critical medical anthropology, which focuses on political-economic determinants of health, as well as the public health concepts of "syndemics" and "oppression illness." Dr. Singer has won the SMA's Rudolph Virchow Prize and George Foster Memorial Award for the Practice of Medical Anthropology, the Anthropology of North America Prize for Distinguished Achievement in the Critical Study of North America, and the Solon T. Kimball Award from the American Anthropological Association.

EMILY A. WENTZELL is Assistant Professor of Anthropology at the University of Iowa. Her work combines approaches from medical anthropology, gender studies, and science and technology studies to examine the gendered social consequences of sexual health interventions. Her book on working-class Mexican men's experiences of masculinity as they age and encounter sexual health difficulties is forthcoming from Duke University Press. She is also beginning a new project exploring the co-construction of heterosexuality, illness identity, and "Mexicanness" among couples enrolled in a longitudinal study of human papillomavirus (HPV) transmission in central Mexico. She recently completed a postdoctoral fellowship at Yale University, where she co-organized the SMA conference that formed the basis for this book.

MARCIA C. INHORN is William K. Lanman Jr. Professor of Anthropology and International Affairs at Yale University. She is the author of *The New Arab Man: Emergent Masculinities, Technologies, and Islam in the Middle East* and *Local Babies, Global Science: Gender, Religion, and In Vitro Fertilization in Egypt*, among numerous other titles.

EMILY A. WENTZELL is Assistant Professor of Anthropology at the University of Iowa. She is the author of *Maturing Machos: Aging, Illness, and Viagra in Mexico*, forthcoming from Duke University Press. Her current research addresses the relationships between gender, ethnicity, and spouses' experiences of participation in longitudinal sexual health research.

Library of Congress Cataloging-in-Publication Data
Medical anthropology at the intersections : histories, activisms, and futures / Marcia C. Inhorn and Emily A. Wentzell, editors.
    p. cm.
Includes bibliographical references and index.
ISBN 978-0-8223-5251-8 (cloth : alk. paper)
ISBN 978-0-8223-5270-9 (pbk. : alk. paper)
    1. Medical anthropology. 2. Medical anthropology—
Study and teaching. 3. Medical anthropology—Research.
I. Inhorn, Marcia Claire, 1957– II. Wentzell, Emily A., 1980–
GN296.M424   2012
306.4'61—dc23   2011053300